CULTURE AND
THE EVOLUTION
OF MAN

CONTRIBUTORS

PAUL T. BAKER, Pennsylvania State University

GEORGE A. BARTHOLOMEW, Jr., University of California, Los Angeles

JOSEPH B. BIRDSELL, University of California, Los Angeles

C. LORING BRACE, University of California, Santa Barbara

ALICE BRUES, University of Oklahoma

M. R. A. CHANCE, Birmingham University

Th. DOBZHANSKY, Columbia University

LOREN C. EISELEY, University of Pennsylvania

WILLIAM ETKIN, Albert Einstein College of Medicine

J. B. S. HALDANE, Indian Statistical Institute

JULES HENRY, Washington University

A. IRVING HALLOWELL, University of Pennsylvania

FRANK B. LIVINGSTONE, University of Michigan

FRED A. METTLER, Columbia University

M. F. ASHLEY MONTAGU, Columbia University

KENNETH P. OAKLEY, British Museum (Natural History)

D. H. STOTT, Glasgow University

SHERWOOD L. WASHBURN, University of California, Berkeley

LESLIE A. WHITE, University of Michigan

CULTURE AND c 2

THE EVOLUTION

OF MAN

EDITED BY M. F. ASHLEY MONTAGU

OXFORD UNIVERSITY PRESS
New York

OXFORD UNIVERSITY PRESS

London   Oxford   New York
Glasgow   Toronto   Melbourne   Wellington
Cape Town   Ibadan   Nairobi   Dar es Salaam   Lusaka   Addis Ababa
Delhi   Bombay   Calcutta   Madras   Karachi   Lahore   Dacca
Kuala Lumpur   Singapore   Hong Kong   Tokyo

© Oxford University Press, Inc., 1962
Library of Congress Catalogue Card Number: 62-9827
First issued as an Oxford University Press paperback, 1962
This reprint, 1972
Printed in the United States of America

P89139

CONTENTS

INTRODUCTION vii

A DEFINITION OF MAN 3
KENNETH P. OAKLEY

TOOLS AND HUMAN EVOLUTION 13
SHERWOOD L. WASHBURN

ECOLOGY AND THE PROTOHOMINIDS 20
GEORGE A. BARTHOLOMEW JR. AND JOSEPH B. BIRDSELL

THE CONCEPT OF CULTURE 38
LESLIE A. WHITE

THE ARGUMENT FROM ANIMALS TO MEN: AN
EXAMINATION OF ITS VALIDITY FOR ANTHROPOLOGY 65
J. B. S. HALDANE

SOCIAL BEHAVIOUR AND PRIMATE EVOLUTION 84
M. R. A. CHANCE

SOCIAL BEHAVIOR
AND THE EVOLUTION OF MAN'S MENTAL FACULTIES 131
WILLIAM ETKIN

NATURAL SELECTION
AND THE MENTAL CAPACITIES OF MANKIND 148
TH. DOBZHANSKY AND M. F. ASHLEY MONTAGU

CULTURE AND THE
STRUCTURAL EVOLUTION OF THE NEURAL SYSTEM 155
FRED A. METTLER

THE SPEARMAN AND THE ARCHER—
AN ESSAY ON SELECTION IN BODY BUILD 202
ALICE BRUES

CULTURE, PERSONALITY, AND EVOLUTION 216
JULES HENRY

THE STRUCTURAL AND
FUNCTIONAL DIMENSIONS OF A HUMAN EXISTENCE 223
A. IRVING HALLOWELL

PERSONALITY STRUCTURE
AND THE EVOLUTION OF MAN 245
A. IRVING HALLOWELL

CLIMATE, CULTURE, AND EVOLUTION 259
PAUL T. BAKER

ANTHROPOLOGICAL IMPLICATIONS OF
SICKLE CELL GENE DISTRIBUTION IN WEST AFRICA 271
FRANK B. LIVINGSTONE

FOSSIL MAN AND HUMAN EVOLUTION 300
LOREN C. EISELEY

TIME, MORPHOLOGY, AND
NEOTENY IN THE EVOLUTION OF MAN 324
M. F. ASHLEY MONTAGU

CULTURAL FACTORS IN THE
EVOLUTION OF THE HUMAN DENTITION 343
C. LORING BRACE

CULTURAL AND
NATURAL CHECKS ON POPULATION-GROWTH 355
D. H. STOTT

INTRODUCTION

It is an interesting fact that discussions of the evolution of man have almost always been devoted to the evolution of his physical traits within an environment virtually exclusively physical. Almost every possible environmental factor that could have been involved in man's physical evolution has been considered, but until the very recent present the role played by cultural factors in the physical evolution of man has received practically no attention. This is all the more surprising in view of the fact that, with the publication in 1871 of *The Descent of Man,* Darwin placed the problem squarely before his contemporaries. He did more than that. Darwin devoted a great part of his book to the consideration of the evolution of man's intelligence, the effects of sexual selection, the evolution of man's moral faculties, and the consequences of the action of these factors upon man's physical evolution. Darwin presented his arguments with his usual combination of clarity and cogency. His book was persuasive without being proselytizing. It was widely read and discussed. Nevertheless, the stimulus it provided appears to have evoked little response, at least with respect to further inquiry into the relation between cultural and physical factors in the evolution of man.

This failure to follow the lead so ably provided by Darwin constitutes a puzzling chapter in the history of science. It is quite evident to anyone acquainted with the history and literature, both secular and scientific, of the period that Darwin was not thinking and writing in splendid isolation. The ideas he developed were of considerable interest to his contemporaries. Darwin was not, in fact, thinking ahead of them. Indeed, many of the ideas developed by Darwin in *The Descent of Man* relating cultural factors to man's physical evolution had, in one way or another, already been discussed by such writers as Lord Monboddo in his *Antient Metaphysics,* published in six volumes between 1779 and 1799, by Johann Gottfried Herder in his *Ideen zur Philosophie der Geschichte der Menschheit,* 1784, by Lord Kame in his *Sketches of the History of Man,* published in 1774 in two volumes and in 1791 in an enlarged edition of four volumes, and by Thomas Love Peacock in his *Melincourt,* published in 1817, an enchanting anthropological novel which no reader of this book should do himself the disservice of failing to read, and in a fair number of similar works which appeared prior to and after the publication of *The Origin of Species* in 1859. No one, however, before Darwin, had discussed the relation between cultural factors and the physical evolution of man at such great length and as cogently as he. The times were not, apparently, propitious for the further development of Darwin's ideas by others. The concentration of interest was largely focused upon man's physical evolution, while those who pursued their interest in man's cultural evolution did so as if what they were concerned with was entirely unrelated to that other world of the student of man's physical evolution.

Physical and cultural anthropology developed as two separate disciplines, a specialist in one of these disciplines, in most cases, could not unfairly be described as one who agreed not to know what was going on in the other. In such circumstances it was not surprising that the two seldom met. Historically, physical anthropology grew out of the medical and zoological sciences. For many years its principal representatives were medical men working within the medical or zoological forum. Cultural anthropology, on the other hand, developed largely from the side of the humanities, so that when it became a university subject it was usually pursued in a department which was far removed from that in which the physical evolution of man was being studied. Even when the physical and cultural anthropologists were brought together under the same roof and were subsequently joined by the archaeologists, it took years before some evidences of cross-fertilization were to be observed. But that this was occurring even when it was least obvious should be clear to all who participated in the process. A great deal more was going on in the minds of some of those who were exposed to this triple intellectual climate than, for a time, appeared upon the surface. The latency period lasted about a generation during which time a great many novel ideas were being received and more or less passively allowed to find their proper relations in the heads of those undergoing the experience. It is literally only within the last two decades that these ideas have begun to spark—most of the sparks being reprinted in the present volume. It is the hope of the editor that they will not only ignite a similar interest in others, but will also help them to perceive hitherto unperceived connections between cultural factors and some of the physical structures and functions of man.

In the introduction to *The Origin of Species*, 1859, page 5, Darwin had described the process by which evolutionary change comes about in the principle of natural selection, as follows:

As many more individuals of each species are born than can possibly survive; and as, consequently, there is a frequently recurring struggle for existence, it follows that any being, if it vary however slightly in any manner profitable to itself, under the complex and sometimes varying conditions of life, will have a better chance of surviving, and thus be *naturally selected*. From the strong principle of inheritance, any selected variety will tend to propagate its new and modified form.

It is the demonstration of the validity of this principle that will always remain Darwin's greatest contribution to our understanding of the evolutionary process. Since Darwin's demonstration was, at first, based entirely on physical changes, it was the latter that drew and remained the focus of attention of virtually all evolutionists.

Until very recently physical anthropologists had been busy attempting to relate man's physical traits to the pressures of the physical environment. Every physical trait, it was assumed, must in some manner represent an adaptation to the physical environment, an adaptive trait. What was almost wholly overlooked is that man's principal means of adapting himself to the physical environment is culture.

Culture is an agency not only for controlling but for changing the pressures of natural selection, and thus for influencing the evolution of man both physically and culturally. The cultural processes through which such evolutionary changes are achieved are many, as for example, through the development of tools, marriage regulations, sexual selection, social selection, co-operativeness, economic development, migration, improved care of children, and the like. It is principally through cultural pressures that primate nature, in the case of man, has been changed into human nature. It must be emphasized that this change has been brought about not— among other things—by the suppression of primate instinctual drives, but by their gradual supplantation by an adaptively more effective means of meeting the challenges of the environment, namely, by enhancing the development of intelligence.

The development of intelligence increasingly freed man from the bondage of biologically predetermined response mechanisms, and the limiting effects they exercise upon behavior. In the evolution of man the rewards have gone not to those who could *react* instinctively, but to those who were able to make the best or most successful *response* to the conditions with which they were confronted. Those individuals who responded with intelligence were more likely to prosper and leave progeny than those who were not so able. If there is one thing of which we can be certain it is of the high adaptive value of intelligence as a factor in both the mental and physical evolution of man. In the course of human evolution the power of instinctual drives has gradually withered away, until man has virtually lost all his instincts. If there remain any residues of instincts in man, they are, possibly, the automatic reaction to a sudden loud noise, and, in the remaining instance, to a sudden withdrawal of support; for the rest, man has no instincts.

Instinct has been described as "lapsed intelligence." But instinct as such is no longer intelligence. Intelligence is a far superior instrument to instinct in meeting the requirements of a complex environment. Instinct does not permit of the emergence of novelty, of innovation, or of originality. Intelligence does. The development of high intelligence was conditional upon the liberation from the body-compulsion of instinct.

Instincts are organic, they arise from within the organism, they are parts of its bodily structure. They are somatized, narrowly limited, behavioral responses. It is a main difference between nonhuman animals and man that the former rely upon the body and its capacities as the means by which adaptation to the environment may be implemented, for example, by the development of structures which may be used for defensive or offensive purposes; whereas, man has evolved by the opposite principle, namely, by escape from the restricting bondage of reliance upon organically determined predispositions, to the freedom of what has been called "the superorganic," to culture. This was gradually achieved with the discovery and inventive development of tools.

It is known that some primates will defensively, and sometimes offensively, throw stones and other materials at intruders. It is probable that the precursors of early man used stones in this manner. This is an extra-corporeal, an instrumental, use of an object. A stone used for such a purpose is the crudest of all tools—but it is a tool. The *use*, however, of an object as a tool, and the *making* of a tool to a special design for a particular purpose are two quite different things. I have seen an oran-utan make a tool out of the straw on the floor of its cage. It folded a sheaf of straw into a firm mass, and with it reached food otherwise out of its reach.* That was tool-making. In order to qualify for hominidity, however, it is not enough to make a simple, occasional, tool; it is necessary to play variations upon the raw material from which the tool is made, to improve upon those variations, and perpetuate them. The creature that can do such things differs from all others that cannot. Such a creature is a man. A creature that can create such tools must be capable of mental processes which also serve as tools, mental tools, concepts, words.

The capacity for such mental tools was undoubtedly gradually developed, and it seems highly probable that the development of physical tools went hand-in-hand with the development of mental ones. Tools, physical or mental, open up a world of unlimited possibilities for development; the advantages they confer shift the direction of selection pressure of that development from the body to the mind. The evolutionary result of this is the development of a man-made extra-somatic environment, namely, *culture;* in Leslie White's excellent definition, the class of things and events, dependent upon the symbolic process, considered in an extra-somatic context. It is the influence of the evolution of culture upon the physical evolution of man that is our principal interest in this volume.

* M. F. Ashley Montagu, "A Note on the Behavior of an Oran-Utan," J. Mammal., 11: 231-2, 1930.

With the loss of his instinctual equipment, and as a result of the increasing enlargement of the brain, the human infant is born in both a physically and behaviorally immature condition. In the course of evolution this has rendered him increasingly more dependent upon others for all that he has had to learn as a functioning human being. As such the human child must acquire from the world of human beings outside himself what other animals develop from within themselves. A long dependency period has considerable selective value, in that it favors the prolonged maturation of the organism and the time necessary for learning.

But much of this is to anticipate what is to follow in these pages. There are, however, a few other points that need to be underscored here before turning the reader over to the main body of the book.

It is to be hoped that the reader will perceive that the studies contained in this book are not only of relevance for an understanding of the past evolution of man, but that they are, at least, equally important for a clear understanding of the processes which are at work influencing the evolution of man at the present time.

As we shall see, it is quite erroneous to suggest, as is sometimes done, that natural selection is no longer at work in man, or that he is no longer evolving, or both.

When one considers the conditions among other animals one finds that the members of all species vary in the degree of their adaptive fitness in relation to different aspects of the environment. Among such animals lack of adaptive fitness in a single trait may prove of considerable disadvantage and, in some cases, even lethal. Man, however, has created an environment that is capable of meeting an ever-increasing range of adaptive fitnesses—high or low. A trait of low adaptive fitness under earlier conditions of cultural development, which would have put an earlier end to its bearer, diabetes, for example, today elicits so much support from the man-made environment that it is biologically no longer the extremely disadvantageous trait it once was.

Through cultural means, by the application of scientific discovery and technical advance, man provides an enormous amount of buffering against the impact of defects which in earlier times would have laid him low. Advances in medicine alone have made it possible literally for millions of individuals to survive to a ripe old age who would not otherwise have done so. Insulin and diabetes, liver and pernicious anemia, BCG and tuberculosis, antibiotics and many bacterial diseases, not to mention the successful treatment of many forms of inborn errors of metabolism; these are but a few examples.

Modern civilizations provide an enormous variety of niches for virtually every kind of physical and mental type, and as civilization advances those niches become ever more embracing in scope. With the exception of the individual who is in some way totally incapacitated, there increasingly tends to be a place for everyone in such a society. A wide range of niches is available.

The biologically low adaptive fitness of the individual in one or more traits is compensated for by the proper adjustive medical or social process or both. By this means biological damage is reduced or avoided.

It is on grounds such as these that it has been argued by some that natural selection is no longer operative in man, that it has been nullified or bypassed by man's taking his evolution into his own hands. This is to misunderstand what has, in fact, occurred, and what is continuing to occur, namely, *not* that natural selection has ceased to operate in man, but that, like a refreshing river, its course has simply been redirected to flow in deeper and newer channels. To abandon the metaphor for the reality, natural selection operates in relation to man in the new zone of adaptation into which he has moved, in the new environments which he has created. Fitness is a matter of fitness in relation to an environment, and not to someone's idea of natural selection. It is desirable to dispel the false idea that there is such a thing as absolute fitness. Fitness is always in relation to some part or parts of the environment. No one is ever equally fit in relation to every part of the environment. Natural selection is fitness in relation to the environment as measured by fertility.

At this juncture I should like to conclude on a contemporary note of some urgency. If fertility is a measure of fitness, it may well be asked whether man is not perhaps becoming too fit for his own good? Is he not increasing at too rapid a rate? What has been called "the population explosion" does, indeed, constitute a threat to the welfare of mankind. But it is a threat which man can meet by precisely the same means with which he has met other and even more alarming dangers throughout his history—by the use of his intelligence. Even now agencies all over the world are at work seriously considering methods of controlling population increase. The Japanese have most effectively solved this problem in their own land. There is no reason why men in other lands cannot do likewise. The danger, however, is with us, and the threat to human welfare it constitutes speaks to us with an urgency that demands our most active attention. We are very good at controlling death. We need to be at least equally adept at controlling birth. It would be unthinkable that man should this way be hoist with his own petard.

Such matters are by no means a digression from the main theme of this book. On the contrary, they are in the direct tradition of Darwin's own discussion of them in *The Descent of Man*. In the matter of population increase Darwin wrote, "Natural selection follows from the struggle for existence; and this from a rapid rate of increase. It is impossible not to regret bitterly, but whether wisely is another question, the rate at which man tends to increase; for this leads in barbarous tribes to infanticide and many other evils, and in civilized nations to abject poverty, celibacy, and to the late marriages of the prudent. But as man suffers from the same physical evils as the lower animals, he has no right to expect an immunity from the evils consequent on the struggle for existence" (chapter 5, 2nd ed., 1874; reprint 1901, p. 219).

Darwin was, of course, quite sound in asserting that man had no right to expect immunity from the evils consequent on the struggle for existence, as long as—he might have added—he does nothing to control the rate of natural increase. It is clear that man has no right to expect immunity from smallpox and other diseases as long as he does nothing to protect himself against them. But man can, by controlling his own environment, confer upon himself a lasting immunity against smallpox and similar diseases, and what is more, it is his moral obligation—enforceable by the laws of most civilized states—to do so. Vaccination against smallpox has saved untold millions of lives. In bygone years scarcely anyone was spared, and the stamp of "the pox" was a familiar sight throughout Europe. Since that time man in the western world has progressed so far in the control of this disease that there is today many a physician who has never seen a case of smallpox.

Man possesses the power to achieve a similar immunity from the socially and biologically deteriorative consequences of his own capacity for rapid multiplication. Within the last few years there have been growing indications that man may yet make himself master of his own numbers before it is too late.

In casting a retrospective eye over the role which cultural factors have played in the physical evolution of man, we shall, I trust, have caught more than a glimpse of the manner in which man may control his future evolution. And if the lesson is learned that physical (genetic) and cultural evolution are not mutually exclusive processes, a principal purpose of this book will have been achieved.

But this introduction is already long enough. I wish here to take the opportunity to thank all the authors represented in these pages for their co-operation in making this book possible, and to the editors and publishers of the periodicals and books in which these contributions originally appeared.

Finally, I should like to express my thanks to Mrs. Mary-Louise Weisman and to Miss Barbara Tunmore of the Oxford University Press, New York, for their very substantial help, so efficiently and gracefully rendered, in solving so many of the problems presented in editing and preparing for the press a work of this kind.

Princeton, New Jersey   A.M.
February 1962

EDITOR'S NOTE

Most of the contributions in this volume are reprinted exactly as they were published, except for minor changes designed to bring the text into typographical harmony. The articles by Oakley and Etkin have been slightly rewritten. The article by Chance represents a completely revised version of one originally written by Chance and Mead, and now appearing for the first time in its revised form in the present volume. The article by Brace is published here for the first time, while that by Stott was specially written for this book. A few illustrations have been dropped from some of the articles, and most of the figures have been redrawn.

CULTURE AND
THE EVOLUTION
OF MAN

Australopithecus on the high veldt. Restored and illustrated by Maurice Wilson. (By Permission of the Trustees of the British Museum (Natural History)).

A DEFINITION OF MAN

KENNETH P. OAKLEY

Man has been defined in many ways: he has been described as the reasoning animal, the religious animal, the talking animal, the tool-making animal, and so on. For the most part, these attempts to distinguish man from the rest of brute creation have been philosophical exercises; but from time to time, this question has been a matter of practical concern to scientists interpreting the remains of fossil man-like apes, or ape-like men—supposed "missing links." The latest of these controversies dates from 1924 when a fossil skull of a young ape-like creature, apparently with some human characteristics, was found at Taung in Bechuanaland, and named *Australopithecus africanus* by Professor Raymond Dart. This was the first of a number of fossils which have been discovered in the limestone cave and fissure deposits of South Africa, and are considered by some to date from the beginning of the Pleistocene period. Since 1936, Dr. Robert Broom has been finding skulls and other bones of similar forms (*Pleisanthropus* and *Paranthropus*) at Sterkfontein and elsewhere in Central Transvaal. Recently, Professor Dart has found remains of another species of *Australopithecus* in a cave in the Makapansgat, Northern Transvaal. Some authorities regard these australopithecines as essentially apes, while others interpret them as small "ape-men."

To set this question "What is Man?" in its modern perspective, it is worth considering how zoologists now classify us, remembering that classification in biology is an attempt to express relationship. In addition to our own species, several extinct species of man are now recognized. They are grouped together as Hominidae and regarded by most zoologists as sufficiently close to apes (now collectively called Pongidae) to be placed in the same super-family (Hominoidea). The anatomical similarity between man and the apes of to-day indicates that they have evolved from a common ancestral stock. This conclusion is supported by the findings of palaeontologists, who have shown that some of the fossil types are, in certain features, structurally inter-mediate.

The common stock probably comprised a number of generalized monkey-like apes similar to those of the genus *Proconsul* which inhabited East Africa during early Miocene times, some 25 million years ago. These, it seems,

Reprinted by permission from *Science News*, 20:(edited by A. W. Haslett), Penguin Books, Harmondsworth (1951), pp. 69–81.

were equally capable of climbing trees and of running along the ground on all fours, thus being adaptable enough to spread widely and to evolve along divergent lines of specialization. One line (or group of lines) led to the forest-bound apes of to-day, which have long powerful arms adapted for swinging from bough to bough like trapeze artists (brachiation); another line led to man, with hind limbs specialized for walking upright on open ground. This divergence of the brachiating apes and the immediate ancestors of man probably took place before the end of the Miocene period, around 12 million years ago.

Our problem of defining "man" is resolving itself into two questions. First, what were the hall-marks of the group of "apes" which diverged from the forest-dwellers and became the early Hominidae? Second, to what stage in the evolution of these Hominidae should the status Man be awarded—from the point of view of logical practice?

Man differs from modern apes in a number of striking physical character-istics: in the plan and form of the teeth, in habitually walking erect on two legs, and in having a brain which is considerably larger. The brain increased in size during the evolution of all the Hominoidea. Although man outstripped the forest-bound apes in this respect, it is obvious that there would have been an overlap between the range of brain-size in the earliest Hominidae and in their cousin apes. Brain-size is thus unsuitable as a criterion of relationship.

One would expect to find in "proto-hominids" evidence that their skeleton was being adapted to allow them to leave the forests, and habitually to walk on two feet. However, adaptive characters are usually regarded by biologists as unreliable evidence of relationship. For instance, it might well have hap-pened that more than one line of "apes" acquired the habit of upright bipedal gait, only one of them leading to "man." But it is arguable that even if that were in fact the case, all those lineages could legitimately be grouped as Hominidae. After all, the orang-utan and the gorilla represent separate, parallel lines of descent, but many zoologists do not hesitate to place them in the same family. Even so, one would naturally seek some confirmatory evidence that any fossil biped which came to light was more closely related to *Homo* than to any of the brachiating apes.

Students of fossil mammals have found that the characters of the teeth, especially when the characters are of a non-adaptive kind, are the most useful clues to relationship. Thus, arguing along general lines, one would be in-clined to classify fossil ape-like forms as members of the Hominidae, irrespec-tive of brain-size, if the evidence indicated that they walked upright and had teeth more closely resembling those of man than those of any of the existing apes. The latest discoveries in South Africa have shown that the australo-pithecines, although mostly with brains no larger than those of gorillas, walked upright (this is deduced from their hip bones) and moreover had a dentition of essentially human form. Their canines or eye-teeth were level with the other teeth, even from the earliest stages of wear, and even in males.

Although these fossil creatures are geologically perhaps too recent to be the actual ancestors of man, it is reasonable to suppose that they represent one of the side-branches of the "proto-hominid" stock which persisted in South Africa after the main stem of Hominidae had elsewhere attained an evolutionary level counted as human (e.g., *Pithecanthropus* in the earliest Middle Pleistocene deposits of Java; see below).

But we are still in need of a working definition of man. Without it, we are in this dilemma: that, looked at logically, the South African fossils have good claims to be counted in the same family as *Homo,* yet they are obviously so much more ape-like in the general proportions of their skulls than the roughly contemporary earliest Java Man, that one hesitates to call them "human." Professor Le Gros Clark, who has closely studied this problem, said that "Probably the differentiation of man from ape will ultimately have to rest on a functional rather than an anatomical basis, the criterion of humanity being the ability to speak and to make tools."

It is sometimes assumed that the difference in mental capacity between apes and men is accurately reflected in their respective brain-sizes. Unfortunately the facts do not justify the use of this simple criterion, because mental capacity depends rather more on the quality of the cortical association-areas of the brain than on its size. It is true that the comparative psychology of primates shows that the rating of mental capacity is broadly paralleled by the order of magnitude of the brain. The recorded range of adult brain-size in normal man is from c.750 to 2,800 c.c. Our children are beginning to walk and to talk at the age of two years, when the mean cranial capacity is 1,100 c.c. Since we do not know the range of variation of brain-size at that stage of development in our species, we are not justified in inferring that adult australopithecines whose brains probably ranged in size from 450–750 c.c. were necessarily incapable of speech.

According to recent opinion, no reliable deductions in detail regarding mental aptitudes can be drawn from the pattern of the interior surface of the brain-case. As Weidenreich expressed it, the interpretation of the endocranial cast is no more reliable than any other form of phrenology. Thus it has been claimed that in the brain of an adult australopithecine the association-area for speech was already differentiated; but whether it was qualitatively capable of so functioning is another matter.

The difficulty about accepting the proposal to differentiate man from ape on a functional basis is to find a practical criterion. The definition of man as the tool-making primate has some advantage from this point of view. If deliberately chipped stones (artifacts) had been found in the cave lairs of *Australopithecus* (or allied genera), there would be less hesitation in accepting this fossil as a hominid. The remains of the two Javanese species of *Pithecanthropus* were found in river or lake beds containing no recognizable artifacts; but this genus can be accepted as human because apart from the fact that its brain-size is within the known human range, stone artifacts were associated with the remains of the Chinese species, *Pithecanthropus pekinensis* (Pekin Man). Deliberately broken stones are fairly easily recognized in a cave deposit, particularly if the stones are obvious introductions, such as the pieces of quartz in the limestone caves of Pekin Man. The difficulty of distinguishing between crude stone artifacts and stones chipped by natural agencies, simulating the work of man, is a serious problem only in glacial, river or beach deposits.

The definition of man as the tool-making primate is sometimes criticized on the score that (1) lower primates occasionally make use of tools (2) tool-making is merely one of the by-products of man's mental development, and not a primary characteristic from a zoological point of view. It is worth while to examine these criticisms in some detail.

The *use* of tools and weapons is certainly not confined to man. There are records of monkeys throwing sticks and stones; a baboon will sometimes crack open a scorpion with a pebble; while some of the apes observed by Köhler, used sticks as levers for digging up objects hidden in the ground, and for extending their reach. The use of tools is not even confined to primates: when the sea-otter finds its favourite delicacy on the sea-floor—a sea-urchin (or sea-snail?)—it takes it on shore together with a pebble to crack it open. The *manufacture* of tools requires mental activity of a different order. The chimpanzee is the only ape reliably reported to make tools, and then only in captivity. Sultan, one of the male chimpanzees observed by Köhler, fitted a small bamboo cane into a larger one so as to make a stick long enough to secure a bunch of bananas which could not be reached by the use of either of the rods used singly. Once, he attained the same result by fitting into one of the canes a piece of wood which he pointed for the purpose with the aid of his teeth. Apes are thus evidently capable of improvising tools. But it is important to note that all the improvisations effected by Sultan were carried out with *visible* reward as incentive. Köhler could obtain no indication that apes are ever capable of conceiving the usefulness of shaping an object for use in an imagined future eventuality. He expressed his conclusions as follows:

The time in which the chimpanzee lives is limited in past and future . . . it is in the extremely narrow limits in *this* direction that the chief difference is to be found between anthropoids and the most primitive human beings. The lack of an invaluable technical aid (speech) and a great limitation of those very important components of thought, so-called "images," would thus constitute the causes that prevent the chimpanzee from attaining even the smallest beginnings of cultural development.

In other words, apes are very limited in their capacity for visualizing and thinking about the relationships between objects when those objects are not in sight. The power of abstraction or conceptual thought is basic to the regular manufacture of tools. In apes it is no more than nascent. Mme Kohts in Moscow found that her chimpanzee could select from a collection of objects of extremely varied form those which were of the same shade of colour. This mental isolation of a single feature from a varied field of observation is the dawn of conceptual thought; but Mme Kohts found that ideas such as this rapidly fade in the mind of the ape.

To illustrate more clearly the difference between the mental capacity of an ape and of a human being, the following observations of Köhler are worth quoting. When embarrassed by lack of a stick, a chimpanzee will pull a loose board from an old box and use it. If the boards are nailed together in such a way that they make an unbroken surface, the chimpanzee although strong enough to break up the box will not see "possible sticks" in it—even if his need of a stick is urgent. Men, on the other hand, seeking to make a tool of a form suited to a particular purpose will visualize its shape in a formless lump of stone and chip it until the imagined tool is actualized. There is the possibility of gradation between these two extremes, perceptual thought in apes, conceptual thought in man; but it seems necessary to stress the contrast because one is apt to be so impressed by the occasional manufacture of tools by apes that there is a danger of minimizing the gap in the quality of mind needed for such efforts, compared with even the crudest tools of early man, which indicate forethought.

Language must have greatly facilitated the development of systematic manufacture of tools. Oral tradition, in effect a new kind of inheritance, is sometimes regarded as more distinctive of man than tool-making. But speech itself is really a class of tool, "an invaluable technical aid," in Köhler's description, and depends on a capacity for conceptual thought. The brains of the earliest tool-making Hominidae were probably advanced enough functionally for speech, but nevertheless verbal language may have been a comparatively late cultural development—an invention. The earliest means of communicating ideas was perhaps by gesticulation, mainly of mouth and hands, accompanied by cries and grunts to attract attention ("gesture language").

On the evidence available it appears reasonable to conclude that systematic tool-making, in the broadest sense, would only be possible in primates whose level of cerebral development was in advance of that of modern apes.

It remains to consider at what point in the evolution of the Hominidae did tool-making arise, and whether it can be classed as a fundamental characteristic of man from a zoological point of view. It might be thought that manual dexterity was a limiting factor. Actually, however, the prehensile hands of the less specialized monkeys would be quite capable of most of the ordinary movements in making and using tools, if directed by an adequate brain.

Our unspecialized, five-fingered hands are so well adapted to grasping that they are a clear indication that our remoter ancestors were accustomed to climbing in trees. So long as they continued to lead an arboreal life their prehensile hands, fully occupied by climbing and feeding, had no opportunity or need to develop the habit of using external objects as functional extensions of the limbs. However, some of our early ancestors must have become adapted to spending part of their time walking and sitting on open ground. Their hands thus became free to handle objects, first out of idle curiosity, later perhaps, to some purpose. Some of the Miocene apes were agile monkey-like creatures accustomed to running on the ground as well as climbing trees, and probably capable too of rearing up on hind legs. Such apes may well have been in the habit of improvising tools when circumstances demanded. It is suggestive that the chimpanzee, not known to be a tool-user in its forest environment, makes use of sticks for various purposes as soon as captivity forces it to spend most of its time on the ground.

From a functional point of view tools may be regarded as detachable extensions of the forelimb. Most mammals have evolved specialized bodily equipment suited to some particular mode of life. Horses for example have teeth suited to eating grass, and hoofs adapted for galloping over hard plains and thus avoiding attack. The carnivorous sabre-tooth cats evolved claws like grappling-irons and canine teeth like daggers, perfectly adapted for killing prey. In process of evolution the Hominidae avoided any such extreme specialization, their teeth being suited to an omnivorous diet, while they retained the pliant five-fingered hands which were so useful to their small tree-dwelling ancestors. When the forerunners of man acquired the ability to walk upright habitually, their hands became free to use tools.

One can imagine that "proto-hominids" may have remained at the stage of occasional tool-using for millions of years. Systematic tool-making would not have followed until the brain had attained the complexity of organization requisite for conceptual thought; and even then, this activity would be unlikely to become regular until new habits were demanded by circumstances.

Probably within the Pliocene period, certainly by early Pleistocene times, the human level of cerebral development had been reached, and stone artifacts of standardized types were being made. These indicate that the manufacture of tools served certain permanent needs of the earliest human beings. What were these needs? The use of tools and weapons was surely the means whereby the Hominidae kept themselves alive after they abandoned the protection and sustenance provided by forests.

The tree-climbing primates had no use for tools. Tool-using arose in connection with adaptation to life on open ground away from forests. In the evolution of the primates the forelimbs have continually shown a tendency to take on functions performed in their ancestors by the teeth. The use of tools is evidently an extension of this trend, and we may suppose that tools were largely substitutes for teeth.

The apes of to-day are forest creatures, subsisting almost exclusively on fruits, leaves, shoots and insects. All known races of man, on the other hand, include a substantial proportion of animal flesh in their diet. We have ample evidence that Pekin Man, Neanderthal Man and Late Palaeolithic races of

Homo sapiens were meat-eaters. The discoveries of broken meat-bones on the Early Palaeolithic camping sites at Olorgesaile in Kenya have shown that the Acheulian handaxe-makers of these sites (perhaps early precursors of *Homo sapiens*) were also hunters. I suggest that meat-eating is as old as man; that with the change from forest living to open country, the diet of proto-men inevitably became more varied and that they changed from being eaters largely of plants and the fruits of plants to being partly meat-eaters.

It seems probable, on the analogy of the baboons, that early Hominidae living in country like the present African savanna may have become addicted to flesh-eating as a result of the struggle for existence being intensified by excessive drought. It may be recalled that baboons, almost the only monkeys completely adapted to life away from woodlands, occasionally prey on lambs and other animals of similar size, using their powerful canine teeth as offensive weapons, and moreover that this habit is liable to become more prevalent when conditions of existence are hard. Owing to the extensive folk-lore associated with baboons, reports of the carnivorous habits of those in South Africa have been discounted by some zoologists, but information from many different observers, recently collected by my friend Mr. F. E. Hiley, leaves no doubt that such reports are substantially true. A report from Captain H. B. Potter, Game Conservator in Zululand, is typical of those received:

The following are my personal observations over a period of twenty years' wardenship in the Hluhluwe Game Reserve: I have seen full-grown poultry killed and actually eaten by baboons, mostly however by aged individuals. Eggs and chickens are taken by the dozen, by old and young baboons. I have on many occasions actually witnessed apparently organized hunts which often result in the death of the intended victim. The baboons, usually led by a veteran of the troop, surround an unsuspecting three-parts grown Mountain Reedbuck, or Duiker, as the case may be, and on one occasion a young Reedbuck doe was the victim. It would appear that on a given signal the baboons close in on their quarry, catch it and tear it asunder. As a matter of interest I have refrained from interference in these grim encounters so that I would be in a position authentically to record the results. In nine cases out of ten the game animal is devoured limb by limb and after the affair is over all that is to be found are the skull and leg bones.

Baboons, like some other monkeys and apes too, have powerful canine teeth, serving mainly for defence against carnivores and for attack in mating duels. It has been suggested that the reduction of the canine teeth in man was an outcome of the use of hand-weapons. But judging by their condition in the australopithecines, the canine teeth were reduced in the Hominidae at an evolutionary stage below that of tool-making. Certainly the "proto-hominids" would have needed some means of defending themselves in the open, and having their hands free may well have used stones as missiles and sticks or animal long-bones as clubs.

In dry open country (such, for instance, as that inhabited by the australopithecines) the "proto-hominids," like baboons, might readily have taken to

9

eating flesh particularly in times of drought. Although they lacked teeth suited to carnivorous habits they could easily have killed small mammals. Life in the open set a premium on co-operation. Drawing on our knowledge of the mentality and social life of other primates, it seems not unreasonable to suppose that hunting in hordes the "proto-hominids" could have killed medium-sized mammals, say by cornering them and using improvised hand-weapons such as they might earlier have learnt to improvise for their own defence. This is frankly speculation. Is there any real evidence that the early Hominidae were carnivorous and that they passed through a tool-using stage, before becoming tool-makers?

Even if the australopithecines are geologically too late to be actual ancestors of Man, their "morphological dating" is plain—structurally, they may be viewed as slightly modified descendants of our Pliocene forebears. There are indications that they may have been carnivorous, and that possibly they used improvised tools and weapons. The quantities of broken animal bones and fragments of egg shells found with *Australopithecus* in the cave deposits at Taung suggest a "midden" of food refuse; but the possibility cannot be ruled out that the bones were introduced by a carnivore which left no other trace of its presence. Professor Dart claims that some of the long-bones of antelopes found in the australopithecine layer at Makapan show signs of having been used as weapons. But again, although there is a strong probability that these bipedal primates were tool users, the evidence remains *sub judice*.

By the time that the Hominidae had evolved into tool-makers they were evidently largely carnivorous—quantities of meat-bones were associated with the remains of *Pithecanthropus pekinensis*. It is easy to see how the one habit led from the other. Although the killing of game may have been accomplished easily enough in some such way as that suggested above, the early hominids must often have encountered difficulty in removing skin and fur, and in dividing the flesh. In the absence of strong canine teeth the solution would have been overcome most readily by using sharp pieces of stone. Here surely was the origin of the tradition of tool-making. Where no naturally sharp pieces of stone lay ready to hand, some of the more intelligent individuals saw that the solution was to break pebbles and produce fresh sharp edges. Once the tradition of tool-making had begun, the manifold uses of chipped stones became obvious; they were useful for sharpening sticks for use in digging out burrowing mammals, for making spears sharp enough to be effective weapons in hunting larger game, for scraping meat from bones, splitting them to get at the marrow, chopping the meat into convenient mouthfuls. All the main uses of stone tools were, I suggest, connected in the first place with adoption of semi-carnivorous habits.

From the endowment of nature we should be vegetarians. We lack the teeth evolved by true carnivores, and we have the long gut associated with a herbivorous diet. Furthermore, we are the only members of the Hominoidea which are accustomed to eat meat on any considerable scale. It is true that anthropoid apes, like many herbivores, consume small quantities of animal protein; some of them occasionally rob birds' nests of eggs and fledglings, but by and large they are fruit and plant eaters.

One can well imagine that a changing environment, for instance during a period of desiccation, may have produced an abnormal appetite in the early hominids. Gorillas in captivity quickly develop a liking for meat, and this appears to be due to a change in the flora and fauna of their intestines. Normally their intestines are richly supplied with ciliate protozoa (Infusoria), which serve to digest cellulose. According to Reichenow, under the abnormal conditions of captivity the Infusoria are ingested, and with their disappearance from the intestine the animal develops an abnormal appetite, and readily takes to eating meat—and may even prefer meat to its normal fare.

By widening his diet and becoming a tool-maker man became the most adaptable of all primates. The change from herbivorous to semi-carnivorous habits was important from the point of view of the use of energy. To obtain a given amount of energy a carnivore subsists on a smaller quantity of food than a herbivore. Instead of eating almost continuously like their ancestors, the Hominidae spent much of their time in hunting. This led to increased interdependence. New skills and aptitudes were developed through this new way of life, and with increasing control of environment through the use of tools, man became the most adaptable of all creatures, and free to spread into every climatic zone.

An important step in the control of environment in northern climes was the making of fire. This could only have been discovered as an outcome of tool-making, but we do not know when or how. Professor Dart's claim to have found evidence of the use of fire by *Australopithecus* is not accepted. Pekin Man regularly used fire, and presumably knew how to make it. The much later Acheulian hunters of Olorgesailie do not appear to have been fire-users; probably, like some Eskimo tribes at the present time, they ate meat raw.

To sum up: I think it may fairly be claimed that tool-making is one of man's fundamental characteristics from a biological point of view. But the definition of man as the tool-making primate carries the implication that one should apply the term human only to the later members of the family Hominidae, which had attained a certain level of cerebral development, and which for convenience should perhaps be included in the single genus *Homo* (with *Pithecanthropus* one of the subgenera).

The Hominidae as a whole are bipedal primates with a distinctive dentition, which probably became differentiated during the Miocene period. The australopithecines, probably of early Pleistocene age, are believed to be slightly aberrant descendants of Pliocene Hominidae. Through following various indirect lines of evidence it appears to the author most probable that in course of adaptation to life in open country the early Hominidae relied to some extent on the use of improvised hand-weapons for defence; that they became addicted to flesh-eating during periods of aridity; and that when a certain level of cerebral development had been reached in their evolution this change of dietary habit led to regular manufacture of tools and weapons.

POSTSCRIPT

The australopithecine described by Broom under the name *Plesianthropus* is now referred to as *Australopithecus*.

The discovery in 1957 of pebble-tools in the top layer of australopithecine breccias at Sterkfontein, and the finding in 1959 by Dr. and Mrs. L. S. B. Leakey of an australopithecine skull (*Zinjanthropus*) with pebble-tools in Lower Pleistocene lake-beds at Olduvai in Tanganyika, have gone far toward establishing that the australopithecines were tool-making hominids, and therefore by definition "human."

REFERENCES

CLARK, W. E. LE GROS 1950 History of the Primates, 2nd ed. London, British Museum (Natural History). 6th ed. 1958.

DART, R. A. The predatory implemental technique of australopithecus. Am. J. Phys. Anthrop., 7(N.S.), 1 (1950).

KÖHLER, W. 1927 The Mentality of Apes, 2nd ed. London, Kegan Paul.

LEAKEY, L. S. B. The early history of man. Science News 17, p. 36.

REICHENOW, E. Arch. f. Protistenk. 41, 1 (1920).

YERKES, R. M., and A. W. 1929 The Great Apes. New Haven, Yale University Press.

ZUCKERMAN, S. Taxonomy and human evolution. Biol. Rev., 25, 435 (1950).

TOOLS AND HUMAN EVOLUTION

SHERWOOD L. WASHBURN

A series of recent discoveries has linked prehuman primates of half a million years ago with stone tools. For some years investigators had been uncovering tools of the simplest kind from ancient deposits in Africa. At first they assumed that these tools constituted evidence of the existence of large-brained, fully bipedal men. Now the tools have been found in association with much more primitive creatures, the not-fully bipedal, small-brained near-men, or man-apes. Prior to these finds the prevailing view held that man evolved nearly to his present structural state and then discovered tools and the new ways of life that they made possible. Now it appears that man-apes—creatures able to run but not yet walk on two legs, and with brains no larger than those of apes now living—had already learned to make and to use tools. It follows that the structure of modern man must be the result of the change in the terms of natural selection that came with the tool-using way of life.

The earliest stone tools are chips or simple pebbles, usually from river gravels. Many of them have not been shaped at all, and they can be identified as tools only because they appear in concentrations, along with a few worked pieces, in caves or other locations where no such stones naturally occur. The huge advantage that a stone tool gives to its user must be tried to be appreciated. Held in the hand, it can be used for pounding, digging or scraping. Flesh and bone can be cut with a flaked chip, and what would be a mild blow with the fist becomes lethal with a rock in the hand. Stone tools can be employed, moreover, to make tools of other materials. Naturally occurring sticks are nearly all rotten, too large, or of inconvenient shape; some tool for fabrication is essential for the efficient use of wood. The utility of a mere pebble seems so limited to the user of modern tools that it is not easy to comprehend the vast difference that separates the tool-user from the ape which relies on hands and teeth alone. Ground-living monkeys dig out roots for food, and if they could use a stone or a stick, they might easily double their food supply. It was the success of the simplest tools that started the whole trend of human evolution and led to the civilizations of today.

From the short-term point of view, human structure makes human behavior possible. From the evolutionary point of view, behavior and structure form an interacting complex, with each change in one affecting the other. Man

Reprinted by permission from *Scientific American*, 203: (1960), 63–75.

began when populations of apes, about a million years ago, started the bipedal, tool-using way of life that gave rise to the man-apes of the genus *Australopithecus*. Most of the obvious differences that distinguish man from ape came after the use of tools.

The primary evidence for the new view of human evolution is teeth, bones and tools. But our ancestors were not fossils; they were striving creatures, full of rage, dominance and the will to live. What evolved was the pattern of life of intelligent, exploratory, playful, vigorous primates; the evolving reality was a succession of social systems based upon the motor abilities, emotions and intelligence of their members. Selection produced new systems of child care, maturation and sex, just as it did alterations in the skull and the teeth. Tools, hunting, fire, complex social life, speech, the human way and the brain evolved together to produce ancient man of the genus *Homo* about half a million years ago. Then the brain evolved under the pressures of more complex social life until the species *Homo sapiens* appeared perhaps as recently as 50,000 years ago.

With the advent of *Homo sapiens* the tempo of technical-social evolution quickened. Some of the early types of tool had lasted for hundreds of thousands of years and were essentially the same throughout vast areas of the African and Eurasian land masses. Now the tool forms multiplied and became regionally diversified. Man invented the bow, boats, clothing; conquered the Arctic; invaded the New World; domesticated plants and animals; discovered metals, writing and civilization. Today, in the midst of the latest tool-making revolution, man has achieved the capacity to adapt his environment to his need and impulse, and his numbers have begun to crowd the planet.

This article is concerned with the beginnings of the process by which, as Theodosius Dobzhansky says, biological evolution has transcended itself. From the rapidly accumulating evidence it is now possible to speculate with some confidence on the manner in which the way of life made possible by tools changed the pressures of natural selection and so changed the structure of man.

Tools have been found, along with the bones of their makers, at Sterkfontein, Swartkrans and Kromdraai in South Africa and at Olduvai in Tanganyika. Many of the tools from Sterkfontein are merely unworked river pebbles, but someone had to carry them from the gravels some miles away and bring them to the deposit in which they are found. Nothing like them occurs naturally in the local limestone caves. Of course the association of the stone tools with man-ape bones in one or two localities does not prove that these animals made the tools. It has been argued that a more advanced form of man, already present, was the toolmaker. This argument has a familiar ring to students of human evolution. Peking man was thought too primitive to be a toolmaker; when the first manlike pelvis was found with man-ape bones, some argued that it must have fallen into the deposit because it was too human to be associated with the skull. In every case, however, the repeated discovery of the same unanticipated association has ultimately settled the controversy.

This is why the discovery by L. S. B. and Mary Leakey in the summer of 1959 is so important. In Olduvai Gorge in Tanganyika they came upon traces of an old living site, and found stone tools in clear association with the largest man-ape skull known. With the stone tools were a hammer stone and waste flakes from the manufacture of the tools. The deposit also contained the bones of rats, mice, frogs and some bones of juvenile pig and antelope, showing that even the largest and latest of the man-apes could kill only the smallest animals and must have been largely vegetarian. The Leakeys' discovery confirms the association of the man-ape with pebble tools, and adds the evidence of manufacture to that of mere association. Moreover, the stratigraphic evidence at Olduvai now for the first time securely dates the man-apes, placing them in the lower Pleistocene, earlier than 500,000 years ago and earlier than the first skeletal and cultural evidence for the existence of the genus *Homo*. Before the discovery at Olduvai these points had been in doubt.

The man-apes themselves are known from several skulls and a large number of teeth and jaws, but only fragments of the rest of the skeleton have been preserved. There were two kinds of man-ape, a small early one that may have weighed 50 or 60 pounds and a later and larger one that weighed at least twice as much. The differences in size and form between the two types are quite comparable to the differences between the contemporary pygmy chimpanzee and the common chimpanzee.

Pelvic remains from both forms of man-ape show that these animals were bipedal. From a comparison of the pelvis of ape, man-ape and man it can be seen that the upper part of the pelvis is much wider and shorter in man than in the ape, and that the pelvis of the man-ape corresponds closely, though not precisely, to that of modern man. The long upper pelvis of the ape is characteristic of most mammals, and it is the highly specialized, short, wide bone in man that makes possible the human kind of bipedal locomotion. Although the man-ape pelvis is apelike in its lower part, it approaches that of man in just those features that distinguish man from all other animals. More work must be done before this combination of features is fully understood. My belief is that bipedal running, made possible by the changes in the upper pelvis, came before efficient bipedal walking, made possible by the changes in the lower pelvis. In the man-ape, therefore, the adaptation to bipedal locomotion is not yet complete. Here, then, is a phase of human evolution characterized by forms that are mostly bipedal, small-brained, plains-living, tool-making hunters of small animals.

The capacity for bipedal walking is primarily an adaptation for covering long distances. Even the arboreal chimpanzee can run faster than a man, and any monkey can easily outdistance him. A man, on the other hand, can walk for many miles, and this is essential for efficient hunting. According to skeletal evidence, fully developed walkers first appeared in the ancient men who inhabited the Old World from 500,000 years ago to the middle of the last glaciation. These men were competent hunters, as is shown by the bones of the large animals they killed. But they also used fire and made complicated tools according to clearly defined traditions. Along with the change in the structure of the pelvis, the brain had doubled in size since the time of the man-apes.

The fossil record thus substantiates the suggestion, first made by Charles Darwin, that tool use is both the cause and the effect of bipedal locomotion. Some very limited bipedalism left the hands sufficiently free from locomotor functions so that stones or sticks could be carried, played with and used. The advantage that these objects gave to their users led both to more bipedalism and to more efficient tool use. English lacks any neat expression for this sort of situation, forcing us to speak of cause and effect as if they were separated, whereas in natural selection cause and effect are interrelated. Selection is based on successful behavior, and in the man-apes the beginnings of the human way of life depended on both inherited locomotor capacity and on the learned skills of tool-using. The success of the new way of life based on the use of tools changed the selection pressures on many parts of the body, notably the teeth, hands and brain, as well as on the pelvis. But it must be remembered that selection was for the whole way of life.

In all the apes and monkeys the males have large canine teeth. The long upper canine cuts against the first lower premolar, and the lower canine passes in front of the upper canine. This is an efficient fighting mechanism, backed by very large jaw muscles. I have seen male baboons drive off cheetahs and dogs, and according to reliable reports male baboons have even put leopards to flight. The females have small canines, and they hurry away with the young under the very conditions in which the males turn to fight. All the evidence from living monkeys and apes suggests that the male's large canines are of the greatest importance to the survival of the group, and that they are particularly important in ground-living forms that may not be able to climb to safety in the trees. The small, early man-apes lived in open plains country, and yet none of them had large canine teeth. It would appear that the protection of the group must have shifted from teeth to tools early in the evolution of the man-apes, and long before the appearance of the forms that have been found in association with stone tools. The tools of Sterkfontein and Olduvai represent not the beginnings of tool use, but a choice of material and knowledge in manufacture which, as is shown by the small canines of the man-apes that deposited them there, derived from a long history of tool use.

Reduction in the canine teeth is not a simple matter, but involves changes in the muscles, face, jaws and other parts of the skull. Selection builds powerful neck muscles in animals that fight with their canines, and adapts the skull to the action of these muscles. Fighting is not a matter of teeth alone, but also of seizing, shaking and hurling an enemy's body with the jaws, head and neck. Reduction in the canines is therefore accompanied by a shortening in the jaws, reduction in the ridges of bone over the eyes and a decrease in the shelf of bone in the neck area. The reason that the skulls of the females and young of the apes look more like man-apes than those of adult males is that, along with small canines, they have smaller muscles and all the numerous structural features that go along with them. The skull of the man-ape is that of an ape that has lost the structure for effective fighting with its teeth. Moreover, the man-ape has transferred to its hands the functions of seizing and pulling, and this has been attended by reduction of its incisors. Small canines and incisors are biological symbols of a changed way of life; their primitive functions are replaced by hand and tool.

The history of the grinding teeth—the molars—is different from that of the seizing and fighting teeth. Large size in any anatomical structure must be maintained by positive selection; the selection pressure changed first on the canine teeth and, much later, on the molars. In the man-apes the molars were very large, larger than in either ape or man. They were heavily worn, possibly because food dug from the ground with the aid of tools was very abrasive. With the men of the Middle Pleistocene, molars of human size appear along with complicated tools, hunting and fire.

The disappearance of brow ridges and the refinement of the human face may involve still another factor. One of the essential conditions for the organization of men in co-operative societies was the suppression of rage and of the uncontrolled drive to first place in the hierarchy of dominance. Recently it has been shown that domestic animals, chosen over the generations for willingness to adjust and for lack of rage, have relatively small adrenal glands, as Curt P. Richter of Johns Hopkins University has shown. But the breeders who selected for this hormonal, physiological, temperamental type also picked, without realizing it, animals with small brow ridges and small faces. The skull structure of the wild rat bears the same relation to that of the tame rat as does the skull of Neanderthal man to that of *Homo sapiens*. The same is true for the cat, dog, pig, horse and cow; in each case the wild form has the larger face and muscular ridges. In the later stages of human evolution, it appears, the self-domestication of man has been exerting the same effects upon temperament, glands and skull that are seen in the domestic animals.

Of course from man-ape to man the brain-containing part of the skull has also increased greatly in size. This change is directly due to the increase in the size of the brain: as the brain grows, so grow the bones that cover it. Since there is this close correlation between brain size and bony brain-case, the brain size of the fossils can be estimated. On the scale of brain size the man-apes are scarcely distinguishable from the living apes, although their brains may have been larger with respect to body size. The brain seems to have evolved rapidly, doubling in size between man-ape and man. It then appears to have increased much more slowly; there is no substantial change in gross size during the last 100,000 years. One must remember, however, that size alone is a very crude indicator, and that brains of equal size may vary greatly in function. My belief is that although the brain of *Homo sapiens* is no larger than that of Neanderthal man, the indirect evidence strongly suggests that the first *Homo sapiens* was a much more intelligent creature.

The great increase in brain size is important because many functions of the brain seem to depend on the number of cells, and the number increases with volume. But certain parts of the brain have increased in size much more than others. As functional maps of the cortex of the brain show, the human sensory-motor cortex is not just an enlargement of that of an ape. The areas for the hand, especially the thumb, in man are tremendously enlarged, and this is an integral part of the structural base that makes the skillful use of the hand possible. The selection pressures that favored a large thumb also favored a large cortical area to receive sensations from the thumb and to control its motor activity. Evolution favored the development of a sensitive, powerful, skillful thumb, and in all these ways—as well as in structure—a human thumb differs from that of an ape.

The same is true for other cortical areas. Much of the cortex in a monkey is still engaged in the motor and sensory functions. In man it is the areas adjacent to the primary centers that are most expanded. These areas are concerned with skills, memory, foresight and language; that is, with the mental faculties that make human social life possible. This is easiest to illustrate in the field of language. Many apes and monkeys can make a wide variety of sounds. These sounds do not, however, develop into language. Some workers have devoted great efforts, with minimum results, to trying to teach chimpanzees to talk. The reason is that there is little in the brain to teach. A human child learns to speak with the greatest ease, but the storage of thousands of words takes a great deal of cortex. Even the simplest language must have given great advantage to those first men who had it. One is tempted to think that language may have appeared together with the fine tools, fire and complex hunting of the large-brained men of the Middle Pleistocene, but there is no direct proof of this.

The main point is that the kind of animal that can learn to adjust to complex, human, technical society is a very different creature from a tree-living ape, and the differences between the two are rooted in the evolutionary process. The reason that the human brain makes the human way of life possible is that it is the result of that way of life. Great masses of the tissue in the human brain are devoted to memory, planning, language and skills, because these are the abilities favored by the human way of life.

The emergence of man's large brain occasioned a profound change in the

18

plan of human reproduction. The human mother-child relationship is unique among the primates as is the use of tools. In all the apes and monkeys the baby clings to the mother; to be able to do so, the baby must be born with its central nervous system in an advanced state of development. But the brain of the fetus must be small enough so that birth may take place. In man adaptation to bipedal locomotion decreased the size of the bony birth-canal at the same time that the exigencies of tool use selected for larger brains. This obstetrical dilemma was solved by delivery of the fetus at a much earlier stage of development. But this was possible only because the mother, already bipedal and with hands free of locomotor necessities, could hold the helpless, immature infant. The small-brained man-ape probably developed in the uterus as much as the ape does; the human type of mother-child relation must have evolved by the time of the large-brained, fully bipedal humans of the Middle Pleistocene. Bipedalism, tool use and selection for large brains thus slowed human development and invoked far greater maternal responsibility. The slow-moving mother, carrying the baby, could not hunt, and the combination of the woman's obligation to care for slow-developing babies and the man's occupation of hunting imposed a fundamental pattern on the social organization of the human species.

All these family functions are ultimately related to tools, hunting and the enlargement of the brain. Complex and technical society evolved from the sporadic tool-using of an ape, through the simple pebble tools of the man-ape and the complex toolmaking traditions of ancient men to the hugely complicated culture of modern man. Each behavioral stage was both cause and effect of biological change in bones and brain. These concomitant changes can be seen in the scanty fossil record and can be inferred from the study of the living forms.

Surely as more fossils are found these ideas will be tested. New techniques of investigation, from planned experiments in the behavior of lower primates to more refined methods of dating, will extract wholly new information from the past. It is my belief that, as these events come to pass, tool use will be found to have been a major factor, beginning with the initial differentiation of man and ape. In ourselves we see a structure, physiology and behavior that is the result of the fact that some populations of apes started to use tools a million years ago. The pebble tools constituted man's principal technical adaptation for a period at least 50 times as long as recorded history. As we contemplate man's present eminence, it is well to remember that, from the point of view of evolution, the events of the last 50,000 years occupy but a moment in time. Ancient man endured at least 10 times as long and the man-apes for an even longer time.

ECOLOGY AND THE PROTOHOMINIDS

GEORGE A. BARTHOLOMEW, Jr. and JOSEPH B. BIRDSELL

Although the word ecology is used in both the biological and the social sciences, attempts to bring the biologist and students of human society together by analogical reasoning are beset with traps for the unwary. The biological world lies primarily within genetic and physiological limits while that of the social sciences lies within cultural limits. However, whatever else man is, he is first an animal and hence subject, although usually indirectly, to environmental and biological factors.

It is generally agreed that the ecological generalizations and points of view which have proved helpful in interpreting the natural history of most mammals can be applied virtually intact to all primates except man. It should, therefore, be possible to extrapolate upward from ecological data on other mammals and suggest the biological attributes of the protohominids and to extrapolate downward from ethnological data on hunting and collecting peoples and suggest the minimal cultural attributes of the protohominids.

We propose first to discuss in general terms some aspects of mammalian ecology which appear to be applicable to the protohominids; second, to apply these ideas to the available data on the australopithecines; and third, to discuss the application of a few ecological ideas to preagricultural humans. A history of the development of ecology and suggestions for its applications to anthropology which has recently been published by Bates (1953) provides basic historical orientation and perspective for such an effort.

Protohominids and tools. In retrospect, the vast sweep of evolution appears to lead inevitably to the appearance of man, but a rational interpretation of the evidence refutes this. During the Cenozoic there have been three separate mammalian evolutionary complexes, one in Australia, one in South America, and one in Eurasia, Africa, and North America. Of these complexes, only the last has produced organisms of the hominid level. Further, since the major orders of mammals were already distinct in the Eocene, each has had a separate genetic history for approximately 70,000,000 years, and only one, primates, has produced an organism at the hominid level of organization.

Since a number of mammalian orders have shown a strong independent

Reprinted by permission from *American Anthropologist*, 55: (1953), 481-98.

evolutionary trend toward a large brain size, this trend is by no means peculiar to the order primates (Edinger 1948). This striking parallelism is presumably related to the fact that large brain size favors varied behavior and learning as supplements to genetically fixed responses. Why then did not the primates, like the other mammals, reach an apparent evolutionary dead end in the Pliocene? The familiar and reasonable ideas concerning the importance of arboreal life in setting the stage for the appearance of man, i.e., dependence on vision, grasping hands, and the lack of restrictive skeletal adaptations, need not be labored here, but the importance of bipedalism can profitably be re-examined.

The primates comprise the only major order of mammals which is characteristically arboreal. There can be no doubt that this arboreal heritage has been of vital importance in human evolution, but the critical stage in the transition from ape to protohominid involves the assumption of a unique terrestrial mode of life. A number of cercopithecids have successfully invaded the terrestrial habitat, but these all show quadrupedal adaptations. This level of adaptation, while obviously effective if one may judge by the fossil record and by present abundance, appears to represent a stable, long-surviving, adaptive equilibrium.

The terrestrial adaptations of the hominid line represent a step into a new and previously unexploited mode of life in which the critical feature was bipedalism. Among mammals changes of this magnitude have occurred only rarely since the middle Cenozoic. Aside from the saltatorial rodents such as the jerboas and kangaroo rats, all placental terrestrial mammals other than man use both hind and front legs for locomotion. The extreme rarity of bipedalism among mammals suggests that it is inefficient except under very special circumstances (Hatt 1932; Bartholomew and Caswell 1951). Even modern man's unique vertical bipedal locomotion, when compared to that of quadrupedal mammals, is relatively ineffective, and this implies that a significant nonlocomotor advantage must have resulted from even the partial freeing of the forelimbs. This advantage was the use of the hands for efficient manipulation of adventitious tools such as rocks, sticks, or bones. Of course, the terrestrial or semi-terrestrial living primates have their hands free when they are not moving, but only man has his locomotion essentially unimpeded while carrying or using a tool. Man has been characterized as the "tool-using animal," but this implies a degree of uniqueness to man's use of tools which is unrealistic. Not only do other primates use tools—the use of sticks and rocks by chimpanzees and baboons is generally familiar—but such unlikely animals as the sea otter (Fisher 1939) and one of the Galapagos finches (Lack 1945) routinely use rocks or sticks to obtain food. Indeed, the natural history literature is replete with instances of the use of tools by animals, and there really is no clear-cut boundary between web-spinning, nest-building, and stick-wielding on the one hand, and tool use at the simplest human level on the other. However, in contrast to all other mammals, the larger arboreal primates are, in a sense, tool users in their locomotion. As they move through the maze of the tree tops, their use of branches anticipates the use of tools in that they routinely employ levers and angular momentum. The grasping hands on which the locomotion and feeding of primates depends, are of course obviously pre-adapted for tool use.

Rather than to say that man is unique in being the "tool-using" animal, it is more accurate to say that man is the only mammal which is continuously dependent on tools for survival. This dependence on the learned use of tools indicates a movement into a previously unexploited dimension of behavior, and this movement accompanied the advent of bipedalism. With the assumption of erect posture regular use of tools became obligatory; the ability occasionally to use tools must have preceded this in time.

Protohominids and body size. The conditions of terrestrial life for a bipedal tool-using mammal virtually demanded that the protohominids be big mammals, i.e., at least in the 50 to 100 pound range, for large size of itself offers important biological advantages (Carter 1951:293). In the case of the protohominids two such advantages at once suggest themselves: First, large size would remove them from the category of potential prey for all carnivorous birds, reptiles, and all mammals except the big cats and the pack-hunting dogs; second, it would allow them to utilize without restrictive anatomical specialization and with simple instrumentation, virtually the entire range of food size utilized by all other terrestrial mammals.

Sociality. Social behavior is inextricably interwoven with ecology, and although it is not possible to review the subject in detail here, certain aspects of it are basic to the development of later ideas.

The transitional protohominids must have been social to the extent of forming relatively stable family groups. Even in the absence of direct evidence, such a statement can be made with complete confidence from knowledge of the other members of the suborder Anthropoidea. First, there is the absence of seasonal sexual periodism in man and the great apes. Thus sexual ties form a bond of sustained and continuing attraction which provides a biological basis for the long-surviving family unit. As has frequently been pointed out this is a central element in human sociality. Second, there is a long period of growth and maturation. The long childhood of man and the great apes is not a mere function of size—the blue whale, the largest mammal that has ever lived, grows to sexual maturity and to a length of 70 or more feet in two years (Mackintosh and Wheeler 1929)—but it is related to the unique dependence for survival on learning in the higher primates. The acquisition of competence for independent life demands several years of parental care in the chimpanzee and a decade or more in man. Hence, survival requires a mother-offspring relation which is sustained through many years and, like sexual attraction, is not just a seasonal interlude as in other social mammals. Since these factors shape the social behavior of both the great apes and man, they must have shaped the social life of the proto-hominids.

Other cohesive forces, by analogy with living primates, must have supplied integration to the social organization of the protohominids. Important among these must have been dominance-subordinance relationships. The concept of social dominance has proved to be a touchstone to the understanding of the social behavior of vertebrates. It is a key factor in the social behavior of mammals as diverse as deer (Darling 1937), seals (Bartholomew 1952), and primates (Yerkes 1939).

In every case in which it has been studied in mammals, dominance is established at least in part on the basis of aggressive behavior (Collias 1944), of which a large component is either directly or indirectly dependent on reproductive physiology. In mammals the male sex hormones stimulate ag-gressive behavior and contribute to greater body size, while the female sex hormones inhibit the former and do not contribute to the latter. Conse-quently, males tend to be dominant over females in most situations. In the higher primates, as in many other social mammals, sexual dimorphism in size reinforces the greater aggressiveness of the male and insures his superior social status in situations where force is involved. In most social mammals, gregariousness overcomes the disruptive effect of dominance-subordinance relations and maintains the social unit. In primates dominance is not an exclusively disruptive force, since the dominant animal may protect the subordinate animal which looks to it for protection as well as leadership (Noble 1939).

In nonprimate social mammals, the resolution of the forces produced by dominance and gregariousness typically produces a seasonal breeding unit which consists of a dominant male and a harem of females and which usually excludes the young of previous years.

The social unit in nonhuman primates is variable, and too few detailed field studies have been published to allow extrapolation from living anthro-poids to the protohominids. In modern hunting and collecting groups of man the smallest unit is the biological family including immature offspring, and in many cultures the most important functional group is the extended family, or band. In the case of man, even at the simplest level, social dominance is not based exclusively on successful aggressive behavior. The distance between nonprimate mammals and man is too broad to be spanned by the bracketing technique previously used, but the semi-permanent biological family, includ-ing offspring, must have been a basic unit among the protohominids. Inte-gration on any more extensive scale must have depended upon the degree of cultural attainment. It should be observed however, that fairly large groups have been reported for living nonhominid anthropoids (Carpenter 1942: Nissen 1951).

23

Territoriality. No aspect of the social behavior of wild vertebrates has attracted more attention than territoriality, a concept which includes the entire complex pattern of behavior associated with the defense of an area. The display of ownership of places and objects is very highly developed among human beings, but this behavior pattern is not peculiar to modern man. It is almost universally present in terrestrial vertebrates, either on a permanent or seasonal basis. The large literature on the subject with regard to birds has been reviewed by Nice (1941). Its status in mammals has been discussed by Burt (1943), and its relation to vertebrate populations has been examined by Errington (1946).

Territoriality springs from the necessity for finding and maintaining environmental conditions suitable for survival and reproduction. The techniques of territory maintenance, the precise factors immediately responsible for it, and the immediate significance of it vary from species to species.

The maintenance of territories either by individuals or by social groups has profound effects on distribution. Birds and mammals tend to be neither continuously distributed nor irregularly grouped, but to be spaced at more or less regular intervals through ecologically suitable habitat. This spacing is determined by conflicts between pairs of individuals or between interacting groups of animals. Thus, territorial boundaries are learned and vary in time and space. If anthropologists were willing, this might almost be considered protocultural behavior at a subhuman level; in any event, it emphasizes the continuity of human behavior with that of other vertebrates.

As a result of the centrifugal effects of aggressive behavior, territory maintenance forces animals to disperse into adjacent areas. It distributes the individual organisms or social units of a species throughout the entire accessible area of suitable habitat. Should the population increase, local population density does not continue to build up indefinitely. Instead territorial defense forces individuals out into marginal situations, and thus the resources of the optimal habitat are not exhausted. Most of the displaced individuals do not survive, but some many find unexploited areas of suitable habitat and thus extend the range of the species. The result is that a population tends to be maintained at or below the optimum density in the preferred habitat, and the excess individuals are forced to marginal areas to which they must adapt or die.

Thus territoriality is one of the primary factors which determine the density of population. It organizes a local population into a well-spaced array that allows adequate living conditions for all successful individuals. It limits the breeding population which can exist in suitable habitats and thus helps to prevent increase beyond the long-term carrying capacity of the range. This dispersive effect of territoriality can hardly help but be an important causal factor both in migration and in the spread of genes through a population. Hence, it must contribute importantly to rate of evolutionary change (Burt 1949).

The question of the importance of territoriality to the biology of proto-hominids at once presents itself. Carpenter (1934; 1940) has demonstrated that howler monkeys and gibbons maintain territory by group action. It is clear that territoriality exists in all complex human societies, and it is clearly established that group territoriality is also important at the simplest levels of human culture. It is, therefore, reasonable to assume that protohominids similarly possessed a well-developed territoriality, presumably on the basis of the family or extended family.

Population equilibrium. One of the most critical ecological factors which can be determined about an animal is the density of its population. The number of variables which contribute to the determination of population density is enormous; a complete analysis for even the best known of living wild mammals is difficult, perhaps impossible. Nevertheless, the framework within which such an analysis can be made is known, for the factors involved in population dynamics have been studied intensively in recent years. A useful discussion of populations from the point of view of the ecologist is given by Bodenheimer (1938), and Allee *et al.* (1949).

Since organisms are transient biochemical systems which require con-tinuous expenditure of energy for their maintenance, the struggle for existence becomes, in one sense at least, a struggle for the free energy avail-able for doing physiological work. This fact offers a point of view from which to approach the problem of estimating the population of .proto-hominids, or any other mammal.

There exists a series of nutrient or trophic levels that expresses the energy relations which tie together the various organisms of the terrestrial environ-ment. The primary trophic level is that of the green plants, for only they can use radiant energy to synthesize significant quantities of organic material. The trophic level of the herbivores includes all animals directly dependent on plants for food. The next higher trophic level, that of the meat-eaters which may be primary carnivores (eaters of herbivores), secondary carnivores (eaters of other carnivores), and so on. The final trophic level, the eaters of dead organic material, eventually returns materials to the inorganic state depleted of biologically available energy.

Materials which are used as building blocks and sources of energy by organisms cycle continuously through these trophic levels, and at each level there is an endless competition for them. There are a number of obvious corollaries which follow from these relationships. An important one is that nutrition plays a primary role in determining the major functional adapta-tions of animals. Life demands a continuous expenditure of energy, and this energy is available only through nutrition. These energy relations involve a sustained long-term pressure sufficiently constant to maintain and give direction to the major evolutionary trends apparent in the adaptive changes of the sort shown by hoofed mammals and the carnivorous mammals. As

Simpson (1944:31) and others have pointed out, these nutritive adaptations have for the most part led not only to greater efficiency but also to more and more specialization, with a consequent reduction in potentiality for new major nutritive adaptations. Thus adaptations toward increased efficiency in food getting, or toward avoidance of becoming food for other organisms, are largely restrictive from the standpoint of future evolutionary change.

The total weight of biological materials produced by one trophic level must necessarily be less than that of the level below it on which it depends, and greater than that of the level above, which it supports. Each nutritive level must in the long run live on the interest, not the capital, of the trophic level below it. From this there follows a maxim which allows of no exception. On a long-term basis the mean population of a species is in equilibrium with the trophic levels both above it and below it, as well as with the total limiting effects of the inorganic environment. This means that the birth rate must be great enough to balance the death rate from disease (a nutritive phenomenon from the standpoint of the disease-causing organism), predation, and accident. Consequently, birth rate is a factor subject to natural selection, and all natural populations represent approximate equilibria between biotic potentials and total resistance of the biological and physical environments. Short-lived mammals of high fecundity, such as rabbits and mice, are sometimes characterized by drastic short-term fluctuations in population size, the causes for which are still subject to active controversy (Cole 1951). However, in this paper we shall ignore the problem of population cycles, for drastic cyclic fluctuations have rarely been observed in large tropical mammals with low reproductive potentials.

It has been generally appreciated since the time of Darwin that animals, despite their capacity to increase in numbers, tend to maintain a population which fluctuates around some equilibrium figure. This idea is of such a basic nature that it forms a foundation for the concept of natural selection which now appears to be an omnipresent evolutionary force. The factors involved in the maintenance of these equilibria are complex and variable. Since, as pointed out above, an animal population cannot possibly permanently exceed its food resources, these fix an upper limit. The determination of the actual equilibrium figure is a subtle problem which must be solved independently for each population. A thoughtful analysis of the factors limiting population in a nonhominid primate under natural conditions is presented by Collias and Southwick (1952) in their study of howling monkeys. For a population to maintain itself above that lower critical level which means inevitable extinction (Darling 1938), many factors (which may vary independently) must be simultaneously satisfied. Such things as a suitable habitat which will include adequate food resources, water, and home sites, and climatic conditions that do not exceed the tolerance of the group must be present.

Since biological factors vary with time, values for population equilibria are not to be measured at a given point in time. They fluctuate about a balance which is determined, not by the mean condition, but by the extremes. Indeed, one of the most firmly established ecological generalizations is Liebig's law of the minimum, which states that a biological reaction at any level is controlled not by the factors which are present in excess, but by that essential factor which is present in minimal quantity. Since, as was previously pointed out, population density is the most critical single ecological datum, anthropologists studying the simpler cultures characterized by few storage techniques would do well to search for those critical limiting factors which do determine density. Such limiting factors are not necessarily either obvious or conspicuous at all points in time, and even when they occur their expression may be subtle or apparently indirect. A semi-arid area may have many fruitful years in succession, but a single drought year occurring once in a human generation may restrict the population to an otherwise inexplicably low density. For example, the Papago Indians of the lower Colorado River were forced in drought years to revert to a desert hunting and collecting economy for survival (Castetter and Bell 1942). Thus, their population density appears in part to have been strongly affected by the preagricultural carrying capacity of this area. In some cases the size of a population will be determined not by the availability of an abundance of food during ten months of the year but by a regular seasonal scarcity in the remaining two months.

The reproductive potential of animals is such that under favorable conditions, such as having available a previously unexploited habitat, the size of a population can increase at an essentially logarithmic rate. This capacity for rapid increase makes possible the recovery of populations following drastic population reduction. In a stable population, on the other hand, the reproductive potential is expressed only as a one-to-one replacement of adult individuals.

Anthropologists are properly impressed with the complexity of learned behavior in human groups, but may fail to appreciate its significance among other mammals. Even on the nonhuman level, population density may be controlled by behavioral factors, either genetic or learned. Territoriality and dominance relations, which are dependent on learned behavior, contribute to the determination of group relations and population density. Under certain circumstances behavioral factors may be more important than nutritive factors in determining population density. For example, recent work discussed by Calhoun (1952) has shown that the Norway rat under controlled experimental conditions, in which food is present in excess at all times, reaches a population equilibrium that is determined by strictly behavioral factors related to territoriality and competition for suitable home sites. Thus, experimental work confirms extensive field observations on a variety of vertebrates. Since learned behavior operates as an important factor determining density in all terrestrial mammals which have been studied, and in modern man, it must have been an important factor in determining the population density of the protohominids. The importance of learned behavior increases directly with its complexity, and in man at cultural levels above the hunting and collecting stage of economy it becomes increasingly difficult to identify the ecological factors affecting population size.

ECOLOGY AND THE AUSTRALOPITHECINES

The dating of the australopithecines has proved troublesome, and final decision is not now possible. Dart and Broom have suggested that these protohominids lived during a period extending from the Villafranchian into the middle Pleistocene. This time span overlaps the datings of early man in other parts of the world, and implies a collateral relationship with more evolved hominids. Another view has recently been given by de Chardin (1952), who places the australopithecines in Villafranchian time, and thus removes them from contemporaneity with known African hominids. Breuil (1948) seems to reflect a similar point of view. In the former case the australopithecines would have been competing in their closing phase with more advanced forms of man, and hence would have been decreasing in numbers and range. In the latter instance the australopithecines would apparently have been the sole occupants of the protohominid niche over wide areas in South Africa, with the resultant possibility of having an expanding population and range. For purposes of an ecological discussion it is necessary to assume one dating or the other; it is not important to decide whether or not the australopithecines were in fact ancestral to more advanced hominid types, but it is important to determine whether or not they were the sole occupants of the hominid niche in South Africa.

As de Chardin (1952) points out, the australopithecine-bearing breccias and the human industry-bearing deposits have never been found conformably associated in the same site. This assumes, as did de Chardin, that *Telanthropus* is but a variant of the australopithecine type. Therefore, for purposes of discussion we shall assume that the australopithecines are Villafranchian in date and hence earlier than the markers of the pebble-cultures of South Africa. By analogy with the ecology of other animals it would be surprising if man and the australopithecines had remained contemporaries in the same area over very long periods of time, for closely-related forms with similar requirements rarely occupy the same area simultaneously.

Use of tools. Neither the archeological nor morphological evidence concerning australopithecines suggests an alternative to the assumption, which we made earlier, that protohominids were dependent on the use of tools for survival. It is generally agreed that the australopithecines were bipedal. Referring to our previous discussion, this strongly implies that the australopithecines routinely utilized adventitious or perhaps even slightly modified tools. Dart's evidence (1949) for the use of ungulate humeri as clubs offers empirical support for this theoretical position. Unmodified rocks used as tools can rarely be identified except by context. Familiar evidence from both archeology and ethnology shows that at the simplest level, rough tools commonly are discarded after initial use. Hence, a lack of recognizable stone tools in the breccias does not indicate that these were not used. Time alone precludes the survival of wooden implements such as clubs and digging sticks, although their use by australopithecines is certainly to be expected, for even the living great apes use sticks spontaneously.

The dentition of the partly carnivorous australopithecines (see section on food size) is uniformly characterized by reduced canines and incisors, and by nonsectorial premolars and molars (Le Gros Clark 1949). These dental characteristics are unique to them among all the large carnivorous mammals. The absence of teeth adapted for stabbing or shearing clearly implies the killing of game by weapons and butchering by simple tools. This observation would hold true even if the assignment of carnivorous habits to australopithecines were based only upon the abundant evidence that baboons were an important item in their diet. It is not dependent on the controversial question of their killing large hoofed mammals.

The dentition of australopithecines offers further evidence concerning their dependence on tools. As pointed out previously, intrasexual combat is characteristic of the males of virtually all strongly dimorphic mammals. Australopithecines are dimorphic, but they do not have the large piercing canines so characteristic of most of the larger living primates. This striking reduction of canines strongly implies that even in intrasexual (and intraspecific) combat, the australopithecines placed primary dependence on tools.

Scale of food size. It should be possible on theoretical grounds to fix the approximate upper and lower size limits of the food which could economically be handled by the australopithecines with nothing more elaborate than a crude stick for digging and a limb bone for a club. Their capabilities would allow the utilization of the following animal foods: virtually all terrestrial reptiles and the smaller aquatic ones; eggs and nesting birds; some fish; fresh-water mollusks and crustaceans; insects; all of the smaller mammals including some burrowing forms, and larger mammals up to and including baboons. It is difficult, perhaps impossible to determine whether or not the remains of the large giraffids and bovids reported from the bone breccias (Dart 1948), represent kills by australopithecines or their scavenging from the kills of the larger cats. Since few meat-eaters are loath to scavenge, and the implementation which would allow the australopithecines to kill such large animals is not apparent, we suggest that scavenging from the kills of the larger carnivores may have been systematically carried out.

Like most present-day hunting and collecting peoples, the australopithecines probably used plants as their major source of food. Without imputing to the australopithecines any cultural capabilities beyond the use of a simple stick for digging, at least the following types of vegetable food would be available to them: berries, fruits, nuts, buds and shoots, shallow-growing roots and tubers, and fruiting bodies of fungi. Some of the very small vegetable foods exploited by modern human groups were probably not extensively used. Effective utilization of grass seeds and other hard-shelled small seeds require specialized gathering implements and containers, and processing by grinding or cooking.

Such activties imply technologies which cannot be assigned *a priori* to the australopithecines, and for which there is no archeological indication until much later times. In this connection it may be noted that the evidence for the use of fire by *Australopithecus prometheus*, though impressive, is still regarded by some as controversial (Barbour 1949; Broom 1950). In summary, it seems reasonable to treat the australopithecines as generalized carnivorous animals for which the freeing of hands and the use of simple implements enormously broadened the scale of food size to include a surprisingly large proportion of the total food resources of the terrestrial environment.

Social behavior. The biological bases for the family and social organization at the protohominid level which have already been discussed should apply to the australopithecines. Group organization beyond the family level is not indicated by the archeological context of the finds, because the rather large number of individuals recorded from Swartkrans and Sterkfontein might result from sampling of family-sized groups over many generations. However, there is at least one line of archeological evidence which suggests social organization beyond the simple family level. Since baboons travel in large aggregations and were a significant item of australopithecine diet, it would seem likely that the latter hunted in bands. A single australopithecine, even armed with a club, would not be a serious threat to a band of baboons (Dart 1949). Such group hunting does not necessarily imply a high level of communication, such as speech, or permanence of organization, for it is characteristic of a number of nonprimate carnivorous vertebrates—many canids, some fish-eating birds, and killer-whales. Broom (1950) has shown that the australopithecines were characterized by sexual dimorphism, a widespread trait in the primates, including man. In social mammals, sexual dimorphism is almost invariably a product of the sexual selection associated with competition between males for females. Characteristically this sexual selection produces males which are larger, and more aggressive than females, and which have specialized structures for offense and defense. Although these dimorphic characters are a product of competition between males, they usually result in the males assuming the role of group defender. We propose that the sexual dimorphism of the australopithecine males may have favored a secondarily-derived function related to aggressive behavior, namely the hunting of large prey, including perhaps other australopithecines (Dart 1949). Thus it may be that a sexual division of labor such as is present in all known hunting peoples was foreshadowed at this early level of hominid evolution.

The primates which first began to exploit a bipedal tool-using mode of life were establishing a level of adaptedness of enormous potentiality which had previously been inaccessible. They were entering a period of rapid change leading to a new kind of adaptedness. In the terminology of Simpson (1944) they were a group undergoing quantum evolution. It is to be expected that, like other similarly rapidly evolving groups, they would be represented in the fossil record not by a uniform long-persistent type, but by a variable group of related forms. The australopithecines, which probably occupy a stage near the end of a step in quantum evolution, fit this theoretical prescription nicely. The various australopithecine forms which have been named can be considered representatives of a highly polymorphic assemblage. Their polymorphism is consistent with the idea of a rapidly evolving and radiating group and thus favors the probability of the Villafranchian dating.

It is reasonable to assume that most of the recovered australopithecine fossils date from a period prior to the time they faced competition from more highly evolved hominid types. When, as they inevitably must have, the australopithecines came in contact with culturally advanced hominids, they must have been subject to rapid replacement in terms of geological time.

DISCUSSION

A paper such as this necessarily can be of only temporary utility. We feel that its principal contribution lies in raising questions, the answering of which may require orientation toward new points of view, the collection of new kinds of data, and perhaps the use of new techniques.

Students of animal ecology have developed a number of points of view which could be profitably applied to the study of preagricultural man. Two are particularly attractive. The first of these is that the basic problem of human behavior, like the behavior of other animals, is the obtaining of food, for the human body requires a continuous input of energy both for maintenance and for propagation. The second point of view involves the idea that population density normally is a complexly maintained equilibrium, dependent upon environmental as well as behavioral (and in the case of man, cultural) forces.

Anthropologists and archeologists to date have shown great ingenuity in utilizing the meager data for paleolithic and mesolithic man to establish tentative chronologies and outline cultural relationships. However, at the simplest level, the significance of material culture lies neither in the establishment of chronology nor as a measure of relationships, but as an indicator of efficiency in obtaining food. The lack of data concerning the food-getting effectiveness of the various items of material culture primarily results from

31

preoccupation with typology rather than function. Even the best of typological labels tend to restrict functional interpretations and to ignore the role of varied behavior and human ingenuity in extending an implement's utility. Furthermore, functional interpretations can be determined only by studies of living peoples, and the ethnologist has not yet generally been stimulated to the realization of the basic importance of such data.

It is of interest that some food-getting devices which we presume to have been available to the australopithecines remain important today in the economy of hunting and gathering peoples. But there is little systematic quantitative information concerning the proportion of food obtained through the use of the hands alone, or that added by the use of the simple digging stick, club, or wooden spear. Nor at a more culturally sophisticated level are there quantitative data available to measure the increase in efficiency made possible by the invention of such devices as the spear-thrower and the bow and arrow. In making such analyses it would be useful to distinguish between the contributions of the relatively limited variety of primary tools and the more varied secondary tools. For example, the ecological significance of the fist-axes of the lower and middle Pleistocene varies enormously depending upon whether they are to be interpreted as primary tools used to make wooden implements such as clubs, digging sticks and spears, or whether they are regarded in the unlikely light of hand-held striking implements (see, for example, Tindale 1949).

As pointed out previously, all animal populations, including human populations, depend on radiant energy stored chemically by photosynthesis. Animals compete endlessly between themselves for the one per cent of incident solar energy which plants are able to capture. The competitive success of an individual animal can be determined from its metabolism and the success of a population can be expressed quantitatively as the product of population density times individual metabolism.

If one can obtain even approximate figures for (1) the production of organic material by plants, (2) population densities and, (3) metabolism, one can evaluate from one point of view the biological success of different organisms. One can compare lions and elephants, earthworms and mice, humans and all other organisms, or more pertinent to anthropologists, one can compare simple cultures existing in either similar or different environmental situations. Since human beings comprise a single species, inter-group comparisons can be made on the basis of weight per unit area. An instructive analysis of this sort for small North American mammals has been made by Mohr (1947).

To our knowledge this quantitative approach to human ecology has not been exploited by anthropologists; indeed, few attempts have been made by zoologists. Pearson (1948) has gathered figures which allow a comparison of Indians of northeastern United States with other animals common in the same area. Indians had less metabolic impact than deer, about the same impact as long-tailed shrews. Deevey (1951) presents calculations which show the amazing trophic impact of the present human population of the world. Both these efforts are frankly exploratory and depend on approximations, but they point up an approach which merits consideration by anthropologists. If one could obtain for given areas even crude figures for human population density and for the production of organic material by the flora, he could compare the nutritive efficiencies of rainforest and grassland cultures, or the efficiency of Great Basin Indians and Australian Aborigines even though the two peoples live in arid regions of a very different character. Similarly one could obtain quantitative estimates for the effects of rivers, lakes, sea shore, and particularly vegetation types (i.e., oak woodland) on the capacity of an area to support human populations at a simple cultural level.

As discussed earlier, natural populations tend to fluctuate about some equilibrium figure. This fact has long been recognized by biologists, but to date, despite the perspectives which it supplies, it has not significantly influenced the approach of most anthropologists. From a short-term point of view, populations are in only approximate equilibrium, but viewed from the time scale of the Pleistocene, slowly expanding populations of man can be considered as being essentially in equilibrium. It appears to us that the idea that the populations of early man were in approximate equilibrium with the environment can supply a point of view from which to interpret the dynamics of technologically simple human populations. It should greatly facilitate qualitative exploration of such considerations as spatial variation of population density; growth or decline in numbers; rates of movement as influenced by migration and gene flow; and, shifts of populations into new climatic situations which demand new modes of life and may involve biological as well as cultural changes in adaptedness. As such qualitative interpretations are refined it may be possible to develop models which depict these processes semi-quantitatively and thus allow crude predictions.

Population density is a key to these dynamic processes, for either directly or indirectly it controls all of the others. As discussed in the sections on territoriality and population equilibrium, the density of early human populations, while immediately determined by a complex of variables in which behavior plays a central role, was ultimately controlled by the environment. Even in the most favorable environments the equilibrium density attained by natural populations is somewhat below the maximum which the environment can support. The factors restricting density are behavioral in an immediate sense and involve such things as aggressive behavior and territoriality. These behavioral factors must have brought dispersive forces to bear on Pleistocene man just as they do on other mammals. The existence of such dispersive forces suggests that the evolving australopithecines must have spread with great rapidity (i.e., almost instantaneously in terms of geological time) throughout the continental tropics and subtropics of the Old World.

33

Such an expansion would leave no suitable and accessible areas unoccupied. Consequently all subsequently evolved hominids in these regions must have expanded at the expense of already established populations. The replacement of the australopithecines by somewhat more advanced but related hominids may have followed the usual mammalian pattern of the gradual expansion of the more efficient form, and the slow reduction of the numbers of the less efficient. In many instances, however, population change must have resulted from gradual genetic penetration, and much of human evolution in the Pleistocene could easily have been powerfully affected by introgressive hybridization. In this regard it should be remembered that anatomical differences do not necessarily indicate genetic incompatability between groups, and that there is no evidence of reluctance to hybridize even between widely different human types. If rapid and dramatic group replacement did occur it must have been a rare event occurring in special circumstances.

Although mammals are less affected by climate in a direct physical sense than are most organisms, physiological differences among mammals adapted to different climatic conditions have been clearly demonstrated (Scholander, et al., 1950). Distributionally the primates are an order characteristic of the tropics or subtropics. Modern man himself appears to be unable to invade the higher latitudes without fairly elaborate cultural accoutrements. It may therefore be concluded that during the Pliocene, the evolving protohominids occupied only the tropics, subtropics and perhaps the fringes of the temperate zones. The only place in which human populations could have expanded into a vacuum was at the margins of the then habitable areas. Thus changing cultural, and possibly changing biological, adaptedness would have allowed hominid expansion from the tropics into the temperate regions and ultimately into the arctic regions of the Old World. Aside from the initial continental expansion of the Old World protohominids, man expanded into major vacuums in populating Australasia, the New World, and much later, Micronesia and Polynesia. Once entered, these areas must have become filled rapidly, so that subsequent immigrants were faced for the most part with the problem of replacing established populations. Migrations, although spectacular, were probably of less importance in the Pleistocene than the processes discussed previously, which proceed normally without local catastrophic environmental change.

The anthropologists' lack of concern with the idea of population equilibrium in the simpler and more static human cultures is explicable in historical terms. Anthropologists, reacting to the claim by some anthropogeographers that extreme environmental determinism was operative on man, soon demonstrated that details of culture were not controlled directly by the environment. This broad denial overlooked man's nutritive dependence upon the environment, and long inhibited quantitative investigation of the relationship between man's population density and environmental factors.

The present interpretation of the mechanism of evolution is based upon natural selection which demands that populations be in a state of approximate equilibrium at a given time. To unravel the evolution of Pleistocene man, inevitably hampered as one is with inadequate data, one must necessarily use the idea of a population in equilibrium with the carrying capacity of the environment.

Most ecologists agree that no data are more crucial than those bearing upon population size, structure and density. Anthropologists, even though generally unconcerned with population equilibria, in some instances have been aware of the concept (Krzywicki 1934; Steward 1938; and Evans-Pritchard 1940). But in general the importance of an ecological approach has not been appreciated. Some archeologists have hoped to reconstruct pre-agricultural population figures from studying the temporal and spatial distribution of sites, but the inescapable sampling errors in this approach render it unreliable. We suggest that an analysis of the energy relationships and the efficiency of the techniques for obtaining food offer a promising approach.

For several years it has been apparent that an ecological approach is imperative for all studies in population genetics, including those pertaining to man. It also offers a potentially useful point of view to the physical anthropologist, the ethnologist, and the archeologist, and it should provide an important integrative bridge between the various fields of anthropology.

REFERENCES

ALLEE, W. C., A. E. EMERSON, O. PARK, T. PARK, and K. P. SCHMIDT   1949 Principles of animal ecology. W. B. Saunders Co., Philadelphia.

BARBOUR, G. B.   1949   Ape or man? Ohio Journal of Science 49: 129–145.

BARTHOLOMEW, G. A., JR.   1952   Reproductive and social behavior of the northern elephant seal. University of California Publications in Zoology 47: 369–472.

BARTHOLOMEW, G. A., JR., and H. C. CASWELL, JR.   1951   Locomotion in kangaroo rats and its adaptive significance. Journal of Mammalogy 32: 155–169.

BATES, M.   1953   Human ecology. Anthropology Today: An Encyclopedic Inventory, ed. by A. Kroeber. University of Chicago Press, Chicago.

BODENHEIMER, F. S.   1938   Problems of animal ecology. Oxford University Press, London.

BREUIL, ABBE HENRI   1948   Ancient raised beaches and prehistoric civilisations in South Africa. South African Journal of Science 44: 61–74.

BROOM, R.   1950   The genera and species of the South African ape-man. American Journal of Physical Anthropology n.s. 8: 1–13.

BURT, W. H.   1943   Territoriality and home range concepts as applied to mammals. Journal of Mammalogy 24: 346–352.

——— 1949   Territoriality. Journal of Mammalogy 30: 25–27.

CALHOUN, J. B.   1952   The social aspects of population dynamics. Journal of Mammalogy 33: 139–159.

CARPENTER, C. R.   1934   A field study of the behavior and social relations of howling monkeys. Comparative Psychology Monographs 10: 1–168.

——— 1940   A field study of the behavior and social relations of the gibbon. Comparative Psychology Monographs 16: 1–212.

——— 1942   Societies of monkeys and apes. Biological Symposia 8: 177–204.

CARTER, G. S.   1951   Animal evolution. Sedgwick and Jackson Ltd., London.

CASTETTER, E. F., and W. H. BELL   1942   Pima and Papago Indian agriculture. Inter-American Studies I. Univ. of New Mexico Press, Albuquerque.

COLE, LA MONT C.   1951   Population cycles and random oscillations. Journal of Wildlife Management 15: 233–252.

COLLIAS, N. E., and C. SOUTHWICK   1952   A field study of population density and social organization in howling monkeys. Proceedings of the American Philosophical Society 96: 143–156.

DARLING, F. F.   1937   A herd of red deer. Oxford University Press, London.

———   1938   Bird flocks and the breeding cycle. Cambridge University Press.

DART, R. A.   1948   A (?) promethean *Australopithecus* from Makapansgat Valley. Nature 162: 375–376.

———   1949   The predatory implemental technique of *Australopithecus*. American Journal of Physical Anthropology n.s. 7: 1–38.

DE CHARDIN, P. T.   1952   On the zoological position and evolutionary significance of australopithecines. Transactions of the New York Academy of Sciences Ser. II 14: 208–210.

DEEVEY, E. S., JR.   1951   Recent textbooks of human ecology. Ecology 32: 347–351.

EDINGER, TILLY   1948   Evolution of the horse brain. Geological Society of America Memoirs 25: 1–177.

ERRINGTON, P. A.   1946   Predation and vertebrate populations. Quarterly Review of Biology 21: 144–177 and 221–245.

EVANS-PRITCHARD, E. E.   1940   The Nuer: a description of the modes of livelihood and political institutions of a Nilotic people. Oxford University Press, London.

FISHER, EDNA M.   1939   Habits of the southern sea otter. Journal of Mammology 20: 21–36.

HATT, R. T.   1932   The vertebral columns of ricochetal rodents. Bulletin of the American Museum of Natural History 63: 599–738.

KRZYWICKI, L.   1934   Primitive society and its vital statistics. Macmillan and Co., London.

LACK, D.   1945   The Galapagos finches (Geospizinae). A study in variation. Occasional Papers of the California Academy of Sciences 21: 1–151.

LE GROS CLARK, W. E.   1949   New palaeontological evidence bearing on the evolution of the Hominoidea. Quarterly Journal of the Geological Society of London 105: 225–264.

MACKINTOSH, N. A., and J. F. G. WHEELER   1929   Southern blue and fin whales. Discovery Reports 1: 257–540.

MOHR, C. O.   1947   Table of equivalent populations of North American small mammals. American Midland Naturalist 37: 223–249.

NICE, MARGARET M.   1941   The role of territory in bird life. American Midland Naturalist 26: 441–487.

NISSEN, H. W.   1951   Social behavior in primates. Chapt. 13 (pp. 423–457) *in* Comparative Psychology (3rd edit.), edited by C. P. Stone. Prentice-Hall, Inc., New York.

NOBLE, G. K.   1939   The experimental animal from the naturalist's point of view. American Naturalist 73: 113–126.

PEARSON, O. P.   1948   Metabolism and bioenergetics. Scientific Monthly 66: 131–134.

SCHOLANDER, P. F., R. HOCK, V. WALTERS, and L. IRVING   1950   Adaptation to cold in arctic and tropical mammals and birds in relation to body temperature, insulation, and basal metabolic rate. Biological Bulletin 99: 259–271.

Simpson, G. G. 1944 Tempo and mode in evolution. Columbia University Press, New York.

Steward, J. H. 1938 Basin-plateau aboriginal sociopolitical groups. U. S. Government Printing Office, Washington, D. C.

Tindale, N. B. 1949 Large biface implements from Mornington Island, Queensland and from South Western Australia. Records of the South Australian Museum 9: 157–166.

Yerkes, R. M. 1939 Social dominance and sexual status in the chimpanzee. Quarterly Review of Biology 14: 115–136.

THE CONCEPT OF CULTURE

LESLIE A. WHITE

Virtually all cultural anthropologists take it for granted, no doubt, that *culture* is the basic and central concept of their science. There is, however, a disturbing lack of agreement as to what they mean by this term. To some, culture is learned behavior. To others, it is not behavior at all, but an abstraction from behavior—whatever that is. Stone axes and pottery bowls are culture to some anthropologists, but no material object can be culture to others. Culture exists only in the mind, according to some; it consists of observable things and events in the external world to others. Some anthropologists think of culture as consisting of ideas, but they are divided upon the question of their locus: some say they are in the minds of the peoples studied, others hold that they are in the minds of ethnologists. We go on to "culture is a psychic defense mechanism," "culture consists of *n* different social signals correlated with *m* different responses," "culture is a Rohrschach of a society," and so on, to confusion and bewilderment. One wonders what physics would be like if it had as many and as varied conceptions of energy!

There was a time, however, when there was a high degree of uniformity of comprehension and use of the term culture. During the closing decades of the nineteenth century and the early years of the twentieth, the great majority of cultural anthropologists, we believe, held to the conception expressed by E. B. Tylor, in 1871, in the opening lines of *Primitive Culture*: "Culture . . . is that complex whole which includes knowledge, belief, art, morals, law, custom, and any other capabilities and habits acquired by man as a member of society." Tylor does not make it explicit in this statement that culture is the peculiar possession of man; but it is therein implied, and in other places he makes this point clear and explicit (Tylor 1881:54, 123, where he deals with the "great mental gap between us and the animals"). Culture, to Tylor, was the name of all things and events peculiar to the human species. Specifically, he enumerates beliefs, customs, objects— "hatchet, adze, chisel," and so on—and techniques—"wood-chopping, fishing . . . , shooting and spearing game, fire-making," and so on (Tylor 1913: 5–6).

The Tylorian conception of culture prevailed in anthropology generally

Reprinted by permission from *American Anthropologist*, 61: (1959), 227–51.

for decades. In 1920, Robert H. Lowie began *Primitive Society* by quoting "Tylor's famous definition." In recent years, however, conceptions and definitions of culture have multiplied and varied to a great degree. One of the most highly favored of these is that *culture is an abstraction*. This is the conclusion reached by Kroeber and Kluckhohn in their exhaustive review of the subject: *Culture: a Critical Review of Concepts and History* (1952: 155, 169). It is the definition given by Beals and Hoijer in their textbook, *An Introduction to Anthropology* (1953:210, 219, 507, 535). In a more recent work, however, *Cultural Anthropology* (1958:16, 427), Felix M. Keesing defines culture as "the totality of learned, socially transmitted behavior."

Much of the discussion of the concept of culture in recent years has been concerned with a distinction between culture and human behavior. For a long time many anthropologists were quite content to define culture as behavior, peculiar to the human species, acquired by learning, and transmitted from one individual, group, or generation to another by mechanisms of social inheritance. But eventually some began to object to this and to make the point that culture is not itself behavior, but is an abstraction from behavior. Culture, say Kroeber and Kluckhohn (1952:155), "is an abstraction from concrete human behavior, but it is not itself behavior." Beals and Hoijer (1953:210, 219) and others take the same view.[1]

Those who define culture as an abstraction do not tell us what they mean by this term. They appear to take it for granted (1) that they themselves know what they mean by "abstraction," and (2) that others, also, will understand. We believe that neither of these suppositions is well founded; we shall return to a consideration of this concept later in this essay. But whatever an abstraction in general may be to these anthropologists, when culture becomes an "abstraction" it becomes imperceptible, imponderable, and not wholly real. According to Linton, "culture itself is intangible and cannot be directly apprehended even by the individuals who participate in it" (1936:288–89). Herskovits also calls culture "intangible" (1945:150). Anthropologists in the imaginary symposium reported by Kluckhohn and Kelly (1945:79, 81) argue that "one can see" such things as individuals and their actions and interactions, but "has anyone ever seen 'culture'?" Beals and Hoijer (1953:210) say that "the anthropologist cannot observe culture directly; . . ."

If culture as an abstraction is intangible, imperceptible, does it exist, is it real? Ralph Linton (1936:363) raises this question in all seriousness: "If it [culture] can be said to exist at all. . . ." Radcliffe-Brown (1940:2) declares that the word culture "denotes, not any concrete reality, but an abstraction, and as it is commonly used a vague abstraction." And Spiro (1951:24) says that according to the predominant "position of contemporary anthropology . . . culture has no ontological reality. . . ."

Thus when culture becomes an abstraction it not only becomes invisible and imponderable; it virtually ceases to exist. It would be difficult to construct a less adequate conception of culture. Why, then, have prominent and influential anthropologists turned to the "abstraction" conception of culture?

A clue to the reason—if, indeed, it is not an implicit statement of the reason itself—is given by Kroeber and Kluckhohn (1952:155):

Since behavior is the first-hand and outright material of the science of psychology, and culture is not—being of concern only secondarily, as an influence on this material—it is natural that psychologists and psychologizing sociologists should see behavior as primary in their field, and then extend this view farther to apply to the field of culture also.

The reasoning is simple and direct: if culture is behavior, then (1) culture becomes the subject matter of psychology, since behavior is the proper subject matter of psychology; culture would then become the property of psychologists and "psychologizing sociologists"; and (2) nonbiological anthropology would be left without a subject matter. The danger was real and imminent; the situation, critical. What was to be done?

The solution proposed by Kroeber and Kluckhohn was neat and simple: let the psychologists have behavior; anthropologists will keep for themselves abstractions from behavior. These abstractions become and constitute *culture*.

But in this rendering unto Caesar, anthropologists have given the psychologists the better part of the bargain, for they have surrendered unto them real things and events, locatable and observable, directly or indirectly, in the real external world, in terrestrial time and space, and have kept for themselves only intangible, imponderable abstractions that "have no ontological reality." But at least, and at last, they have a subject matter—however insubstantial and unobservable—of their own!

Whether or not this has been the principal reason for defining culture as "not behavior, but abstractions from behavior," is perhaps a question; we feel, however, that Kroeber and Kluckhohn have made themselves fairly clear. But whatever the reason, or reasons—for there may have been several —may have been for the distinction, the question whether culture is to be regarded as behavior or as abstractions from it is, we believe, the central issue in recent attempts to hammer out an adequate, usable, fruitful, and enduring conception of culture.

The present writer is no more inclined to surrender culture to the psychologists than are Kroeber and Kluckhohn; indeed, few anthropologists have taken greater pains to distinguish psychological problems from culturological problems than he has.[2] But he does not wish to exchange the hard substance of culture for its wraith, either. No science can have a subject matter that consists of intangible, invisible, imponderable, ontologically unreal "abstractions"; a science must have real stars, real mammals, foxes, crystals, cells, phonemes, gamma rays, and culture traits to work with.[3] We believe that we can offer an analysis of the situation that will distinguish between psychology, the scientific study of behavior on the one hand, and culturology, the scientific study of culture, on the other, and at the same time give a real, substantial subject matter to each.

Science makes a dichotomy between the mind of the observer and the external world [4]—things and events having their locus outside the mind of this observer. The scientist makes contact with the external world with and through his senses, forming percepts. These percepts are translated into concepts which are manipulated in a process called thinking [5] in such a way as to form premises, propositions, generalizations, conclusions, and so on. The validity of these premises, propositions, and conclusions is established by testing them in terms of experience of the external world (Einstein 1936: 350). This is the way science proceeds and does its work.

The first step in scientific procedure is to observe, or more generally to experience, the external world in a sensory manner. The next step—after percepts have been translated into concepts—is the classification of things and events perceived or experienced. Things and events of the external world are thus divided into classes of various kinds: acids, metals, stones, liquids, mammals, stars, atoms, corpuscles, and so on. Now it turns out that there is a class of phenomena, one of enormous importance in the study of man, for which science has as yet no name: this is the class of things and events consisting of or dependent upon symboling.[6] It is one of the most remarkable facts in the recent history of science that this important class has no name, but the fact remains that it does not. And the reason why it does not is because these things and events have always been considered and designated, not merely and simply as the things and events that they are, in and of themselves, but always as things and events in a particular context.

A thing is what it is; "a rose is a rose is a rose." Acts are not first of all ethical acts or economic acts or erotic acts. An act is an act. An act becomes an ethical datum or an economic datum or an erotic datum when—and only when—it is considered in an ethical, economic, or erotic context. Is a Chinese porcelain vase a scientific specimen, an object of art, an article of commerce, or an exhibit in a lawsuit? The answer is obvious. Actually, of course, to call it a "Chinese porcelain vase" is already to put it into a particular context; it would be better first of all to say "a glazed form of fired clay is a glazed form of fired clay." As a Chinese porcelain vase, it becomes an object of art, a scientific specimen, or an article of merchandise when, and only when, it is considered in an esthetic, scientific, or commercial context.

Let us return now to the class of things and events that consist of or are dependent upon symboling: a spoken word, a stone axe, a fetich, avoiding one's mother-in-law, loathing milk, saying a prayer, sprinkling holy water, a pottery bowl, casting a vote, remembering the sabbath to keep it holy—"and any other capabilities and habits [and things] acquired by man as a member of [human] society" (Tylor 1913:1). They are what they are: things and acts dependent upon symboling.

We may consider these things-and-events-dependent-upon-symboling in a number of contexts: astronomical, physical, chemical, anatomical, physiological, psychological, and culturological, and, consequently, they become astronomic, physical, chemical, anatomical, physiological, psychological, and culturological phenomena in turn. All things and events dependent upon symboling are dependent also upon solar energy which sustains all life on this planet; this is the astronomic context. These things and events may be considered and interpreted in terms of the anatomical, neurological, and physiological processes of the human beings who exhibit them. They may be considered and interpreted also in terms of their relationship to human organisms, i.e., in a somatic context. And they may be considered in an extrasomatic context, i.e., in terms of their relationship to other like things and events rather than in relationship to human organisms.

When things and events dependent upon symboling are considered and interpreted in terms of their relationship to human organisms, i.e., in a somatic context, they may properly be called *human behavior*, and the science, *psychology*. When things and events dependent upon symboling are considered and interpreted in an extrasomatic context, i.e., in terms of their relationships to one another rather than to human organisms, we may call them *culture*, and the science, *culturology*. This analysis is expressed diagrammatically in Fig. 1.

In the middle of the diagram we have a vertical column of circles, O_1, O_2, O_3, etc., which stand for things (objects) and events (acts) dependent upon

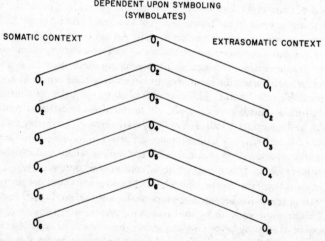

THINGS AND EVENTS
DEPENDENT UPON SYMBOLING
(SYMBOLATES)

SOMATIC CONTEXT   EXTRASOMATIC CONTEXT

HUMAN BEHAVIOR
SCIENCE OF PSYCHOLOGY

CULTURE TRAITS
SCIENCE OF CULTURE

Fig. 1

symboling. These things and events constitute a distinct class of phenomena in the realm of nature. Since they have had heretofore no name we have ventured to give them one: *symbolates*. We fully appreciate the hazards of coining terms, but this all-important class of phenomena needs a name to distinguish it from other classes. If we were physicists we might call them "Gamma phenomena." But we are not physicists, and we believe a simple word would be better—or at least more acceptable—than a Greek letter. In coining our term we have followed a well-established precedent: if an *isolate* is something that results from the process or action of isolating, then something that results from the action or process of symboling might well be called a symbolate. The particular word with which we designate this class of phenomena is not of paramount importance, and perhaps a better term than symbolate can be found. But it is of paramount importance that this class has a name.

A thing or event dependent upon symboling—a symbolate—is just what it is, but it may become significant in any one of a number of contexts. As we have already seen, it may be significant in an astronomic context: the performance of a ritual requires the expenditure of energy which has come from the sun. But within the sciences of man we may distinguish two significant contexts: the somatic and the extrasomatic. Symbolates may be considered and interpreted in terms of their relationship to the human organism, or they may be considered in terms of their relationships to one another, quite apart from their relationship to the human organism. Let us illustrate with some examples.

I smoke a cigarette, cast a vote, decorate a pottery bowl, avoid my mother-in-law, say a prayer, or chip an arrowhead. Each one of these acts is dependent upon the process of symboling; [7] each therefore is a symbolate. As a scientist, I may consider these acts (events) in terms of their relationships to me, to my organism; or, I may treat them in terms of their relationships to one another, to other symbolates, quite apart from their relationship to my organism.

In the first type of interpretation I consider the symbolate in terms of its relationship to my bodily structure: the structure and functions of my hand, for example; or to my stereoscopic, chromatic vision; or to my needs, desires, hopes, fears, imagination, habit formation, overt reactions, satisfactions, and so forth. How do I feel when I avoid my mother-in-law or cast a ballot? What is my attitude toward the act? What is my conception of it? Is the act accompanied by heightened emotional tone, or do I perform it in a mechanical, perfunctory manner? And so on. We may call these acts *human behavior*; our concern is *psychological*.

What we have said of acts (events) will apply to objects (things) also. What is my conception of a pottery bowl, a ground axe, a crucifix, roast pork, whisky, holy water, cement? What is my attitude and how do I react toward each of these things? In short, what is the nature of the relationship between each of these things and my own organism? We do not customarily call these things human behavior, but they are the embodiments of human behavior; the difference between a nodule of flint and a stone axe is the factor of human labor. An axe, bowl, crucifix—or a haircut—is congealed human labor. We have then a class of objects dependent upon symboling that have a significance in terms of their relationship to the human organism. The scientific consideration and interpretation of this relationship is *psychology*.

But we may treat symbolates in terms of their relationships to one another, quite apart from their relationship to the human organism. Thus, in the case of the avoidance of a mother-in-law, we would consider it in terms of its relationship to other symbolates, or symbolate clusters, such as customs of marriage—monogamy, polygyny, polyandry—place of residence of a couple after marriage, division of labor between the sexes, mode of subsistence, domestic architecture, degree of cultural development, etc. Or, if we are concerned with voting we would consider it in terms of forms of political organization (tribal, state), kind of government (democratic, monarchical, fascist); age, sex, or property qualifications; political parties and so on. In this context our symbolates become *culture*—culture traits or trait clusters, i.e., institutions, customs, codes, etc., and the scientific concern is *culturology*.

It would be the same with objects as with acts. If we were concerned with a hoe we would regard it in terms of its relationships to other symbolates in an extrasomatic context: to other instruments employed in subsistence, the digging stick and plow in particular; or to customs of division of labor between the sexes; the stage of cultural development, etc. We would be concerned with the relationship between a digital computer and the degree of development of mathematics, the stage of technological development, division of labor, the social organization within which it is used (corporation, military organization, astronomical laboratory), and so on.

Thus we see that we have two quite different kinds of sciencing [8] with regard to things and events—objects and acts—dependent upon symboling. If we treat them in terms of their relationship to the human organism, i.e., in an organismic, or somatic context, these things and events become *human behavior* and we are doing *psychology*. If, however, we treat them in terms of their relationship to one another, quite apart from their relationship to human organisms, i.e., in an extrasomatic, or extraorganismic, context, the things and events become *culture*—cultural elements or culture traits—and we are doing *culturology*. Human psychology and culturology have the same phenomena as their subject matter: things and events dependent upon symboling (symbolates). The difference between the two sciences derives from the difference between the contexts in which their common subject matter is treated.[9]

The analysis and distinction that we have made with regard to things and events dependent upon symboling in general is precisely like the one that linguists have been making for decades with regard to a particular kind of these things and events, namely, words.

A word is a thing (a sound or combination of sounds, or marks made upon some substance) or an act dependent upon symboling. Words are just what they are: words. But they are significant to scientific students of words in two different contexts: somatic or organismic, and extrasomatic or extra-organismic. This distinction has been expressed customarily with the terms *la langue* and *la parole,* or language and speech.[10]

Words in a somatic context constitute a kind of human behavior: speech behavior. The scientific study of words in a somatic context is the psychology (plus physiology, perhaps, and anatomy) of speech. It is concerned with the relationship between words and the human organism: how the words are produced and uttered, the meanings of words, attitudes toward words, perception of and response to words, and so on.

In the extrasomatic context, words are considered in terms of their relationships to one another, quite apart from their relationship to the human organism. The scientific concern here is linguistics, or the science of language. Phonetics, phonemics, syntax, lexicon, grammar, dialectic variation, evolution or historical change, etc., indicate particular focuses, or emphases, within the science of linguistics.

The difference between these two sciences may be illustrated by citing two books: *The Psychology of Language* by Walter B. Pillsbury and Clarence L. Meader (New York, 1928), and *Language* by Leonard Bloomfield (New York, 1933). In the former we find chapter titles such as "The Speech Organs," "The Senses Involved in Speech," "Mental Processes in Speech," etc. In the latter the chapter headings are "The Phoneme," "Phonetic Structure," "Grammatical Forms," "Sentence-Types," etc. We illustrate the distinction between these two sciences in Fig. 2.

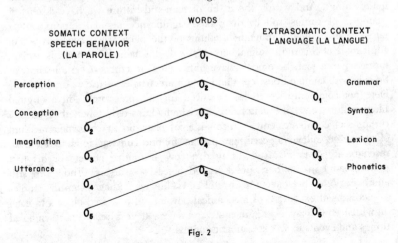

Fig. 2

Figures 1 and 2 are fundamentally alike. In each case we are concerned with a class of things and events dependent upon symboling. In Fig. 1, we are concerned with a general class: symbolates; in Fig. 2 we are dealing with a particular class: words (a subclass of the class symbolates). In each case we refer the things and events to a somatic context on the one hand, and to an extrasomatic context on the other, for purposes of consideration and interpretation. And in each case we have two distinct kinds of science, or sciencing: the psychology of human behavior or of speech; and the science of culture or of language.

Culture, then, is a class of things and events, dependent upon symboling, considered in an extrasomatic context. This definition rescues cultural anthropology from intangible, imperceptible, and ontologically unreal abstractions and provides it with a real, substantial, observable subject matter. And it distinguishes sharply between behavior—behaving organisms—and culture; between the science of psychology and the science of culture.

It might be objected that every science should have a certain class of things per se as its subject matter, not things-in-a-certain-context. Atoms are atoms and mammals are mammals, it might be argued, and as such are the subject matter of physics and mammalogy, respectively, regardless of context. Why therefore should cultural anthropology have its subject matter defined in terms of things in context rather than in terms of things in themselves? At first glance this argument might appear to be a cogent one, but actually it has but little force. What the scientist wants to do is to make intelligible the phenomena that confront him. And very frequently the significant thing about phenomena is the context in which they are found. Even in the so-called natural sciences we have a science of organisms-in-a-certain-context: parasitology, a science of organisms playing a certain role in the realm of living things. And within the realm of man-and-culture we have dozens of examples of things and events whose significance depends upon context rather than upon the inherent qualities of the phenomena themselves. An adult male of a certain animal species is called a man. But a man is a man, not a slave; a man becomes a slave only when he enters a certain context. So it is with commodities: corn and cotton are articles of use-value, but they were not commodities—articles produced for sale at a profit—in aboriginal Hopi culture; corn and cotton become commodities only when they enter a certain socioeconomic context. A cow is a cow, but she may become a medium of exchange, money (*pecus*, pecuniary) in one context, food in another, mechanical power (Cartwright used a cow as motive power for his first power loom) in another, and a sacred object of worship (India) in still another. We do not have a science of cows, but we do have scientific studies of mediums of exchange, of mechanical power, and of sacred objects in each of which cows may be significant. And so we have a science of symboled things and events in an extrasomatic context.

If we define culture as consisting of real things and events observable, directly or indirectly, in the external world, where do these things and events exist and have their being? What is the locus of culture? The answer is: the things and events that comprise culture have their existence, in space and time, (1) within human organisms, i.e., concepts, beliefs, emotions, attitudes; (2) within processes of social interaction among human beings; and (3) within material objects (axes, factories, railroads, pottery bowls) lying outside human organisms but within the patterns of social interaction among them.[11] The locus of culture is thus intraorganismal, interorganismal, and extraorganismal (see Fig. 3).

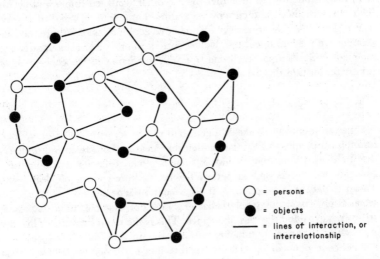

○ = persons

● = objects

── = lines of interaction, or interrelationship

Fig. 3 The locus of culture.

But, someone might object, you have said that culture consists of extrasomatic phenomena and now you tell me that culture exists, in part, within human organisms. Is this not a contradiction? The answer is, No, it is not a contradiction; it is a misunderstanding. We did not say that culture consists of extrasomatic things and events, i.e., phenomena whose locus is outside human organisms. What we said is that culture consists of things and events considered within an extrasomatic context. This is quite a different thing.

Every cultural element has two aspects: subjective and objective. It might appear that stone axes are "objective," and ideas and attitudes are "subjective." But this is a superficial and inadequate view. An axe has a subjective component; it would be meaningless without a concept and an attitude. On the other hand, a concept or an attitude would be meaningless without overt

47

expression, in behavior or speech (which is a form of behavior). Every cultural element, every culture trait, therefore, has a subjective and an objective aspect. But conceptions, attitudes, and sentiments—phenomena that have their locus within the human organism—may be considered for purposes of scientific interpretation in an extrasomatic context, i.e., in terms of their relation to other symboled things and events rather than in terms of their relationship to the human organism. Thus, we may consider the subjective aspect of the mother-in-law taboo, i.e., the conceptions and attitudes involved, in terms of their relationship, not to the human organism, but to other symbolates such as forms of marriage and the family, place of residence after marriage, and so on. On the other hand, we may consider the axe in terms of its relationship to the human organism—its meaning; the person's conception of it; his attitude toward it—rather than to other symboled things and events such as arrows, hoes, and customs regulating the division of labor in society.

We shall now pass in review a number of conceptions of culture, or conceptions with regard to culture, widely current in ethnological literature, and comment critically upon each one from the standpoint of the conception of culture set forth in this paper.

CULTURE CONSISTS OF IDEAS

Some anthropologists like to define culture in terms of ideas only. The reason for this, apparently, is the notion that ideas are both basic and primary, that they are prime movers and as such originate behavior which in turn may produce objects such as pottery bowls. "Culture consists of ideas," says Taylor (1948:98–110, passim), it "is a mental phenomenon . . . not . . . material objects or observable behavior. . . . For example, there is present in an Indian's mind the idea of a dance. This is the trait of culture. This idea influences his body so that he behaves in a certain way," i.e., he dances.

This conception of sociocultural reality is a naive one. It is based upon a primitive, prescientific, and now obsolete metaphysics and psychology. It was Thought-Woman among the Keresan Pueblo Indians who brought about events by thinking and willing them to happen. Ptah created Egyptian culture by objectifying his thoughts. And God said "Let there be light," and there was light. But we no longer explain the origin and development of culture by simply saying that it has resulted from man's ideas. To be sure, an idea was involved in the invention of firearms, but we have explained nothing when we say that firearms are the fruit of thought, because the ideas themselves have not been accounted for. Why did the idea occur when and where it did rather than at some other time and place? And, actually, ideas —matter of fact, realistic ideas—enter the mind from the outside world. It was working with soils that gave man, or woman, the idea of pottery; the calendar is a by-product of intensive agriculture. Culture does indeed consist in part of ideas; but attitudes, overt acts, and objects are culture, also.

We return now to the presently popular definition: "culture is an abstraction, or consists of abstractions." As we observed earlier, those who define culture in these terms do not tell us what they mean by "abstraction," and there is reason to believe that they are not very clear as to what they do mean by it. They make it emphatically clear, however, that an abstraction is not an observable thing or event. The fact that doubts have been raised as to the "reality" of an abstraction indicates that those who use this term are not sure what "it means," i.e., what they mean by it. We do have some clues, however.

Culture is "basically a form or pattern or way," say Kroeber and Kluckhohn (1952:155, 169), "even a culture trait is an abstraction. A trait is an 'ideal type' because no two pots are identical nor are two marriage ceremonies ever held in precisely the same way." The culture trait "pot" therefore appears to be the ideal form of which each particular pot is an exemplification—a sort of Platonic idea, or ideal. Each and every pot, they reason, is real; but the "ideal" is never realized in any particular pot. It is like the "typical American man": 5'8½" high, weighs 164.378 pounds, is married, has 2.3 children, and so on. This is, we suppose, what they mean by an abstraction. If so, we know it well: it is a conception in the mind of the observer, the scientist.

There is a slightly different way of looking at an "abstraction." No two marriage ceremonies are ever held in precisely the same way. Well, let us tabulate a large sample of marriage ceremonies. We find that 100 percent contain element a (mutual acceptance of spouses). Ninety-nine percent contain element b. Elements c, d, and e appear in only 96, 94, and 89 percent, respectively, of the cases. We construct a distribution curve and determine an average or norm about which all particular instances are distributed. This is the typical marriage ceremony. But, like the typical American who has 2.3 children, this ideal is never fully and perfectly realized in any actual instance. It is an "abstraction," that is, a conception, worked out by the scientific observer and which exists in his own mind.

The failure to recognize the fact that abstractions are conceptions has led to confusion both as to their locus and their reality. Recognition of the fact that the so-called abstractions of science (such as a "rigid body" in physical theory; rigid bodies do not exist in actuality) are conceptions in the mind of the scientist clears up both these points: cultural "abstractions" are conceptions ("ideas") in the mind of the anthropologist. And as for their "ontological reality," conceptions are none the less real for being in the minds of men —nothing is more real, for example, than an hallucination.

This point was well made by Bidney (1954:488–89) in his review of *Culture, a Critical Review etc.*:

The real crux of the problem centers about what is meant by abstraction and what is its ontological import. Some anthropologists maintain that they are dealing only with logical abstractions and that culture has no reality other than

49

that of an abstraction, but they can hardly expect other social scientists to agree with them, conceding that the objects of their sciences have no ontological, objective reality. *Thus Kroeber and Kluckhohn have confused the concept culture, which is a logical construct, with the actual existential culture . . .* [emphasis ours].

It is interesting to note in this connection that one anthropological theorist, Cornelius Osgood (1951:208; 1940), has defined culture explicitly as consisting of ideas in the minds of anthropologists: "Culture consists of all ideas of the manufactures, behavior, and ideas of the aggregate of human beings which have been directly observed or communicated to one's mind and of which one is conscious." Spiro (1951:24), also, holds that "culture is a logical construct, abstracted from human behavior, and as such, it exists only in the mind of *the investigator*" (Spiro's emphasis).

THERE IS NO SUCH THING AS "MATERIAL" CULTURE

Those who define culture in terms of ideas, or as an abstraction, or as behavior, find themselves obliged logically to declare that material objects are not, and cannot be, culture. "Strictly speaking," says Hoebel (1956:176), "material culture is really not culture at all." Taylor (1948:102, 98) goes farther: ". . . the concept of 'material culture' is fallacious" because "culture is a mental phenomenon." Beals and Hoijer (1953:210): ". . . culture is an abstraction from behavior and not to be confused with acts of behavior or with material artifacts, such as tools. . . ." This denial of material culture is rather awkward in view of the long established tradition among ethnographers, archeologists, and museum curators of calling tools, masks, fetiches, and so on, "material culture." [12]

Our definition extricates us from this dilemma. As we have already seen, it would not be absurd to speak of sandals or pottery bowls as behavior; their significant attribute is not mere deer hide or clay, but human labor; they are congelations of human labor. But in our definition, symboling is the common factor in ideas, attitudes, acts, and objects. There are three kinds of symbolates: (1) ideas and attitudes, (2) overt acts, and (3) material objects. All may be considered in an extrasomatic context; all are to be reckoned as culture. This conception brings us back to long established usage in cultural anthropology: "Culture is that which is described in an ethnographic monograph."

REIFICATION OF CULTURE

There is a kind of conception of culture held by some anthropologists that is much deplored by others who call it "reification." As one who has been especially singled out as a "reifier" of culture,[13] I may say that the term is singularly inappropriate. To reify is to make a thing of that which is not a thing, such as hope, honesty, or freedom. But it is not I who have made culture things. I have merely found real things and events in the external world which are distinguishable as a class by being dependent upon symboling, and which may be treated in an extrasomatic context, and I have called these things and events culture. This is precisely what E. B. Tylor did. It is what Lowie, Wissler, and most early American anthropologists have done. To Durkheim (1938:xliii) "the proposition which states that social facts [i.e., culture traits] are to be treated as things" lay "at the very basis of our method." It is not we who have reified culture; the elements comprising culture, according to our definition, were things to start with.

To be sure, if culture is defined as consisting of intangible, imponderable, ontologically unreal "abstractions," then to transform these wraiths into real, substantial bodies would indeed be to reify them. But we do not subscribe to such a definition.

CULTURE: A PROCESS SUI GENERIS

"Culture is a thing *sui generis* . . ." said Lowie many years ago (1917:66, 17). This view has been held also by Kroeber, Durkheim, and others (for citation of examples see White 1949:89–94). It has been misunderstood and opposed by many. But what Lowie meant by this statement is made clear in the rest of the passage cited above (1917:66): "Culture is a thing *sui generis* which can be explained only in terms of itself . . . the ethnologist . . . will account for a given cultural fact by merging it in a group of cultural facts or by demonstrating some other cultural fact out of which it has been developed." For example, the custom of reckoning descent patrilineally may be explained in terms of customs of division of labor between the sexes, customs of residence—patrilocal, matrilocal, or neolocal—of a married couple; mode of subsistence; rules of inheritance, and so on. Or, to express it in terms of our definition of culture: "a symbolate in an extrasomatic context (i.e., a culture trait) is to be explained in terms of its relationship to other symbolates in the same context."

This conception of culture, like "reification" with which it is closely related, has been much misunderstood and opposed. In general, it has been regarded as "mystical." How can culture grow and develop by itself? ("Culture . . . seems to grow of itself"; Redfield 1941:134.) "It seems hardly necessary," says Boas (1928:235), "to consider culture a mystic entity that exists outside the society of its individual carriers, and that moves by its own force." Bidney (1946:535) brands this view of culture as a "mystical metaphysics of fate." And it has been opposed by Benedict (1934:231), Hooton (1939:370), Spiro (1951:23), and others.

But no one has ever said that culture is an entity that exists and moves by, and of, itself, quite apart from people. Nor has anyone ever said, as far as we know, that the origin, nature, and functions of culture can be understood without taking the human species into consideration. Obviously, if one is to understand culture in these aspects he must consider the biological nature of man. What has been asserted is that, given culture, its variations in time and place, and its processes of change are to be explained in terms of culture itself. This is precisely what Lowie meant when he said that "culture is a thing [process would have been a better term] *sui generis*," as the above quotation from him (1917:66) makes clear. A consideration of the human organism, individually or collectively, is irrelevant to an explanation of processes of culture change. "This is not mysticism," says Lowie (1917:66), "but sound scientific method." And, as everyone knows, scholars have been working in accordance with this principle of interpretation for decades. One does not need to take human organisms into account in a scientific explanation of the evolution of currency, writing, or of Gothic art. The steam engine and textile machinery were introduced into Japan during the closing decades of the nineteenth century and certain changes in social structure followed; we add nothing to our explanation of these events by remarking that human beings were involved. Of course they were. And they were not irrelevant to the events which took place, but they are irrelevant to an explanation of these events.

IT IS PEOPLE, NOT CULTURE, THAT DOES THINGS

"Culture does not 'work,' 'move,' 'change,' but is worked, is moved, is changed. It is people who do things," says Lynd (1939:39). He supports this argument with the bold assertion that "culture does not enamel its fingernails . . . but people do . . ." (ibid.). He might have clinched it by demonstrating that culture has no fingernails.

The view that "it is people, not cultures, that do things" is widely held among anthropologists. Boas (1928:236) tells us that "the forces that bring about the changes are active in the individuals composing the social group, not in the abstract culture." Hallowell (1945:175) remarks that "in a literal sense cultures never have met nor will ever meet. What is meant is that peoples meet and that, as a result of the processes of social interaction, acculturation—modifications in the mode of life of one or both peoples—may take place. Individuals are the dynamic centers of this process of interaction." And Radcliffe-Brown (1940:10–11) pours fine scorn on the notion that cultures, rather than peoples, interact:

A few years ago, as a result perhaps of re-defining social anthropology as the study, not of society, but of culture, we were asked to abandon this kind of investigation in favor of what is now called the study of "culture contact." In place of the study of the formation of new composite societies, we are supposed to regard what is happening in Africa as a process in which an entity called African culture comes into contact with an entity called European or Western culture, and a third new entity is produced . . . which is to be described as Westernized African culture. To me this seems a fantastic reification of abstractions. European culture is an abstraction and so is the culture of an African tribe. I find it fantastic to imagine these two abstractions coming into contact and by an act of generation producing a third abstraction.

We call this view, that people rather than culture do things, the fallacy of pseudo-realism. Of course culture does not and could not exist independently of people.[14] But, as we have pointed out earlier, cultural processes can be explained without taking human organisms into account; a consideration of human organisms is irrelevant to the solution of certain problems of culture. Whether the practice of mummification in pre-Columbian Peru was indigenous or the result of Egyptian influence is an example of a kind of problem that does not require a consideration of human organisms. To be sure the practice of mummification, its invention in Peru, or its diffusion from Egypt to the Andean highlands, could not have taken place without the action of real, flesh-and-blood human beings. Neither could Einstein have worked out the theory of relativity without breathing, but we do not need to take his respiration into account when we trace the history, or explain the development, of this theory.

Those who argue that it is people, not culture, that do this or that mistake a description of what they see for an explanation of these events. Seated in the Senate gallery they see men making laws; in the shipyards men are building freighters; in the laboratory human beings are isolating enzymes; in the fields they are planting corn, and so on. And, for them, a description of these events, as they observe them, is a simple explanation of them: it is people who pass laws, build freighters, plant corn, and isolate enzymes. This is a simple and naive form of anthropocentrism.

A scientific explanation is more sophisticated. If a person speaks Chinese, or avoids his mother-in-law, loathes milk, observes matrilocal residence, places the bodies of the dead on scaffolds, writes symphonies, or isolates enzymes, it is because he has been born into, or at least reared within, an extrasomatic tradition that we call culture which contains these elements. A people's behavior is a response to, a function of, their culture. The culture is the independent, the behavior the dependent, variable; as the culture varies so will the behavior. This is, of course, a commonplace that is usually expounded and demonstrated during the first two weeks of an introductory course in anthropology. It is indeed people who treat disease with prayers and charms or with vaccines and antibiotics. But the question, "Why does one people use charms while another uses vaccines?" is not explained by saying that "this people does this, that people does that." It is precisely this proposition that needs to be explained: why do they do what they do? The scientific explanation does not take the people into account at all. And as for the question, Why does one extrasomatic tradition use charms while another uses vaccines, this also is one to which a consideration of people, of human organisms, is irrelevant; it is answered culturologically: culture, as Lowie has observed, is to be explained in terms of culture.

Culture "cannot be realistically disconnected from those organizations of ideas and feelings which constitute the individual," i.e., culture cannot be realistically disconnected from individuals, says Sapir (1932:233). He is quite right, of course; in actuality culture is inseparable from human beings. But if culture cannot be realistically (in actuality) disconnected from individuals it most certainly can be disconnected in logical (scientific) analysis, and no one has done a better job of "disconnecting" than Edward Sapir: there is not a single Indian—or even a nerve, muscle, or sense organ—in his monograph, *Southern Paiute, a Shoshonean Language* (1930). Nor are there any people roaming about in his *Time Perspective in Aboriginal American Culture* (1916). "Science must abstract some elements and neglect others," says Morris Cohen (1931:226) "because *not all things that exist together are relevant to each other*" (emphasis ours). Comprehension and appreciation of this fact would be an enormous asset to ethnological theory. "Citizenship cannot be realistically disconnected from eye color," i.e., every citizen has eyes and every eye has a color. But, in the United States at least, color of eyes is not relevant to citizenship: "things that exist together are not always relevant to each other."

And so it is perfectly true, as Hallowell, Radcliffe-Brown, and others say, that "it is *peoples* who meet and interact." But this should not keep us from confining our attention, in the solution of certain problems, to symbolates in an extrasomatic context: to tools, utensils, customs, beliefs, and attitudes; in short, to culture. The meeting and mixing of European culture with African culture and the production thereby of a mixture, Euro-African culture, may seem "a fantastic reification of abstractions" to Radcliffe-Brown and others. But anthropologists have been concerned with problems of this sort for decades and will continue to deal with them. The intermingling of customs, technologies, and ideologies is just as valid a scientific problem as the intermingling of human organisms or genes.

We have not asserted, nor do we imply, that anthropologists in general have failed to treat culture as a process sui generis, i.e., without taking human organisms into account; many, if not most, cultural anthropologists have in fact done this. But some of them, when they turn to theory, deny the validity of this kind of interpretation. Radcliffe-Brown himself provides us with examples of purely culturological problems and culturological solutions thereof—in "The Social Organization of Australian Tribes" (1930–31), "The Mother's Brother in South Africa" (1924), etc. But when he dons the philosopher's cap he denies that this procedure is scientifically valid.[15]

However, some anthropologists have recognized, on the theoretical level, that culture can be scientifically studied without taking human organisms into account, that a consideration of human organisms is irrelevant to the solution of problems dealing with extrasomatic traditions. We have cited a number —Tylor, Durkheim, Kroeber, Lowie, et al.—who have done this.[16] But we may add one or two new references here. "The best hope . . . for parsimonious description and 'explanation' of cultural phenomena," say Kroeber and Kluckhohn (1952:167) "seems to rest in the study of cultural forms and processes as such, largely . . . abstracted from individuals and personalities." And Steward (1955:46) remarks that "certain aspects of a modern culture can best be studied quite apart from individual behavior. The structure and function of a system of money, banking, and credit, for example, represents supra-individual aspects of culture." Also, he says: "form of government, legal system, economic institutions, religious organizations, educational systems," and so on, "have aspects which are national . . . in scope and which must be understood apart from the behavior of the individuals connected with them" (ibid.:47).

There is nothing new about this; anthropologists and other social scientists have been doing this for decades. But it seems to be difficult for some of them to accept this as a matter of theory and principle as well as of actual practice.

IT TAKES TWO OR MORE TO MAKE A CULTURE

There is a conception, not uncommon in ethnological theory, that whether a phenomenon is an element of culture or not depends upon whether it is expressed by one, two, or "several" individuals. Thus Linton (1945:35) says that "any item of behavior . . . which is peculiar to a single individual in a society is not to be considered as a part of the society's culture. . . . Thus a new technique for weaving baskets would not be classed as a part of culture as long as it was known only to one person." Wissler (1929:358), Osgood (1951:207–08), Malinowski (1941:73), Durkheim (1938:lvi), et al., have subscribed to this view.

Two objections may be raised against this conception of culture: (1) if plurality of expression of learned behavior be the significant distinction between culture and not-culture, then the chimpanzees described by Wolfgang Köhler in *The Mentality of Apes* (New York, 1925) had culture, for innovations made by a single individual were often quickly adopted by the whole group. Other subhuman species also would have culture according to this criterion. (2) The second objection is: if expression by one person is not enough to qualify an act as a cultural element, how many persons will be required? Linton (1936:274) says that "as soon as this new thing has been transmitted to and is shared by even one other individual in the society, it must be reckoned as a part of culture." Osgood (1951:208) requires "two or more." Durkheim (1938:lvi) needs "several individuals, at the very least." Wissler (1929:358) says that an item does not rise to the level of a culture trait until a standardized procedure is established in the group. And Malinowski (1941:73) states that a "cultural fact starts when an individual interest becomes transformed into public, common, and transferable systems of organized endeavor."

Obviously such a conception does not meet the requirements of science. What agreement could one find on the point at which an "individual interest becomes transformed into public, common, and transferable systems of organized endeavor"? Or, suppose an ornithologist said that if there were but one specimen of a kind of bird it could not be a carrier pigeon or a whooping crane, but that if there were an indefinite number then they could be pigeons or cranes. Or, suppose a physicist said that if there were but one atom of a certain element that it could not be copper, but if there were "a lot of such atoms" then it might properly be called copper. One wants a definition that says that item x belongs to class y or it does not, regardless of how many items of x there may be (and a class, in logic, may have only one member, or even none).

Our definition meets the requirements of a scientific definition: an item —a conception or belief, an act, or an object—is to be reckoned an element of culture (1) if it is dependent upon symboling, and (2) when it is considered in an extrasomatic context. To be sure, all cultural elements exist in a social context; but so do such nonhuman (not dependent upon symboling) traits as grooming, suckling, and mating exist in a social matrix. But it is not sociality, duality, or plurality that distinguishes a human, or cultural, phenomenon from a nonhuman or noncultural phenomenon. The distinguishing characteristic is symboling. Secondly, whether a thing or an event can be considered in an extrasomatic context does not depend upon whether there is only one such thing or event, or two, or "several." A thing or event may be properly considered an element of culture even if it is the only member of its class, just as an atom of copper would still be an atom of copper even if it were the only one of its kind in the cosmos.

And, of course, we might have pointed out in the first place that the notion that an act or an idea in human society might be wholly the work of a single individual is an illusion, another one of the sorry pitfalls of anthropocentrism. Every member of human society is of course always subjected to sociocultural stimulation from the members of his group. Whatever a man does as a human being, and much of what he does as a mere animal, is a function of his group as well as of his organism. Any human act, even in its first expression in the person of a single individual, is a group product to begin with.[17]

CULTURE AS "CHARACTERISTIC" TRAITS

"Culture may be defined," says Boas (1938:159), "as the totality of the mental and physical reactions and activities that *characterize* the behavior of the individuals composing a social group . . ." (emphasis ours). Herskovits (1948:28) tells us that "when culture is closely analyzed, we find but a series of patterned reactions that characterize the behavior of the individuals who constitute a given group." (Just what "close analysis" has to do with this conception is not clear.) Sapir (1917:442): "The mass of typical reactions called culture. . . ." This view has, of course, been held by others.

Two objections may be raised against this conception of culture: (1) how does one determine which traits characterize a group and which traits do not —how does one draw the line between the two classes, culture and not-culture? And, (2) if we call the traits that characterize a group *culture,* what are we to call those traits that do not characterize it?

It seems probable that anthropologists who hold this view are really thinking of *a* culture, or cultures, plural, rather than of culture in general, culture as a particular kind of phenomena. Thus, "French culture" might be distinguished from "English culture" by those traits which characterize each. But if, on the one hand, the French and the English may be distinguished from each other by differences of traits, they will on the other hand be found to be very similar to each other in their possession of like traits. And the traits that resemble each other are just as much a part of the "way of life" of each people as the traits that differ. Why should only one class be called culture?

These difficulties and uncertainties are done away with by our conception of culture: culture consists of all of the ways of life of each people which are dependent upon symboling and which are considered in an extrasomatic context. If one wished to distinguish the English from the French on the basis of their respective culture traits he could easily specify "those traits which characterize" the people in question. But he would not assert that nontypical traits were not culture.

In this connection we may note a very interesting distinction drawn by Sapir (1917:442) between the behavior of individuals and "culture."

It is always the individual that really thinks and acts and dreams and revolts. Those of his thoughts, acts, dreams, and rebellions that somehow contribute in sensible degree to the modification or retention of the mass of typical reactions called culture we term social data; *the rest, though they do not, psychologically considered, in the least differ from these, we term individual and pass by as of no historical or social moment* [i.e., they are not culture]. It is highly important to note that the differentiation of these two types of reaction is essentially arbitrary, resting, as it does, entirely on a principle of selection. The selection depends on the adoption of a scale of values. Needless to say, the threshold of the social (or historical) [i.e., cultural] *versus* the individual shifts according to the philosophy of the evaluator or interpreter. I find it utterly inconceivable to draw a sharp and eternally valid dividing line between them [emphases ours].

Sapir finds himself confronted by a plurality, or aggregation, of individuals. (He would have preferred this wording rather than "society," we believe, for he speaks of "a theoretical [fictitious?] community of human beings," adding that "the term 'society' itself is a cultural construct"; Sapir, 1932:236.) These individuals do things: dream, think, act, and revolt. And "it is always the individual," not society or culture, who does these things. What Sapir finds then is: individuals and their behavior; nothing more.

Some of the behavior of individuals is culture, says Sapir. But other elements of their behavior are not-culture, although, as he says, psychologically considered they do not differ in the slightest from those elements which he calls culture. The line thus drawn between "culture" and "not-culture" is purely arbitrary, and depends upon the subjective evaluation of the one who is drawing the line.

A conception of culture could hardly be less satisfactory than this one. It says, in effect: "culture is the name that we give to some of the behavior of some individuals, the selection being arbitrary and made in accordance with subjective criteria."

In the essay from which we have been quoting, "Do We Need a Super-organic?" (1917), Sapir is opposing the culturological point of view presented by Kroeber in "The Superorganic" (1917). He (Sapir) virtually makes culture disappear; it is dissolved into the totality of the reactions of individuals. Culture becomes, as he has elsewhere called it, a "statistical fiction" (Sapir 1932:237). If there is no significant reality that one can call culture, then there can be no science of culture. Sapir's argument was skillful and persuasive. But it was also unsound, or at least misleading.

Sapir's argument was persuasive because he bolstered it with authentic, demonstrable fact. It was unsound or misleading because he makes it appear that the only significant distinction between the behavior of individuals and culture is the one that he had made.

It is perfectly true that the elements which comprise the human behavior of individuals and the elements which comprise culture are identical classes of things and events. All are symbolates—dependent upon man's unique ability to symbol. It is true, also, that "psychologically considered," they are all alike. But Sapir overlooks, and by his argument effectively obscures, the fact that there are two fundamentally different kinds of contexts in which these "thinkings, actings, dreamings, and revolts" can be considered for purposes of scientific interpretation and explanation: the somatic and the extrasomatic. Considered in a somatic context, i.e., in terms of their relationship to the human organism, these acts dependent upon symboling constitute *human behavior*. Considered in an extrasomatic context, i.e., in terms of their relationships to one another, these acts constitute *culture*. Instead, therefore, of arbitrarily putting some in the category of culture and the rest in the category human behavior, we put all acts, thoughts, and things dependent upon symboling in either one context or the other, somatic or extrasomatic, depending upon the nature of our problem.

SUMMARY

Among the many significant classes of things and events distinguishable by science there is one for which science has had no name. This is the class of phenomena dependent upon symboling, a faculty peculiar to the human species. We have proposed that things and events dependent upon symboling be called symbolates. The particular designation of this class is not as important, however, as that it be given a name of some kind in order that its distinction from other classes be made explicit.

Things and events dependent upon symboling comprise ideas, beliefs, attitudes, sentiments, acts, patterns of behavior, customs, codes, institutions, works and forms of art, languages, tools, implements, machines, utensils, ornaments, fetiches, charms, and so on.

Things and events dependent upon symboling may be, and traditionally have been, referred to two fundamentally different contexts for purposes of observation, analysis, and explanation. These two contexts may properly and appropriately be called somatic and extrasomatic. When an act, object, idea or attitude is considered in the somatic context it is the relationship between that thing or event and the human organism that is significant. Things and events dependent upon symboling considered in the somatic context may properly be called human behavior—at least, ideas, attitudes, and acts may; stone axes and pottery bowls are not customarily called behavior, but their significance is derived from the fact that they have been produced by human labor; they are, in fact, congelations of human behavior. When things and events are considered in the extrasomatic context they are regarded in terms of the interrelationships among themselves rather than in terms of their relationship to the human organism, individually or collectively. Culture is the name of things and events dependent upon symboling considered in an extrasomatic context.

Our analysis and distinctions have these advantages. The distinctions made are clear cut and fundamental. Culture is clearly distinguished from human behavior. Culture has been defined as all sciences must define their subject matter, namely, in terms of real things and events, observable directly or indirectly in the actual world that we live in. Our conception rescues anthropology from the incubus of intangible, imperceptible, imponderable "abstractions" that have no ontological reality.

Our definition extricates us, also, from the dilemmas in which many other conceptions place us, such as whether culture consists of ideas and whether these ideas have their locus in the minds of peoples studied or in the minds of anthropologists; whether material objects can or cannot be culture; whether a trait must be shared by two, three, or several people in order to count as culture; whether traits have to characterize a people or not in order to be culture; whether culture is a reification or not, and whether a culture can enamel its fingernails.

Our distinction between human behavior and culture, between psychology and culturology, is precisely like the one that has been in use for decades between speech and language, between the psychology of speech and the science of linguistics. If it is valid for the one it is valid for the other.

Finally, our distinction and definition is in very close accord with anthropological tradition. This is what Tylor meant by culture as a reading of *Primitive Culture* will make clear. It is the one that has actually been used by almost all nonbiological anthropologists. What is it that scientific field workers among primitive peoples have studied and described in their monographs? Answer: real observable things and events dependent upon symboling. It can hardly be said that they were studying and describing imperceptible, intangible, imponderable, ontologically unreal abstractions. To be sure, the field worker may be interested in things and events in their somatic context, in which case he would be doing psychology (as he would be if he considered words in their somatic context). And anthropology, as this term is actually used, embraces a number of different kinds of studies: anatomical, physiological, genetic, psychological, psychoanalytic, and culturological. But this does not mean that the distinction between psychology and culturology is not fundamental. It is.

The thesis presented in this paper is no novelty. It is not a radical departure from anthropological tradition. On the contrary, it is in a very real sense and to a great extent, a return to tradition, the tradition established by Tylor and followed in practice by countless anthropologists since his day. We have merely given it concise and overt verbal expression.

NOTES

[1] One of the earliest instances of regarding culture as an abstraction is Murdock's statement: "realizing that culture is merely an abstraction from observed likenesses in the behavior of individuals . . ." (1937:xi).

[2] Several of the essays in *The Science of Culture* (1949)—"Culturological vs. Psychological Interpretations of Human Behavior," "Cultural Determinants of Mind," "Genius: Its Causes and Incidence," "Ikhnaton: The Great Man vs. the Culture Process," "The Definition and Prohibition of Incest," etc.—deal with this distinction.

[3] I made this point in my review of Kroeber and Kluckhohn, "Culture: a Critical Review etc." (1954:464–65). At about the same time Huxley was writing (1955:15–16): "If anthropology is a science, then for anthropologists culture must be defined, not philosophically or metaphysically, nor as an abstraction, nor in purely subjective terms, but as something which can be investigated by the methods of scientific inquiry, a phenomenal process occurring in space and time."

[4] "The belief in an external world independent of the perceiving subject is the basis of all natural science," says Einstein (1934:6).

[5] Thinking, in science, means "operations with concepts, and the creation and use of definite functional relations between them, and the co-ordination of sense experiences to these concepts," according to Einstein (1936:350). Einstein has much to say in this essay about the manner and process of scientific thinking.

[6] By "symboling" we mean bestowing meaning upon a thing or an act, or grasping and appreciating meanings thus bestowed. Holy water is a good example of such meanings. The attribute of holiness is bestowed upon the water by a human being, and it may be comprehended and appreciated by other human beings. Articulate speech is the most characteristic and important form of symboling. Symboling is trafficking in nonsensory meanings, i.e., meanings which, like the holiness of sacramental water, cannot be comprehended with the senses alone. Symboling is a kind of behavior. Only man is capable of symboling.

We have discussed this concept rather fully in "The Symbol: the Origin and Basis of Human Behavior," originally published in The Philosophy of Science, Vol. 7, pp. 451-63, 1940. It has been reprinted in slightly revised form in *The Science of Culture*. It has also been reprinted in Etc., A Review of General Semantics, Vol. 1, pp. 229-37, 1944; *Language, Meaning, and Maturity*, S. I. Hayakawa ed. (New York, 1954); *Readings in Anthropology*, E. Adamson Hoebel et al. eds. (New York, 1955); *Readings in Introductory Anthropology*, Elman R. Service ed. (Ann Arbor, Mich., 1956); *Sociological Theory*, Lewis A. Coser and Bernard Rosenberg eds. (New York, 1957); and in *Readings in the Ways of Mankind*, Walter Goldschmidt ed. (1957).

[7] "How is chipping an arrowhead dependent upon symboling?" it might be asked. I have answered this question in "On the Use of Tools by Primates" (Journal of Comparative Psychology, Vol. 34, pp. 369-74, 1942; reprinted in White, *The Science of Culture*; in *Man in Contemporary Society*, prepared by the Contemporary Civilization staff of Columbia University (New York, 1955); and in *Readings in Introductory Anthropology*, E. R. Service ed. (Ann Arbor, Mich., 1956). There is a fundamental difference between the tool process in the human species and the tool process among subhuman primates. This difference is due to symboling.

[8] "Sciencing," too, is a kind of behavior. See our essay, "Science is *Sciencing*" (Philosophy of Science, Vol. 5, pp. 369-89, 1938; reprinted in *The Science of Culture*).

[9] Importance of context may be illustrated by contrasting attitudes toward one end the same class of women: as mothers they are revered; as mothers-in-law, reviled.

[10] "According to [Ferdinand] de Sassure the study of human speech is not the subject matter of *one* science but of two sciences. . . . De Sassure drew a sharp line between *la langue* and *la parole*. Language (*la langue*) is universal, whereas the process of speech (*la parole*) . . . is individual" (Cassirer 1944:122). Huxley (1955:16), citing Cassirer's discussion of de Sassure's distinction between *la langue* and *la parole*, speaks of the former as "the super-individual system of grammar and syntax," and of the latter as "the actual words or way of speaking used by particular individuals." He goes on to say that "we find the *same distinction in every cultural activity*—in law, . . . ; in art . . . . in social structure . . . ; in science . . ." (emphasis ours).

[11] "The true locus of culture," says Sapir (1932:236), "is in the interactions of . . . individuals and, on the subjective side, in the world of meanings which each one of these individuals may unconsciously abstract for himself from his participation in these interactions." This statement is like ours except that it omits objects: material culture.

[12] It is interesting to note that Durkheim (1951:313-14), who uses the term "society" when many an American anthropologist would say culture, or socio-cultural system, remarks that "it is not true that society is made up only of individuals; it also includes material things, which play an essential role in the common life." He cites as examples such things as houses, instruments and machines used in industry, etc. "Social life . . . is thus crystallized . . . and fixed on material supports . . . externalized. . . ."

[13] Max Gluckman "reifies structure in precisely the way that White reifies culture . . ." says Murdock (1951:470). Strong (1953:392) feels that "White reifies, and at times almost deifies, culture. . . ." See, also, Herrick 1956:196.

[14] "To be sure, these cultural events could not have taken place had it not been for human organisms . . . the culturologist knows full well that culture traits do not go walking about like disembodied souls interacting with each other . . ." (White, *The Science of Culture*, pp. 99-100).

[15] Cf. White, *The Science of Culture*, pp. 96–98, for further discussion of this point.

[16] In our essays "The Expansion of the Scope of Science" and "The Science of Culture," in *The Science of Culture*.

[17] More than one hundred years ago Karl Marx wrote: "Man is in the most literal sense of the word a *zoon politikon*, not only a social animal, but an animal which can develop into an individual only in society. Production by isolated individuals outside of society . . . is as great an absurdity as the idea of the development of language without individuals living together and talking to one another," *A Contribution to the Critique of Political Economy* (Charles H. Kerr & Co., Chicago, 1904), p. 268.

REFERENCES

BEALS, RALPH L., and HARRY HOIJER 1953 An introduction to anthropology. New York, The Macmillan Co.

BENEDICT, RUTH 1934 Patterns of culture. Boston and New York, Houghton, Mifflin Co.

BIDNEY, DAVID 1946 The concept of cultural crisis. American Anthropologist 48:534–552.

——— 1954 Culture: a critical review of concepts and definitions, by Kroeber and Kluckhohn. American Journal of Sociology 59:488–489.

BOAS, FRANZ 1928 Anthropology and modern life. New York, W. W. Norton and Co., Inc.

——— 1938 The mind of primitive man, revised edition. New York, The Macmillan Co.

CASSIRER, ERNST 1944 An essay on man. New Haven, Yale University Press.

COHEN, MORRIS R. 1931 Fictions. Encyclopedia of the Social Sciences 7:225–228. New York, The Macmillan Co.

DURKHEIM, EMILE 1938 The rules of sociological method, George E. G. Catlin ed. Chicago, The University of Chicago Press.

——— 1951 Suicide, a study in sociology, George Simpson ed. Glencoe, Ill., The Free Press.

EINSTEIN, ALBERT 1934 The world as I see it. New York, Covici, Friede.

——— 1936 Physics and reality. Journal of the Franklin Institute 221:313–347, in German; 349–382 in English.

HALLOWELL, A. IRVING 1945 Sociopyschological aspects of acculturation. *In* The science of man in the world crisis, Ralph Linton ed. New York, Columbia University Press.

HERRICK, C. JUDSON 1956 The evolution of human nature. Austin, University of Texas Press.

HERSKOVITS, MELVILLE J. 1945 The processes of cultural change. *In* The science of man in the world crisis, Ralph Linton ed. New York, Columbia University Press.

——— 1948 Man and his works. New York, Alfred A. Knopf.

HOEBEL, E. ADAMSON 1956 The nature of culture. *In* Man, culture and society, Harry L. Shapiro ed. New York, Oxford University Press.

HOOTON, EARNEST A. 1939 Crime and the man. Cambridge, Mass., Harvard University Press.

HUXLEY, JULIAN S. 1955 Evolution, cultural and biological. Yearbook of Anthropology, Wm. L. Thomas, Jr. ed.

KEESING, FELIX M. 1958 Cultural anthropology. New York, Rinehart and Co., Inc.

KLUCKHOHN, CLYDE, and WM. H. KELLY 1945 The concept of culture. *In*

The science of man in the world crisis, Ralph Linton ed. New York, Columbia University Press.

KROEBER, A. L.   1917   The superorganic. American Anthropologist 19:163–213; reprinted in The nature of culture. Chicago, University of Chicago Press.

KROEBER, A. L., and CLYDE KLUCKHOHN   1952   Culture, a critical review of concepts and definitions. Papers of the Peabody Museum of American Archaeology and Ethnology, Harvard University, 47(1):1–223. Cambridge, Mass.

LINTON, RALPH   1936   The study of man. New York, D. Appleton-Century Co.

———   1945   The cultural background of personality. New York, D. Appleton-Century Co.

LOWIE, ROBERT H.   1917   Culture and ethnology. New York, Boni and Liveright.

LYND, ROBERT S.   1939   Knowledge for what? Princeton, N. J., Princeton University Press.

MALINOWSKI, BRONISLAW   1941   Man's culture and man's behavior. Sigma Xi Quarterly 29:170–196.

MURDOCK, GEORGE P.   1937   Editorial preface to Studies in the science of society, presented to Albert Galloway Keller. New Haven, Conn., Yale University Press.

———   1951   British social anthropology. American Anthropologist 53:465–473.

OSGOOD, CORNELIUS   1940   Ingalik material culture. Yale University Publications in Anthropology No. 22.

———   1951   Culture: its empirical and non-empirical character. Southwestern Journal of Anthropology 7:202–214.

RADCLIFFE-BROWN, A. R.   1924   The mother's brother in South Africa. South African Journal of Science, 21:542–555. Reprinted in Structure and function in primitive society.

———   1930–31   The social organization of Australian tribes. Oceania 1:34–63; 206–246; 322–341; 426–456.

———   1940   On social structure. Journal of the Royal Anthropological Institute 70:1–12; reprinted in Structure and function in primitive society. Glencoe, Ill., The Free Press.

———   1952   Structure and function in primitive society. Glencoe, Ill., The Free Press.

REDFIELD, ROBERT   1941   The folk culture of Yucatan. Chicago, The University of Chicago Press.

SAPIR, EDWARD   1916   Time perspective in aboriginal American culture. Canada Department of Mines, Geological Survey Memoir 90. Ottawa.

———   1917   Do we need a superorganic? American Anthropologist 19:441–447.

———   1930   Southern Paiute, a Shoshonean language. Proceedings of the American Academy of Arts and Sciences 65:1–296.

———   1932   Cultural anthropology and psychiatry. Journal of Abnormal and Social Psychology 27:229–242.

SPIRO, MELFORD E.   1951   Culture and personality. Psychiatry 14:19–46.

STEWARD, JULIAN H.   1955   Theory of culture change. Urbana, Ill., University of Illinois Press.

STRONG, WM. DUNCAN   1953   Historical approach in anthropology. In Anthropology today, A. L. Kroeber ed. Chicago, The University of Chicago Press, pp. 386–397.

TAYLOR, WALTER W.   1948   A study of archeology. American Anthropological Association Memoir No. 69.

TYLOR, EDWARD B.   1881   Anthropology. London.

———   1913   Primitive culture. 5th ed., London.

WHITE, LESLIE A. 1949 The science of culture. New York, Farrar, Straus and Cudahy; paperbound, 1958, New York, The Grove Press.

—— 1954 Culture: a critical review of concepts and definitions, by Kroeber and Kluckhohn. American Anthropologist 56:461–468.

WISSLER, CLARK 1929 Introduction to social anthropology. New York, Henry Holt and Co.

THE ARGUMENT

FROM ANIMALS TO MEN: AN EXAMINATION

OF ITS VALIDITY FOR ANTHROPOLOGY

J. B. S. HALDANE

In honouring me by associating my name with that of Thomas Henry Huxley, the Royal Anthropological Institute has given me the opportunity to assess the value for anthropology today of the standpoint of this great man. In *Man's Place in Nature* he argued not only for man's close morphological resemblance to other members of the order Primates, but for his descent from members of that order who could reasonably have been described as monkeys. His opponents in his own day of course accused him of degrading men to animals. And in his famous Romanes Lecture he went out of his way (some may think too far) to contrast the ethical process operating in humanity with the cosmic process operating in nature generally.

My theme today will be the legitimacy or otherwise of arguments from what we know of animals to our own species. Such arguments are not, of course, novel. Solomon, Aesop, and the authors of the mediaeval bestiaries, who were undoubtedly influenced by the *Pançatantra,* to mention no more, used them. Above all, Plato argued from dog breeding to the possibility of human eugenics. But with the acceptance of Huxley's thesis that we are descended from non-human animal species such arguments gained in force, and it is desirable to examine them in some detail.

A whole lecture could be devoted to such arguments in the field of anatomy, of physiology, of pharmacology, pathology, or psychology. But I am speaking to anthropologists. And the smattering of anthropology which I have acquired leads me to the conclusion that anthropologists are mainly interested in the differences between human groups, less so in the differences within groups, and rather little in the characters which are common to all groups, and to almost all members of these groups. This is in no way a reproach. An anthropologist must know some anatomy, physiology, medicine, psychology, statistics, and so on. But he or she is not expected to be an expert in all these fields, even though he may be in one of them. Nor need he be an expert comparative philologist, though again, he may be. I shall therefore devote this lecture mainly to the contributions made by animal studies to physical anthropology and to cultural anthropology.

First delivered as The Huxley Memorial Lecture at the Rooms of the Royal Society, Piccadilly, November 1956, this article is reprinted by permission from the *Journal of the Royal Anthropological Institute of Great Britain and Ireland,* 36: (1956), 1–14.

I hope however that I will be forgiven if I touch very briefly on those human studies which are not the specific business of anthropologists. The gross anatomy of man is better known than that of any other animal. The microscopic and ultramicroscopic anatomy and embryology are not. If for example we want the best possible preparations of the internal ear we must kill animals by special methods and begin to fix the tissues before they are completely dead. If we want to examine nerve cells with an electron microscope we must do much the same. If we want to follow the details of an embryological process we shall be well advised to use mice or rats. In all these cases enough human material is available to justify or to rebut the argument from animal to human structure.

Again, in so far as they can be studied without danger to life, human physiology, pharmacology, and pathology are better known than those of any other animal. Thanks particularly to my late father, we know that human physiology can be extremely accurate: Nevertheless we must often rely on animal experiments. But these seldom give us quantitative information applicable to men. The human heart will probably respond to a drug in the same way as a dog's heart, but it may be a good deal more or less responsive to an equivalent dose in milligrams per kilogram. Still, animal experiments are very helpful in these spheres because in the last ten million years of its evolution the line ancestral to our species has not altered as much in its anatomy, physiology, and so on as some other mammalian lines, except in the physiology of the brain.

The situation in psychology is very different. Human psychology is perhaps as different from that of a chimpanzee as a chimpanzee's is from a bird's. This difference is emphasized by some religions, though Hindus and Buddhists seem to me to evaluate it fairly correctly. Conversely some zoologists class every attempt to argue from human to animal psychology as anthropomorphism. In Huxley's lifetime Darwin and Romanes among others tried to trace the origin of human psychological traits in animals. So, a little later, did Freud, particularly in *Beyond the Pleasure Principle*. A new epoch began with Pavlov, and his approach, based on experiment, has been vigorously followed up, especially in the U.S.S.R. and the U.S.A. From a study of how animals alter their conduct, a process called conditioning, learning, forgetting, and so on, we can, I believe, learn a good deal about how individual human beings alter their conduct, and this has applications to human psychiatry.

Nevertheless, I think that a different approach to the study of animal behaviour may ultimately be at least equally valuable to anthropologists. We are living in a wholly exceptional period, in which human adults have got to continue learning. A failure to learn the meaning of traffic signals is an offence for which the punishment may be death. But in most human cultures of the past, and in a few relict cultures which anthropologists can still study, this was not so. The culture did not change appreciably during a lifetime, and an adult did not have to alter his schedule of conduct in given circumstances. Now it is possible to study the behaviour of animals in an approximately steady state, during which, so far as we can see, they learn nothing and forget nothing. Such a study must however be statistical. Moreau's (1939) observations on the nesting behaviour of birds, and those of Kinsey, Pomeroy & Martin (1948) on human sexual behaviour fall nearly into this class.* Moreau measured the mean times during which swallows stayed on their nests and away from them, and their variation. He found, for example, that the periods of absence were much less variable than those of incubation. Presumably a bird feels the need to return to its eggs even if it has caught few insects, but may not feel the need to leave its eggs. This is an obvious adaptation to the need for keeping the eggs at a fairly constant temperature. A similar study of more or less rhythmical behaviour in human beings in cultures where there is no "clocking in" is much to be desired.

With these prolegomena I pass to my main topics. The differences with which physical anthropologists are concerned are in part genetically determined. How far they are so can only be determined from the results of geographic or social migration. Thus Suski (1933) found that the children of Japanese origin born and bred in California were about as tall, on average, as Californian children of European descent. Mahalanobis, Majumdar & Rao (1949) showed that well-to-do members of other castes resembled Brahmins in many physical characters. When all such allowances have been made it is clear that most of the differences with which physical anthropologists had concerned themselves are mainly determined genetically. A fundamental question is at once posed. Are the principles of human genetics the same as those of animal genetics? And if so was not Plato fully justified in arguing from dog breeding to human breeding? Should not human breeding be controlled scientifically? I have tried to answer some of these questions elsewhere (Haldane 1956b). Perhaps more interesting to anthropologists are such questions as these. Are the biological differences between human groups comparable with those between groups of domestic animals such as grey-hounds and bulldogs, or between related species or subspecies living in different areas or habitats, such as wolves and jackals?

I have no doubt that the fundamental principles of genetics, discovered largely by Mendel, and first applied to men by Bateson and Garrod, are valid for men, as they are for animals and plants. But the applications of these principles to men and the animals so far studied are very different, perhaps as different as the application of the fundamental principles of chemistry to iron and to wood. Let us try to see some reasons why this is so. There are several different reasons. Most work on animal genetics has been done on domesticated animals. Since *Drosophila melanogaster* has 30 or 40 generations a year it has been bred under human control for about as many gener-

* To quote these authors (p. 446): "Exceedingly few males modify their attitudes on sex or change their patterns of overt behavior in any fundamental way after their middle teens."

ations as the cow, and must be regarded as domesticated. Now one of the first things which anthropologists investigate in a culture is its mating system: who has children by whom. The mating system of domestic animals is quite peculiar. In most domestic species there is a number of strictly endogamous breeds. The parents of a member of the breed must be members of the same breed. An Aberdeen Angus can no more become a Jersey on account of her meritorious milk yield than a sudra can become a brahmin by learning or asceticism. We might expect that the Indian castes would differ as much *inter se* as breeds of domestic animals. So perhaps they might but for one fundamental fact. The children of brahmins who could not learn the Vedas were not drowned, castrated, or even demoted to a lower caste. But it is only by such methods as these that the characters of animal breeds are preserved. The same applies to social classes in other societies. Individuals from lower classes may enter a higher one by intelligence, valour, or beauty. But human beings commonly look after the interests of their children, even if they do not resemble their parents. Hence much of the effort of members of a ruling class is devoted to finding niches within it for those of their children who do not possess the characters needed to enter it from below. Were it not for this fact humanity might by now have divided into several subspecies corresponding to social classes, and aristocracy would be the only possible form of government.

We might however expect that the inheritance of physical characters such as hair and eye colour within a polymorphic race such as Western Europeans would be as simple as it is in mice or poultry. There is a good reason why this is not so. A white hen appears by mutation in a previously black breed. It may be eaten. Or its descendants may be mated together to form a new white breed. It is therefore usually found that the genetical basis of white plumage in all members of a breed is the same. But nothing comparable occurs in our own species. Blue eye colour is, on the whole, recessive to brown. But there are enough well-authenticated cases of brown-eyed children of blue-eyed parents to show that several different gene substitutions may determine the development of blue rather than brown eyes.

However, Spurway (1953b) found that many of the taxonomic differences between geographical subspecies of the newt *Triturus cristatus* were due to single gene differences. We might have hoped that the colour differences between Europeans and West Africans would have been as simply based, though this would seem *a priori* improbable to an anthropologist who considered the almost continuous cline of skin colour found as we travel overland from Ukraine to Nigeria. In fact the colour difference in question has not been analysed genetically. It appears to depend on a number of gene pairs. The analysis will become possible as, on the one hand increasing racial equality makes for unions where paternity is neither doubtful nor likely to be concealed, and on the other, biochemical work such as that of Rothman, Krysa & Smiljanic (1946) and of Kikkawa, Ogito & Fujito (1955; see also

Kikkawa 1956) opens up the possibility of distinguishing, by biochemical methods, between genes with similar effects on pigmentation.

But meanwhile genetics has made little contribution to physical anthropology as our grandparents understood it. The reason is, I believe, simple. Domestic animals are the product of artificial selection, combined with intense inbreeding. The newts in a river basin, as Spurway (1953b) has argued on cytological grounds, may all be descended from the first fertilized female to cross a watershed into it. Perhaps in palaeolithic times human tribes were so endogamous that one could have argued from the genetics of domestic animals, had they existed, to that of men. Today the human mating system is more like that of moderately mobile mammals such as field voles. Since their genetics have not been studied, we cannot argue from it to human genetics.

At this point it may be worth saying a few words on animal mating systems. They may be utterly different in nearly related species. Thus in the mallard duck *Anas platyrhynchos* a brood disperses in its first year, and its members may breed hundreds or thousands of miles apart. This species is not divided into local races or subspecies. But young geese of the genera *Anser* and *Branta* normally migrate with their parents. There are local races with colour differences which have been given sub-specific rank, e.g. *Anser caerulescens caerulescens* and *A. c. hyperboreus,* the blue and lesser snow geese, the latter of which is almost white. Their breeding areas are adjacent but probably do not overlap. Lorenz (1943a) has claimed that wild geese brought up together will not mate, the brother-sister relationship inhibiting sexual attraction. This observation seems to need confirmation. If confirmed it is clearly of great interest for anthropologists.

If genetics has done little for classical anthropology it has revealed a wholly new and unexpected set of anthropological characters, the antigens and haemoglobins of the red corpuscles, whose genetic determination is very simple. As a reader of Mourant's (1954) book can readily verify, their geographical distribution is not. What is worse, no such character sharply differentiates two populations, as skin colour or hair structure may. It is nevertheless true that some antigens, or combinations of antigens, are rare and probably absent in some populations, and very common in others. Thus the Henshaw, Hunter, and Diego antigens have not been found in Europeans, but the first two are common in West Africans, the latter in South American Amerindians. These antigens seem to have very little adaptive value, and just for this reason are particularly valuable as an index of racial origins. Whereas the fact that skin cancer in Bombay is almost confined to Europeans leaves little doubt of the adaptive value of skin pigmentation, and the work of Schreider (1950) is making it more and more probable that many metrical characters are adaptations to climate. Thus we cannot argue that the very dark pigmentation of African negroes and Melanesians indicates common ancestry. However, from the absence of a very dark indigenous race in tropical America we can suggest that the evolution of such a race requires over 10,000 years, and that the ancestors of negroes and Melanesians have mainly lived in the tropics for more than that time.

There is no reason to think that our knowledge of the erythrocyte antigens is anywhere near complete. But if it were so, we know that there are many other antigens found in cells of other types, of which we know nothing in man, except that they differ so much as to render organ grafts impossible. We know a good deal about them and their genetics in mice. It is safe to prophesy that if biology exists fifty years hence they will have provided us with anthropological data of the greatest importance. Recent work (Layrisse & Arends 1956; Lewis, Ayukawa & Chown 1956) which shows that the Diego antigen, commonest in South American Amerindians, is also found in 10 per cent of Chippewas in North America, and of Japanese, and 5 per cent of a smaller sample of south Chinese, fully confirms the usual theory of the derivation of the Amerindians. A search for this antigen among Polynesians and Eskimos will be rewarding. The discovery that the Basques and the Swiss of the Canton of Wallis, with their excess of the d antigen, can be considered as representatives of a proto-European stock, is an example of what we may hope for. I shall speak later of the abnormal haemoglobins.

In recent years Plato's argument from dogs to men has been expanded into the statement, both by zoologists such as Lorenz (1934b) and by anthropologists such as Mead (1954), that man, and civilized man in particular, is a domestic animal. From this premise Lorenz (p. 502) proceeded to argue that civilized peoples must inevitably perish "unless selfconscious, scientifically based race politics prevents it" (p. 302). Such politics are based on "the value of racial purity" (p. 311), "the function of the intolerant value-judgment" (p. 308), and other tenets of the *National Sozialistische Arbeiter Partei*. I believe that the statement that man is a domestic animal is almost wholly false. Let us see where it is correct. Civilized men, like domestic animals, are sheltered from the predation of other vertebrate species. They are sheltered from some violent natural forces such as storms and frosts, though more liable than houseless men to be killed by earthquakes. They are, or were till very recently, particularly liable to be killed by infectious diseases promoted by overcrowding. Their food is relatively soft. As against this, domestic animals, with rare exceptions such as reindeers, cats, and bees, are divided into endogamous groups, the differences between which have been produced and are maintained by artificial selection. They have in consequence become highly specialized, and have usually lost many of the characters of their wild ancestors. From a purely animal point of view, man is unspecialized in many important ways. No other animal can swim a mile, walk twenty miles, and then climb forty feet up a tree. Many civilized men can do this without much difficulty. If so it is rather silly to regard them as physically degenerate. It is characteristic of Lorenz' argument (p. 303) that beside the picture of a wolf he gives that of a bulldog with the caption

"Reduction of the locomotory organs in the domestic form." He was not, perhaps, aware of the existence of borzois and Irish wolf-hounds, which run quicker than wolves; nor had it yet been revealed to him that dogs are mainly descended from jackals.

Perhaps the greatest difference between men and domestic animals is a very simple one. The wild ancestors of every domesticated land vertebrate have been at least somewhat social, and their tame descendants exhibit to men some at least of the patterns of behaviour which the wild ancestors exhibited to members of their own species. But as the result of domestication they have ceased to a greater or less extent to communicate with members of their own species (Spurway 1955). In particular, with the abolition of mating choice, sexual communication, including the activities called courtship, has atrophied or been grossly simplified (Lorenz 1940). A few domestic animals, such as sheepdogs, understand some human communications, but even these communicate less with their own species than did their wild ancestors. Whereas man has hypertrophied communication. He speaks, writes, gesticulates, draws, performs rituals, and so forth. The religions of others—not of course our own—can even be described in the language of comparative ethology (Lorenz 1950) as vacuum activities of communication in which human beings communicate with non-existent hearers.

Biologists generally accept Huxley's thesis that man has evolved. But the evolution of our ancestors in the last few million years has been of an unusual kind, involving a considerable increase in the volumes of some parts of the brain. It is difficult to answer the question, "Has man evolved more rapidly or more slowly than the average mammalian species?" Of course this question can only be answered on the morphological level. I shall try to answer it provisionally on this level. At first sight one would undoubtedly answer "Yes." The forms described as *Pithecanthropus, Sinanthropus, Atlanthropus,* and *Meganthropus* probably lived less than a million years ago. Indeed, recent work suggests that the Pleistocene period only lasted for about 300,000 years. The South African Australopithecines are not very much, if at all, older. It is not yet sure that our ancestors belonged to any of these genera, but some cannot be far off our ancestral line. If we accept the validity of the generic distinctions, it would appear that a genus of the Hominidae has a mean life of less than a million years. This would be very rapid evolution. Simpson (1944) finds the mean life of the genus of Carnivora to be about eight million years, and in many other groups it is much longer. But I think the generic distinctions are very doubtful. We have overclassified the Primates. Mayr (1951), who is one of the world's leading taxonomists, may have gone too far in the other direction when he suggested that the genus *Homo* should consist of three species, *sapiens* including the subspecies *neanderthalensis* and *soloensis, erectus* including *Pithecanthropus* and *Sinanthropus,* and *transvaalensis* including the Australopithecines. I should personally incline to put some at least of the latter in separate genera. But if

Mayr's view is anywhere near correct, human evolution has not been very rapid on a taxonomic basis.

Some years ago I introduced (Haldane 1949b) a more quantitative measure of evolutionary rate. I defined the unit, a darwin, as the increase or decrease in the mean dimension of a structure by a factor of e per million years, or what comes to the same thing, by a factor of 1.001 per 1,000 years. Average rates for tooth evolution in the ancestors of the horse since the Eocene are about 40 millidarwins, and Dinosaur lengths gave similar figures. But if *Sinanthropus* is in any way representative, human skull height has increased at a rate of about one darwin during the Pleistocene. The length and breadth have of course changed very little. But it appears that evolution of height has been abnormally quick. When we have adequate fossil material it will be of the greatest interest to discover whether the human hand evolved as quickly.

I believe, with T. H. Huxley, that the main agent of human evolutionary change has been natural selection. The most varied views have been expressed as to how far, if at all, men are, or have been, exposed to natural selection. I shall not review them, but state my own opinions. Firstly, man, like every other species, is subject to centripetal selection which weeds out extreme variants. These variants are of two kinds genetically. On the one hand there are rare mutants such as haemophilics and microcephalics. The selection approximately balances the mutation rate. On the other hand where the heterozygote for a pair of allelomorphs is fitter in the Darwinian sense than either homozygote, an equilibrium is reached where only a minority of the population is of the most favoured genotype. Penrose (1955b) has developed this notion in some detail. Secondly mankind is subject to natural selection of the type considered by Darwin, producing changes in gene frequencies, with evolutionary consequences. This however is usually a slow process, and much harder to observe, let alone to measure accurately, than centripetal selection. Thirdly, as I have suggested elsewhere (Haldane 1949a) the main selective agency acting on mankind during the last few thousand years has been infectious disease. The inventions of husbandry, of agriculture, and finally of cities, greatly increased the density of populations, and hence the death rate from infectious diseases. Trade led to the exchange of pathogens between different populations.

It is probable that during most of the Pleistocene period mankind was divided into small endogamous tribes. Sewall Wright (1949 and earlier) has produced strong *a priori* arguments that evolution can be very rapid in a population so divided. Keith (1948) later reached the same conclusion independently. We should expect to find very considerable physical diversity between different contemporaneous peoples, and the data assembled by Vallois (1954) support this view; however, the fossil record of the lower and middle palaeolithic is meagre, and the artefacts suggest a considerable uniformity. It is much too early to be dogmatic.

We still know too little of the biochemical basis of resistance to most diseases to say much as to their genetics, except that congenital resistance to disease appears to be specific. A person congenitally resistant to measles is not thereby rendered congenitally resistant to tuberculosis, or conversely. But we are beginning to learn something of the biochemical basis of resistance to malaria, or rather to the various malarias due to different sporozoan species. In the malarious regions of the world large fractions of human populations have red blood corpuscles abnormal in their structure (thalassaemia minor) or in the nature of their haemoglobin (haemoglobin S, C, E, etc.). Beet (1946) was probably the first to suggest that the sickle-cell trait, or in modern terminology, haemoglobin S, conferred resistance to malaria. Allison (1954) showed that the resistance, which is not however so complete as he first believed, is only or at least mainly to *Plasmodium falciparum*. Haldane's (1949c) suggestion that thalassaemia minor has a similar function has not been confirmed or disproved, though the geographical distribution in Italy and Greece supports it. Lehmann (1956) thinks that haemoglobins D and E may give some protection against ankylostomiasis. These abnormal conditions are transmitted as dominants over the normal state of the erythrocytes, the resistant persons being heterozygous. However, in the case of thalassaemia minor and the sickle-cell trait the progeny of two heterozygotes include one quarter abnormal homozygotes who generally die young of severe anaemia. Homozygotes for C and E haemoglobins are less handicapped. In consequence the frequency of resistant heterozygotes seldom exceeds about 20 per cent, in which case about one per cent of all children die of anaemia.

The gene for thalassaemia appears to be most frequent round the Mediterranean, though it extends at least to Indochina and Indonesia (Brumpt, de Traverse & Coquelet 1956). Haemoglobin S stretched from West Africa to the Nilgiris in Southern India, but is now found wherever African slaves were brought. Haemoglobin C seems to be mainly confined to West Africa, haemoglobin D to North-western India, haemoglobin E to South-eastern Asia and Indonesia. Lehmann (1956) gives the latest data. Once such a gene is present in a population it will spread if the appropriate malarial parasite gives it an advantage, until its further spread is checked by its lethal effect when homozygous. But since haemoglobin C is almost confined to West Africa, though it would be advantageous in East Africa, while haemoglobin E stretches from Indonesia to Ceylon, but has not been found in Africa, and thalassaemia is at least rare south of the Sahara, it is probable that such genes arise very rarely indeed by mutation, less than once in a thousand million gametes, as compared to about once in fifty thousand for the more mutable human loci. If so Lehmann and his colleagues (cf. Lehmann 1953) are justified in drawing conclusions as to racial origins from the presence of haemoglobin S in Southern India and Arabia as well as in Africa.

I shall not develop this topic further, but I think the time has come when a discussion of such matters between anthropological geneticists and animal geneticists like myself who have studied mutation and selection might achieve unanimity on the validity of arguments of this kind.

It is reasonable to hope that within some of our life-times infectious diseases will become sufficiently rare to be unimportant as agents of selection. If so a chapter in human evolution will close. The abnormal haemoglobins will slowly disappear. So probably will a number of other characters which are only advantageous in presence of specific infective agents. As Penrose (1955a) has pointed out, hygiene is more likely to have a eugenic effect than the dysgenic one usually attributed to it. No doubt however it will have a dysgenic effect as regards non-infectious but at least partly hereditary diseases such as diabetes. We do not know what will be the main agents of natural selection among our descendants. In certain circumstances resistance to high-frequency radiation will become as important as was resistance to disease in the past. There is unfortunately no reason to believe that exceptional men, if such there be, who can survive a dose of 1000 roentgens are any more desirable in other respects than those who recover from plague.

I must now pass to the topic of cultural anthropology. The diversity of human behaviour depends both on innate differences and on differences of culture. There are presumably differences in the median innate capacities of human groups for various forms of achievement. But the differences between members of a group are much greater than the differences between group medians. Hence environment, and particularly tradition, are more important than innate differences in determining the differences between human cultures. The study of animal tradition is therefore important to anthropologists. Unfortunately the statements made about it by some distinguished anthropologists seem to me to be inaccurate.

In my classification of human cultural features I shall use a Hindu classification rather than a modern European or American one for the following reason. Modern cultural anthropology is a by-product of colonialism. It consists of accounts given by persons almost all of European origin of the behaviour of members of other cultural groups over which they exerted dominance, largely through the greater efficiency of their weapons. Colonialism lasted for about four centuries, and is now drawing to a close. Hindu anthropology is similarly a by-product of the caste system, which is now also drawing to a close, but which lasted for over two thousand years. Soviet anthropology is a by-product of yet a third system. We do not know how long it will last, but it is not yet forty years old, and some of its tenets are taken over from Morgan's study of the Iroquois, which was a by-product of colonialism. I shall therefore employ a terminology of respectable antiquity, in the form given to it by my friend Professor Nirmal Kumar Bose in his *Cultural Anthropology* (reprinted 1953). I shall thus annoy not only British and Soviet anthropologists, but the majority of Indian ones, who may very reasonably object to a terminology associated with ideas which are a hindrance to progress in India. On the other hand I am emboldened to use the terminology of Indian cultural anthropology because some Western anthropologists ignore it completely. Pocock (1956) may be consulted as to the ignoration of recent Indian work.

According to the Hindu classics, human desires can be classified according as they are concerned with *artha,* economic needs, *kama,* reproductive needs, and *moksha,* the need for emancipation from these other needs. Perhaps there is also a *dharma* concerned with beauty, *sundara.* A culture is characterized by various *dharmas* which satisfy these needs to a greater or less extent. Each *dharma* acts through five agencies, *vastu* or material object, *kriya* or habitual action, *samhati* or social grouping, *vicharamalaka tattwa,* namely "knowledge based on experience and subject to criticism," and *viswasamalaka tattwa* or knowledge based on faith. These interact with the *svadharma* of each individual, which, to some extent, corresponds with our notion of genotype. I do not of course suggest that this is the only Hindu classification. Some authors would deny the existence of a *kamadharma.*

Anthropologists study all five of these agencies, and it is clear that the differences between them in different cultures are due mainly to differences of tradition, rather than of biological heredity. A human being brought up in one culture can adopt the traditions of another, though with some difficulty. Perhaps the change is easiest for those who have most nearly achieved *moksha,* to whom the *dharma* of one culture appears as devoid of absolute value as that of another. Such a person is unlikely to wear a *dhoti,* a kilt, or a pair of trousers with full elegance, but may be prepared to wear any of them.

Does tradition exist among animals? Many animal activities are instinctive, by which I mean that many complicated social activities are performed by animals which have been brought up in isolation from members of their own species, and in particular have not perceived other members of it carrying out these activities. Honeybees have a language or set of symbolical movements, first interpreted by von Frisch (1950 and earlier), which enable them to communicate the distance of a food source with considerable accuracy, and its direction rather more accurately than a man can do by such words as "Northeast by east" (Haldane & Spurway 1954). This communication is both made and understood without learning, though Lindauer (1951, 1953) has shown that bees often misinterpret their first instructions for a flight, and usually exaggerate the distance when first reporting a discovery of food. We shall learn little from insects as to the transmission of culture, though we can learn something.

But culture is certainly transmitted in birds and mammals. Von Pernau (1702) and Barrington (1773) founded cultural ornithology, but little further progress was made before the work of the Heinroths (1924–6) and Promptov (e.g. 1949) in this century. It is now being vigorously prosecuted by Thorpe (1951, 1954) and his colleagues in England. These investigations have mainly been concerned with vocal, or linguistic tradition. In some species, for example the blackbird, *Turdus merula,* there is apparently no tradition. Males brought up by human beings from the egg sing a perfect song. This represents a human aspiration. Several mythical personages were born with a knowledge of the Vedas. But I wish to suggest that it may once have been a human reality. During the lower palaeolithic period, techniques of flint chipping continued with very little change for periods of over 100,000 years. It seems to me possible that they may have been as instinctive as the making of spiders' webs, even if most flint chippers saw other men chipping flints. To assume that these techniques were learned seems to me an anthropo-. morphic interpretation of beings who were hardly quite human. The contrary assumption is of course equally temrarious. In my opinion we do not know.

Other birds such as the skylark (*Alauda arvensis*) and chaffinch (*Fringilla coelebs*) must learn their song. Reared in isolation the lark's song is said to be unrecognizable, that of the chaffinch very imperfect. Marler (1952) found that within Great Britain he could recognize five local chaffinch dialects, with considerable overlap, and considerable variation within a given area. But the chaffinches of the Azores sing a dialect differing from any of the British dialects far more than they differ from one another.

We can ask what are the conditions for the development of a local dialect given that young song-birds disperse widely during their first year, whereas in later years they generally return to the same area to nest, even if they have migrated southwards in autumn. The answer is not quite obvious. The song must of course be learned. If it were determined genetically local dialects within a country of the size of England would be no more possible than local colour varieties. And the song must not be learned by nestlings from their father, as it is in robins (*Erithacus rubecula*). Such learning has the same observable effects as one type of biological inheritance. The condition for the formation of local dialects is that male birds should learn the song from neighbouring males at the end of their first year, when they are already attached to particular localities.

I have dealt with this case in some detail because the conditions for the development of local cultures differ from one species to another, and a consideration of them may at least give anthropologists a background. In our own species unduly precocious learning is probably inimical to culture. No doubt we learn some very important things from our mothers, but we learn still more important ones from society, and many cultures mark the transition from one type of learning to the other by special rites, which are fortunately not required by chaffinches.

Now let me go back to Bose's classification. Do social animals transmit *vastu* (material objects) from one generation to another? Most certainly. The most striking example is the transmission by females (queens) of the agricultural ant genus *Atta* of pieces of the fungus *Rhozites* which they cultivate. Each piece is carried in a special cavity near the mouth and deposited in the new fungus garden. The analogy with seeds in human cultures is obvious. The immense emotional valence of plant seeds for men is shown by the fact that the word for them in many languages also designates the male reproductive fluid. This is so in a variety of Aryan and Semitic languages, in Magyar (where it is also a reflexive pronoun), and also in Mundari, though Professor Bose tells me that in Mundari the word also means acculturation, a custom being described as "Hindu seed," or "English seed." But as might be expected, this equivalence is absent in Fulani, the language of a pastoral people. Sanskrit has two other official words for the reproductive fluid, and many languages have unofficial words. A world-wide study on this topic would be worth while, unless indeed I am displaying my ignorance and it has already been made.

Do animals use material objects for communication? They do so both to communicate with other members of their species, and with themselves in the future, as men use writing for both purposes. Hediger (1955) in a book which every cultural anthropologist should read, though its title hardly suggests its relevance, gives surprising but probably true answers to two questions: "In what way do men most resemble other mammals psychologically, apart from physiological needs, and in what way do they most differ?" He states (cf. Spurway 1956) that they resemble them most in their sense of property, and differ most in not being chronically afraid. Non-human mammals, particularly males, characteristically mark their property with their individual scent, sometimes, but by no means always, using excretions or glands near the anus for this purpose. You have only to look at a male chamois, black buck, or hyaena to see scent glands on the head. It is even possible to distinguish the marks made by individual hyaenas visually. These odours serve as a warning to other males, and a source of satisfaction to the rightful owners. Other species such as several bears and the domestic dog communicate by depositing odours and scratching objects outside their territories. These odours and marks are material objects whose main function is to arouse certain emotions. Such objects are of course familiar to anthropologists, though in our species they usually act by being seen rather than smelt.

The *kriya* or habitual action is quite often learned. Kuo's (1938) experiments showed that cats would not generally kill mice or rats unless taught to do so by their parents. Chernomordikov (1944) found that young lizards of the genera *Anguis* and *Eumeces* only eat insect larvae if their skin has been broken, and only hunt moving insects if they have previously tasted them. Evans (1955) describes maternal care in *Eumeces*, and it is probable that members of this genus are taught what to eat by their mothers. More remarkably Reyniers (1953) reported that young rats isolated from their parents die from retention of urine unless the external opening of the urethra is mechanically stimulated. After this has been done once or twice they respond to distension of the bladder. Let no psychoanalyst claim that the human species is unique in having psychological difficulties connected with infantile excretion.

Some member of an animal species may invent a new *kriya,* and it can spread, apparently by imitation. A few years ago a Stevin or Watt among great tits (*Parus major*) invented the practice of opening milk bottles left on human doorsteps. This has become common in England (Fisher & Hinde 1949) and has now spread to Holland, whether by cultural diffusion or by independent invention we do not know. Similarly Petterson (1956) reports that greenfinches (*Chloris chloris*) are taking to eating immature seeds of *Daphne mezereum.* This had not been reported till very recently, although the opportunity has probably existed for ten thousand years or so. I need not emphasize the interest of such facts for students of human cultural change.

On the other hand it is more doubtful that *samhati,* or social organization, is traditional in mammals. Vertebrates have to learn their functions in the society into which they are born. And the structure of this society varies with its numbers, its environments, the temperament of dominant individuals, and so on. But there is as yet little evidence that unusual economic circumstances or unusual individuals can induce a change in social structure lasting through many generations, as they can in human societies. The best piece of evidence on this question is Elton's (1933) statement that the muzzling order of 1895 by which dogs were prevented from biting one another for some months has permanently lowered the acerbity of fights between British dogs. It would perhaps be rash to build too large a theoretical superstructure on this foundation.

The question of a traditional *tattwa,* or knowledge, in animals is difficult, because we can only infer knowledge from habitual actions. But there is an analogy with the two types in Bose's classification. A bird on first leaving the nest where it was hatched already knows that some objects, which it has seen, such as caterpillars or seeds, are edible, while others, such as sticks, are not. This knowledge is however subject to critical revision. De Ruiter (1953) showed that birds can very rapidly learn that stick-like caterpillars are edible, and most vertebrates can be taught (or "conditioned") to avoid food with particular visual or odorous characters. We do not know whether some kinds of infantile learning in vertebrates are as difficultly effaceable as moral and religious notions learned from the mother are in some human beings.

But this seems to be so in insects. Thorpe (1938) made the remarkable discovery of larval conditioning, where there is no question of even such elementary teaching as the offering of a caterpillar to a nestling. Female insects of several species which have spent their larval life eating food with a particular odour will search for food of this odour in which to lay their eggs. It is doubtful whether adult learning can overcome this larval conditioning, which can be compared with *viswasamalaka tattwa.* In such species the choice of food plants and animals is to some extent traditional, and Thorpe was able to alter the tradition. Where such experiments have not been done, egg-laying preference is generally thought to be instinctive, as no doubt it is in some cases.

If we speak of an insect knowing where to lay her eggs as the result of experience, we can also speak of instinctive knowledge, or in deference to philosophers who think that knowledge cannot err, instinctive opinion. Such knowledge or opinion exists in our own species. Every baby "knows" that sweet things are good to eat. This "knowledge" may of course be erroneous, as when a child poisons itself with lead acetate. But the scope of human instinctive knowledge is limited, and we feel the lack of it. Free will is a hard burden to bear. We try to lighten it with knowledge based on faith. We know, according to the culture in which we have been brought up, either that the eating of human flesh is an abomination, or that it is necessary for the acquisition of certain qualities. We also claim to know the truth of some most detailed and complicated assertions about the structure of the universe, its past and its future. It is not known whether human societies can exist without traditional *viswasamalaka tattwa*. They can certainly exist with very different and mutually contradictory ones, and the "knowledge" acquired in this way need not include supernatural elements. It can however be argued that beliefs in the rightness and wrongness of certain actions, held without rational foundations, are essential for the stability of any human society. I shall come back later to the question whether any elements in such beliefs are not of traditional origin.

Returning once more to Bose's classification, a few animals, such as bower birds, show *sundaradharma*, behaviour satisfying aesthetic needs. This is most marked in the bower birds, where Marshall (1954) regards it as a derivative, or displacement activity, of sexual behaviour, as it is in men according to some Freudians. It does not appear to be traditional. Have animals a *mokshadharma*? So far as I know this question has not been asked. It is too seldom asked concerning human cultures. *Moksha* means the state of a human being unaffected by external stimuli such as heat and cold, or internal stimuli (Pavlov 1928) such as those causing hunger and lust. It has a special theological significance for Hinduism, but it can be equated with the ἀταραξία of Epicurus, and the contemplative life of Christian mystics. I do not doubt that some at least of the primitive religions help their adherents towards it, but it is perhaps the hardest function of a religion for field anthropologists to investigate. I think it conceivable that some higher animals can perform *mokshadharma* in their post-reproductive period, but there is no evidence for its cultural transmission.

I hope that I have shown that we can legitimately ask the question whether the equivalent of a human social activity is found in a particular animal species, and if so how far it depends on tradition. It always depends on heredity, in the broad sense of that word. Even those songbirds which must learn their song learn the song characteristic of their own species when a choice is offered to them. The examples which I have given are few because zoologists have only recently begun to ask this question systematically, and no comprehensive review of animal tradition exists. I claim that even our very meagre knowledge furnishes a background for cultural anthropology. Perhaps anthropologists may sometimes be able to put a question more clearly if they do so in a form which would be applicable to an animal species, though I trust that they will never imitate some psychologists in thinking that such a form is obligatory.

I also think that the data of animal ethology can throw some light at least on the origins of human behaviour, and above all on its extreme adaptability. Social behaviour in most mammals depends largely on odour signals. That is one reason why we understand their social behaviour less well than that of birds, which, like our own, is mainly based on visual and auditory signals. Odorous signals still have some valence for us men. But when our ancestors took to arboreal life animal odours became less important to them, and plant ones more so. They doubtless developed a set of instincts appropriate to arboreal life. They probably came down from the trees more than a million years ago, and may have gone through a more or less quadrupedal phase before a change in pelvic shape made bipedal running and the emancipation of the hands possible. The great development of the brain probably occurred quite soon after the adoption of the bipedal posture. Man did not arise with a set of instincts as detailed as those of most other vertebrates, from which he had to emancipate himself. Wordsworth described this human absence of instinct as

> "Blank misgivings of a creature
> Moving about in worlds not realised."

Had our ancestors had a few million years in which to develop instincts appropriate to a bipedal mammal I doubt if they could have become men. If our descendants ever achieve a stable and permanent culture lasting with little change over some millions of years, they may develop instincts suited to it, and cease to be men. Our relative lack of instincts has so far enabled us to adapt ourselves to the changes which we have made and are making in our environments. We do however find traces of instinct, by which I mean in this context the release of characteristic emotions and actions by somewhat arbitrary sign-stimuli, in unexpected quarters. I am inclined to accept Jung's conclusion that human beings in different cultures independently produce similar symbols which have for them a high emotional valence and are often incorporated into religions. For reasons given elsewhere (Haldane 1956a) I see no reason to adopt his theory of a collective unconscious. I give just one example, which I believe is novel. Michael Angelo's frescos in the Sistine Chapel are generally regarded as one of the masterpieces of European art. So far as I know my wife was the first to remark that the attitude of Christ in the Last Judgement is that of Siva in one of his destructive aspects. The attitude is certainly rare in Christian art, and it is most unlikely that it was copied from a Hindu original. But it evokes similar emotions in Christians and Hindus.

And here let me return to Hediger's point that man differs from most animals in not being chronically slightly frightened. Our ancestors clearly were so as long as large carnivora were a danger. With their disappearance we have peopled the world with hobgoblins and supernatural beings whose characters inspire fear. They appear to fulfil an emotional need. It is a gross oversimplification to present the needs which are served by mythology in such words as:

> "This life cannot be all, they swear
> For how unpleasant if it were."

I suggest that man, or a great many men, demands an object of fear, as some animals appear to do (Spurway 1953a), and that it may be better to believe in Kali, Maryamma or our adversary the Devil than to make foreign governments our principal object of fear. No doubt it would be better still to concentrate on bacteria, but a primitive emotion of this type seems too often to need an object which can be readily imagined. To conclude, I think that the study of animals may tell us a good deal about the human unconscious, and thus about irrational human behaviour.

I must end up by apologizing for my subject matter and my treatment of it. An adequate treatment would have filled several books. I hope that I may stimulate a zoologist to write a book on "Animal Tradition." I have inevitably been both superficial and dogmatic. I have doubtless displayed my ignorance of anthropology. But the sciences are becoming specialized, and it is of immense importance for their healthy development that contact should be preserved between them. The price of such contact is a measure of inaccuracy and superficiality. But the cost of avoiding it is even more serious. Thomas Henry Huxley was primarily an anatomist. But he was not afraid of stating his opinions on physiology, anthropology, theology, and philosophy. I should like to see professional anthropolgoists trespassing on the fields of other sciences, and particularly, perhaps, on the study of animal behaviour. If I have irritated some of my audience into such a counter-attack this lecture will have been justified.

REFERENCES

ALLISON, A. C.   1954   Notes on sickle-cell polymorphism. Ann. Eugen. 19:39–57.

BARRINGTON, D.   1773   Experiments and observations on the singing of birds. Phil. Trans. Roy. Soc. 63:249–91.

BEET, E. A.   1946   Sickle cell disease in the Balovale district of Northern Rhodesia. E. African Med. J. 23:75.

BOSE, N. K.   1953   Cultural Anthropology and Other Essays. Calcutta.

BRUMPT, L., M. DE TRAVERSE, P. M. COQUELET   1956   Interaction entre hémoglobine E et trait thalassémique au Cambodge. C.R. Soc. Biol. 150:147–61.

CHERNOMORDIKOV, V. V. 1944 On inherent and acquired food reactions in reptiles. *C. R.* (Doklady) Ac. Sci. *U.R.S.S.* 43:174.

ELTON, C. S. 1933 The Ecology of Animals. London.

EVANS, L. T. 1955 In Group Processes. New York.

FISHER, J., and R. A. HINDE 1949 The opening of milk bottles by birds. British Birds, 42:347.

FRISCH, K. VON 1950 Bees, Their Vision, Chemical Senses and Language. Ithaca, N.Y.

HALDANE, J. B. S. 1949a Disease and evolution. La Ric. Sci. Suppl. 19:68–76.

———— 1949b Suggestions as to the quantitative measurement of rates of evolution. Evolution, 3:51–6.

———— 1949c The rate of mutation of human genes. Proc. VIII Int. Congr. Genet. (Hereditas suppl.) 267–73.

———— 1956a Time in biology. Sci. Progr. 175:385–402.

———— 1956b The prospects for eugenics. New Biol. 22 (in press), and Proc. Roy. Institution (in press).

HALDANE, J. B. S., and H. SPURWAY 1954 A statistical analysis of communication in Apis mellifera, and a comparison with communication in other animals. Insectes sociaux, 1:247–83.

HEDIGER, H. 1955 Studies of the Psychology and Behavior of Captive Animals in Zoos and Circuses. London.

HEINROTH, O., and M. HEINROTH 1924–26. Die Vögel Mitteleuropas. Berlin.

KEITH, A. 1948 A New Theory of Human Evolution. London.

KIKKAWA, H. 1956 Relation between hair color and metals in human hair. Human Biology, 28:59–66.

KIKKAWA, H., Z. OGITO, and S. FUJITO 1955 Nature of pigments derived from tyrosine and tryptophan in animals. Science, 121:43–7.

KINSEY, A. C., W. B. POMEROY, and C. E. MARTIN 1948 Sexual Behavior in the Human Male. Philadelphia and London.

KUO, Z. Y. 1938 Further study on the behavior of the cat towards the rat. J. Comp. Psychol. 25:1–8.

LAYRISSE, M., and T. ARENDS 1956 The Diego blood factor in Chinese and Japanese. Nature, London, 177:1084–7.

LEHMANN, H. 1956 Distribution of abnormal haemoglobins. J. Clin. Path. 9:180–81.

LEWIS, M., H. AYUKAWA, and B. CHOWN 1956 The blood group antigen Diego in North American Indians and Japanese. Nature, London, 177:1087.

LINDAUER, M. 1951 Bienentänze in der Schwarmtraube. Die Naturwissenschaften, 38:509–13.

———— 1953 Bienentänze in der Schwarmtraube. Die Naturwissenschaften, 40:379.

LORENZ, K. Z. 1940 Durch Domestikation verursachte Störungen arteigener Verhalten. Z. angew. Psychol. Characterkunde, 59:1–81.

LORENZ, K. Z. 1943a Der Kumpan in der Unwelt des Vogels. J. Ornith. 83:137–413.

———— 1943b Die angeborenen Formen möglicher Erfahrung. Z. Tierpsychol. 5:235–409.

———— 1950 The comparative method in studying innate behaviour patterns. Symp. Soc. exp. Biol. 4:221–68.

MAHALANOBIS, P. C., D. N. MAJUMDAR, and C. R. RAO 1949 Anthropometric survey of the United Provinces 1941 A statistical study. Sankhya, 9:90–324.

MARLER, P. 1952 Variation in the song of the chaffinch *Fringilla coelebs*. Ibis, 94:458–72.

MARSHALL, A. J.   1954   Bower Birds, their Display and Breeding Cycles. Oxford.
MAYR, E.   1951   Taxonomic categories in fossil hominids. Cold Spring Harbor Symposia on Quantitative Biology, 15:109-28.
MEAD, M.   1954   Some theoretical considerations on the problem of mother-child separation. Am. Jour. Orthopsych. 24:471-83.
MOREAU, R. S.   1939   Numerical data on African birds' behaviour at the nest: Hirundo s. smithii Leach, the Wire-tailed swallow. Proc. Zool. Soc. 109A: 109-25.
MOURANT, A. E.   1954   The Distribution of the Human Blood Groups. Oxford.
PAVLOV, I. P.   1928   Lectures on Conditioned Reflexes, vols. 1 and 2. New York and London.
PENROSE, L. S.   1955a   Genetics and medicine. Adv. Sci. London, 11:387.
――――   1955b   Evidence of heterosis in man. Proc. Roy. Soc. B 144:203-12.
PERNAU, E. A. VON   1702   Unterricht, was mit dem lieblichen Geschoepff denen Voegelen, auch ausser dem Fang, nur durch Ergruendung deren Eigenschaften und Zahmmachung oder anderer Abrichtung man sich vor Lust und Zeitvertreib machen koenne.
PETTERSON, M.   1956   Diffusion of a new habit among greenfinches. Nature, London, 177:709-10.
POCOCK, D. F.   1956   The social anthropology of India. Man, 1956, 169.
PROMPTOV, A. V.   1949   Vocal imitation in the Passeriformes. C. R. (Doklady) Ac. Sci. U.R.S.S. 45:261.
REYNIERS, J. A.   1953   Germ-free life. (Report of a lecture) Lancet II:933-4.
ROTHMAN, S., A. F. KRYSA, and A. M. SMILJANIC   1946   Inhibitory action of human epidermis on melanin formation. Proc. Soc. exp. Biol. Med. 62:208-9.
RUITER, L. DE   1953   Some experiments on the camouflage of stick caterpillars. Behaviour, 4:222-32.
SCHREIDER, E.   1950   Les variations raciales et sexuelles du tronc humain. L'Anthrop. 54:67-81, 228-61.
SIMPSON, G. G.   1944   Tempo and Mode in Evolution. New York.
SPURWAY, H.   1953a   The escape drive in domestic cats and the dog and cat relationship. Behaviour, 5:81-4.
――――   1953b   Genetics of specific and subspecific differences in European newts. Symp. Soc. exp. Biol. 7:200-37.
――――   1955   The causes of domestication: an attempt to integrate some ideas of Konrad Lorenz with evolution theory. J. Genet. 53:325-62.
――――   1956   Cultural mammalogy. (Review of Studies of the Psychology and Behavior of Captive Animals in Zoos and Circuses, by H. Hediger, 1955). New Biol. 20:104-11.
SUSKI, P. M.   1933   The body-build of American-born Japanese children. Biometrika, 25:323-52.
THORPE, W. H.   1938   Further experiments on olfactory conditioning in a parasitic insect. The nature of the conditioning process. Proc. Roy. Soc. B. 126:370-97.
――――   1951   The learning abilities of birds. Ibis, 93:1-42, 252-96.
――――   1954   The process of learning in the chaffinch as studied by means of the sound spectrograph. Nature, London, 173, 465.
VALLOIS, HENRI V.   1954   Neandertals and Praesapiens. Huxley Memorial Lecture 1954   J. R. Anthrop. Inst. 84:111-30.
WRIGHT, S.   1949   Adaptation and selection. In Genetics, Paleontology and Evolution. Princeton.

SOCIAL BEHAVIOUR

AND PRIMATE EVOLUTION

M. R. A. CHANCE

INTRODUCTION

It is now possible to state clearly the anatomical features which differentiate man from the other primates (Straus, 1949; Clark, 1949), and the fossil evidence makes clear the major changes, if not the actual stages, which have led to his emergence from the primitive mammalian state to his present taxonomic position. Yet we are still without an adequate theory to explain this process in terms of adaptive evolution. Man's anatomical characteristics appear to be the culmination of the evolutionary trend which distinguishes primates from other mammals. Zuckerman (1933) has said of the primates that their morphological characters "are generally believed to represent a primitive mammalian condition, so that it may be truly said that the primate, except for its general tendency to cerebral development, is relatively a non-specialized mammal." No adequate explanation has been put forward, how-ever, to account for the development of so large a cerebrum as that found in man.

Evolutionary theory will provide an explanation of the fossil record only in terms of specific selective processes. Hence, the most pertinent question in this context is: What were the selective forces acting on man's ancestors? A survey of the relevant literature shows that in no instance has this question been formulated. This may be due to the fact that evolutionary theory up to the present has been based almost exclusively upon anatomical consider-ations. The evidence bearing upon this problem is of two kinds. The direct evidence is founded upon the fossil record in an attempt to identify fossil sequences. The indirect evidence comes from consideration of the features exhibited by related living primates and mammals, and entails arguments by analogy from them. It is not possible to deduce the selective forces acting upon man's ancestors from anatomical studies alone, although essential evidence is obtained about the changes that have taken place in anatomical structures. In view of this it is necessary to examine the nature of the indirect evidence more closely.

Anatomical evidence enables inferences to be drawn from fossil material about the functions and changes in function of particular parts of the body; but interpretation of the fossil record involves the use of two components of knowledge, both of which are derived from observations of contemporary processes, made either in the laboratory or in nature. From our knowledge of physics, it is possible to state that processes are performed to greater mechanical advantage by particular anatomical changes observed in the fossil record; and also it can be shown that certain other functions may have been lost. These deductions can be verified by reference to the behaviour of living forms, which show resemblances to the fossil types.

The interpretation of the fossil record is thus incomplete without reference to the evidence obtained from contemporary processes. Every instance in which the selective forces have been deduced requires an understanding of the principles underlying the function of the particular organ which has undergone change. In the primates the enlargement of the neocortex is the most prominent feature, requiring explanation in terms of adaptive evolution (Straus, 1949). We require, therefore, a clear idea of the principles underlying the function of the central nervous system, on the one hand; and on the other, an understanding of the way in which the behaviour of the primate has consequences for the evolution of the central nervous system. From these it may be possible to infer the reason for the enlargement of the neocortex. Modern neurophysiology is in the process of elucidating the first point, and studies in primate behaviour help us to understand the second. Behaviour studies in primates help us in two ways: first, by showing the behaviour patterns characteristic of primates, and secondly, by defining the circumstances of their lives, which precipitate particular stresses requiring a type of adaptive response not dependent upon the possession of specialized effector organs.

Great progress has been made in our understanding of the behaviour of birds and insects; so that, as Julian Huxley has put it, we now have some idea of the anatomy of the behaviour of these animals. The same cannot be said of mammals. Throughout the class Mammalia, the similarities are more pronounced than the differences, since no anatomical features or physiological factors, comparable to differences between phyla, exist to be considered. Differences between mammals reflect quantitative elaboration of parts, relative disproportion of parts, and alteration in physiological timing of events. It must, therefore, be possible to show that there are basic forms of behaviour, characteristic of all mammals, which have become modified in the different orders and genera under the influence of natural selection. These forms of behaviour would facilitate direct comparison of one animal with another, in evolutionary as well as in behavioural contexts.

It can be shown, from existing knowledge of the natural mode of life of mammals, that the primates are subject to a large element of conflict in their social relations. They differ from all other mammals, in that the particular type of social conflict is an ever-present element in the life of several species. We can infer that, in the setting of primate society, this conflict has a pronounced selective action on the breeding performance of individuals within

85

the group, and thus will have evolutionary consequences of a very high order. An attempt is made to suggest what these will be.

In order to do this, however, an adequate conceptual framework is required. How far this is provided by existing theoretical interpretations of mammalian behaviour must now be examined.

CONCEPTS IN BEHAVIOUR STUDIES

There are at present in the field of animal behaviour studies, concerned with conflict, three distinct types of research. In America, Maier (1949) and Masserman (1946) have studied the effect of conflict on the subequent behaviour pattern of the individual animal. These two workers derive their theoretical approach from human psychology, which has now revealed that "conflict" (originating from situations in which choice is eliminated, and motive satisfaction prevented) is a prime factor in human psychopathology. This work provides no information relevant to our inquiry. Miller (1944), on the other hand, has used the runway for the analysis of conflict resolutions. His findings are directly relevant to this thesis, and are referred to again later. These groups are analytical, in that they are investigating behaviour under conditions designed to elicit the capabilities of animals in specified conditions. They are little concerned whether the types of behaviour examined occur in natural environments. Their work has, therefore, no connotation with evolutionary theory.

In contrast to them, in Europe, Lorenz (1937), Tinbergen (1942) and Thorpe (1948) have emphasized the need to construct a theory of animal behaviour, based upon observations of the animal in the natural environment. They have devised methods for making experiments in natural surroundings, or in isolated replicas of the normal environment. These experiments are designed to make the original observations of behaviour in the wild more precise, and in this way to analyse the underlying mechanisms. Their studies thus have an evolutionary connotation, and they are interested in the role of behaviour in natural selection, but they have not worked with mammals.

The concept of a goal (Russell, 1945) as the end-state of a particular type of behaviour is widely used throughout biology, and has been used in this way in the studies already mentioned. In a maze, the consummatory act takes place at a predetermined place, by virtue of the experimental set-up, and the goal-directed behaviour is taken as the positive response to an attractive stimulus object. A great degree of restriction on the movement of the animal is also a feature of such experiments. Except in the experiments of Neal Miller, objects which tend to repel the animal are considered as obstructions to the completion of a positive response; there is no negative goal. As we are concerned with the interaction within the animal of attractive and repellant stimuli, it is unlikely that it will be found possible to use existing concepts to define the situations in which an act is consummated and conflict arises in a community of free-ranging animals like the primates.

In view of the diverse nature of these studies we have felt the need to develop a new approach, which will serve to link analytical studies on mammals with field studies, so that it may be possible to deduce evolutionary consequences from the combined approach. This approach is the logical continuation of the field studies of Elton & Chitty and their co-workers, who are commencing analytical experiments in the laboratory on mammalian behaviour, to elucidate some of the problems they have thrown up from studies on the field ecology of mammalian populations.

Before we come to the problem of the type of theoretical structure required for these studies, we must define the way in which we propose to establish a theoretical link between analytical studies on the one hand, and observations of the behaviour of mammals in the natural habitat on the other. The concept underlying the linkage is that of biological appropriateness (Thorpe, 1948; Sommerhoff, 1950).

Biological appropriateness refers to the extent to which the particular type of behaviour actually facilitates the biological processes towards which it is directed, or around which it is grouped.

It is clear that laboratory analysis has revealed patterns of behaviour which have not been recorded from field studies, and which, therefore, play only a slight, if an appreciable, role in the behaviour of an animal in its natural surroundings. It is also possible that types of behaviour discovered in the laboratory may be of real importance in the normal environment, even though field workers have not discovered them. Extreme experimental conditions, however, are required to evoke some of these aspects of behaviour. It is possible to understand, therefore, that the central nervous system of mammals holds potentialities, which only particular circumstances can evoke (Lashley, 1949; Chance, 1957; Chance & Russell, 1959). These circumstances may or may not exist in the environment of the animal; and accordingly the behaviour appropriate to them may play a prominent part in the life of one animal, and enter only slightly into the life of another. Therefore, in studies in comparative behaviour, it must be borne in mind that the circumstances employed in the study of a form of behaviour in one mammal may not be directly applicable to the study of the same form in another mammal. We must be careful to ensure that the same element of behaviour is studied in each animal, and this may entail the utilization of the stimulus situation normally evoking the response in its natural environment.

Not all naturally occurring stimulus situations will have selective consequences, but there are some in which these consequences are very great. Where an animal is in such a relation to its environment that slight changes in its behaviour bring about a relatively high degree of inappropriateness, this is a situation of behaviour stress. This behaviour may have evolutionary consequences, in proportion to the influence it has on the breeding performance.

The stress in the life of subhuman primates arises out of an element of conflict, to which they are continuously subjected by the nature of their social relations. It is now necessary to consider the terms in which this can be defined.

THEORETICAL FRAMEWORK FOR ANALYSIS
OF MAMMALIAN BEHAVIOUR IN FREE RANGING CONDITIONS

We are here concerned with the formulation of a general statement governing the relationship of the organism (in this instance a mammal) to the environment, therefore the variation of structure which allows one animal to perform movements, wholly or partly different from those performed by others, is not relevant.

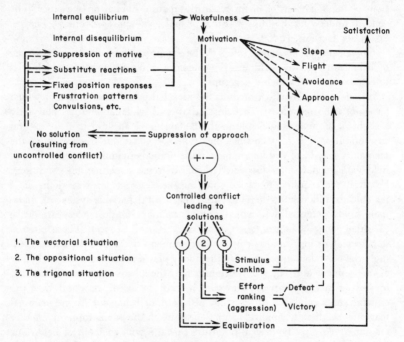

Fig. 1 Scheme of conflict analysis.

The diagram (Fig. 1) is an attempt to illustrate the role conflict plays in normal, as well as in abnormal, behaviour, so that it can be interpreted within a single framework of ideas. Conflict occurs in situations in which a repellent influence affects the behaviour of an animal, which is subject to a persistent drive, orienting its behaviour with respect to a spatially identifiable point in the environment. Conflict at this stage can, therefore, be defined as the state of simultaneous opposition of attractive and repellent stimuli operating on an animal. Aberrant behaviour resulting from such

88

situations arises when the resolution of the conflict is without reference to the positive or negative goal. Conversely, normal conflict resolution involves an orientation component derived from the relevant environmental stimuli. The most elementary type of conflict resolution takes the form of *stimulus-ranking* behaviour, in which the intensity of the prevailing external stimulation determines the path of the behaviour. When opposition between two animals engenders conflict, however, the overt effort of the animals may exert a predominant influence in the form of the resolutions, by virtue both of the animal's physical attributes, and the intensity of its reaction to the stimuli; such resolutions we call *effort ranking*. The meaning of *equilibration*, which appears to be peculiar to primate societies, will become clear later, but essentially both components are modulated in order to allow a temporal extension of the conflict. The effect of conflict on the behaviour of animals can be studied through the observation of movement; and, therefore, this scheme will enable us to describe, and later to interpret, the control of movement as movement towards, or away, from a satisfying object; or around or away from an object, which contains a potential threat to the organism, in conditions where no restriction is placed on movement. In this way all the types of movement are resolved in terms of movement towards an object. In Fig. 1 the paths denoting movement towards a stimulus are indicated by the continuous lines; those leading away from it are indicated by the dotted lines. Thus, flight or avoidance are actions initially concerned with movement away from or around a stimulus; once started, they are satisfying in that the stimulus disequilibrium is diminished. Where a combination of positive and negative stimulation arises, the activities indicated in the diagram appear in response to the predominant stimulus. Thus an animal, the approach of which is suppressed oppositionally, and which is defeated in the subsequent test of strength, is, by movement away from the scene, satisfying the more predominant stimulus (viz. the negative). Exactly similar is the approach of the victor. It is interesting to note that in all activities leading to a solution, other than equilibration behaviour, the solution is immediate, and is made in terms of either the negative or the positive stimulus, whichever predominates. Equilibration behaviour, however, involves appropriate action in terms of both the negative and positive aspects of the situation simultaneously, and brings about a temporal extension of the conflict. The nature of behaviour appropriate to the vectorial and trigonal situations is explained later.

For the purposes of analysis, the organism environment relationship can be considered in two ways. Thus the behavioural state of the organism constitutes the variable on one side of the relation, and the other is the nature of the environment.

(*a*) *The behavioural state of the organism.* The behavioural state of the organism is probably dependent on the activity of particular brain centres, which take their place as organizers of the behaviour into a sequence. The components of this sequence, when environmental factors are constant and freedom of movement is possible, show definite relations in time to each other (Richter, 1927).

In using the terms drive and motivation, it is necessary to specify the meanings we attach to them in this discussion, since in some degree the meaning is altered by the context in which it is used by each group of workers.

When an animal develops a physiological need, the activity resulting is said by psychologists to be an expression of "drive." When this activity has become directed towards some need reducing incentive, it is said to be an expression of "motive." "Drives as such are usually blind. They activate, it is true, but most of them do not, until learning has occurred, turn activity into appropriate channels" (Munn, 1950). Since it appears that some drives are structured into motives by virtue of innate qualities of the animal, and others become specified by learning, we shall assume that the term motivation covers both types.

The findings of Richter (1927) summarized by Tolman (1949) suggest that motivation provides both non-directed activity as well as specification.

The rat lived in an activity cage which had attached to it by a short funnel a very small cramped food cage. The movements of the animal in both cages were recorded automatically. It was found that after each eating period in the small cage, the rat went back into the main one, cleaned itself and went to sleep. After some relatively constant time period of, say, two hours,' quiescence, the rat would wake up and begin exploring the larger cage, and indulging in a variety of other general activities. Only some half hour later would he finally, when his hunger drive became really strong, pass into the small cage and eat. (Tolman, 1949.)

This experiment showed that in caged rats, when there is present a slight barrier to be overcome by virtue of the smallness of the aperture leading to the food, the drive first of all produces non-specific activity. Only later, when the activity is more intense, does it become specifically directed towards a point at which need reduction can occur. Whenever the response is not subject to a barrier the behaviour of the rat readily terminates the response, and this obscures the effect of the drive in determining the amount of activity shown by the rat. Therefore, when an animal is motivated (subject to an internal disequilibrium in the presence of an appropriate external stimulus) either a specific response may be evoked or an increase in activity may take place. Specificity of response may, therefore, be regarded separately from activity in some instances.

We recognize three classes of stimuli—the positive or attractive, evoking approach responses in an appropriately activated animal, the negative evoking movement away, and the neutral including all stimuli not evoking approach or withdrawal movements. These last include stimuli controlling postural responses, the various sounds, smells, sights and touches encountered by the animal as the background Gestalt of its environment, within which the more specific positive and negative signs govern its approach and suppression of approach movements.

A positive attraction arises from either or both of two sources, and varies in strength according to the contribution from each; these are the level of drive due to internal disequilibria and the degree of attraction of the external stimulus. The sum of these produces the degree of motivation. The responses to negative stimuli are dependent on the value of the external negative stimuli, and probably also on the responsiveness of the animal to them.

Awareness of a negative sign alone may lead to flight or avoidance activity; similarly, a positive sign may lead to approach. The presence of a negative sign, together with a positive sign, can lead to the suppression of approach, i.e. to slowing of the movement towards, arrest of all movement, or retreat, all of which are regarded in this context as three degrees of the suppression of approach. The external form of the resolution between the two conflicting elements expresses the relative movement values of the positive and of the negative signs. This is expressed schematically in Fig. 2, which summarizes the basic elements of approach and suppression of approach situations.

In diagrams 1–6 the situation is expressed with respect to animal A; in diagram 7, one primate social situation is expressed in terms of the vectors illustrated in 1–6. In diagram 1 the positive internal motivation of the animal, and the induced motivation, by virtue of the attractiveness of the object, are added. In diagram 2 all approach movements of the animal are controlled by the predominant stimulus in that they represent an attempt to find whether the positive elements of the situation are greater than the negative, leaving excess positive elements, or vice versa (i.e. stimulus ranking behaviour). This leaves a predominant sign in control of the action, except in the case of conflict where solution is not quite so simple, thus:

$$A+ + O+ > A- + O- \text{ approach,}$$
$$A+ + O+ = A- + O- \text{ conflict,}$$
$$A+ + O+ < A- + O- \text{ withdrawal (Miller's avoidance),}$$

where $A+$ $A-$ represents the internal conflict components of the animal independent of the qualities of the object in question and $O+$ $O-$ represents the degree of induced negative and positive elements based on the degree of attractiveness or otherwise of the object.

Exactly similar is the bivectorial suppression of approach involving two animals and a common objective, except that the movement of one animal will have a bearing on the resolution of the situation by the other. Bivectorial approach is probably rare in that a situation involving two animals engaged on a common activity is unlikely to lead to complete expression of the motivation of each animal in terms of movement. The reciprocality of such movements is shown in the film *Feeding Behaviour of Rats,* by the Ministry of Agriculture and Fisheries Infestation Department (Barnett, 1950).

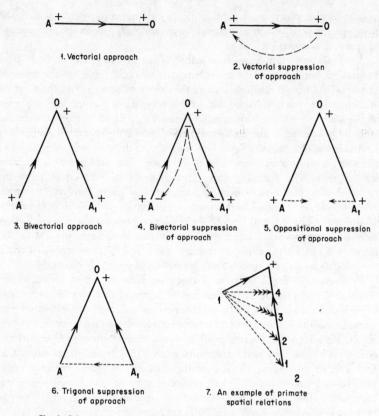

1. Vectorial approach

2. Vectorial suppression
of approach

3. Bivectorial approach

4. Bivectorial suppression
of approach

5. Oppositional suppression
of approach

6. Trigonal suppression
of approach

7. An example of primate
spatial relations

Fig. 2 Scheme for analysis of social relations based on spatial organization.

The oppositional situation is more likely to be common in cases where the object does not bear a negative sign, an oppositional vector being set up between the two animals. Stags in rut frequently express effort ranking behaviour in its simplest form when they test their strength by putting their antlers together and exerting all their strength in an attempt to push their opponent backwards. If one is much weaker than the other, he is pushed back, disengages and retreats. If neither is strong enough to oust the other, a fight ensues (Darling, 1937). The solution of such a situation is immediate, and momentary with respect to the life span of the animal. It is likely that, in nature, situations of suppression of approach involving more than one animal and a common activity, which lead to an immediate solution, will be found to be a complex involving situations 3–5 in varying degrees.

The trigonal situation is expressed in terms of the animal A, his approach being suppressed by an oppositional vector from another animal, with no immediate resolution of the situation. This demands that all movements must be made in terms of the positive common motivation and the oppositional vector.

(*b*) *The nature of the environment.* There are two major subdivisions of the environment which influence the behaviour of animals: the *reactive* and the *non-reactive.* The *reactive environment* comprises all living organisms, the behaviour of which is correlated with that of the animal under consideration. It is subdivided according to whether the encounter is with a member of another species or of the same species, in which event the encounter may constitute a social event. The *non-reactive environment* includes all the rest of the surroundings. The characteristics of these two different aspects of the environment require the participation of different mechanisms, involved in the approach of the animal to the two different parts. The distinction is, therefore, fundamental for behaviour studies.

In approaching a non-reactive component, an essentially sequential approach is biologically appropriate, i.e. one type of act follows another, as the sensory impressions give the clues the animal receives in approaching an objective. The exact timing of the approach, in relation to the impressions derived from the object, does not have any relevance to the success or failure of the approach. In the behaviour relating an organism to the reactive environment, i.e. to the behaviour of another organism, an effective approach can only be made at a particular moment in the behaviour of the animate environment or other animal. In all these circumstances proper timing of movements involved in the behaviour during approach enhances its biological appropriateness. Suppression as well as acceleration of all movements, and a gradation of them, are thus necessary for correct timing, as well as precise spatial control of movement in an approach to the reactive environment. This involves the "suppression of approach."

THE NATURE OF THE SOCIAL ENVIRONMENT

Social life grows up only when there is a mutual interrelationship between the members of a group. Loose associations, of which there are many types, occur; and it appears that where these associations can give rise to social activity, as in primates and wolves, these groupings are based upon social activities subserving a common motive, e.g. reproduction or hunting for food (Darling, 1937). Some authorities (Alverdes, 1927) consider that all social groupings arise as reproductive associations, and that this explains the formation of ungulate herds which now show a common social behaviour in self-defence. It is clear from the work of Allee (1939) that animal associations exist at many systematic levels, and that these may be based upon a diversity of factors; nevertheless, the existence of an association profoundly affects the behaviour of the individuals in all instances, and it is necessary, therefore, to note how this can occur in mammals.

It will be at once apparent that at times most of the animals will be involved in the *same* activity, and at others different animals will be occupied *differently*. When the animals pursue the *same* activity for whatever reason, the possibility of mutual interference arises, especially when the common activity is focused at a point. In these circumstances, one animal takes precedence over another, and the phenomenon of dominance arises.

These precedence relations are early established between members of the peck order in hens; and this governs the behaviour of any one bird in all subsequent encounters with any other particular bird in the group. Variations in dominance relations between any two mice occur much more frequently than in birds (Allee, 1942).

THE SIGNIFICANCE OF A HIERARCHY

A hierarchy is created by means of the degree of dominance between animals. This provides order by means of which the individuals' activities are related to those of the group. Wherever, therefore, the same activity exists contemporaneously in the behaviour of all the members of a group, those animals may be said to be socially integrated. This condition is usually accompanied by some degree of mutual activation. Social activities, therefore, can be inferred from the existence of dominance between animals, or where two or more animals are involved in the same activity.

The existence of a society, therefore, requires that at least during part of the behaviour pattern of the individuals their activities will coincide with those of other individuals, so that for a period the same activity sets up a system of vectors orienting the behaviour of the individuals one with another. The new element in societies is the emergence of oppositional vectors on top of already established links.

Associations between animals meet certain essential biological needs. These are protection against enemies, obtaining food, reproduction etc. These essential needs are met by a variety of activities. Fish, equidae, ungulates and birds live an open existence in shoals, herds or flocks which provide mutual protection and gregariousness itself is a way of reducing the likelihood of attack from predators. Wolves and many other species of canines hunt together. These associations are continuous, even though the activities they support are, in fact, periodic.

Social activation is the mutual stimulation of one individual by another, which leads to common activities, and the satisfaction of the same motive together. In this way, instead of each animal having its own cycle of motivation, overlapping in time that of another, all animals tend to be similarly motivated at the same time. Where satisfaction is achieved at a particular point in the environment, these circumstances inevitably create the conditions in which conflict arises.

(c) *Definition of conflict situations.* Conflict situations, produced by experimental inanimate environments, place a high degree of restriction on investigatory behaviour. In natural surroundings, on the other hand, if unpleasant or painful stimuli are received from the unfamiliar object, they are immediately reduced by avoidance activity. The response engendered by an unfamiliar inanimate object tends to diminish, even if on the initial approach to it a painful stimulus was received; since it then assumes the role of a negative stimulus which diverts the movements away from rather than towards the object.

Clearly, if suppression of approach can be expressed in behaviour, the consequent movement (for example, the arrest of forward movement) is the resultant of two opposing forces, the magnitude of which will vary. Miller (1937, 1944) has demonstrated that, in the rat, approach and avoidance are opposing responses which vary in strength with the strength of their underlying drives (i.e. with the strength of hunger and punishment in his experiments). He has also shown that these responses are graded, being stronger the nearer the animal is to the causal stimulus, and that the avoidance gradient is steeper than the approach gradient. These experiments have been verified by Brown (1942). Here we have an experimental illustration of the quantification of the responses to positive and negative signs in the environment. Moreover, Miller has studied their responses simultaneously in the same animal, and found that when a rat was conditioned to first approach, and then to avoid a light, the typical response on a subsequent time with both stimuli present was for the animal to approach a certain distance and then stop. Miller states that the position at which the animal stopped was a function of the relative strengths of the opposing responses, a stronger hunger or weaker shock (the reinforcing avoidance stimuli) allowing the animal to approach the light more closely. It is clear from this work that these tendencies can be balanced to produce the cessation of movement as a typical suppression of approach response.

We further postulate that approach and avoidance can be balanced at different levels to produce, for example, the same conflict position on the part of a rat in relation to a light. As we show later, behaviour in such situations does not always take the form of a direct response to the predominant stimulus; and that it is necessary to postulate compensatory mechanisms which participate in an equilibrational reaction, depending on conditions within the animal. If other factors in the situation require that the animal move away from the point of intersection of the two gradients, additional stimulation from an internal source can act as a compensating mechanism, providing additional freedom of movement in these circumstances. Thus in this way the overt response to a situation of suppression of approach may be due to either the quantitative values resulting from the sensory data involved, or to the change in negative/positive balance brought about by such compensatory mechanisms. It is now possible to link the processes underlying a purely quantitative solution of two opposing stimuli (stimulus ranking) to those underlying the resolution of a spatial problem (equilibration), and possibly to other forms of problem resolution. It should be remembered that our conception of conflict involves the idea that as there are levels of positive attraction and negative avoidance, there may also be levels of balance between them. Conflict is used in this context and represents the absolute level of the balance at any one time. Therefore, we must assume degrees of conflict due to the fact that the level of balance will vary, even though this may not be clearly shown in the overt behaviour of the animals under conflict.

In an approach/avoidance situation, a rat is not behaving appropriately if its movements terminate in a conflict position at the intersection of the approach/avoidance gradients. For a successful and naturally relevant solution, the movements of the rat must lead eventually to the completion of either the approach or avoidance response.

It is most appropriate for a primate however to move into the conflict position, in which he neither disturbs the social equilibrium by his presence, nor yet subjects himself to stimulation which would lead him to transgress the social equilibrium. In the rat, the ability to assume a conflict position can be demonstrated in restricted experimental conditions, and studies by E. C. Grant (in preparation) have shown that for relatively short periods during combat between two rats the behaviour involves a temporal extension of the conflict between approach and avoidance. It is probable that it is the respective natural circumstances of the rat and the primate, which determines whether or not such responses become a part of their natural mode of behaviour, and what forms they take.

The spatial contexts within which conflict can arise are:

(1) Restriction on avoidance. (2) Vectorial, i.e. when a motivated animal meets a negative sign, as well as a positive sign, on the object to which it is oriented. (3) Trigonal, i.e. when a motivated animal receives a positive sign from one object, and a negative sign from another. This occurs when two animals simultaneously, for example, meet at a single point for the satisfaction of the same motive.

Number 1 is an essential component of frustration behaviour. Number 2 can be considered as being resolved by a simple estimate of the strengths of the two opposing stimuli, and the third requires constant equilibration in terms of spatial as well as of strength components.

(d) *Approach to the familiar and unfamiliar.* By definition, familiar situations are those which enable an adequate response, satisfying a primary motive, to be made by an organism. Conversely, unfamiliar objects and situations do not provide an immediate clue to action. The organism is thus forced in these new circumstances to arrest its approach, or possibly make investigatory movements. The immediate effect of the unfamiliar, however, is to arrest the approach of an animal. The environment thus consists of two aspects, a part within which the animal moves freely, and a part which arrests the movements. Sudden movements in the inanimate environment are rare, and unfamiliarity in the environment usually initiates investigatory behaviour. The animal is now in a potential conflict situation; it is motivated to go forward and simultaneously inhibited, but conflict does not normally develop under these circumstances, because as investigatory movement proceeds the unfamiliarity drops away.

Chitty & Shorten (private communication) have demonstrated the great importance of unfamiliar aspects of the environment in their studies on rats, and have summarized these features of the behaviour as new object reactions. A well-used run will be avoided for a matter of days following the introduction of a new object on or close to the run. Thompson (1948) has demonstrated the existence of this suppression of approach to the unfamiliar, when he found that the number of visits to food in a new situation were initially widely spaced, and of short duration, until after a few days, when the visits occurred earlier and were compressed into a short space of time. Barnett (1948) has reviewed the application of this knowledge successfully in rodent control.

We note that in general the normal environment of the rat does not provide conflict situations. That is to say, a persistent negative sign is rare, restriction on possible patterns of avoidance is rare, and the occurrence of a negative sign simultaneously with a positive sign is also rare. This is probably true of most mammals.

MATING BEHAVIOUR IN MAMMALS

General. Zuckerman (1932) has recognized three types of mating behaviour in mammals. The first group is polyoestrous and includes some rodents. In them the male is always potent, and the female passes through a reproductive cycle from anoestrus to oestrus. She is receptive only during oestrus. Mating in these animals takes place when any male meets a receptive female. The approach of the male to the anoestrous female is suppressed or prevented from proceeding to completion by the response of the female. In these animals, therefore, regular mating occurs as a result of random encounters between males and females of the same population. It is a brief occurrence with respect to the life span of the animal.

The second type, which is represented in the behaviour of the seals and ungulates, consists of anoestrus demarcated breeding seasons. In these animals the males and females come into season approximately simultaneously, usually a few times a year, and the males also go out of season with the females. In them the oestrous period is very much shorter than the anoestrous interval. Fights may occur between the males for possession of females during the rutting season.

In the third type, characteristic of anthropoid primates, the female can be receptive throughout the whole cycle and the male is continually potent. Mating, therefore, can occur throughout the cycle, although in the primate stock there is every gradation between mating behaviour only exhibited at the discrete oestrous period and that of man where there is only slight evidence of a cyclic influence on the behaviour.

A later paper by Eckstein (1949) reveals that the mating systems of mammals consist of a number of combinations of the features exhibited by the mammals as a group. The spontaneously ovulating examples mentioned above are differentiable on the presence or absence of pseudopregnancy. The advent of periods of pseudopregnancy prevents temporarily the appearance of mating behaviour and will, therefore, have a limiting effect upon the mating behaviour of a population. A similar state of affairs exists in the group of induced ovulators in that the proportion of pregnancies to matings is likely to be much higher than in spontaneously ovulating groups. A further limiting effect occurs amongst the spontaneously ovulating groups in which a seasonal period of anoestrus is characteristic. Further, it is said that the primates are characterized by the presence of at least some anovular cycles, and this has been demonstrated in the macaque (Hartman, 1930–2), which means that the mating behaviour of other spontaneous ovulators compared with the primates will be limited by pregnancy.

It appears that in the primates the combination of features comprising their mating system (a continuously potent male in association with a spontaneously ovulating polyoestrous female, with no seasonal anoestrus, no pseudopregnancy and some anovular cycles) is physiologically limitless in respect of their mating behaviour.

The new feature of mating behaviour in the primate is, according to Beach (1947), the "emancipation" of the mating behaviour of the female from the cyclic control of oestrous hormones. This statement by itself is insufficiently explicit for our purposes, since two distinct elements, either of which may be present to a different degree in different primates, are responsible for the most extreme form of this new type of reproductive behaviour as it is found in man.

On the one hand in the subhuman primates the postures, movements and gestures forming the mating complex have, to various degrees in different species, become part of the repertoire of behaviour at the disposal of the primates. In some of the subhuman primates these constitute a repertoire of communicative social gestures which regulate the relations between animals engaged in other types of social behaviour, other than specific sexual activities. This is most highly developed in the baboons and macaques; it is also evident in some genera of platyrrhines (howler and spider monkeys), but appears to be largely absent in gibbons. While this particular use of the sexual gestures as a means of social communication is a specific adaptation found in some species of subhuman primates, the employment of sexual gestures as one element in the social behaviour is nevertheless discernible in all primates above the lemurs.

The second and unique feature by which the sexual repertoire of the females has been brought up to the status in the male is the extension of female receptivity to cover a larger proportion of the reproductive cycle.

Amongst rodents which have the same type of mating relation consisting of a continuously potent male and cycling female, the rat has a cycle of 4 days, out of which oestrus occupies not more than 12 hr. (Snell, 1941). The cycle for the mouse occupies approximately 5 days with an oestrous period of the same length. Thus in these two species oestrus occupies an eighth or less of the total cycle. A greater proportion of the total cycle is spent in oestrus by the primates.

No really adequate study of the initiation of sexual behaviour by monkeys in a social group is yet available for us to be certain what the function of the swollen sexual skin in either baboon or macaque is; for to say it is attractive to the male in the sense that we would consider sexual attributes attractive would be to ignore the two ways in which a female may court her prospective overlord. Both Carpenter (1942a) and Chance (1956) report that besides soliciting with facial gestures females initiate relations with prospective mates by being aggressive towards them, and since presenting is an agonistic gesture, in which stance alone the sexual skin is turned towards the male, much more study is needed before its role in courtship is understood. All that is common to both forms of courtship is that they both draw the attention of the male towards the female and subsequently he may become "attracted" to follow her, but what prompts him is not yet clear. The term "attractive" is used here to denote his following her whichever way the female has drawn his attention.

"All female old world Primates experience approximately four-weekly menstrual cycles" (Zuckerman, 1930). The character of the cycle can be judged in some species by the sexual swelling. In the *Hymadryas* and yellow baboons "the sexual skin . . . begins to swell either during or immediately after menstrual bleeding, and is suddenly absorbed soon after the middle of the cycle." "In the *Hymadryas* baboon the average duration of the phase of sexual skin swelling is about seventeen days; and that of sexual skin quiescence, which is less variable in length, fifteen days."

"In some species the maximum of swelling is reached in about a week, in others, the skin continues to swell until the point when absorption suddenly begins" (Zuckerman, 1932).

In the baboon, therefore, the female gradually becomes more and more sexually attractive for a period slightly in excess of half the cycle, and in some species is maximally attractive for one-third of the cycle.

In macaques "the length of the receptive period, as observed" in the Santiago Island colony "ranged from four to fifteen days with an average duration of 9.2 days." Thus "the average length of the oestrous period is approximately one-third of the average total length of the cycle" (mean 28 days) (Carpenter, 1942).

Out of a mean of 36.2 days for the cycle in ten captive chimpanzees, the sexual skin was quiescent for 15 days, during which menstruation occurred. Enlargement of the sexual skin occupies 7 days, maximal swelling and enhanced sexual receptivity 10 days, ovulation occurring towards the end of the 10-day period (Yerkes & Elder, 1936a). Oestrus lasted, therefore, for 10 days out of 36, or between one-quarter and one-third of the cycle. In the chimpanzee, therefore, enhanced sexual receptivity occupies a period of time slightly shorter than that during which the sexually attractive anatomical changes of oestrus are apparent, maximal receptivity lasting only half the period.

The significance of these figures is not immediately apparent from a comparison of their magnitude with those of a rat for example. This, however, can be revealed if a table is constructed for the proportion of time during which two males are likely to be in the presence of, and therefore, in competition for, an oestrous female, in a society in which there are approximately the same number of each sex at maturity, but in which the female's oestrus period is of different lengths.

TABLE I

RELATION BETWEEN PROPORTION OF REPRODUCTIVE CYCLE SPENT IN OESTRUS BY THE FEMALES TO PROPORTION OF TOTAL TIME UNDER MATING PROVOCATION FOR THE MALES IN A SOCIETY OF EQUAL SEX RATIO

| | | | Mating provocation time | |
Number of females in the group (N)	Fraction of total time spent in oestrus by any female (p)	Percentage of total time when no female is in oestrus (t)	Type I Percentage of time in which at least one female is in oestrus (100 − t)	Type II Percentage of time in which more than one female is in oestrus
2	1/2	25	75	25
	1/3	44	56	12
	1/4	56	44	6
	1/8	77	23	1
4	1/2	6	94	69
	1/3	20	80	40
	1/4	32	68	26
	1/8	59	41	8

Calculated from: $100 \times \binom{N}{R} \times (p)^R \times (q)^{N-R}$

(percentage of time R females are together in oestrus, where the cycles occur independent of each other), when R = number of females in oestrus, p = fraction of total time spent in oestrus by any one female, $q = (1 - p)$.

Table 1 shows calculation for the smallest unit of society capable of setting up a trigonal relation between the sexes, and for twice that number, we see that, in those primate societies in which the female is in oestrus for more than one-quarter to one-third of the cycle, the males will be under mating provocation (type 1) longer than out of it, but that the reverse is true for other societies in which the oestrous interval in the female is less. In those species, therefore, where more than one-quarter of the cycle is spent in oestrus, an element of conflict is the rule rather than the exception, and when it reaches one-half, conflict is likely to be an ever-present element. Since a preponderance of females in the heterosexual groups of subhuman primates is the rule, the disparity between proportion of total time under provocation between primates and other mammals will be more pronounced than the table suggests. In these conditions the probability of continual sexual provocation and competition between males is thus very high.

It should also be noted that under these conditions where encounters occur or where unfamiliar antagonistic components are present, mating behaviour becomes more and more an integral part of the social responses between primates. Beach (private communication) has noted that of 174 paired matings between chimpanzees recorded by Yerkeş & Elder (1936b), one-third occurred outside the period of tumescent sexual skin. These matings are ascribed to social factors, amongst which dominance has been identified as in certain instances an important factor, after the observations were made on caged individuals. Yerkes & Elder (1936b) make the following comment:

Normally and typically the multiparous female will mate with a male with whom she is intimately acquainted and on friendly or affectionate terms only during a few days of the period of genital swelling about and including the sexual time of ovulation. At other times, the female as a rule is ignored sexually by the male, or, if approached or solicited, she avoids him. Every word in this statement is important, *for social relationships as well as the physiological status of the consorts are important determinants of response.* (Our italics.) If either mate be recently matured sexually, relatively inexperienced in mating, or if the two be strangers, slightly acquainted, or hostile mutually of one to the other, mating may occur under any condition of sexual status and seemingly irrespective of biological appropriateness and reproductive requirement, or on the other hand, it may not occur even under entirely appropriate physiological conditions?

Moreover, Carpenter (1942a) ascribes the prolongation of oestrus in the consorts of the dominant macaque males to the influence of dominance as well as to perseveration.

Since in man the sexual propensities of the female are only slightly, if at all, dependant, as in subhuman primates, on fluctuating anatomical or behavioural features, her attractiveness for the male originates from the sociosexual status of her behaviour. This represents the culmination of the process of the modification of sexual gestures and postures into overt form of social communication, establishing sociosexual status, which has originated in the primates.

The development of flexibility in the control of sexual behaviour and the consequent reduction of control by stereotyped anatomical and hormonal mechanisms as a result of the transfer of function to cortical mechanisms is shown to be a pre-eminent evolutionary process in the progress from mammals, through subhuman primates to man, in a well-documented review by Beach (1947).

In conclusion, it can be stated that the majority of contemporary primates exhibit a characteristic combination of reproductive features which create the possibility of continuous mating provocation. In no other mammalian group does such continuous mating provocation occur, for all other combinations of reproductive features lead to the limitation of mating behaviour to certain physiologically defined periods, even when the animals come together in groups (*vide* red deer with seasonal anoestrus).

Therefore, we suggest that the advent of such a combination paves the way for the development of social groupings in which continuous mating behaviour, and, therefore, the continuous suppression of mating behaviour through competition, may occur. This in turn leads to the modification of sexual gestures, and even copulation itself, into a system of socially specialized forms of overt behaviour. In open terrain this will lead to the development of visual conflict and forms of socially determined behaviour in a spatial context.

Thus we believe that the following combination of factors

(1) A continuously sexually potent male
(2) A female characterized by:
    Spontaneous ovulation
    Polyoestrous cycles
    Absence of pseudopregnancy
    No seasonal anoestrus
    Proportion of heat to cycle one-quarter or more
    Anovular cycles for at least part of the time (first year and periodically in macaque)
(3) An environment in which open terrain allows the development of a visual conflict which can be resolved in spatial terms in a social context

has led to the development of the social behaviour and selective processes we are about to describe.

Mating provocation in the macaque. From the work of Hartman (1930–32) on reproductive patterns of the macaque it is possible to construct a model of the mating relations in the wild from which an estimate of the proportion of time occupied by mating provocation type 1 (see Table 1) can be calculated. The essential information provided by Hartman is as follows:

(1) That anovular cycles (which are characteristic of primates as a group; Eckstein, 1949) occur throughout the first year of life in a captive

colony and constitute an appreciable proportion of the cycles throughout the adult life of the females both in captivity and in the wild.

(2) That during pregnancy which lasts approximately 5 months sexual skin and, by inference, receptivity cycles occur at only slightly reduced intensity.

(3) That mating (noted in other species, e.g. the chimpanzee) is likely to occur during pregnancy, but not during lactation which lasts 11–13 months.

Thus, if we assume that in the wild the adult life of a macaque is 5–15 years and that the number in a group will average forty individuals of which ten are young, then there will be an adult population of thirty individuals. With a socionomic index (see below) of 5 there will be twenty-five females, and of these at least 2.5 will be in their first year of adult life during which anovular cycles occur. If we allow for the additional 5 months of sexual provocation exerted by them during the first pregnancy and for the fact that rather more than 2.5 will contribute to the population of first year adult females due to the relatively large proportion of younger age groups in the population as a whole, the effective provocation time will be derived from a population of approximately three females possessing an oestrous phase one-third of the cycle in length. From Table 1 it can be seen that mating provocation type 1 will be more often present than absent, occupying a fraction between 56 and 80% of the total time.

SOCIAL STRUCTURE AND ITS CONSEQUENCES
FOR THE BREEDING PERFORMANCE OF THE MALES

The special features of the females' sexual behaviour in the social monkeys has profound consequences on the breeding performances of the males, arranged as they are in an order of dominance. As a result of this, and the spatial relations within the different classes of individual within the group, equilibration and the ability to withstand conflict become essential prerequisites to successful breeding by the maturing males which, for part of their life at least, must occupy a subordinate position. Let us consider these different features of the situation separately.

(a) *Dominance.* Grant & Chance (1958) showed that dominance is the result of the resolution of social encounters or combats between male rats caged together and that females did not develop a rank order even though encounters between them were about as frequent. The rank of any one of the male rats in a group can be assessed by simply observing the proportion of wins to losses sustained by any one rat in encounters with any other. So far as could be ascertained this was competition simply for status and gave rise in the male cages to a stable order of rank in many cages.

The problem of assessing rank order in primate societies becomes difficult as soon as an attempt is made to define the components of the behaviour which distinguish one member of a hierarchy from another. On several occasions I have seen visitors to the London colony say, "Look at the boss!" "He's the boss" or words to that effect. In every instance they showed that they were able to identify the overlord male with assurance. In the London Zoo macaque colony (Chance 1956) there were only two adult males which eventually consorted with eight adult females as they became sexually receptive and showed sexual swellings, thus forming the breeding hierarchy. These males could readily be noticed because of certain features which marked them out from all the others in the colony, but these features did not present the same pattern in the colony at the West of England Zoo in Bristol.

By the time the breeding hierarchy had been established in the London Colony the males were sleek and thick of fur with muscular body contours, tipped and edged by lines of darkened fur. In fact, they looked the part! The overlord macaque at Bristol showed perhaps the greatest likeness to his opposite number in London, but was much fatter and with his skin there were no distinctive markings, though his fur was both sleek and thick.

In London these two dominant males set themselves apart from the rest of the colony; as they were surrounded by a space several feet across from all other monkeys except their consorts most frequently resting within a few feet of each other. Each of these males was free to roam anywhere, other monkeys always giving them a free path and keeping at a distance. In the Bristol colony these features of the dominant males were much less evident, though both were present if looked for.

Much the same point is made by Kummer (1957). He could not find a "pervading general criterion of rank" in the colony of Hamadryas baboons in the Zurich Zoo. The criteria of social position only applied to groups of a certain age and sex. Thus the usual rank order of feeding does not, for example, appear since larger young never take away the smaller one's food, nor are the smaller ones timid in helping themselves to food in the presence of older young animals. This behaviour contrasts very sharply with that of older and younger males in the colony of Japanese macaques observed by Itani.

Kummer continues "Each category of individuals of the same age and sex (for example the adult females) has an order of rank which is relatively easily identified. In its largely uniform inventory of behaviour there are constant individual elements of behaviour which are indications of rank. These same elements, however, may appear in the behaviour of another category without showing any correlation of rank, or else they may be missing altogether. Threat, for example, is a good criterion of rank amongst adult females, but appears without reference to rank in the play of 2–3 year olds and is quite absent from the one-year old's behaviour."

Despite these differences one or more of the features are usually present and this enables one to select the most likely candidates for pride of place in a group of monkeys. The characters of this selected few can then be subjected to closer study and differences of rank can then be assessed. In the London Colony the most constant central feature of the social structure was the order of rank between the males of the breeding hierarchy. This has also been found by Altmann (1959) for the macaques on Cayo Santiago Island and by Itani (1954) for the "provisionized" wild group of Japanese macaques of Takasakiyama.

From the study of the London Zoo colony and later studies of the Whipsnade colony (Reynolds, personal communication) and of the West of England colony at Bristol, it is clear that the rank of a male macaque of the breeding hierarchy can be assessed from his poise, posture and the degree to which he takes note of other members of the hierarchy. It appears, therefore, that dominance is a result of direct interaction between monkeys and that it leads to a stabilized rank order between the males, which on occasion, and in suitable circumstances, leads to priority of access in proportion to the status of the individual.

In the family parties of gibbons, dominance, which is seldom manifest, is not found predominantly in conjunction with competition for the same female, though this does occur (Carpenter, 1940). The main effect of dominance is to exclude the maturing male from the group. The fact that mating behaviour is a part of a primate's repertoire of activity enabling copulation and foreplay components to be initiated at any time in the cycle, makes it likely that the relation between the sexes will be more flexible than in lower mammals. This is true of the gibbons, howler and spider monkeys (Carpenter, 1934, 1935) in contrast to the baboons (Zuckerman, 1932) and macaques (Carpenter, 1942a), and a greater individual variation in reactions is evident in the individual behaviour of the chimpanzees reported by Yerkes & Elder (1936b). In these circumstances initiatory, aggressive, antagonistic and receptive behaviour may be shown by animals of either sex in their mating behaviour. On the other hand, the amount of interference between animals of the same sex for access to a member of the opposite sex is likely to be pronounced where the attractiveness of the female is high, or lasts at a moderately high level for a long time. Since the interference will be highest where attraction is most pronounced, we shall expect to find dominance exerting a marked influence when pronounced sexual activity is present. This will be more marked when more than one female is in oestrus at the same time (mating provocation type II, see Table 1). With lower degrees of motivation or with a rapidly varying intensity of sex drive, some degree of alternating mating may participate alongside dominance in the control of this aspect of social activity, e.g. spider and howler monkeys.

The mating provocation of primate societies constitutes what we have termed a bivectorial situation between the attractive female, and two or more males. In these circumstances we have noted that the behaviour of the two males must either be regulated by sequential mating or by some form of exclusive matings. These exclusive associations may either be the result of previous conditioning, or of dominance. The evidence from studies in the wild goes to show that dominance plays some part in many species, and a very prominent part in regulating the sociosexual behaviour of the group in others.

Dominance or the type of behaviour, which gains preferential access for the animal manifesting it, can be identified in every sphere of primate social life. It controls feeding behaviour in many species, and can be seen to influence the play of many young primates. It is also exerted between groups of primates inhabiting neighbouring territories, and may enable one group to extend its territory at the expense of another, but for our purposes the part it plays in regulating the sexual behaviour is of the greatest importance. Dominance can be recognized by the various ways in which one male temporarily, or for prolonged periods, interferes with, or wholly prevents, mating behaviour between a particular female or a group of females, and other males. For example, in the gibbon, the young male on reaching maturity is gradually compelled to leave the family group, either together with a sibling, or singly, in which event pairing may take place with a female which can be attracted away from another group. Sexual approach to the adult female of the family is prevented by the dominant male as soon as the young gibbon reaches maturity. In the societies of howler monkeys, one male may form a temporary consort relation with a female simultaneously preventing the approach of another. In macaques and baboons, dominance establishes a rigid male hierarchy, which in different ways allows the dominant male or overlord exclusive access to the greatest number of females at the peak of heat. In these ways dominance is recognized in the relation between individuals, but it can also be inferred from the numbers of each type of individual constituting a group.

Carpenter has carried out an extensive survey of the types of associations found in different species of monkeys. Zuckerman's work on the *hamadryas* baboon in captivity, and in the wild state, is an intensive study of the relations between individual primates in a typical primate society. From these studies it is clear that the primate social organization arises from a group within which it is possible to identify a dominant male, or overlord, a number of females attached to him termed the harem, the young animals and the surplus males or bachelors. The existence of surplus males arises from the appropriation of more than one female by the overlord.

Carpenter (1942*b*) has termed the ratio of males to females in the societies of different primates the socionomic index. This index is roughly characteristic of each genus. For example, in the howler monkey (*Alouatta palliata*) there is a ratio of 1 male to 2.3 females. The excess males are solitary. In the spider monkey (*Ateles geoffoyi*), on the other hand, there is a ratio of 1 male to 1.6 females. The group is less cohesive than in the howler monkey, and the excess males are found in groups.

The socionomic index for macaques has not been recorded from the wild, but in the Santiago colony established by Carpenter the ratio of females to males was 6:1.

The number of females predominate over the number of males in every observed group of macaques, and for all species except *Macaca nemestrinus*, which is little known. Within organised groups, the males dominate all other individuals, but exclusive dominance like that described by Zuckerman for the baboon, is not found, unless *Macaca nemestrinus* be an exception. Extra group males in the large genus of macaques live both temporarily isolated, and also, more frequently, in uni-sexual male groupings. (Carpenter, 1942b.)

Figures for two groups of the Japanese macaque obtained by Imanishi (1959) showed a preponderance of adult females over males of nearly 2:1 in the colony at Arashiyama which totaled 70 monkeys in all; a very slight excess of adult males over adult females 11:9 for the group at Koshima, showing that the socionomic index varies depending on the conditions from approximate unity to a figure indicating a marked preponderance of females.

Carpenter summarizes Zuckerman's evidence on baboons in these terms "in organised heterosexual groupings one may assume that the socionomic sex ratio is even more unequal than that of 'Howlers' and 'Spiders'; there are more intra-group females than males."

He also makes the following statements:

Orang outans. While on the west coast of Sumatra, I was fortunate enough to be able to observe a group of orang outans. This group consisted of two adult females with young babies, judged to be about two years of age, and a large adult male.

Chimpanzees and gorillas. Although complete information is still lacking on these important African anthropoids, it would seem from the reports of Bingham and Nissen that their grouping patterns are somewhat similar. Available information would suggest that the typical group consists of a dominant male with several other less dominant males, and a larger number of females, plus a series of young.

This brief survey indicates several important characteristics of groupings in monkeys and apes:

(1) There is a marked variability from genus to genus among the non-human primates, both in total size, and in patterning of groups.

(2) Organised groups of primates usually contain more adult females than males. The Gibbon, which lives in families is a known exception, and there may be other species which have different grouping patterns.

(3) Extra group males are found to live temporarily alone or in uni-sexual groupings, and, in some instances, females also are found to live temporarily alone. (Carpenter, 1942b.)

Since the information available to us suggests that the sex ratio at birth is equal, and that the viability of males and females does not differ to any marked extent, we must assume that the existence of a socionomic index in these monkeys is a consequence of the degree of dominance of the overlord males. Even if this were not so, the existence of male bands and solitary males is itself sufficient evidence of the exclusion of some males from the heterosexual groupings, and thus of the appropriation of the females by a few males.

The existence of this socionomic index can be inferred despite the fact that these groups may exist singly or in association with one another, and with the surplus males. The heterosexual group appears to exist singly in the gorilla, chimpanzee and orang-outan. They are observed associated together as troops in the baboons and langurs. We have seen that there will be surplus males to be accounted for in any primate population. In many cases these males are associated diffusely with single heterosexual groups and troops, as in the baboon. In some genera of *Macaca, Cerococebus* and *Cercopithecus,* males living alone have been observed.

Fighting is often a consequence of competition for females between animals of many species, and Beach (private communication) has also shown that aggressive behaviour is closely associated and is a part of mating behaviour in many mammals, including the primates.

It is natural, therefore, to inquire to what extent the primate mating relations engender fights between the males, and then it becomes clear that dominance also plays an important role in controlling intragroup fights between males. Zuckerman noted that in the captive colonies of *hamadryas* baboons fighting occurred between the males from time to time. But since mating provocation continually exists in such a colony, we must inquire further why this type of fighting was not continuous.

From time to time the colony at the London Zoo was disrupted by fights which began between some of the bachelor males over the possession of females. Zuckerman noted that this usually occurred when the overlord failed to exert his dominance over the subordinate males, and thus had failed to maintain the possession of all his females. When this occurred, it sometimes came about that having failed on one occasion, he was successfully ousted from the dominant position by one of the subordinate males. In these circumstances, the stability of the group was maintained, and various members took up their positions under the new overlord. If, however, one of the bachelors was not successful in this attempt, fighting broke out throughout the whole colony, and continued for as long as a week or two. During this time periodic fights would occur for possession of the females, and this would often lead either to an encounter between two males, or to the physical dismemberment of the female over which it had developed. In these fights it also sometimes happened that the young were maltreated or killed.

These fights do not appear to be restricted to baboons in captivity, since Zuckerman found that many adult males of a wild baboon troop shot in Africa bore severe skin lesions. Since it is known that in those regions in which the specimens were shot man had almost eliminated the larger carnivores which are their natural predators, and also that they do not fight with other species of animals, it is inferred from the high incidence of these lesions that intragroup fights occur in the wild state, and thus that the captive colonies were in this important respect representative of the wild populations.

The behaviour of macaque males is essentially similar, as it is possible to identify a male dominance hierarchy which is maintained without fights between the males, despite the provocative and aggressive behaviour of the females coming into heat. Unlike the baboon females, which remain attached to one male in a number proportional to the dominance of the male, macaque females, after exhausting the copulatory potentialities of a low-ranking male, solicit the attention of other males higher up the scale by aggressive as well as sexually assertive behaviour. The change in their social status often calls forth attacks by still more dominant males, but in these encounters the male to whom the advance has been made often remains neutral. Moreover, his reluctance immediately to respond sexually is considered by Carpenter to be an expression of the restraining influence of the male dominance hierarchy on the behaviour of the subordinate males.

It is possible, therefore, to show that the social relations of mature males is regulated by the dominance of one male over another in all species of infrahuman primates on which observations have been made in the wild or in comparable free-ranging conditions. This dominance is exerted by threat which in many instances is directed by facial expression, but which may also be expressed in the body posture of the high-ranking males (Carpenter, private communication). [Chance, 1956.]

The existence of relatively prolonged periods of stable relations within the group must, therefore, be ascribed to the dominance relations within it, and this implies in turn that one animal is suppressing his approach with respect to another.

(b) *Spatial behaviour patterns.* The factors that have been identified in primate societies provide the essential elements of conflict, as this was defined earlier. The sexual attractiveness of the female is matched and balanced by the threat of a more dominant male. It should, therefore, be possible to describe the social behaviour of primates in spatial terms, similar to those we found adequate for orientation behaviour about a single object where this is also the site of goal achievement.

Zuckerman's description of the baboons suggests this. "Family parties move independently of one another, and seldom come into contact. They act as separate groups in all their activities as a rule, mingling with other members of the colony only when engaged in communal feeding, or when participating in some quarrel" (Zuckerman, 1932). Carpenter has described the characteristics in a way which confirms this inference:

An important clue to social relations in primate societies is the observed spatial relation of individuals, sub-groups or organised groups. The strength of the attachment between two individuals may be judged, or actually measured, by observing for a period of time the average distance which separates the two animals. In group 1 of the Santiago Rhesus Colony, for example, the most dominant male and the next most dominant male were on the average less closely associated than the second most dominant male and the third one in the male dominance hierarchy. During oestrus, females seek the closest possible spatial association with responsive males, so that the short distance separating the two animals, and the continuance of this close association are reliable indicators of oestrus in the female. (Carpenter, 1942*b*.)

When these two social forces occur together, the region close to a dominant male where the most attractive oestrous females are situated is also the region of maximum conflict for subordinate males subject to the dominance of the overlord. This region in its simplest form is trigonal, consisting of the overlord, an oestrous female, and a subordinate male. Within such a group of individuals it should be possible to observe that in the movement of the group as a whole, the spatial relations will be maintained approximately constant in response to the attraction exerted for the males by the female, counterbalanced in the case of the subordinate animals by threat from the dominant male. Evidence of this was provided by the following observation which was made during studies of a free-ranging macaque colony. Four adults were close to the edge of an enclosure on our arrival at this colony.

The social status of these individuals was easily recognized. The situation of this group is illustrated in Fig. 3. The configuration shown in A was evidently one of equilibrium. The dominant male and a female showing maximal sexual skin were together copulating at intervals. A young male was in the vicinity watching this, while a pregnant female was grooming herself. A peanut was then offered as indicated in B (by a cross) through the bars. Female 1 immediately came to the bars, male 1 making no attempt to secure the peanut. Male 2 moved towards the nut and towards female 1. Female 2 was greatly interested and came to the bars. Immediately the situation became unstable. Female 2 refused to come nearer the peanut intimidated by the more dominant female. Male 1 stood up and threatened male 2 who had moved to a position very close to female 1. The nearer female 1 moved towards the peanut the farther away from it moved female 2. The two oppositional vectors shown in B were clearly demonstrated by the behaviour of these animals, each watching the other closely throughout. Immediately equilibration occurred. Male 2 moved back towards the centre of the enclosure, stopping at about the same distance from male 1 as before. Male 1 approached female 1 who had by now obtained, and was eating, the peanut. Female 2 moved around the perimeter for several yards before moving to her original position. During the entire period of observation, the rapid movements of the eyes of the animals never ceased, and reached a peak just before the situation became once more stable, after the changes of position had ceased.

The effect of this situation on the spatial relations is clearly of a triangular character, since the farther the subordinate male is from the female, the closer it is possible for the two males to approach each other without pre-

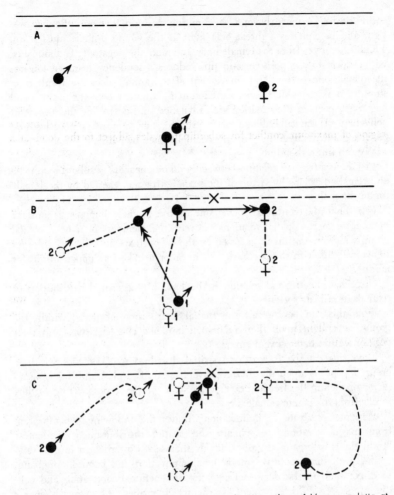

Fig. 3 Diagrammatic representation of observations made on a colony of Macaca mulatta at the Dudley Zoo. Changes in position of animals within the trigonal region resulting from the introduction of food at position X. (Animals' tracks indicated by broken lines; threats indicated by double-arrowed straight lines.)

cipitating antagonism between them, and vice versa. It is trigonal in the sense originally defined, because a negative sign provided by the dominant male inhibits the approach of a subordinate male to the attractive female. This is expressed spatially in Fig. 2 (diagram 7). As the subordinate male primate moves from positions 1–4, the negative sign he receives from the overlord male will increase. Clearly there is a limiting position of proximity to the female at which the positive and negative signs represent a social equilibrium. To move beyond the limiting position increases the negative sign, and precipitates a threat or a fight as the young primate must learn. The farther away from the female he is, the more the negativity is diminished with respect to the positive, and this induces a tendency to move towards the female once more. Thus movement of the animal does not result from stimulus ranking, which leaves a predominant stimulus; both the positive and negative aspects of the situation are in balance, and determine the locomotor behaviour of the subordinate male primate, and appear as negative and positive gradients with the properties demonstrated by Miller.

We can infer, therefore,

(1) That a trigonal relation between a dominant male, a subordinate male and female develops by virtue of the sexual attraction exerted by the female for all the males.

(2) That the continual movement of the animals imposes a constant fluctuation in the spatial relations between the members of a heterosexual group which is continually assessed by the subordinate animal: (a) in order to avoid fights with the overlord, (b) in order to take any opportunities for mating.

(3) That the trigonal relation is the basis of the spatial distribution of animals in primate societies.

From this can be forecast the spatial distribution of males within the group, dependent upon their relative dominance characteristics, and their position within heterosexual groups.

From this can be forecast the spatial distribution of females within a group depending upon the rhythm of their oestrous cycles, and this is also a factor restricting the freedom of movement of the developing young as they recede from the parent female.

Carpenter (private communication) draws the following generalization from his observations to explain the spatial distribution of primates: "Individuals in organised groups deploy themselves in space in inverse ratio to the strength of positive interactional motivation and conditioning, and, in direct ratio to the degree of negative interactional motivation and conditioning." In this statement Carpenter identifies the same elements as postulated here. It is necessary to distinguish, however, between the motivational and conditioned elements in assessing the nature of these interactions. An animal may tend to move away from another to which it is negatively conditioned, and thus in a group of which it is a member to remain at a distance from the first. This does not imply a conflict component, but merely an avoidance reaction. The relations within the trigonal sphere, on the other hand, involve true antagonistic motivational forces in balance with one another. Carpenter maintains that "any single relationship involves a complex of both negative and positive elements" (1942). Mother, young, or consort relations, however, cannot involve negatives of the type normally causing spatial deployment of individuals within the group. In such relations the positive elements must by far outweigh any negatives present. Otherwise on his interpretation the spatial relations would be different.

Carpenter considers the presence of the negative and positive elements to be general. This is true. The unique element of primate society, however, appears to be the persistent interaction between negative and positive elements in the trigonal sphere of the primate social environment, which is thereby distinguished from other mammalian environments.

In the life of baboons and macaques at least *this conflict is an ever-present element* requiring reassessment from moment to moment, during active foraging activities for example (Zuckerman, 1932).

(c) *The evolutionary significance of the behaviour of the subordinate male.* The forces operating in the trigonal situation can, we have seen, be deduced from the existence of equilibration behaviour which provides a means of avoiding unpremeditated fights with dominant males. We should, therefore, expect to find that the behaviour of animals in this region is conspicuous by the absence of fights or other agonistic social behaviour.

The possibility of testing this hypothesis arose while studying the macaque monkey colony at the London Zoo in 1950 (Chance, 1953), when on the 17th September observers who had been working together on the colony were all present. To obtain as much uniformity as possible between the different observers all of us reported for a short while on the behaviour of the same monkey. After this each observer noted the number of times any one of the six postures occurred in social encounters during the same 50 minute period. The results listed in Table II show how very much less socially active the overlord male was compared with the second in rank of

TABLE 2

NUMBER OF VARIOUS TYPES OF BEHAVIOUR RECORDED DURING AGONISTIC ENCOUNTERS IN THE BEHAVIOUR OF MEMBERS OF THE BREEDING HIERARCHY DURING THE SAME FIFTY-MINUTE PERIOD

| Description of Monkey | Date of Observation in September | Types of Agonistic Behaviour | | | | | | Total |
		Attack-ing	Chas-ing	Threat-ening	Sexual Gestures Dominant and Submissive	Equili-bration	Retreat-ing	
D1	17th	2		3	1			6
D2	17th		4	7		3	1	15
♀ consort of D1	17th		2			3		5
An anoestrus ♀	17th	3	3	10	1	4	2	23
Anoestrus ♀ Rank I	18th	1	3	11		1		16
Anoestrus ♀ Rank II	18th	6	9		23	10		48

the adult males who went in for 2½-times as many encounters. The same was true for females of different rank on both the 17th and 18th.

Carpenter (private communication) concludes that this is so in the Santiago Rhesus Colony.

Much of the constantly operative social control of individual over individual, and individuals over individuals, is exercised in groups through *sign-signal communication*. Not only individuals as such, but also their statuses are evidently perceived as signalised and appropriately responded to by most other individuals of organised groups. For example, it is a significant fact that the supremely dominant males of all groups of the Santiago Colony fought other group members less frequently than the males subordinate to them. The supreme males were often without disfiguring injuries. They were sleek of coat and full in flesh. Their stances, postures, carriage, especially the upward flexed tails, seemed to function as signs of their statuses, rights and privileges relative to other animals of their groups. Only infrequently did the need arise to reinforce their statuses by actual fighting. When this became necessary, it was done with telling effect. Whereas due deference is shown for animals with high statuses, weak, sickly or cringing animals may be attacked repeatedly by a wide range of the group's members.

Awareness of these elements is required of the subordinate male, and to some extent by the non-oestrous female, even when their behaviour is primarily directed towards the satisfaction of other needs besides mating. This is by virtue of the danger that is involved in too close an approach (be it undirected) to the trigonal sphere. It is unlikely that any other mammals (except some species of seals in the mating season) are subject to anything like such *persistent threat* in their normal environment; certainly not to such *persistent conflict.*

The above spatial analysis of the relations between members of primate societies suggests that the dominant male occupies a unique position, and that the area around him is a special region of the activity of the group; this is because the oestrous females are in his vicinity.

Owing to the fluctuating attractiveness of the females they pass into the sphere of the trigonal relations during oestrus, and pass out of it in dioestrus. Since during oestrus they mate only with the overlord, it should follow that all or most of the progeny at any one time are the offspring of the overlord and the females of the whole group. Mating, however, occurs between animals outside the trigonal sphere, but it is without breeding consequences. Thus, *in its extreme form,* this relation requires that for a male primate to produce offspring, he must occupy the overlord's position at least once in his life. In primates, therefore, the breeding/mating relations are dissociated. In this respect they are not alone amongst mammals; the same essential relation is found in the herd of wild cattle observed by Darling (private communication) at Chillingham Park, but the other attributes of behaviour associated with successful breeding in herds of cattle are different.

It should be noted that in primate society, a breeding premium is achieved by those animals whose attraction for the oestrous females is matched by an ability to withstand the conflict arising from the dominance of a more mature male. This ability to withstand conflict arises out of the constant equilibrational component present in their movements within the society, their stances, postures and carriage, and the absence of fighting in their behaviour. This means that these animals possess an ability to control aggressive responses under conflict. Selection of those animals which control aggressive behaviour in this region can be deduced from the disastrous effect of non-equilibrational behaviour on the fate of the maturing male primate. These are not restricted to a possible early demise, but mistakes in movements of the maturing male within the social field will affect his subsequent chances of reaching a sufficient degree of dominance to bring him within sight of the breeding position. (This is clearly a case of sexual selection as proposed by Darwin (1875) involving the intrasexual selection component distinguished by Huxley (1938).) This may be inferred from the work of Allee (1942), who has observed that success in fights makes for continued success, and failure for continued failure in fights between mice. If, as in primates, success in breeding depends upon success in a challenge, if not in a fight, then clearly those animals which do not challenge before the likelihood of success in a fight is reasonably assured will be more likely to reach a high status in the dominance hierarchy from which position most breeding is possible. There is more evidence bearing on this point. Miller (1950) has provided two examples of the consequences of fights between male mammals on their subsequent mating behaviour. He was describing experiences at an Artificial Insemination Centre where "on one occasion two stallions broke out of control and got together in an enclosure, and fought for twenty minutes before they were finally separated, without the fight having reached a conclusion." Nevertheless, the younger male suffered permanent interference with its ability to mate on subsequent occasions, whereas the older animal showed no change in its behaviour. A similar sequel was the result of a fight between two bulls, following which the vanquished animal refused to mate with females on heat. It may be assumed, therefore, that the immature male primate is not only in danger of failing to reach a sufficient degree of dominance, but also of serious impairment of its mating behaviour, if the equilibrational behaviour is not adequate.

Owing to the emergence of mature mating behaviour at puberty before the maximum strength and size of the primate has been reached, failure to equilibrate for a considerable time following puberty may prevent the male reaching a social position from which he can exert his potential dominance.

These new conditions render mating behaviour *per se* inappropriate for reproductive functions, so that it becomes necessary for the young primate to antedate his major reproductive activity by behaviour appropriate for the achievement of a social status, adequate for a successful association of mating behaviour with full dominance. This in turn leads to a succession of sires for the females, and thus to a rapid succession of generations sired at any one time by the male which, in each generation, displayed appropriate forms of behaviour at different times in his maturation.

Following this line of argument Altman (1959) in his study of the macaques of Cayo Santiago Island noted the length of time each female associated with a particular male and found that—

During oestrous periods of several days, female rhesus monkeys associated very closely with one male at a time. Some females associated with only one male throughout one or more oestrous periods; others, with a series of two or more males.

Differential reproduction is one of the major factors altering the gene frequencies of populations. We will try to explicate the relation between the dominance status of rhesus males and their access to sexually receptive females. Let us first consider the biological premises of our model. As we acquire more knowledge about this species, doubtless some of these premises will have to be amended. However, they are probably sufficiently accurate for a first approximation. The premises are as follows:

First, the menstrual cycles of the female are independent, i.e. diachronic.

Second, the mean probability (p) that a female is in oestrus is one third, i.e. the period of sexual receptivity of the female is, on the average, one third of her menstrual cycle. In contrast, males are continually potent.

Third, if only one oestrous female is available to two males, she will consort with the more dominant male of the two.

Fourth, males do not consort with more than one female at a time.

From the first two premises it follows that, in a population of a certain number of sexually mature non-pregnant females the probability that any given number will be in oestrus at one time can be calculated. This will determine the opportunities for mating open to males in the hierarchy; the higher the status of the individual the more frequently will mating opportunities occur. This has been computed, see Graph I and footnote, page 118.

It shows "the chance that the male of each rank will have access to a receptive female in groups of various sizes."

These results have several interesting features. First, there is a sharp change in the probability of access to females where the rank of the males equals one third the number of sexually mature, non-pregnant females. The males are sharply demarcated into the 'haves' and 'have nots.' Second, the equability of the distribution of the receptive females among the males depends upon the total number of females in the group, as well as on the ratio of males to females. To the extent that access to sexually receptive females is directly correlated with reproductive success, the intensity of sexual selection can be expected to be a function of the total number of sexually mature females in the group. Unfortunately, the two groups of monkeys that were on Cayo Santiago do not provide enough data to test this model. Data from a series of groups in their native habitat are highly desirable.

This mathematical prediction is illustrated and its essential feature, namely the class division of the sub-human primate society confirmed by the study of Itani on the structure of the macaques of Takasakiyama, wherein the separation of the breeding from the non-breeding males can be seen taking on the special form due to the special characteristics of these monkeys. (See Fig. 4.)

There is a total adult male population of 18, divided into three parts. The central breeding hierarchy of six dominant males occupies the centre of the group and associated with it (i.e. free to move round and about the dominant males) are all the adult females with young and juvenile males.

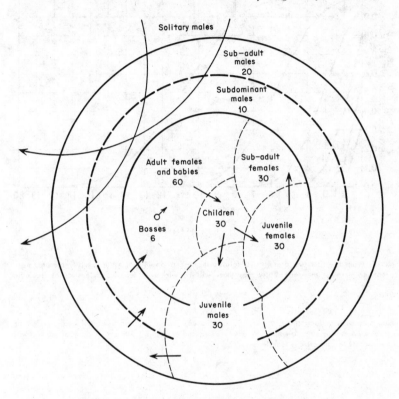

Fig. 4 Social structure of the macaque monkeys of Takasakiyama.

On the periphery of the group are the remainder of the adult males, 10 in all, which are unable to enter the space occupied by the dominant set; with these are associated the group of 20 sub-adult (i.e. adolescent) males. Finally, living a solitary existence but attached to the group, are two other adult males.

Itani says that the six adult males are very clearly set apart from the other adult males; and he notes that they may be recognised because, as a rule, they have a stronger body, more majestic gait and the hind part of the body is better developed than it is in the subordinate males.

GRAPH I DOMINANCE RANK OF MALE

The effect of relative dominance rank (r) and the number of sexually mature, non-pregnant females in the group (n) on the probability of a rhesus male's access to a sexually receptive female. The value of n is shown adjacent to each curve. Based on a model described in the text.

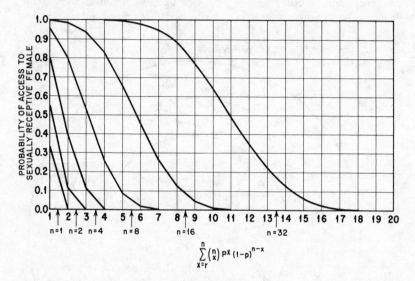

$$\sum_{x=r}^{n} \binom{n}{x} p^x (1-p)^{n-x}$$

NOTE: From the first two premises, it follows that, in a population of n sexually mature, non-pregnant females, the probability that there will be exactly x females in oestrus at any one time is—

$$f(n, x; p) = \binom{n}{x} p^x (1-p)^{n-x}.$$

The male of any dominance rank, r, will have access to an oestrous female if and only if r or more females are simultaneously in oestrus, i.e., the probability that the male of rank r will have access to an oestrous female is—

$$\sum_{x=r}^{n} f(n, x; p).$$

(d) *Social conflict in other mammals.* In the preceding sections we have demonstrated the relationship between the combination of factors in mating systems and the development and resolution of social conflict. The emphasis has been placed upon the continual provocation and ability to mate and the perpetual nature of the conflict thus engendered for the maturing animals of a primate group. Unfortunately, there is insufficient information for an exhaustive review of the mating systems of mammals and their social consequences, but the information available (Eckstein, 1949; Asdell, 1946) is sufficient for us to state that the time available to all other mammals for mating is restricted, in comparison with the primates, by virtue of a periodicity imposed on this activity by different circumstances. That such restriction exists does not rule out the possibility that social conflict may develop in all mammals, but as no other mammal is able to mate continually we should infer that the social conflict engendered in other mammals may not be precisely the same as that in primates, and when it arises it may be resolved in different ways.

In any situation in which two males compete for a female it can be said that a conflict situation develops, but as we have seen in the stag (Darling, 1937) such conflict is not maintained for very long and is resolved by effort-ranking forms of behaviour. At the start of rut in the deer the males are not hierarchically arranged and cannot be said to be in a society (our definition), as there is one male to each harem at any one time. In the anoestrous herds, there is an identifiable hierarchy, but, as the animals are then sexually neutral, social conflict of the type described does not develop.

Thus it would appear that the conditions necessary for the development of social conflict, perpetual or periodic, are the presence of a masculine dominance hierarchy together with sexual provocation on the part of the females. We wish to focus attention on this aspect of mammalian sociology, for although sufficient information has been gathered for us to state that in many mammals this does not occur, there is not enough data for an adequate comparison to be made between mammals in this respect.

In the deer, as we have shown, these two conditions are present, but do not coincide to produce social conflict. A similar situation occurs in the wolf. The formation of packs, as hunting units, occurs at a particular time of year, and both male and female hierarchies are formed (Murie, 1944; Schenkel, 1948). In the pack studied by Schenkel in the Zoological Gardens at Basle the presence of both sexes intensified the rigour with which the hierarchical order was enforced by the different animals, but both Schenkel and Murie state that at the reproductive season the dominant animals segregate in pairs from the pack. Thus in the wolf there can be but little development of social conflict.

However, in the Alaska fur seal of the Pribilov Islands a situation occurs in which a form of social conflict not unlike that of the primate arises. This animal has been described by Charles Mulvey, Scheffer & Kenyon (1945) and other authorities, and an excellent documentary film of the breeding habits of this animal has recently been made by Walt Disney.

The male seals come ashore on the Pribilov Islands towards the end of June and territories become clear along the foreshore in July, many males, because of the intense competition, being segregated to the higher ground behind the foreshore. The females come ashore throughout August and September and are appropriated to the territories of the males by force, where they drop their young and mate. After parturition the females are able to mate after 24 hr. and the males spend these two months appropriating, maintaining and mating with their harems.

The situation is so intense that the males holding territory do not leave them over a period of 54–57 days (Scheffer & Kenyon), during which they digest the 200 lb. of fat which constitutes roughly one-third of their weight at the start of the mating season. Intense fighting occurs during the maintenance of the harems, and the animals are often severely injured or killed.

The males without territories and harems are able to move down to the sea from the rear of the shore by means of channels between the territories. The presence of other animals in these neutral zones does not provoke a challenge from the neighbouring males, and, indeed, Mulvey used these channels to get close to the animals and observe their behaviour. If, however, an animal transgresses the boundaries of one of these territories he is immediately challenged by the overlord male, and the only alternatives are to flee, escape into the neutral zones or stay and fight. Such challenges between hitherto subordinate animals and overlords have been observed and either may be the victor.

Thus we have a situation in the seal in which the provocation to mate and the suppression of such mating behaviour by the male hierarchy exist contemporaneously. The masculine hierarchy is expressed territorially and hence in the number per harem (which may consist of from 1 to 100 females). The suppression of sexual approach is also expressed territorially in the neutral zones behind the foreshore and the channels between territories to the sea. The maturing male is only liable to threat when actually transgressing the territorial boundaries, and hence the visual social conflict is not continuous throughout the season, but is expressed in the exclusion, challenge and fighting that occurs between males.

There are probably many examples in mammals of forms of resolution of social conflict, and it would be of considerable significance to have to hand more information about the societies of mammals. Also it is said that the seal has a large convoluted cortex, but this has not been adequately reported comparatively as yet, and hence information about the social life of animals together with comparative knowledge of their neuro-anatomy might give us considerably more information as to the functions and evolution of various parts of the nervous system.

As a result of the prolonged mating provocation of the males in primate society, the appropriateness of mating behaviour for reproductive efficiency becomes dependent not only on adequate sexual behaviour, but on other forms of social behaviour. These we have seen are the ability to withstand conflict by equilibration and the control of aggression. How far is it possible to identify the anatomical features underlying these functions?

THE BRAIN AND SOCIAL BEHAVIOUR

In the present state of knowledge in neurology and related studies, the relationship between the functions of many parts of the brain and the behaviour of mammals is equivocal. Much of the evidence is contradictory. There are also considerable difficulties in interpretation. For instance, a certain lesion may produce some behavioural change, but such a change may not persist. This may be due to the effects of operative shock, transfer of functions, or other reasons. The behavioural effect, moreover, may not occur until after some time. Disregarding time relations, it is not possible to be sure, except in the case of very careful and extensive studies, just what part is played in the behaviour of an animal by specific regions in the brain, the removal of which causes a change in the behaviour pattern.

There is also a paucity of information in comparative studies which at present renders most evolutionary comparisons suspect, and tends to detract from the value of their intrinsic concepts. Systems of reference such as brain/body weight ratios cannot be accepted at their face value (von Bonin, 1937). At present, therefore, it is impossible to seek supporting evidence for the basic concepts expressed here from a mass of conflicting material. It is more profitable, and this has been our intention, to suggest new interpretations in order that attention be focused on a need for more relevant neurological information.

For the sake of simplicity hitherto, we have used the term enlargement to express those changes in the brain accompanying the selective processes we have described. It is clear that the neocortex has enlarged in proportion both to the somatic mass and to the rest of the subcortical neural structures in man. The term enlargement, therefore, is descriptive rather than analytical. We must here discuss what is the significance of this enlargement. The neocortex is composed typically of six layers of cells, and their connexions with, in addition, glial tissue. It takes the form of a layer of a certain volume. The first fundamental question is, therefore, whether the cell/volume ratio remains constant in mammals which have undergone greater or less development of the neocortex in the course of their evolution. This cannot be completely answered, as information is lacking. However, in *Cebus,* although the total number of cells is smaller than that of man, the cell/volume ratio is higher than that of man (von Bonin, 1938). This suggests that, within a cortical layer of uniform thickness, an increase in size of the cortex, and decrease in cell/volume ratio, indicates an increase in the other elements of the cortex. If the enlargement of the neocortex has been significantly accompanied by a proportionately greater increase in total connexions than of total neurones, this is a fundament in the evolution of man. There is, as we have stated, no complete evidence relating to this.

The criteria for assessing the significance of neocortical enlargement is yet another open question. Which relation between parts of the central nervous system are of significance? Whilst we feel that expressions of area, volume, or mass of parts of the cortex to brain or spinal cord would be of interest, they would be of doubtful evolutionary significance, in that increase in the size of parts of the brain in evolutionary development may only occur *pari passu* with similar developments in the rest of the brain. The structure and function of homologous parts also change in evolution (e.g. red nucleus); therefore, simple mass comparisons between such changing structures, or between ganglia and laminae, are not significant measures of evolutionary development, as the changes taking place in these structures are qualitative as well as quantitive. It is likely, however, that a comparison of the proportion of the different functional areas to the total cortical surface would be a measure which might be of more significance in evolutionary studies than encephalometric studies by themselves (von Bonin, 1941). This will be discussed in more detail later.

It should be also borne in mind that with enlargement of the cortex a change in the functional relationships between it and other brain structures may have taken place. This change in the relationship between parts of the brain may also be of significance in this context.

In the great majority of neurological studies, the animals have not been kept in conditions which would facilitate subsequent analysis of social behaviour following brain lesions. In many studies on primates, the experimental animals have been kept in cages, singly or in pairs, and subsequently used in retention or aptitude tests for comparison with normal animals. Such investigations are of very great interest, but are not relevant to the questions raised here. In the remainder of this section such evidence as is relevant to this discussion will be presented. It must be remembered that the value of such a discussion depends largely upon the amount of general information available which, as we have attempted to show, is frequently lacking in relevant detail.

On present evidence, it is virtually impossible to estimate the proportion of the neocortical surface subserving a particular function. This is because, as von Economo states (1926), two-thirds of the cortical surface resides in the sulci and most of the localization studies using strychninization or placed electrodes are confined to the remaining one-third which is exposed on the outer surface. On the assumption, however, that the sulci represent invaginations of the functional areas represented on the surface, it is clear that total autonomic representation in man's cortex is of a much higher order than that of the areas concerned with special senses and motor function. At present, comparative data is lacking to enable us to say whether this fact, on which Fulton (1949) lays so much emphasis from a functional point of view, has any evolutionary significance, i.e. represents any exceptional enlargement of these functions in man in comparison with other primates and mammals. Nevertheless, the social circumstances in which the evolution of the primates must, by inference, have taken place is just such as to require the development of a differentiated control of autonomic functions.

In particular, since the hypothalamus functions as a centre concerned with the reflex maintenance of the internal environment, and also contains the centres which are the source of efferent impulses, providing the expression of specific patterns of emotional behaviour, e.g. rage and sleep (involving as they do major shifts in the constitution of the internal environment), both aspects of its function will have to be brought under the control of the cortex. Here reside the neurons with definite pathways, bringing about localized and circumscribed autonomic changes in parts and organs of the body concerned with particular functions (Fulton, 1949).

There are, however, other aspects to the question of the adaptations necessary for life in the primate social environment. Equilibration behaviour tends to lead the maturing male primate away from situations liable to evoke emotional responses in him. However, under the extreme provocation exerted by the trigonal situation, the ability to diminish emotive responses, e.g. rage and fear reaction, would thus minimize the chances of impairment to his breeding potential. We noted earlier that dominant males do not become involved in as many social encounters (invloving emotional arousal) as do animals lower in social status. It would be reasonable, therefore, to expect that, during primate evolution, enlargement of those structures mediating the control of emotive responses would take place.

In this connexion, the work of Bard & Mountcastle (1948) focuses our attention on the amygdaloid nucleus and its connexions. These authors point out that when the neocortex is removed from cats, leaving intact allocortical and mesocortical structures (amygdala, hippocampus, pyriform lobe and cingular gyrus), a state of extreme placidity or refractiveness to rage-provoking stimuli develops. On the further removal of midline cortex (area 24), or by further ablation of pyriform lobe, amygdala and hippocampus, the slightest stimulus provokes intense rage. An extraordinary and lasting depression of rage responses was produced by bilateral removal of the amygdala and much of the pyriform lobe. From this work it appears that the amygdala is a centre maintaining a continual state of inhibition on the hypothalmic centres concerned with rage responses in the cat, being innervated from mesocortical, allocortical and neocortical structures. In the *macaque* electrolytic lesions in the region of the amygdala produces long-lasting placidity (E. A. Turner, 1952, private communication). It is thus evident that this region participates in the control of rage reactions in these widely different types of mammals. It may, therefore, be significant that in man this structure is more prominent than in other primates, and that in the macaque and man in that order the baso-lateral nuclei have increased in proportion relative to the cortico-medial when compared with the amygdala of the rabbit (Figs. 5, 6 and 7). This prominence is a reflexion of a selective enlargement of those nuclei (baso-lateral) of the amygdala with pyriform lobe connexions which mediate the control of emotion; a reduction in size and relative importance having taken place in the nuclei with olfactory origin and connexions (cortico-medial) (Crosby & Humphrey, 1941).

It is equally significant for our understanding of the structure of the control of autonomic function that the anatomical basis exists for equilibra-

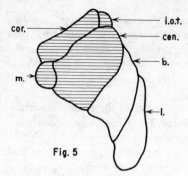

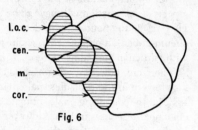

Fig. 5

Fig. 6

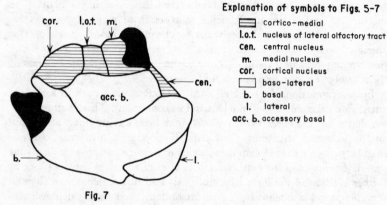

cortico-medial
l.o.t.   nucleus of lateral olfactory tract
Cen.   central nucleus
m.   medial nucleus
cor.   cortical nucleus
baso-lateral
b.   basal
l.   lateral
acc. b.   accessory basal

Fig. 7

Fig. 5 Schematic diagram of amygdala of rabbit (from Johnston, 1922–4).
Fig. 6 Schematic diagram of amygdala of rhesus monkey, *Macaca mulatta* (from Johnston, 1922–4).
Fig. 7 Transverse section of the most highly differentiated region of amygdala of man (from Crosby & Humphrey, 1941).

tory circuits to provide the mechanism of emotional control. "Papez (1937) traced a path from the gyrus cinguli, through the hippocampus and fornix, to the mammillary body and thence, via the mammilothalamic tract, to the anterior nuclei of the thalamus, and back to the starting point in the gyrus cinguli." Moreover, another "feedback" circuit from the mammillary body (concerned with sympathetic efferent discharges) to the hippocampus, and thence back to the mammillary nucleus, enlarges as we trace the changes in it from reptile through the mammal to the primate (Le Gros Clark, 1952). The greatest enlargement occurs in the retroactive circuit which feeds back impulses leaving the mammillary body to the hippocampus. This is evidence that the anatomical basis for sympathetic control is most highly developed in the group we are discussing, and that the characteristic trend of their evolution represents in this respect, as in their enlargement of the neocortex, a continuation of those changes which brought the mammals into existence and first enlarged the cortex in the tetrapods.

We have postulated that the enlargement of the neocortex is an anatomical adaptation to the circumstances requiring an equilibrational response, and that, therefore, the neocortex facilitates equilibration. In one of the few instances in which social behaviour has been studied following brain lesions, the subsequent behaviour of the animal is of very great interest. Ward (1948a) has given the following description of changes in social behaviour of macaques following frontal lobe operation.

Immediately following either unilateral or bilateral subpial resection of the rostral cingular gyrus in the monkey, there is an obvious change in personality (Ward, 1948b).

In a large cage with other monkeys of the same size it (the monkey) showed no grooming or acts of affection towards its companions. In fact, it behaved as if they were inanimate, it would walk over them, walk on them if they happened to be in the way, and would even sit on them. It would openly take food from its companions, and appeared surprised when they retaliated, yet this never led to a fight for it was neither pugnacious nor even aggressive, seeming merely to have lost its "social conscience" (Ward, 1948a).

It is thus evident that, following removal of the anterior limbic area, such monkeys lose some of the social fear and anxiety which normally govern their activity, and thus lose the ability to accurately forecast the social repercussion of their own actions (Ward, 1948b).

Ward also states that the behaviour changes produced by unilateral operation lasted at least a month, and there was no difference between the effects of lesions placed on the left- or right-hand sides. Bilateral operation, however, produced a slightly more marked change which, he states, was permanent. This example clearly illustrates that in *Macaca mulatta* the neuro-anatomical basis for the pattern of primate behaviour, the evolutionary implication of which has already been discussed, has neocortical components.

Equilibration demands of the animal an intensification of the control over its emotional responses, both facilitatory and inhibitory. It seems reasonable, therefore, to suggest that one of the major differences between a lower mammal, such as a rat, and a primate may be that in the former the control of approach and the evocation of emotion are two aspects of a single response to a negative sign, and that the capacity to differentiate these responses is limited by a physiological and possibly anatomical feature. In the primate, these two elements appear to be less rigidly associated.

CONSPECTUS

We have identified two aspects to the uniqueness of primate behaviour. The first arises out of the fact that in those primates in which the female is receptive for longer than one-third of the cycle, mating becomes a form of behaviour possible at most times, and thus becomes of equal rank to other behavioural activities of the group. The second is the element of conflict which arises out of this situation and affects all the other activities of the group. In the evolution of the primates, these two elements combine to produce the unique type of selection. However, in studies of the behaviour of contemporary primates these two components are separable.

Consider the form of the argument. We have drawn attention to two prominent characteristic features of the primates. One is an aspect of their behaviour, and the other comprises the enlargement of a certain structure in the brain. This parallel in itself is not especially significant, since similar parallel developments could be identified in the primates. What is significant is, first, that the anatomical changes in the brain are of a generalized type in a region concerned with the integration of all other brain functions; the new form of behaviour which we have described is also generalized. This means that it is possible to relate one to the other. The second point is, that these two features are also comparable in an evolutionary context, since we have adduced arguments to show that the behaviour will be selected, and we know that the anatomical enlargement has, in fact, been selected. We have, therefore, suggested a causal link between the two. Whether or not the facts we have discussed have the significance we have placed on them, requires careful consideration in any theory of primate evolution.

Conflict, as Neal Miller has shown, results from the equalization of the two opposing variables at the intersection of their gradients. Moreover, this intersection we have suggested can itself exist at various absolute intensities of the negative and positive elements. Conflict is thus a graded element, which, in primate behaviour and in the behaviour of a rat under the conditions of Miller's experiments, determines the position the animal takes up. At a given intensity of conflict, a greater facility for input from sources within the animal will increase the freedom of movement within the confines of the social environment. This is a single quantitative aspect of the enlargement of the neocortex and its dependent structures, which must be kept in sight, and may mean that in evolution the ability to withstand conflict was a simple function of the increasing number of connexions between the cells throughout these structures as a whole. In these circumstances we may usefully consider the hypothesis that man's elaborate behaviour is the consequence of enlargement of the cortex, which process lends to the particular regions of the cortex a functional potential far greater than that exhibited by the cortices of other mammals.

The neuro-anatomical evidence, however, points to the localization of specific functions in distinct, but in the case of autonomic functions widely placed, areas of the cortex. An alternative hypothesis is thus available, namely, that the conditions of conflict create the circumstances, which require the continual reintegration of a variety of separate functions into a number of combinations for correct behaviour of any kind in the primate social setting. For example, we have observed that feeding behaviour is structured by the presence of equilibration in response to or even in the absence of threat from the dominant animals. However, in these circumstances fear-provoking stimuli do not cause the animal to stop eating, but having secured food to equilibrate before eating it. We can see, therefore, that on our definition of conflict, the animal which, having equilibrated to a particular spot and settled down to eat, is nevertheless under a degree of sympathetic tone, and yet simultaneous specific parasympathetic activity is required to facilitate the digestive processes. Here, therefore, while general sympathetic tone may be raised, specific parasympathetic outflows may also be brought into operation by a mechanism revealed by Fulton's studies of cortical anatomy (1949).

Carpenter's studies of primate society make it clear that not all males are occupied in sexual behaviour to the same extent as others. Indeed, great variety in individual behaviour is apparent in all subhuman primate societies. Moreover, major differences in behaviour separate those males gathered in the trigonal sphere of influence, surrounding the dominant male from those in the periphery of the group. In some societies the element of conflict, as represented by the male hierarchy, grades outwards from this point to the periphery (e.g. macaques). Even in the societies of this monkey (Itani 1954 & Altmann 1959) the evidence shows that this conflict is concentrated round the central breeding hierarchy of a few males. In others (e.g. baboons) the region of conflict appears to be confined to the trigonal sphere itself. Thus, not all animals are sexually motivated to the same extent, or behave in such a way that they possess this element of drive as a permanent feature in their behaviour. We have chosen to emphasize the regions of the social environment where this is so, since the great majority of the breeding activity takes place there, and thus the animals in this region are those whose behaviour patterns have evolutionary consequences.

Mammalian behaviour is the outcome of the interaction between mechanisms inherent in behaviour structure, the environmental circumstances, and the learning processes. We have dealt here with unlearned behaviour, i.e. the outcome of the interaction between behaviour structure and the environment. The evidence which has been presented is not primarily concerned with the relationship between equilibration behaviour and the learning processes, as it is not relevant to the present discussion to attempt to specify the exact nature of the relationship between the features which we have discussed and the evolution of the learning processes in primates.

The conditions in which equilibration behaviour has been observed to-day require that the animals be free to move and still remain in contact with each other. This is essential if the element of conflict is to be ever present, as it is in groups of free-ranging monkeys. It may, therefore, be assumed that the ancestors of man and other primates showing cortical enlargements must have developed this feature while living in groups inhabiting relatively open country, which would necessitate the development of such spatial behaviour patterns. So far, little is known of the actual site of the development of the primates for any evidence to be brought to bear on this point.

It must be made clear that we have not attempted to provide a complete explanation of the evolution of man. It has been our intention to provide an explanation of the orthoselective processes in the evolution of the primates up to the stage of constitutional preadaptation on the part of some of them for man's present exploitation of the environment (see Huxley, 1942). In this instance, the primary selective advantage lay in an appropriate form of behaviour; the consequent adaptation gives a greater diversity of potential behaviour and capacities.

We therefore conclude that the ascent of man has been due in part to a competition for social position, giving access to the trigonal sphere of social activity in which success was rewarded by a breeding premium, and that at some time in the past, a group of primates, by virtue of their pre-eminent adaptation to this element and consequent cortical enlargement, became pre-adapted for the full exploitation of the properties of the mammalian cortex.

ACKNOWLEDGEMENT

I wish to thank F. A. Beach and P. B. Medawar for their most helpful criticism, and am indebted to W. E. Le Gros Clark for recent information on neuro-anatomy and to C. R. Carpenter for additional information on sub-human primate sociology, and to C. White for assistance in constructing Table 1. Discussions with L. L. Whyte were also of great assistance.

REFERENCES

ALLEE, W. C. 1939 The Social life of animals. London, Heinemann.
—— 1942 Social dominance and subordination among vertebrates. Biol. Symp. 8:139–63.
ALTMANN, S. A. *in* The Roots of Behavior, ed. E. L. Bliss. (in the Press.)
ALVERDES, F. R. 1927 Social Life in the Animal World. London, Kegan, Paul, Trench, Trubner.
ASDELL, S. A. 1946 Patterns of Mammalian Reproduction. Ithaca, N.Y., Comstock Publ.
BARD, P., and V. B. MOUNTCASTLE 1948 Some forebrain mechanisms involved in the expression of rage, etc. Res. Publ. Ass. Nerv. Dis. pp. 362–404.
BARNETT, S. A. 1948 Principles of rodent control. F.A.O. Agric. Publ., Wash., 2:1–20.
—— 1950 Film: Feeding Behaviour of the Rat. From meeting of Society for Experimental Biology, Queen Mary College, London.
BEACH, F. A. 1947a Hormones and mating behaviour in vertebrates. Proc. Laur. Hormone Conf. 1:27–64.
—— 1947b Evolutionary changes in the physiological control of mating behaviour in mammals. Psychol. Rev. 54:297–315.
BONIN, G. VON 1937 Brain weight and body weight of mammals. J. Gen. Psychol. 16:279–89.
—— 1938 The cerebral cortex of the Cebus monkey. J. Comp. Neurol. 69:(2)181.
—— 1941 On encephalometry. J. Comp. Neurol. 25: 287–316.

Brown, S. S. 1942 Factors determining conflict reactions in difficult discriminations. J. Exp. Psychol. 31:272–92.

Carpenter, C. R. 1934 A field study of the behaviour and social relations of howling monkeys (Alouatta palliata). Comp. Psychol. Monogr. 10:48–168.

——— 1935 Behaviour of red spider monkeys in Panama. J. Mammal. 16: 171–80.

——— 1940 A field study in Siam of the behaviour and social relations of the gibbon (Hylobates lar). Comp. Psychol. Monogr. 16:5.

——— 1942a Sexual behaviour of free ranging rhesus monkeys (Macaca Mulatta). I. Specimens, procedures, and behavioural characteristics estrus. II. Periodicity of estrus, homosexual, autoerotic and nonconformist behaviour. J. Comp. Psychol. 23, no. 1.

——— 1942b Societies of monkeys and apes. Biol. Symp. 8:177–204.

Chance, M. R. A. 1956 Social structure of a macaque colony. Brit. J. Anim. Behav. IV 1.

——— 1957 The role of convulsions in behaviour. Behav. Sci.

Chance, M. R. A., and W. M. S. Russell 1959 Protean displays: a form of allaesthetic behaviour. Proc. Zoo. Soc. (Lond) 132. pt. 1. 65–70.

Clark, W. E. Le Gros 1949 History of the primates. Publ. Brit. Mus. Nat. Hist.

——— Acta neerl. morph. (In the Press.)

Crosby, E. C., and T. Humphrey 1941 Studies of the vertebrate telencephalon. II. J. Comp. Neurol. 74:309.

Darling, F. Fraser 1937 A Herd of Red Deer. Oxford University Press.

Darwin, Charles 1875 The Origin of Species by means of Natural Selection etc. London, John Murray.

Eckstein, P. 1949 Patterns of mammalian sexual cycle. Acta anat. 7:389–410.

Economo, G. Von 1926 Ein Koeffizient für die Organisationshöhe der Grosshirnrinde. Klin. Wschr. 5:593.

Fulton, J. F. 1949 Functional localisation in the Frontal Lobes and Cerebellum. Oxford, Clarendon Press.

Grant, E. C. in preparation.

Grant, E. C., and M. R. A. Chance 1958 Rank order in caged rats. Anim. Behav. VI 304.

Hartman, C. G. 1930–2 Studies in the reproduction of the monkey Macacus rhesus, with special reference to menstruation and pregnancy. Contr. Embryol. Carneg. Instn. 134:22–3.

Huxley, J. S. 1938 Darwin's theory of sexual selection and the data subsumed by it in the light of recent research. Amer. Nat. 72:416–33.

——— 1942 Evolution. The Modern Synthesis. London, Allen and Unwin.

Imanishi, K. 1959 Primates. 2. No. 2.

Itani, J. 1954 The monkeys of Takasakiyama. Tokyo. Kobunsha.

Johnston, J. B. 1922–4 Further contributions to the study of the evolution of the forebrain. J. Comp. Neurol. 35–36, 337–481.

Lashley, K. S. 1949 Persistent problems in the evolution of mind. Quart. Rev. Biol. 24 (1): 28–42.

Lorenz, K. 1937 Über den Begriff der Instinkthandlung. Folia biotheor., Leiden, II, 17–50.

Maier, N. R. F. 1949 Frustration—A study of Behaviour without a Goal. McGraw Hill Publ. Psychol.

Masserman, J. M. 1946 Behaviour and Neurosis. Chicago University Press.

Miller, N. E. 1937 Analysis of the form of conflict reaction. Psychol. Bull. 34:720.

——— 1944 Experimental studies of conflict. In Personality and the Behavior Disorders, ed. J. McV. Hunt. New York, Ronald.

MILLER, W. C. 1950 Communication to a meeting of the Institute for the Study of Animal Behaviour. (Private communication.)

MUNN, N. L. 1933 An Introduction to Animal Psychology; the Behaviour of the Rat. Boston, Houghton, Mifflin Co.

—— 1950 Handbook of Psychological Research on the Rat, p. 84. Boston, Houghton Mifflin Co.

MURIE, A. 1944 The wolves of Mount McKinley. U.S.G.P.O. Publ. Wash.

PAPEZ, J. W. 1937 A proposed mechanism of emotion. Arch. Neurol. Psychiat. 38:725–43.

RICHTER, C. P. 1927 Animal behaviour and internal drives. Quart. Rev. Biol. 2 (3):302–43.

RUSSELL, E. S. 1945 The Directiveness of Organic Activities. Cambridge University Press.

SCHEFFER, V. B., and K. W. KENYON 1952 The fur seal comes of age. Nat. Geogr. Mag. 101 (4):491–512.

SCHENKEL, R. 1948 Ausdrucks-studien an Wolfen. Behaviour, I, 81:130.

SNELL, G. D. (Ed.) 1941 Biology of the Laboratory Mouse. Philadelphia, Blakiston.

SOMMERHOFF, G. 1950 Analytical Biology. Oxford University Press.

SPENCE, K. W., and R. LIPPIT 1946 An experimental test of the sign theory of trial and error learning. J. Exp. Psychol. 36:491–502.

STRAUS, W. J. 1949 Riddle of man's ancestry. Quart. Rev. Biol. 24 (3): 200–223.

THOMPSON, H. V. 1948 Studies in the behaviour of the common brown rat. I. Bull. Anim. Behav. 6:26–40.

THORPE, W. H. 1948 Modern concept of instinctive behaviour. Bull. Anim. Behav. 7:1–12.

TINBERGEN, N. 1942 An objectivistic study of the innate behaviour of animals. Bibl. Biotheor., Leiden, I (2), 39–98.

TOLMAN, E. C. 1949 The psychology of social learning. J. Soc. Iss. 3.

WARD, A. A. (Jr.) 1948a The cingular gyrus-area 24. J. Neurophysiol. II: 13–23.

—— 1948b The anterior cingular gyrus and personality. Res. Publ. Ass. Nerv. Ment. Dis. 27:438–45.

YERKES, R. M., and J. H. ELDER 1936a The sexual reproductive cycles of chimpanzees. Proc. Acad. Nat. Sci., Wash. 22:276–85.

—— 1936b Oestrus, receptivity and mating in the chimpanzee. Comp. Psychol. Monogr. 13 (5):39.

ZUCKERMAN, S. 1930 The menstrual cycle of the primates. I. General nature and homology. Proc. Zool. Soc. Lond. 1930, pp. 691–754.

—— 1932 The Social Life of Monkeys and Apes. London, Kegan, Paul, Trench, Trubner.

—— 1933 Functional Affinities of Man, Apes and Monkeys. New York, Harcourt.

SOCIAL BEHAVIOR AND THE EVOLUTION

OF MAN'S MENTAL FACULTIES

WILLIAM ETKIN

INTRODUCTION

The concept of the uniqueness of man is again in the forefront of biological thought. The basis of that uniqueness is recognized as man's capacity for culture, its accumulation and transmission. This capacity in turn is the resultant of the unique mental qualities man displays, qualities which set him off from even his nearest relatives among the primates. This point of view has been brilliantly elaborated by several modern students of evolution, particularly by Julian Huxley (1941) and by G. G. Simpson (1949). Henry Nissen (1951) has phrased it (p. 426) in behavioral terms.

With one notable exception the phylogenetic course of behavioral development has been gradual; that it has been a continuous affair, proceeding by quantitative rather than qualitative changes. The one exception is that which makes the transsition from the highest nonhuman primates to man (that is, "modern man"). At this point a new "dimension" or mode of development emerges, culture or "social heredity."

If this uniqueness of man is to be understood in terms of evolutionary biology it can only be as the resultant of a biological history that includes unique conditions under which the basic driving forces of evolution have operated in his history. Since modern biology has returned to considering natural selection as the basic driving force in evolution we must expect to find the explanation of man's separateness in some features of his history by which a selective pressure was accorded to the particular forms of intelligence and cooperative behavior which mark man as a culture-capable organism. Furthermore these selective pressures must have come into play upon an organism which provided the kind of genetic variability which permitted evolution to progress in the requisite direction. Any adequate theory of human evolution must specify both of these factors.

The general discussions of the post-Darwinian era sought an explanation of man's culture-accumulating ability in pointing out the general survival value of intelligence, particularly in such activities as tool using. The recent emphasis on the biological significance of cooperative behavior by Allee (1951), Montagu (1950) and others stresses the value to the group of such

Reprinted by permission from *The American Naturalist*, 88: (1954), 129–42.

intra-group cooperation. These generalized discussions while of course valid do not offer an explanation of the special characteristics of man's intelligence or social cooperation since they do not qualify on either of the two counts mentioned above. Indeed in their more enthusiastic presentations these points of view lead one to wonder why all animals are not as intelligent as Einstein and as moral as Schweitzer.

Whereas biologists are mostly content to treat the problem of the evolution of human mentality from that of a primate ancestor in general terms, anthropologists usually skip over it entirely and assume the culture-accumulating capacity of man as the basis from which their discussions start. For example, Tappen (1953) writing recently on a mechanistic theory of human evolution states:

Ancestors of the human group must have made the shift over to symbolic communication to initiate specifically human evolution. Such an adaptive change corresponds to Simpson's evolutionary mode, the *quantum evolution*. Once such a shift toward this new adaptive zone was initiated, a high selective advantage for individuals better adapted to learned behavior and symbolic communication must have ensued.

It is evident that from the biological point of view the crux of the matter is the explanation of the shift over to symbolic communication which is assumed as given by Tappen.

Dobzhansky and Montagu (1947) have briefly considered this problem and have offered the suggestion that human intelligence and cooperative behavior have developed in connection with the adjustment of individuals to each other within the social group. They emphasize that this dependence of human mentality upon social behavior implies that the same essential factor has operated on the evolution of mentality in all human groups in contradistinction to the variety of environmental factors which have operated to produce physical diversity in different races. Their fundamental contribution is thus to account for the general conformity of all races in mental characteristics in spite of a degree of physical distinctiveness. Their point of view is also important in that it orients the search for the selective factors in the evolution of man's mentality toward the analysis of social behavior. But their brief consideration does not attempt to specify the behaviors involved in the selective process.

Chance and Mead (1953) * in a recent study have attempted to specify the social behavioral factors involved in man's evolution. They point out the role of the cortex in control of the function of the autonomic nervous system. They consider that the young primate male, subject to competition for place in an autocratic primate society such as that of the baboon, has a high survival value placed upon the cortical control of his relations, particularly the autonomic control of emotional behavior. Hence they suppose a considerable selection pressure is exerted for the expansion of the cortex. Apparently

* Reprinted in this Volume as revised by Chance, pp. 84–130.

their concept is that human mentality, otherwise than as it is characterized by cortical dominance of autonomic function, is an incidental product of the expansion of the cortex. They say (p. 437):

> We therefore conclude that the ascent of man has been due in part to a competition for social position, giving access to the trigonal sphere of social activity in which success was rewarded by a breeding premium, and that at some time in the past, a group of primates, by virtue of their pre-eminent adaptation to this element and consequent cortical enlargement became pre-adapted for the full exploitation of the properties of the mammalian cortex.

This theory seems of limited applicability for a number of reasons. It is based on one aspect of social behavior, intense male competition for dominance in a polygamous group. This, though characteristic of baboon and macaque society, is not universal among primates. It hardly seems applicable to precultural man for reasons to be discussed later. Perhaps a more fundamental defect of the theory is that it is non-adaptational, making the various aspects of human intelligence incidental to selection in respect to other characteristics which, it should be pointed out, operate in the male sex only. Such a view is hardly consistent with modern emphasis on selection pressure as the basic motive power of evolution (Dobzhansky, 1937; Mayr, 1942).

THE BASIS FOR A SELECTION PRESSURE THEORY

Any attempt to develop a theory to account for the distinctive traits of intelligence and cooperative behavior as shown by man is necessarily highly speculative. Yet the importance of this subject for an understanding of the biology of man is so great as to justify renewed attempts whenever advances in related fields give new insights that may be helpful. The recent advances in the paleontology of man, particularly in respect to the South African man-apes, the australopithecines, and Pekin man, Sinanthropus, have thrown new and unexpected light on the characteristics of man at the period of the origin of his culture-developing capacities. The recent burgeoning of interest in the study of the comparative psychology and the social behavior of vertebrates, especially of the primates, has afforded new concepts that enable us to deal with the problem in concrete terms. It will be our purpose here to draw upon these fields for materials from which to formulate a theoy of some of the selective factors operating on man in the transition from the non-cultural to the cultural level.

It is not necessary for us to accept any fixed notions as to the exact position of the australopithecines in respect to man's evolution. Whether in direct line of evolution of modern man or not, we can accept them as representing a stage or level of evolution in which the anthropoid-to-man line showed the following characteristics. The animal had a brain not much larger than that of our present great apes, with a cranial capacity of perhaps 600–800 cc., a body somewhat smaller than modern man's (about 100 lbs.), canines not conspicuously enlarged nor dimorphic, erect posture and bipedal locomotion leaving the hands free of locomotor use. The abundance of baboon and other mammalian bones and evidence of cracking of long bones and the skulls in a way to permit extraction of their contents as food strongly suggest that these African man-apes hunted baboons and smaller mammals as food.

On the basis of these aspects of his australopithecine finds, Dart (1949) inferred that these man-apes were hunters who lived in part by killing fairly large and ferocious mammals (the baboons of the kitchen-middens were somewhat larger than present-day types). He reasoned that the man-ape could not have effectively hunted them unless he used tools. Since no clear stone artifacts are associated with their remains, it must be presumed that such tools were of wood or bone or consisted of naturally occurring stones. Bartholomew and Birdsell (1953) have considered the social organization of australopithecines in connection with population problems and have accepted Dart's point of view. They point out the significance of tool use in exploitation of food resources.

The use of tools was greatly emphasized by Darwin (1871) and other early writers as the basis of the natural selection of intelligence in human evolution. Carveth Read (1920) suggested that precultural man was a wolf-ape, running in wolf-like packs to hunt various moderate and large mammals. He too emphasized the success that would attend those individuals better able to make and use tools in the hunt. But he also stressed the selective value of cooperative behavior in this ecological niche, particularly the development of leadership and discipline in the ranks.

As we have seen, the fossil evidence of australopithecines gives definite support to these older speculations. We can therefore accept as part of the basis for a modern hypothesis of the social organization of precultural man the following points. He was a bipedal terrestrial hunting organism before he developed the human brain. The free use of his hands in tool use and tool production gave a selective advantage to increased intelligence. Possibly he practiced pack hunting and thus was exposed to selection in terms of group cooperative behavior. Such considerations help us to see some of the selective actions that led to the so-called "explosive" evolution of the human brain (Eiseley, 1953; Weidenreich, 1946).

When we turn to consider the Sinanthropus level of human evolution we again may point out that we do not necessarily regard this fossil as in direct line to a modern race but as representative of a particular level of human ancestry. The significant characteristics of that level are a brain of approximately 900–1000 cc., associated with early paleolithic artifacts, and clear evidence of the use of fire in cooking. As Weidenreich remarked of Sinanthropus (1947), his eating habits cannot have differed greatly from those of primitive tribes today. The cultural artifacts associated with Sinanthropus appear to be equivalent to an early paleolithic (Mousterian) level. Davidson Black (1934) remarks on the small improvement seen over the whole extent of the deposits in contrast to the marked improvement shown in Spanish cave deposits covering a much shorter period. This possibly indicates that Sinanthropus brain was functionally, as it was volumetrically, not fully equal to that of modern man.

Middle pleistocene man, either Paleoanthropic (Neanderthaloid) or Neanthropic (Swanscombe, Fontéchevade) displays a brain as large as that of the largest of modern races (Montagu, 1960). It may be that the Neanderthal brain did not show as great a development of frontal and temporal-parietal association areas as that of contemporary man, but certainly the Neanthropic types showed brains which in their gross morphology are completely modern. Culturally too, there appears to be no justification for imputing any inferiority as compared to present-day paleolithic cultural man. Presumably then these fossil men were as capable of absorbing any level of culture, including that of the atomic age, as we presume contemporary primitives to be.

As biologists then we can regard the evolutionary span from australopithecines (presumably late pliocene or earliest pleistocene) to middle pleistocene man as the locale of the evolutionary change in brain and mentality which marks the transition from non-cultural anthropoid society to cultural human society. We can further accept from our knowledge of australopithecines the concept that before his mind made the transition man's ancestors had become erect, ground, perhaps pack running, hunters, dependent upon tools and cooperative pack behavior to supplement the stratagems characteristic of mammalian predators.

Turning now to recent developments in comparative psychology, I would accept two main points from the studies of Köhler, Yerkes and the many others who have explored primate behavior. The first is in regard to their intelligence. The higher apes, the chimpanzee in particular, are capable of insightful solutions of problems. However, these experiments on insight and the results of delayed response and token-using experiments indicate that imagery or ideational behavior are part of the ape's mental equipment. However, the ape is very limited in this respect in comparison to man (Köhler, 1927; Yerkes, 1943). Chimpanzees show considerable individual variation but at best seem to be poorly able to maintain clear images of past events or to form images of future possibilities. Their insightful solutions of problems are good only when they are formed by combining elements already present. This low development of ideation is a principal factor in the failure of apes to develop true speech. One of the characteristics of speech at its lowest level is the representation by a symbol of concrete items not sensually present at the moment. The failure of apes to develop language in the human sense is today recognized as being based on no physical or physiological limitation but rather on psychological inadequacy. This is demonstrated most dramatically in the failure of baby chimpanzees raised in human families to make much progress in developing true speech beyond the use of two or three verbal symbols (Kellogg and Kellogg, 1933; Hayes, 1951). Even these symbols seem to be used chiefly when the objects referred to are present. Of course, the limitations of the ape mentality as compared to human depends on many other factors than the ability to form clear images of past or future events but for our present purpose we shall find this lack, which necessarily limits speech development, the most significant for our own thinking.

A second area in which we will find the concepts of comparative psychology of value is that relating to the socialization of the higher apes. In this connection we wish to point out that though dominance behavior is clearly evident in ape social relations it is subject to modification in a number of respects of which female estrus deserves specific consideration here. Under natural conditions the male of a pair would be expected to dominate the female since, though the species is quite variable, the males generally are larger than females (Nissen, 1931). Under experimental conditions it has been found that the dominant male is modified in his behavior toward a female when she is in estrus (Yerkes, 1939). Then the male yields place to the female thereby permitting her to receive food rewards from which he regularly excludes her when she is not in estrus. Experimentally this relation has been shown to be hormonally controlled (Birch and Clark, 1946) and to apply to female-female pairs as well as to the male-female pairing (Crawford, 1940). Yerkes termed this phenomenon privilege granting, but in view of the demonstration of the complexity of the phenomenon (Birch and Clark, 1950) a more neutral term such as dominance modification is preferable. It is evident that ecologically, dominance modification in estrus fits in with the common phenomenon of a closer social tie between male and female at the time of female estrus. It is a common phenomenon in primates that dominance relations between mates are modified in a way which permits closer socialization of male and female at this period (Carpenter, 1942; Zuckerman, 1932).

From the recent work on social behavior of animals, the primary insight I would select for our purpose here is the realization in concrete terms of the essential role played by social behavior in the adaptation of an animal to its environment.(Tinbergen, 1951). The sexual, parental and other group behaviors are seen to be adjustments to the conditions of the animal's life. They are as necessary to its survival as any of its physiological or structural characteristics and therefore as much subject to natural selection. The classic study of the red deer by Fraser Darling (1936) is an example of the ecological significance of behavior.

A second fundamental proposition is that the elements of the social behavior of an animal form an integrated whole in which each element fits to the others and to the structure of the animal (Scott, 1944; Tinbergen, 1953). Consequently one can make inferences from one aspect, behavioral or structural, to another with the same sort of assurance (or lack thereof) as we are accustomed to do in going from one structure to the other. Illustrations of these propositions are best given as we develop the details of a concrete theory of protohominid social organization and the evidence for it.

THE INTEGRATED FAMILY THEORY OF PROTOHOMINID SOCIOLOGY

The theory that is here suggested is that the protohominid at the australopithecine level of development lived in integrated family units, essentially monogamous, in which the male and female performed separate economic functions but were closely integrated by behavioral mechanisms into a unit in respect to parental functions. The male is visualized as being specialized as a hunter as well as a food gatherer and the female as being a food gatherer and domestic. They shared a more or less permanent domicile. In the following paragraphs the basis for this inference is derived from considerations of the principles of social behavior particularly as seen in other mammals. The selection pressures operating in such a social organization are then analyzed from the point of view of the extent to which they can be seen to be pushing the man-apes in evolution in the direction of truly human mentality.

The male mammal is commonly poorly integrated into such social activities as the species possesses (Alverdes, 1927). In some solitary species as cats and many rodents the male and female associate only during the female's estrus when insemination takes place. The female alone cares for the young. However, there are many types of mammalian societies, particularly in group-living forms, in which the male plays a more conspicuous social role. In the red deer at the rutting season the males leave their own groups and seek out the females. Each one herds as many females as possible into a small harem which he defends from all other males. At the close of the mating season however he breaks contact with the females and returns to the male haunts. The females form well-integrated herds in which the young are raised.

Such a social organization is characterized by males highly dominant over females and extremely aggressive toward other males during the mating season. Such males are obviously subjected to a selection pressure putting a high premium on fighting behavior, strength, aggressive temperament and weapons. This, of course, correlates with the structure of these creatures, sexual dimorphism being especially marked with respect to the male's equipment for fighting and for display.

In primate groups where the males remain with the group of females permanently a modification of this pattern obtains. In some species as the baboons and macaques the dominance and aggressive behavior of the males is as highly developed as in the deer tribe. Such males are larger than females, aggressive in temperament and with conspicuously developed canines. In such cases the males function in the group chiefly as defenders of the group and its territory against outside aggression. They play little or no positive role in domestic affairs, the raising of the young being entirely the burden of the females. In fact the aggressions of the males against each other and against females are a constant source of disturbance within the group, so much so, in fact, as to render impractical the maintenance of the group under semi-natural conditions (Carpenter, 1942; Zuckerman, 1932). Howling monkeys and chimpanzees show considerably less male aggressiveness and a rather greater contribution of the males to group welfare (Carpenter, 1934; Nissen, 1931). Correspondingly these species show less extreme sexual dimorphism.

It is evident that the reason the domestic burden can be effectively carried by the individual females without the help of the male in these primates is because these species live as food-gatherers, eating primarily plant and small animal materials. The young, born usually one at a time, are small enough for the female to carry with her without serious interference with her foraging activities. The young in turn are equipped with grasping limbs enabling them to cling effectively to the belly of the mother with relatively slight danger of dislodgement. When the young attain a size at which they become a burden to the mother they attain independent locomotion.

Such behavioral organization whereby the female carries practically the entire burden of raising the young is possible in carnivorous animals as well but usually requires some special modification of behavior. In the cats such as the cougar, the female continues her hunting after littering but the indications are that she confines her foraging to the immediate neighborhood (Seton, 1929). At any rate the period of infancy is short and the female evidently survives it on limited rations. Later when the young can travel she covers her kill and leads the young to it. In the fur seal, fish-hunting on the part of the nursing female is permitted by a remarkable adaptation. The young can gorge themselves on milk at one feeding to survive several days while the female is away on a fishing expedition in nearby waters (Scheffer and Kenyon, 1952).

Wolves and other canines on the other hand attain a fundamentally different behavioral adjustment (Young and Goldman, 1944; Murie, 1944). In these species the male is integrated into the family group as a cooperating member that assists the female and young. Male and female pair up in the fall, apparently while still members of a pack. Later they separate from the pack, mate and clear out a number of dens. After birth of the young the male not only stands guard for the family but hunts for them as well. He may gorge himself at a kill and then disgorge at the den mouth for the female and young to feed on. Later the pair may hunt together, lead the young to the prey and gradually build them up to a family pack.

It is obvious that in so far as the protohominid was a hunter, the wolf type of behavioral adjustment is more suited to him than is that of the cat or seal. The anthropoid baby is too large to be carried on a hunt and requires too long a developmental period to permit a temporary tiding over of the nursing period. The mature anthropoid female is characterized by the fact that she is almost continuously carrying a child. As one is weaned the next is born. The female therefore cannot be an effective hunter. The development of a hunting economy can occur in an anthropoid only if the male cooperates in feeding and care of the young. The presupposition of monogamy for precultural man which is here made is based on the impracticality of a single male operating successfully as protector and provider for many females. In animal societies in which the male maintains a harem as in the red deer, fur seal or baboon he devotes his continuous attention to guarding his harem against approach of other males. Such continuous guarding is of course impossible in the hunting economy visualized here for precultural man. Such considerations however, do not apply once the cultural level with its distinctive behavioral controls is reached.

The central feature of the social behavior of the "hunter" anthropoid therefore, must be an integration of the male into the monogamous family unit in which he is the primary hunter. This may be described as the wolf-type of behavioral adjustment, not however in the sense of Carveth Read, who apparently thought only of pack behavior and not of the domestic life of the wolf. There is, however, as we saw before, no reason to exclude the idea of pack hunting. It may well be that the males of several family units or of the extended single family covering several generations constituted a clan and hunted together. In that case the reasoning of Read (1920), Keith (1949), Bartholomew and Birdsell (1953) and others regarding the selective factors operating might be applicable.

THE SELECTION PRESSURES OPERATING IN THE INTEGRATED FAMILY UNIT

In this section I will try to show that the biology of the integrated family unit as described above places a premium on the types of intelligence and cooperative activities that characterize human in contradistinction to ape behaviors. Such a selection pressure operating on an ape-like background leads to the first steps in the development of a mind capable of culture.

The male as hunter would necessarily have to use tools as Dart has pointed out for the australopithecines. Since the chimpanzee shows the rudiments of stick use and of the thrown missile, the natural variability upon which selection can act may be presumed to have been present in the protohominids. The effects of this selection pressure need not be further stressed here since they are familiar items in the literature of this topic since the time of Darwin as explained above. It is perhaps well to point out though, that in the integrated family unit the use of fire and tools in the domestic situation by the female would have survival value. Intelligence, therefore, need not have arisen exclusively as a male prerogative!

Another important factor in the development of intelligence is the role of communication by speech which would be favored in an integrated family. Since the sphere of operation of the male and female are separated in space, communication by which specific information concerning items not immediately present such as the nature of the kill, spoors, weapons or fire-use, would be highly valuable. A selection pressure can therefore be visualized operating to activate language at one of its lowest levels, the use of word symbols for objects not immediately present. Such a pressure does not operate to any considerable extent in the lives of group living primates today since each animal is there a self-sufficient economic unit. There is little for them to communicate about except things present such as food or enemies. Such communication is sufficiently accomplished by the attention-attracting and emotion-arousing cries common to many social animals. Thus the alarm cry of apes is an emotional outburst that is highly effective in arousing other members to action against an aggressor. Köhler's account of the attack upon him following the alarm expressed by one of his subjects is an illustration of this. Such a cry need have none of the ideational content of true speech. The social organization of contemporary apes therefore does not favor a selection pressure in the direction of language development.

It may of course, be objected that if this theory is valid the selection pressure for the development of language would operate for the wolf as for the protohominid. The failure of speech to develop in the wolf is, however, not surprising since the wolf's mentality is not well enough developed to provide the basis for selection. In short, it is only after the level of mentality characteristic of the ape is reached where some ideational behavior is already present, that the shift to an integrated family will result in a development of language.

In the evolution of an integrated family economy there must have been some mechanism by which the male aggressiveness and dominance as found in other primates was mitigated to permit the male to become closely associated with the female in the common endeavor of family raising. I suggest that the dominance modification phenomenon as discussed above in the chimpanzee is the basis of such a change. The sexual relation produces a bond of cooperation during estrus in the chimpanzee (Yerkes, 1939). Since the female chimpanzee is in estrus about one third of her cycle this bond is of longer duration here than in lower mammals generally, which have a shorter estrus. In addition in the primates there is some use of sexual behaviors, especially sexual presentation, throughout the cycle as a means of mitigating aggression of a dominant animal. In an integrated family economy an extension of these tendencies would tend to tie the male and female together socially in a highly advantageous way. There would therefore be a strong selective factor making for the diffusion of sexual activity over the entire menstrual period and therefore a loss of the distinctive estrus phase. The development of a diffuse sexual activity between male and female as a type of socializing behavior would further be favored by ventral copulation which makes sexual play more feasible. Thus some of the distinctive characteristics of human sexuality, absence of estrus, relatively extended sexual activity and sexual play can be visualized as a part of the behavioral adaptation to the integrated family.

In lower mammals sexual behavior is predominantly under endocrine control operating through lower nervous centers. In higher mammals more cortical control independent of endocrines appears, particularly in the male. In the human this trend is strikingly accelerated, both male and female showing predominance of cortical rather than endocrine control of sexual behavior (Beach, 1948; Ford and Beach, 1951). It is here suggested that this shift in mechanism is part of the behavioral shift whereby sexual behavior became part of the socializing mechanism of the higher mammals particularly canines and primates. That this shift then is greatly advanced in the human may be one of the results of the selection pressure consequent upon the sociology of the hunting protohominid. Cortical expansion in the human is thus related to sexual behavior control as well as to the intellectual functions. The mode of that sexual control was however quite different than that suggested by Chance and Mead as discussed in the introduction.

The suggestion of Bartholomew and Birdsell (1953) that the australopithecine male may have used tools in sexual competition need not necessarily be accepted. These authors have developed a concept of family organization in the australopithecines very similar to the one proposed here. In such a relation the sexual dimorphism shown by australopithecines may well be related to the differentiation of male and female function with respect to hunting rather than to intrasexual competition. The failure of the canines to enlarge or show dimorphism in the human line in spite of considerable dimorphism in size is consistent with both hypotheses. But the concept of a high level of male intrasexual competition is not consistent with the hypothesis of the integrated family theory proposed here. It may be that the very multiplicity of factors operating in this connection in human evolution accounts for the plasticity cultural man shows in regard to male-male and male-female relations (Mead, 1949).

The selection pressure favoring integration of the male may also have operated on the incipient language development discussed above. In apes we find that an intense devotion to grooming activity serves as a socializing factor between animals in a group. In human groups it is a common observation that speech, mere talking for the sake of talking in gossip and chit-chat serves a similar socializing function. The selection pressure for the integration of members of the family thus favors the development of speech as a socializing technique and helps account for the babbling of the human infant in contrast with the silence of the chimpanzee child (Hayes, 1951). That this socializing function of speech is correlated with the loss of body hair and much, though not all, of the drive for grooming is obvious but whether they are related as cause and effect or merely as concomitants is not clear. Possibly apes have not lost their hairy covering because of its functional value in grooming.

The social organization of the integrated family visualized above would also shift selective pressures with respect to the development of the offspring. For one thing we might anticipate a relaxation of any pressure for rapid maturation. When the mother becomes permanently domiciled, there is no constant migration with which the young must keep up as there is in food-gathering primates. More important, however, than the relaxation of selection pressure for rapid maturation is a positive selection pressure postponing sexual maturation. Such a pressure would be another consequence of the socialization of the male for the following reason.

In baboon and macaque societies the in-group dominant males drive off the young males as they mature. These then tend to form bachelor groups ever alert for the opportunity of breaking into the mixed groups. The competition between the older in-group males and their male offspring is a disruptive factor in primate society and helps prevent the socialization of the primate males. One way to reduce this disruption is by a delay in attaining maturity. Such a delay would have the further advantage that it would permit a longer period for learning on the part of the young. The importance of an extended period of learning can be appreciated better if it is kept in mind that a complex economy involving hunting, food-gathering and domestic activity requires very different activities in different seasons. Several yearly cycles experienced when the youth is far enough developed to take part in these activities would be most directly favorable for the required learning. This applies to the female as well as the male. The inefficiency in maternal behavior of the primiparous chimpanzee is a case in point (Yerkes and Tomlin, 1935). In a permanent domicile as visualized in the integrated family ecology the learning of maternal behavior by the adolescent female would clearly be favored. It may be pointed out that occasionally daughter coyotes den with their mothers so that the possibility of this kind of learning exists in canines (Jackson, 1951).

Admittedly these inferences as to the sociology of fossil man are speculative. Such speculation based on comparative behavior, however, need not be less reliable than that based on comparative anatomy. Both are necessary for the development of an understanding of the evolution and biology of man. The theory offered above attempts to provide the necessary basis in natural selection for explaining the transition of the evolving human organism from the non-cultural anthropoid level to the lowest cultural level.

It is not necessarily implied that the full range of mental capacity as we find it demonstrated in contemporary man is to be explained on this basis. Indeed the data of comparative behavior and the reasoning based upon it as discussed above make it evident that learning abilities and cooperative activities are related to specific functions in the ecology of the animal. Animals do not seem to develop behaviors that go beyond the functional requirements of their mode of life any more than they develop structures or physiological capacities beyond these requirements. This is a basic concept in our understanding of natural selection.

On this basis we expect selection pressure to push language development only to the point where it serves a function of identification of concrete objects and of socialization but not to the level of its use in abstract thought. Similarly the evolution of cooperative behavior can be explained to the point where it permits a degree of stabilization of the male into the family and pack but no further. In this view the origin of abstract thought, for example, mathematical reasoning and truly ethical behavior (the golden rule), is not explicable in the biological terms developed here. I do not propose to elaborate this conception of the limitation of the biological explanation. I mention it because an understanding of the biology of the transition from the non-cultural to the cultural level must include a comprehension of the limits of any theory as well as of its effectiveness.

SUMMARY

A theory is sought to account for the evolution of the features of human mentality that make culture accumulation possible. Such a theory must suggest not only the selection pressures involved but also the basis in behavior of the protohominid upon which selection operated to lead to man's unique mental equipment. The following theory, based upon recent advances in our knowledge of the paleontology of man, of anthropoid psychology, and of the social behavior of vertebrates is offered. The protohominid lived in integrated family units essentially monogamous with a stable domicile. The male specialized as hunter, the female as domestic. A detailed consideration of the selection pressures operative in such an economy reveal the following modifications of the basic anthropoid adaptations: 1. increased intelligence in tool and fire use on the part of both male and female; 2. the beginning of language development; 3. social integration of the male and female through diffuse sexual behavior with increased cortical control; and 4. extension of the developmental period and the integration of the young males as well as females into the group. These biological factors are held to account for only the first steps toward a culture-capable organism.

REFERENCES

ALLEE, W. C.   1951   Cooperation among animals. New York, Henry Schuman.
ALVERDES, F.   1927   Social life in the animal world. New York, Harcourt, Brace & Co.
BARTHOLOMEW, G. A., JR., and J. B. BIRDSELL   1953   Ecology and the proto-hominids. Amer. Anthropol. 55:481–498.
BEACH, F. A.   1948   Hormones and behavior. New York, Paul Hoeber.
BIRCH, H. G., and G. CLARK   1946   Hormonal modification of social behavior. Psychosomatic Medicine 8:320–331.
———   1950   Hormonal modification of social behavior. IV. The mechanism of

estrogen-induced dominance in chimpanzees. Jour. Comp. and Physiol. 43: 181–193.

BLACK, DAVIDSON 1934 On the discovery, morphology and environment of Sinanthropus pekinensis. Roy. Soc. London, Trans. B 223:57–120.

CARPENTER, C. R. 1934 A field study of the behavior and social relations of howling monkeys. Comp. Psychol. Monog. 10:1–168.

—— 1942 Sexual behavior of free-ranging rhesus monkeys (Macaca mulatta). I. Specimens, procedures and behavioral characteristics of estrus. Jour. Comp. Psychol. 33:113–142.

CHANCE, M. R. A., and A. P. MEAD 1953 Social behaviour and primate evolution. In Symposia of Soc. Exper. Biol. VII. Evolution. Edited by R. Brown and J. F. Donielli, pp. 395–439.

CRAWFORD, M. P. 1940 The relation between social dominance and the menstrual cycle in female chimpanzees. Jour. Comp. Psychol. 30:483–513.

DARLING, F. F. 1937 A herd of red deer. New York, Oxford University Press.

DART, R. A. 1949 The predatory implemental technique of Australopithecus. Amer. Jour. Physical Anthrop. N. S. 7:1–38.

DARWIN, Ch. 1871 The descent of man. London.

DOBZHANSKY, T. 1937 Genetics and the origin of species. New York, Columbia University Press.

DOBZHANSKY, T., and M. F. ASHLEY MONTAGU 1947 Natural selection and the mental capacities of mankind. Science 105:587–590.

EISELEY, LOREN 1953 Fossil man. Scientific American 189: No. 6, pp. 65–72.

FORD, C., and F. A. BEACH 1951 Patterns of sexual behavior. New York, Harper and Bros.

HAYES, C. 1951 The ape in our house. New York, Harper and Bros.

HUXLEY, J. 1941 Man stands alone. New York, Harper and Bros.

JACKSON, H. 1951 The clever coyote. Washington, Wildlife Management Inst.

KEITH, A. 1949 A new theory of human evolution. New York, Philosophical Library.

KELLOGG, W. N., and KELLOGG, L. A. 1933 The ape and the child. New York, McGraw-Hill Co.

KOHLER, W. 1925 The mentality of apes. New York, Harcourt Brace and Co.

MAYR, E. 1942 Systematics and the origin of species. New York, Columbia University Press.

MEAD, M. 1949 Male and female. New York, Wm. Morrow and Co.

MONTAGU, ASHLEY 1960 On being human. New York, Henry Schuman.

—— 1960 An introduction to physical anthropology, 3rd ed. Springfield, Ill., C. C. Thomas.

MURIE, A. 1944 The Wolves of Mount McKinley. Washington, D.C.

NISSEN, H. W. 1931 A field study of the chimpanzee. Comp. Psychol. Monographs 8:1–122.

—— 1951 Social behavior in primates. In C. P. Stone, Comparative Psychology, 3rd ed. New York, Prentice-Hall, pp. 423–457.

READ, CARVETH 1920 The origin of man and his superstitions. Cambridge University Press.

SCHEFFER, V. B., and K. W. KENYON 1952 The fur seal comes of age. National Geog. Mag. 101:491–512.

SCOTT, J. P. 1944 An experimental test of the theory that social behavior determines social organization. Science 99:42–43.

SETON, E. T. 1929 Lives of game animals. New York, Doubleday Doran & Co.

SIMPSON, G. G. 1949 The meaning of evolution. New Haven, Yale University Press.

Tappen, N. C. 1953 A mechanistic theory of human evolution. Amer. Anthropologist 55:605–607.

Tinbergen, N. 1951 The study of instinct. Oxford, Clarendon Press.

—— 1953 Social behavior in animals. London, Methuen Co.

Weidenreich, F. 1946 Apes, giants and man. Chicago, Univ. Chicago Press.

—— 1947 The trend of human evolution. Evolution 1:221–236.

Yerkes, R. M. 1939 Social dominance and sexual status in the chimpanzee. Quart. Rev. Biol. 14:115–136.

—— 1943 Chimpanzees. New Haven, Yale University Press.

Yerkes, R. M., and M. Tomilin 1935 Mother-infant relations in chimpanzees. Jour. Comp. Psychology 20:321–359.

Young, S. P., and E. Goldman 1944 The wolves of North America. Washington, Amer. Wildlife Inst.

Zuckerman, S. 1932 The social life of monkeys and apes. New York, Harcourt, Brace and Co.

SUPPLEMENTAL DISCUSSION. DECEMBER 1960

A number of studies have appeared since the above paper was published which bear significantly upon its conclusions. Eiseley (1956) points out a basic hiatus in our presentation in the failure to analyze the psychological pre-adaptations attained by primates for the development of speech. He emphasizes the high development of an integrated space-time perception as a necessary condition of primate arboreal adaptation and urges that this capacity is fundamental for use of symbols in speech. In this connection it is interesting to point to the conclusion of Penfield and Roberts (1959) regarding the functional significance of the right and left parieto-temporal area of the cortex. They identify this in the left cortex as the principal ideational area for speech and in the right they report it functionally concerned with body-scheme and movement in space. This correspondence lends a physiological basis to Eiseley's perceptive suggestion. In agreement with Dobzhansky and Montagu, and others as mentioned in our discussion, Eiseley emphasizes that the early establishment of cultural society provides a basis of selection for human mentality making for the basic similarity in all racial lines. He also points to the possible extension of selective factors operating in this area to the origin of some of those higher mental functions to which we confessed our biological approach unable to penetrate.

Washburn, Spuhler and others have revived the discussion of tool use and manufacture in the evolution of man's mentality (see Spuhler 1959). Furthermore, Washburn (1957) has contended that the australopithecines rather than being hunters were more likely themselves the hunted. He therefore regards them ecologically as food gatherers who may have used artificially fashioned wooden implements to increase their efficiency. In this view, hunting ecology, the basis of our analysis, did not appear until much later in human evolution. The point is not crucial for our contention since the expansion of the brain is largely a post-australopithecine phenomenon in human evolution. However, it must be said that in the opinion of this author, a judicious evaluation of the earlier evidence (for example, Howell 1959) strongly supports Dart's picture of the australopithecines as living at least partly by the hunting of medium-sized game. The more recent writings of Dart (1958, 1960) on the extent of the bone-tool culture associated with these creatures and above all the discovery of Zinjanthropus (Leakey 1959) with the clearly associated paleoliths further strongly support the interpretation of the South African anthropologists that the australopithecines were hunters.

From the point of view of the student of behavior, the revived inclination to consider tools as providing the crucial factor in the early mental development of man seems unfortunate. As long as the basic ecology of the human line of evolution is considered to have remained the same as that of other primates (i.e. food gathering on an individualistic basis) there is no reason to see different selection pressures for mental development in man than in other primates. Tool use can hardly be considered as constituting the outstanding distinction between human and ape mentality, hence, in looking in this direction we are inevitably taking a non-selectionist viewpoint. Selection for tool use might be expected to lead to effective tool use not to language, concept and symbol formation, cooperative and parental disposition in the male, or any of the many other characteristics of human as contrasted to ape mentality. We must suppose man's ecology had changed fundamentally to account for the uniqueness of his mental evolution. This is not to deny that the use of tools did contribute to the evolution of human mentality. It must however have come in a new ecological context, one which involved at the same time a social behavioral revolution promoting the development of language and the characteristic human familial sociality. The evidence from the australopithecines justifies our looking to the change to a hunting ecology as the basis for this development as in the preceding paper.

A neglected point in recent discussions is that of the bipedalism and upright posture of the australopithecines. On morphological grounds this seems well established and generally accepted. Yet there has been little consideration of the ecological significance of this fact. It is hardly consistent with a food gathering ecology for which the oblique position characteristic of the gorilla and chimpanzee with hands on the ground and vision directed downwards while in locomotion seems most suited. The upright posture gives freedom of distant vision, capacity for long sustained movement and above all freedom in the use of the hands while in active movement. These are important assets for hunters rather than gleaners. We believe, therefore, that the more recent development of our knowledge of the australopithecines reinforces our conclusion, spelled out in detail in the 1954 paper, that the social behavioral correlates devolving upon the adoption of a hunting ecology were from that stage of evolution onward among the principal determinants of the direction of man's evolution in mentality.

REFERENCES FOR SUPPLEMENTAL DISCUSSION

DART, RAYMOND   1958   The minimal bone-breccia content of Makapansgat and the australopithecine predatory habit. Amer. Anthropol. 60:923–930.

—— 1960   The bone tool-manufacturing ability of *Australopithecus prometheus*. Amer. Anthropol. 62:134–143.

EISELEY, LOREN C.   1956   Fossil man and human evolution: *in* Thomas (ed.) Yearbook of Anthropology 1955, pp. 61–78. University of Chicago Press.

HOWELL, F. CLARK   1959   The Villafranchian and human origins. Science 130: 831–844.

LEAKEY, L. S. B.   1959   A new fossil skull from Olduvai. Nature 184:492–493.

PENFIELD, WILDER, and L. ROBERTS   1959   Speech and brain mechanisms. Princeton University Press.

SPUHLER, J. N. (ED.)   1959   The evolution of man's capacity for culture. Detroit, Wayne State University Press.

WASHBURN, S. L.   1957   Australopithecines: the hunters or the hunted? Amer. Anthropol. 59:612–614.

NATURAL SELECTION

AND THE MENTAL CAPACITIES

OF MANKIND

TH. DOBZHANSKY and M. F. ASHLEY MONTAGU

The fundamental mechanisms of the transmission of heredity from parents to offspring are surprisingly uniform in most diverse organisms. Their uniformity is perhaps the most remarkable fact disclosed by genetics. The laws discovered by Mendel apply to human genes just as much as to those of the maize plant, and the processes of cellular division and germ cell maturation in man are not very different from those in a grasshopper. The similarity of the mechanisms of heredity on the individual level is reflected on the population level in a similarity of the basic causative factors of organic evolution throughout the living world. Mutation, selection, and genetic drift are important in the evolution of man as well as in amoebae and in bacteria. Wherever sexuality and cross-fertilization are established as exclusive or predominant methods of reproduction, the field of hereditary variability increases enormously as compared with asexual or self-fertilizing organisms. Isolating mechanisms which prevent inter-breeding and fusion of species of mammals are operative also among insects.

Nevertheless, the universality of basic genetic mechanisms and of evolutionary agents permits a variety of evolutionary patterns to exist not only in different lines of descent but even at different times in the same line of descent. It is evident that the evolutionary pattern in the dog species under domestication is not the same as in the wild ancestors of the domestic dogs or in the now living wild relatives. Widespread occurrence of reduplication of chromosome complements (polyploidy) in the evolution of plants introduces complexities which are not found in the animal kingdom, where polyploidy is infrequent. Evolutionary situations among parasites and among cave inhabitants are clearly different from those in free-living forms. Detection and analysis of differences in the evolutionary patterns in different organisms is one of the important tasks of modern evolutionists.

It can scarcely be doubted that man's biological heredity is transmitted by mechanisms similar to those encountered in other animals and in plants. Likewise, there is no reason to believe that the evolutionary development of man has involved causative factors other than those operative in the evolution of other organisms. The evolutionary changes that occurred before

Reprinted by permission from *Science*, 105:2736 (1947), 587–90.

the pre-human could become human, as well as those which supervened since the attainment of the human estate, can be described causally only in terms of mutation, selection, genetic drift, and hybridization—familiar processes throughout the living world. This reasoning, indisputable in the purely biological context, becomes a fallacy, however, when used, as it often has been, to justify narrow biologism in dealing with human material.

The specific human features of the evolutionary pattern of man cannot be ignored. Man is a unique product of evolution in that he, far more than any other creature, has escaped from the bondage of the physical and the biological into the multiform social environment. This remarkable development introduces a third dimension in addition to those of the external and internal environments—a dimension which many biologists, in considering the evoluton of man, tend to neglect. The most important setting of human evolution is the human social environment. As stated above, this can influence evolutionary changes only through the media of mutation, selection, genetic drift, and hybridization. Nevertheless, there can be no genuine clarity in our understanding of man's biological nature until the role of the social factor in the development of the human species is understood. A biologist approaching the problems of human evolution must never lost sight of the truth stated more than 2,000 years ago by Aristotle: "Man is by nature a political animal."

In the words of Fisher, "For rational systems of evolution, that is, for theories which make at least the most familiar facts intelligible to the reason, we must turn to those that make progressive adaptation the driving force of the process." It is evident that man by means of his reasoning abilities, by becoming a "political animal," has achieved a mastery of the world's varying environments quite unprecedented in the history of organic evolution. The system of genes which has permitted the development of the specifically human mental capacities has thus become the foundation and the paramount influence in all subsequent evolution of the human stock. An animal becomes adapted to its environment by evolving certain genetically determined physical and behavioral traits; the adaptation of man consists chiefly in developing his inventiveness, a quality to which his physical heredity predisposes him and which his social heredity provides him with the means of realizing. To the degree to which this is so, man is unique. As far as his physical responses to the world are concerned, he is almost wholly emancipated from dependence upon inherited biological dispositions, uniquely improving upon the latter by the process of learning that which his social heredity (culture) makes available to him. Man possesses much more efficient means of achieving immediate or long-term adaptation than any other biological species: namely, through learned responses or novel inventions and improvisations.

In general, two types of biological adaptation in evolution can be distinguished. One is genetic specialization and genetically controlled fixity of traits. The second consists in the ability to respond to a given range of environmental situations by evolving traits favorable in these particular situations; this presupposes genetically controlled plasticity of traits. It is known, for example, that the composition of the blood which is most favorable for life at high altitudes is somewhat different from that which suffices at sea level. A species which ranges from sea level to high altitudes on a mountain range may become differentiated into several altitudinal races, each having a fixed blood composition favored by natural selection at the particular altitude at which it lives; or a genotype may be selected which permits an individual to respond to changes in the atmospheric pressure by definite alterations in the composition of the blood. It is well known that heredity determines in its possessor not the presence or absence of certain traits but, rather, the responses of the organism to its environments. The responses may be more or less rigidly fixed, so that approximately the same traits develop in all environments in which life is possible. On the other hand, the responses may differ in different environments. Fixity or plasticity of a trait is, therefore, genetically controlled.

Whether the evolutionary adaptation in a given phyletic line will occur chiefly by way of genetic fixity or by way of genetically controlled plasticity of traits will depend on circumstances. In the first place, evolutionary changes are compounded of mutational steps, and consequently the kind of change that takes place is always determined by the composition of the store of mutational variability which happens to be available in the species populations. Secondly, fixity or plasticity of traits is controlled by natural selection. Having a trait fixed by heredity and hence appearing in the development of an individual regardless of environmental variations is, in general, of benefit to organisms whose milieu remains uniform and static except for rare and freakish deviations. Conversely, organisms which inhabit changeable environments are benefited by having their traits plastic and modified by each recurrent configuration of environmental agents in a way most favorable for the survival of the carrier of the trait in question.

Comparative anatomy and embryology show that a fairly general trend in organic evolution seems to be from environmental dependence toward fixation of the basic features of the bodily structure and function. The appearance of these structural features in the embryonic development of higher organisms is, in general, more nearly autonomous and independent of the environment than in lower forms. The development becomes "buffered" against environmental and genetic shocks. If, however, the mode of life of a species happens to be such that it is, of necessity, exposed to a wide range of environments, it becomes desirable to vary some structures and functions in accordance with the circumstances that confront an individual or a strain at a given time and place. Genetic structures which permit adaptive plasticity of traits become, then, obviously advantageous for survival and so are fostered by natural selection.

The social environments that human beings have created everywhere are notable not only for their extreme complexity but also for the rapid changes to which immediate adjustment is demanded. Adjustment occurs chiefly in the psychical realm and has little or nothing to do with physical traits. In view of the fact that from the very beginning of human evolution the changes in the human environment have been not only rapid but diverse and manifold, genetic fixation of behavioral traits in man would have been decidedly unfavorable for survival of individuals as well as of the species as a whole. Success of the individual in most human societies has depended and continues to depend upon his ability rapidly to evolve behavior patterns which fit him to the kaleidoscope of the conditions he encounters. He is best off if he submits to some, compromises with some, rebels against others, and escapes from still other situations. Individuals who display a relatively greater fixity of response than their fellows suffer under most forms of human society and tend to fall by the way. Suppleness, plasticity, and, most important of all, ability to profit by experience and education are required. No other species is comparable to man in its capacity to acquire new behavior patterns and discard old ones in consequence of training. Considered socially as well as biologically, man's outstanding capacity is his educability. The survival value of this capacity is manifest, and therefore the possibility of its development through natural selection is evident.

It should be made clear at this point that the replacement of fixity of behavior by genetically controlled plasticity is not a necessary consequence of all forms of social organization. The quaint attempts to glorify insect societies as examples deserving emulation on the part of man ignore the fact that the behavior of an individual among social insects is remarkable precisely because of the rigidity of its genetic fixation. The perfection of the organized societies of ants, termites, bees, and other insects is indeed wonderful, and the activities of their members may strike an observer very forcibly by their objective purposefulness. This purposefulness is retained, however, only in environments in which the species normally lives. The ability of an ant to adust its activities to situations not encountered in the normal habitats of its species is very limited. On the other hand, social organizations on the human level are built on the principle that an individual is able to alter his behavior to fit any situation, whether previously experienced or new.

This difference between human and insect societies is, of course, not surprising. Adaptive plasticity of behavior can develop only on the basis of a vastly more complex nervous system than is sufficient for adaptive fixity. The genetic differences between human and insect societies furnish a striking illustration of the two types of evolutionary adaptations—those achieved through genetically controlled plasticity of behavioral traits and those attained through genetic specialization and fixation of behavior.

The genetically controlled plasticity of mental traits is, biologically speaking, the most typical and uniquely human characteristic. It is very probable that the survival value of this characteristic in human evolution has been considerable for a long time, as measured in terms of human historical scales. Just when this characteristic first appeared is, of course, conjectural. Here it is of interest to note that the most marked phylogenetic trend in the evolution of man has been the special development of the brain, and that the characteristic human plasticity of mental traits seems to be associated with the exceptionally large brain size. The brain of, for example, the Lower or Middle Pleistocene fossil forms of man was, grossly at least, scarcely distinguishable from that of modern man. The average Neanderthaloid brain was somewhat larger than that of modern man, though slightly different in shape. More important than the evidence derived from brain size is the testimony of cultural development. The Middle Acheulean handiwork of Swanscombe man of several hundred thousand years ago and the beautiful Mousterian cultural artifacts associated with Neanderthal man indicate the existence of minds of a high order of development.

The cultural evidence thus suggests that the essentially human organization of the mental capacities emerged quite early in the evolution of man. However that may be, the possession of the gene system, which conditions educability rather than behavioral fixity, is a common property of all living mankind. In other words, educability is truly a species character of man, *Homo sapiens*. This does not mean, of course, that the evolutionary process has run its course and that natural selection has introduced no changes in the genetic structure of the human species since the attainment of the human status. Nor do we wish to imply that no genetic variations in mental equipment exist at our time level. On the contrary, it seems likely that with the attainment of human status that part of man's genetic system which is related to mental potentialities did not cease to be labile and subject to change.

This brings us face to face with the old problem of the likelihood that significant genetic differences in the mental capacities of the various ethnic groups of mankind exist. The physical and, even more, the social environments of men who live in different countries are quite diversified. Therefore, it has often been argued, natural selection would be expected to differentiate the human species into local races differing in psychic traits. Populations of different countries may differ in skin color, head shape, and other somatic characters. Why, then, should they be alike in mental traits?

It will be through investigation rather than speculation that the problem of the possible existence of average differences in the mental make-up of human populations of different geographical origins will eventually be settled. Arguments based on analogies are precarious, especially where evolutionary patterns are concerned. If human races differ in structural traits, it does not necessarily follow that they must also differ in mental ones. Race differences arise chiefly because of the differential action of natural selection on geographically separated populations. In the case of man, however, the structural and mental traits are quite likely to be influenced by selection in different ways.

The very complex problem of the origin of racial differentiations in structural traits does not directly concern us here. Suffice it to say that racial differences in traits such as the blood groups may conceivably have been brought about by genetic drift in populations of limited effective size. Other racial traits are genetically too complex and too consistently present in populations of some large territories and absent in other territories to be accounted for by genetic drift alone. Differences in skin color, hair form, nose shape, etc. are almost certainly products of natural selection. The lack of reliable knowledge of the adaptive significance of these traits is perhaps the greatest gap in our understanding of the evolutionary biology of man. Nevertheless, it is at least a plausible working hypothesis that these and similar traits have, or at any rate had in the past, differential survival values in the environments of different parts of the world.

By contrast, the survival value of a higher development of mental capacities in man is obvious. Furthermore, natural selection seemingly favors such a development everywhere. In the ordinary course of events in almost all societies those persons are likely to be favored who show wisdom, maturity of judgment, and ability to get along with people—qualities which may assume different forms in different cultures. Those are the qualities of the plastic personality, not a single trait but a general condition, and this is the condition which appears to have been at a premium in practically all human societies.

In human societies conditions have been neither rigid nor stable enough to permit the selective breeding of genetic types adapted to different statuses or forms of social organization. Such rigidity and stability do not obtain in any society. On the other hand, the outstanding fact about human societies is that they do change and do so more or less rapidly. The rate of change was possibly comparatively slow in earlier societies, as the rate of change in present-day nonliterate societies may be, when compared to the rate characterizing occidental societies. In any event, rapid changes in behavior are demanded of the person at all levels of social organization even when the society is at its most stable. Life at any level of social development in human societies is a pretty complex business, and it is met and handled most efficiently by those who exhibit the greatest capacity for adaptability, plasticity.

It is this very plasticity of his mental traits which confers upon man the unique position which he occupies in the animal kingdom. Its acquisition freed him from the constraint of a limited range of biologically predetermined responses. He became capable of acting in a more or less regulative manner upon his physical environment instead of being largely regulated by it. The processes of natural selection in all climes and at all times have favored genotypes which permit greater and greater educability and plasticity of mental traits under the influence of the uniquely social environments to which man has been continuously exposed.

The effect of natural selection in man has probably been to render genotypic differences in personality traits, as between individuals and particularly as between races, relatively unimportant compared to their phenotypic plasticity. Instead of having his responses genetically fixed as in other animal species, man is a species that invents its own responses, and it is out of this unique ability to invent, to improvise, his responses that his cultures are born.

CULTURE

AND THE STRUCTURAL EVOLUTION

OF THE NEURAL SYSTEM

FRED A. METTLER

Two propositions, considered more or less self-evident, have played prominent roles in the consideration of the evolutionary development of man. Indeed, it is often assumed that reference to these propositions is sufficient to decide any doubtful issue as to whether or not man's present structural condition represents an advance over the past. In the first place it has been widely asserted that the size of the brain has steadily increased in those biologic lines leading (and related) to man and that this process has continued until the present and will probably continue through the future. In the second place it is universally assumed that this is or would be a good thing, because, the argument runs, a large brain (especially one with a large frontal lobe) is positively correlated with a high order of intelligence, and the present state of man's development depends upon this alleged cerebral increase.

It will be necessary in the following pages to question the validity of these assumptions, which really are far from self-evident, for there are definite data demonstrating that the size of man's brain has not continued to increase to the present. Moreover, there is good reason to believe that useful or workable intelligence, as we employ the term in day-to-day terminology, is a general aspect of capacity for over-all neural efficiency rather than a localized brain function, and that, in view of the dependence of the individual upon learned cultural traits, the frontal lobe may not be an indispensable substrate for "intelligent" living. I hope then to present certain technical reasons which lead me to question whether *Homo sapiens* can profitably develop a significantly enlarged brain without first undergoing rather radical structural and physiologic alterations in other respects, for it is possible that the size of man's brain might prove to be a limiting factor not merely in his further structural evolution but even in his survival.

Finally I wish to emphasize the role that culture has played in protecting the individual from his natural environment on the one hand (and thus shielding him from the necessity of developing structural adaptations to it) and, on the other, of creating new environmental demands. I shall conclude with a brief inquiry into the nature of these demands and whether or not

The James Arthur Lecture on the Evolution of the Human Brain, New York, American Museum of Natural History, 1955. Reprinted by permission.

the nervous system may be expected to serve as the limiting factor in meeting them.

HAS MAN'S BRAIN CONTINUED TO INCREASE IN SIZE AND
IS BRAIN SIZE POSITIVELY CORRELATED WITH INTELLIGENCE?

One of the basic difficulties in coming to a decision about the evolutionary trend of the brain is the fact that modern man's brain is far from constant in size, shape, or configuration. This situation has long been known, but people, and scientists are no exception, show a strong disinclination to pay attention to data that do not fit into a frame of reference in which the other data are more or less in concurrence (Craik, 1952).

Many years ago Vierordt (1893) brought together the brain-weight data for different geopolitical groups, which are shown here in table 1. In this

TABLE I

ABSOLUTE AVERAGE WEIGHTS (IN GRAMS) OF BRAINS OF EUROPEANS TWENTY TO EIGHTY YEARS OLD FROM DIFFERENT EUROPEAN POLITICO-GEOGRAPHIC DISTRICTS (FROM VIERORDT), 1893)

Investigator	Source of Material	Male	Female
Krause	Hanover	1461	1341
F. Arnold	Grand Duchy of Baden	1431	1312
Reid	Scotland	1424	1262
Peacock	Scotland	1423	1273
Sims	England	1412	1292
Tiedemann	Grand Duchy of Baden	1412	1246
Quain	England	1400	1250
G. H. Bergmann	Hanover	1372	1272
Rud. Wagner	Mixed	1362	1242
Th. von Bischoff	Bavaria	1362	1219
Sappey	France	1358	1256
Huschke	Saxony	1358	1230
Hoffmann	Switzerland	1350	1250
Blosfeld	Russia	1346	1195
Clendinning	England	1333	1197
Dieberg	Russia	1328	1238
Boyd	England	1325	1183
Parchappe	France	1323	1210
Lelut	France	1320	
W. Hamilton	Scotland	1309	1190
Meynert	Austria	1296	1170
Parisot	France	1287	1217
Weisbach	German-Austrian	1265	1112

table variations of well over 10 per cent in brain weight are obvious, not among markedly different races but among white Europeans. Various reasons could be advanced for such differences. They might be due to genotypic variability, having its basis in racial subvarieties and apart from other somatic variation, or they might be a general reflection of differences in corporeal size. (A variation according to sex is explicit in the table.) Again, such variation might be due to age or correlated with differences in intellectual capacity.

In a consideration of the relation of age to brain volume, which is closely related to brain weight, table 2 demonstrates that the brain, whereas it becomes larger with age, reaches its maximum gross size long before the body does and that, beginning around 50 years of age, it ultimately becomes absolutely smaller.

As a result of such an observation, one would expect that body weight would not be a very satisfactory index of brain size, and table 3 shows that beyond a certain point the relationship between these two variables may be

TABLE 2

RELATION BETWEEN AGE AND VOLUME OF BRAIN

	Number of Cases		Volume of Brain (in Cc.)	
Age	Male	Female	Male	Female
0– 6 months	29	28	499	478
7–12 months	19	24	772	700
2 years	9	10	929	976
3 years	11	9	1123	1038
4 years	11	9	1190	1049
5– 6 years	8	11	1300	1147
7–10 years	9	12	1333	1204
11–15 years	9	10	1285	1213
16–19 years	13	10	1289	1099
20–29 years	73	43	1223	1148
30–39 years	74	59	1279	1193
40–49 years	77	60	1264	1164
50–59 years	80	57	1275	1146
60–69 years	84	65	1237	1143
70–79 years	70	55	1212	1088
80–89 years	10	23	1164	1072

TABLE 3

BRAIN WEIGHT CONSIDERED AS A PROPORTION OF TOTAL BODY WEIGHT (FROM VIERORDT, 1893, AFTER BISCHOFF)

Body Weight (in Kilograms)	Brain Weight	
	Male	Female
20		4.47%
30	3.7 %	3.37%
40	2.98%	2.70%
50	2.5 %	2.29%
60	2.16%	1.99%
70	1.99%	
80	1.59%	

TABLE 4

WEIGHT OF THE BRAIN (ENCEPHALON) AND ITS SUBSIDIARY PARTS IN SANE PERSONS, ACCORDING TO SEX, AGE, AND STATURE (FROM DONALDSON, 1895) (a, above average according to age; s, average according to stature.)

	Age	Encephalon	Cerebrum	Cerebellum	Stem
Males					
Stature 175 cm.	20–40	1409	1232	149	28
and upward	41–70	1363	1192	144	27
	71–90	1330	1167	137	26
Stature 172-	20–40	1360	1188	144	28
167 cm.	41–70	1335	1164	144	27
	71–90	1305	1135	142 s	28 a s
Stature 164 cm.	20–40	1331	1168	138	25
and under	41–70	1297	1123	139 a	25
	71–90	1251	1095	131	25
Females					
Stature 163 cm.	20–40	1265	1108	134	23
and upward	41–70	1209	1055	131	23
	71–90	1166	1012	130	24 a
Stature 160-	20–40	1218	1055	137 s	26 s
155 cm.	41–70	1212 s	1055	131	26 s
	71–90	1121	969 s	128	24
Stature 152 cm.	20–40	1199	1045	130	24 s
and under	41–70	1205 a	1051 a	129	25 a s
	71–90	1122	974	123	25 a s

of an inverse nature. Because weight is a poor indication of actual somatic development, stature and degree of muscular development should be correlated with variations in cerebral weight, but tables giving such information have not yet been developed. Because brain volume is obviously influenced by age, some correction for the latter factor must be introduced. Tables of this nature have long been available and show a definite positive correlation between brain weight and stature (table 4) when corrected for age (Donaldson, 1895; Dubois, 1914).

Table 4 may be compared with table 5 to see whether the size of the brain is correlated with condition of rationality. It will be observed that no significant difference is disclosed by comparison of these two sets of old figures. Although the validity of these figures has been abundantly contested in the years which have passed since they were compiled, no one has yet been able to bring forward conclusive data that the brains of insane persons are customarily smaller or lighter than those of a corresponding "normal" population, although, of course, they may be so.

If we cannot explain variation in brain weight on the basis of rationality or its absence, we may ask whether weight variations not accounted for by sex, age, or body size can be explained on the basis of the possession of

TABLE 5

WEIGHT OF THE BRAIN (ENCEPHALON) AND ITS SUBSIDIARY PARTS IN INSANE PERSONS, ACCORDING TO SEX, AGE, AND STATURE (FROM DONALDSON, 1895) (a, above average according to age; s, above average according to stature.)

	Age	Encephalon	Cerebrum	Cerebellum	Stem
400 Males					
Stature 175 cm.	20–40	1378	1192	156	30
and upward	41–70	1354	1170	154	30
	71–90	1333	1158	146	29
Stature 172-	20–40	1363	1186	149	28
167 cm.	41–70	1305	1129	148	28
	71–90	1305	1135 a	142	28
Stature 164 cm.	20–40	1299	1127	144	28
and under	41–70	1285	1119	139	28
	71–90	1216	1047	139	30 s a
325 Females					
Stature 163 cm.	20–40	1220	1056	136	28
and upward	41–70	1215	1053	134	28
	71–90	1240 a	1076 a	136 a	28
Stature 160-	20–40	1189	1027	134	28
155 cm.	41–70	1216 s a	1054 s a	135 s a	27
	71–90	1171	1008	135 a	28 a
Stature 152 cm.	20–40	1141	986	128	28
and under	41–70	1194 a	1036 a	129 a	28 s a
	71–90	1135	985	123	27

unusual intellectual capacities on the part of some of the population. A comparison of the values in table 6, which gives the weights of the brains of certain eminent individuals, with the weights shown in table 1 discloses a range of from 1226 to 1830 grams for eminent individuals between 39 and 82 years of age as compared with 1265 to 1461 grams for average values of samples taken from all over Europe. Moreover, the range encountered in eminence covers the average for insane persons of the same age groups (table 5).

Weidenreich (1946) gives the range of skull capacity for normal individuals in all races of modern man as being from 910 to 2100 cc. As the weight of one cubic centimeter of cerebral tissue is about unity (1.036 grams) and the brain generally occupies two-thirds of the total endocranial capacity, Weidenreich tacitly accepts a weight range of from 625 to 1450 grams as normal. With such figures it would be quite impossible to determine whether any sort of trend in cerebral size has been operative during the last half of the Pleistocene (figs. 1 and 2). Indeed, Weidenreich's range can have really very little meaning even in modern times unless we neglect entirely the influence of age which is operative over a much longer period with regard to skull size (fig. 3) than with regard to brain volume (table 2).

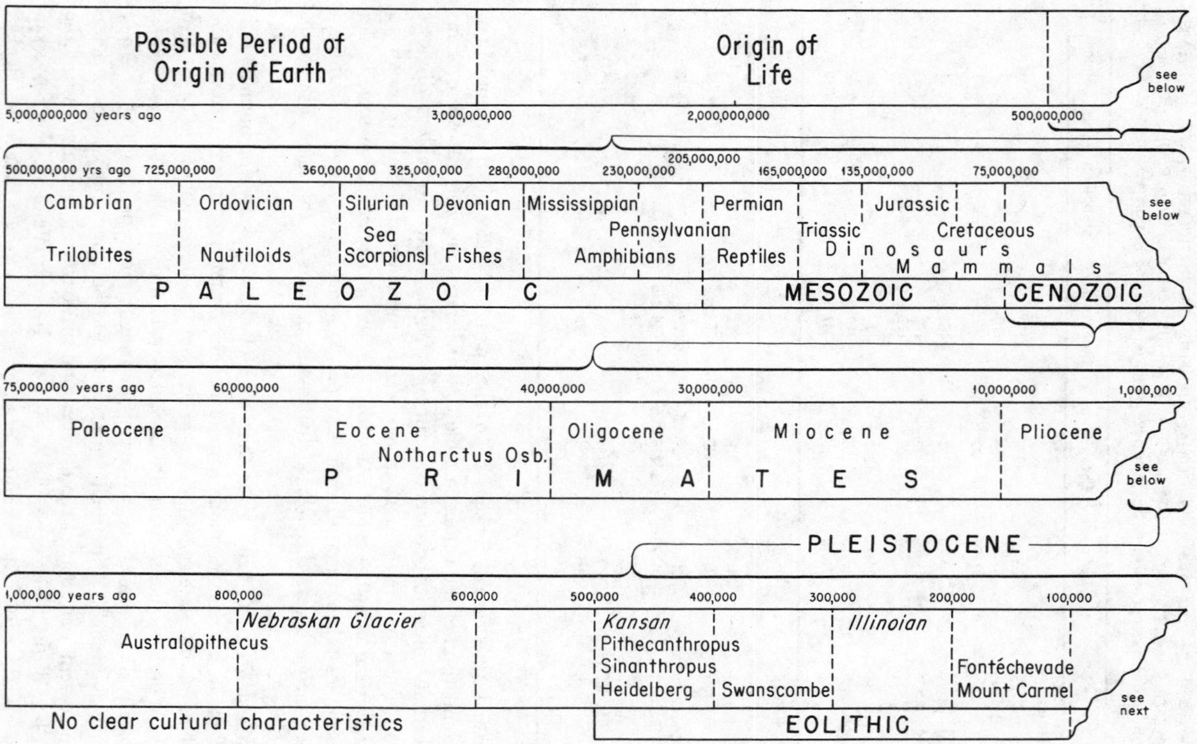

Fig. 1 Approximate time table for origin of man. In second bar graph, right terminal portion of first bar graph is enlarged, as shown by bracketed material. Terminal right portion again enlarged in third bar graph, and so on.

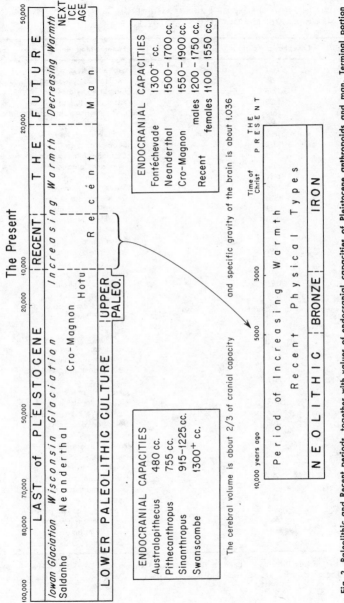

Fig. 2 Paleolithic and Recent periods, together with values of endocranial capacities of Pleistocene anthropoids and man. Terminal portion of last bar graph in figure 1 reproduced in enlarged form.

TABLE 6

BRAIN WEIGHTS (IN GRAMS) OF EMINENT MEN (FROM DONALDSON, 1895, TAKEN FROM MARSHALL AND MANOUVRIER)*

Age	Encephalic Weight	Eminent Men
39	1457	Skobeleff, Russian general
40	1238	G. Harless, physiologist
43	1294	Gambetta, statesmen
45	1403	Assezat, political writer
45	1516	Chauncey Wright, mathematician
49	1468	Asseline, political writer
49	1409	J. Huber, philosopher
5[0]	1312	Seizel, sculptor
50	1378	Coudereau, physician
52	1358	Hermann, philologist
52	1499	Fuchs, pathologist
53	1644	Thackeray, novelist
54	1520	De Morny, statesman
54	1629	Goodsir, anatomist
55	1520	Derichlet, mathematician
56	1503	Schleich, writer
56	1485	Broca, anthropologist
57	1559	Spurzheim, phrenologist
57	1250	v. Lasualx, physician
59	1436	Dupuytren, surgeon
60	1533	J. Simpson, physician
60	1488	Pfeufer, physician
62	1398	Bertillon, anthropologist
62[?]	1415	Melchior Mayer, poet
63	1449	Lamarque, general
63	1332	J. Hughes Bennett, physician
63	1830	G. Cuvier, naturalist
64	1785	Abercrombie, physician
65	1498	De Morgan, mathematician
66	1512	Agassiz, naturalist
67	1502	Chalmers, preacher
70	1352	Liebig, chemist
70	1516	Daniel Webster, statesman
71	1207	Döllinger, anatomist
71	1349	Fallmerayer, historian
71	1390	Whewell, philosopher
73	1590	Hermann, economist
75	1410	Grote, historian
77	1226	Hausemann, mineralogist
78	1492	Gauss, mathematician
79	1254	Tiedemann, anatomist
79	1403	Babbage, mathematician
79	1452	Ch. H. Bischoff, physician
80	1290	Grant, anatomist
82	1516	Campbell, Lord Chancellor

* The entries in this table have been in part revised. Different methods have of course been employed in determining the several weights.

We know, of course, that skull volume does not change appreciably between 50 and 90 years in normal individuals, but we have seen (table 2) that the brain does become atrophic. Now we observe that, although the volume of the brain does not increase notably after the first decade of life, head size does increase quite regularly through and even beyond the second decade. (The skull itself thickens in essentially the same period as skull size increases, if we accept Roche's, 1953, figures for the former dimension.) Estimates of endocranial capacity urgently require qualification, in terms of age at least, and it is impossible to be dogmatic about the age of skulls on the basis of the degree of suture closure (Cobb, 1954).

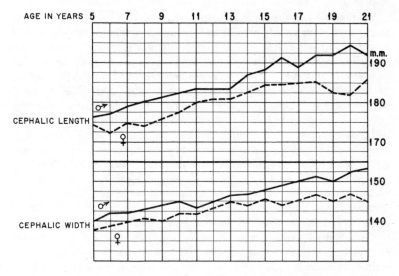

Fig. 3 Age changes in length and breadth of head (from Donaldson, 1895, after West).

Measurements of the volume of the brain are themselves not beyond the possibility of misinterpretation. Physical anthropologists are well aware that large brains often hide dilated, water-containing ventricles. Even brain weights may suffer from artifactual error.

Table 7, the source of which shall remain unidentified by me, is an interesting example of incredible nonsense which might have been produced as the result of the operation of rather simple artifactual principles, notably the post-mortem changes in weight and volume that brains undergo. It is surprising how easily startling results can be achieved as a consequence of artifact.

Some years ago Lewis Rowland and I set out to determine whether the brains of psychotic persons contain fewer cells per unit of cubic volume than do normal brains (Rowland and Mettler, 1949). When we compared our figures, obtained on material from living psychotics, with the values in the literature for normal brains, we came to the astonishing conclusion that the material from our psychotic individuals quite regularly exhibited not merely the same number of cells as, but *more* than, that obtained from normal humans! This curious paradox became explicable when we recalled that all the available figures for the "normal" brain were based upon post-mortem material, whereas our specimens had been obtained from living persons during psychosurgical operations. Although all tissues shrink during histological preparation, the post-mortem material had undergone an intervening swelling which occurred after death and which continued during fixation in the formalin.

Fixation-swelling gradually reverses itself, and the brain returns to and then passes below its original size and weight, depending upon how long it remains in a fixative. It is obvious that in instances in which an investigator was particularly interested in what he considered a rare or valuable brain he would study this as soon as it was adequately fixed and thus at the peak of its artifactual increase in size (von Economo, 1929). On the other hand, the brains of such ordinary folk as "laborers" would be left in a common crock to be weighed and measured at leisure—or, in other words, after they had passed the period of swelling and had begun to shrink. Further, such brains would probably have been removed by less careful assistants who may have ripped off the infundibulum and the membranes of the lateral and median cerebellar recesses so that, with shrinkage, all the contained ventricular fluid would run out to be replaced by air during the process of draining before weighing. I suspect forces of such a nature to have been operative in the development of the data shown in table 7.

Artifactual confusion due to solicitude for "rare" material can be even more profound. It is the custom, when histologic studies are contemplated, to perfuse the tissue to be removed. Until now we have had very little evidence about how such perfusion solutions influence quantitative studies of neural

TABLE 7

EXAMPLE OF MANNER IN WHICH BRAIN WEIGHTS CAN BE EMPLOYED TO BOLSTER AN HYPOTHESIS (see text)

Occupation	Number of Cases	Weight	Percentage Over 1400 Grams
Day laborers	14	1410 ⎫	
Laborers	34	1433 ⎬	26.2
Attendants, supervisors	14	1436 ⎭	
Tradespeople, craftsmen	123	1450	42.8
Minor officials	28	1469	48.5
Major officials, physicians	22	1500	57.2

elements. Professor José Frontera-Reichert of the Department of Anatomy of the Medical School of Puerto Rico has recently shown me figures he has obtained from brains perfused with a variety of mixtures commonly employed for such a purpose. The results clearly indicate that we must reinterpret much "standard" data, for not only do all these fluids engender swelling, but the extent to which cytologic counts of surface elements, such as those in the cerebral cortex, are affected is variably influenced by the magnitude of the radius of the spherical substance which is the brain.

We come therefore to the necessity of concluding that brain size, whether determined by weight or volume, must, like that of other genotypically determined portions of the body, be considered in association not only with factors of handling and age and sex but also in connection with the general bodily characteristics of the individual from whence the material came. There is a direct correlation between the morphology of the brain and race, but that this correlation has any particular meaning in terms of what we call intelligence remains to be demonstrated and, as is shown below, it would be very surprising if a simple correlation could be derived. In attempting to arrive at an opinion as to whether or not modern man's brain has increased in size, we are necessarily forced to deal with endocranial capacities. From what is said above it is clear that a systematic body of data relating encephalon to endocranial capacity has not yet been developed, as this must necessarily be part of the still lacking correlation between brain and body type. Allowing for the shortcomings of the material, we can, however, see if what is available to us discloses any recognizable evolutionary trend.

Endocranial capacity shows variations with regard to sex and bodily development, and these seem to be like those influencing the size of the brain, but we have already commented that the age alterations in endocranial capacity are restricted to the first third of life and progress more slowly than does brain growth. We might expect that, because most primitive races were much smaller than modern man, they might be anticipated to have had smaller endocranial capacities, and this is true. Cro-Magnon man, who was larger than most moderns, had a larger endocranial capacity (fig. 2). In order for us to know whether or not the brains of any of our predecessors were relatively smaller, we should need to have more satisfactory estimates than we possess about the size and weight of many of these Pleistocene forms. Such estimates are only approachable in *Australopithecus, Sinanthropus,* and Cro-Magnon man. The data with regard to the so-called "giant" races of antiquity are confusing. The size of the bones and even of the teeth of the few widely scattered specimens which have given rise to the supposition that giant hominids existed are massive indeed, but the intracranial capacity, where it is determinable, is slight. Le Gros Clark (1954) has pointed out that these so-called giant forms were probably not unusually tall, and Straus (1954) has even suggested that they are merely pathological specimens. If we attempt to correct for differences in bodily magnitude, we do not emerge with very good evidence that man's brain has been increasing. Figures such as those shown in table 1 illustrate the obvious difficulties that arise in an attempt to correlate brain size with something as meaningless as nationality, for it is clear that genotypic variation is more significant than residence in a particular geopolitical locus. This same difficulty arises when we investigate endocranial capacities, for we have only fragmentary knowledge of the movements of genotypically distinct populations of the past. The recent finding, for example, of a group of fifth-century or sixth-century Finnish skulls averaging 1050 cc. for females and 1185 cc. for males of individuals only slightly over 5 feet tall (Blomquist, 1953) discloses remains quite different from others in the area and suggests that these smaller people may have been enslaved Lapps who were imported from another locus or were the remnants of an indigenous group, possibly to be identified with Procopius' Skrithiphinoi. Not all such older people were diminutives with small brain cases. Moreover, Tilly Edinger, who has delivered an earlier James Arthur Lecture, has demonstrated that if there is such a thing as evolution (increase in size and volume) of the brain, it is not related to body size. Among the only slightly taller tenth-century and eleventh-century Slavs of Bed (5½ feet as against 5 feet 2 or 3 inches for Blomquist's material) the intracranial capacity runs about 1437 cc. for males and 1310 cc. for females (Skerlj and Dolinar, 1950). We must therefore conclude that racial (genotypic) variation has long been, as it is now, the major factor in variation in intracranial capacity.

In some districts man has changed very little since the Paleolithic. Torgersen, Getz, Hafsten, and Olsen (1953) report a Bleivik paleolithic skeleton of an individual about 5 feet 4 inches in height and quite similar to modern, mesocephalic Norwegians.

Endocranial casts therefore do not appear to support the notion that the brain of modern man has increased in size. Such casts do show variations, but these variations are all explicable on the basis of age, sex, and the intermingling of genotypically different peoples. There is no evidence of a selective forward march from a smaller to larger brain. As soon as we come upon modern man, some of his representatives have as large a brain case as those of our contemporaries who we consider to be very satisfactorily equipped with regard to both quantity and quality of cerebral substance.

When it becomes apparent in science that a generally accepted hypothesis has really very little to support it, there is always a tendency to look around to discover who the culprit was who brought the suspect hypothesis into polite company. The background for the notion that man's brain has continued a process of progressive forward evolution up to the present is the same as that which lies behind all considerations of homologous structures, i.e., such structures have a lineage and have remained static, regressed, progressed, or have been diverted into quite different forms for performing

TABLE 8

RELATION BETWEEN ENDOCRANIAL CAPACITY AND ENCEPHALIC VOLUME, ABSOLUTE ENCEPHALIC WEIGHT (IN GRAMS), AND RATIO OF WEIGHT OF ENCEPHALON TO THAT OF BODY FOR DIFFERENT SPECIES

Form	Encephalic Volume/Skull Volume	Encephalic Weight	Encephalic Weight/Body Weight
Homo	Ca. 1/1.5	1100–2000	1/30–60
Pitheci			
Simia troglodytes	Ca. 1/1.66	209–463	1/14–213
Macacus	Ca. 1/2.2	56–145	1/25.8–108.6
Cebus capucinus		36–97	1/23–72
Hapale rosalia	Ca. 1/2	7.9	1/30
Prosimii, Lemur	Ca. 1/2.2	14.5–26.3	1/41
Chiroptera, Vespertilio murinus	Ca. 1/2.2	0.13–0.17	1/30–36.6
Carnivora			
Felis domesticus	Ca. 1/2.86	21–35	1/22–185
Meles taxus	Ca. 1/3	46–48	1/128–159
Canis familiaris	Ca. 1/2.5	54–125	1/37–358
Pinnipedia, Phoca vitulina	Ca. 1/2.5	302	1/242
Insectivora, Erinaceus europaeus	Ca. 1/3–4	0.18–3.6	1/43–390
Rodentia			
Mus rattus	Ca. 1/2.6–3	1.8–10.0	1/66–194
Lepus cuniculus **domesticated**		11.20	1/301
Ungulata			
Sus scrofa **domesticated**	Ca. 1/8	105–110	1/630–660
Equus caballus	Ca. 1/7	600	1/379–801
Elephas africanus	Ca. 1/8–10	2536–4000	1/125
Sirenia, Manatus americanus		Ca. 344	
Cetacea			
Phocaena communis		468	1/38–93
Balaenoptera musculus		4700–6700	1/12,000–25,000
Edentata, Dasypus setosus	Ca. 1/3	18	1/141
Marsupialia, Petaurus sciureus	Ca. 1/2.2	3–66	1/40–800
Monotremata, Echidna hystrix and Ornithorhynchus paradoxus		16–32	1/80–130

essentially the same or very different functions. As man's brain is both absolutely and relatively quite large (table 8), it would seem clear that it has not merely failed to participate in the otherwise general degradation of the human form but has, in fact, undergone positive development. Such a conclusion seems sound enough with regard to the animal kingdom as a whole, but difficulty begins to develop when we draw near to man himself. It is not difficult to admit that the brain of man is superior to that found in fish, or in amphibians, or in reptiles, but even some rather lowly primates have relatively more brain than does man (table 8). The notion that there has been a continuous increase in the size of the brain from early, low primates, directly up to and through modern man is explicit in Broca's studies on intracranial volumes (Broca, 1862), but Retzius (1915) expressed, as the title of his article indicates, a distinct doubt about the validity of such an assumption. We have known for a relatively long period of time that the endocranial capacity of Neanderthal man (1500–1700+ cc.) compares very favorably with that of modern man and that Cro-Magnon man's intracranial capacity (1500—1900 cc.) surpassed present day man's, but these observations were ignored. It was emphasized that *Pithecanthropus* had a low endocranial capacity (775+ cc.) and, when *Sinanthropus* was also found to have a small brain case, the difficulties raised by the Neanderthal and Cro-Magnon forms were glossed over, although many serious writers failed to subscribe to Broca's thesis. Among these, besides Retzius, may be mentioned Keith (1925), Tilney and Riley (1928), and especially von Bonin (1934). Von Economo (1929) also expressed the opinion that intracranial capacity and intellectual ability need not parallel each other. Von Bonin expressed himself to the same effect by saying that "the conclusion that there has been a lessening of intelligence throughout the ages is hardly acceptable." (He was ridiculing an oblique statement of Martin's, 1928.) Von Economo (1929) and von Bonin both shifted the search for a correlation between intellectual capacity and structural substratum to a new area by suggesting that the active elements in the brain might increase without any increase in total cerebral dimensions. This argument had been implicit in Flechsig's (1896) and Ferrier's (1890) thesis (see below) that particular cerebral loci were of relatively greater importance than others for intellectual activity and in Parker's (1922) emphasis upon the neurocyte as the critical element.[*] It is the former point of view that has enjoyed popularity among physical anthropologists, as it is not possible to determine how many cells existed in a vanished brain but something can be said about the form of the head which contained that brain.

DOES INTELLECTUAL FUNCTION RESIDE IN A PARTICULAR ASPECT OF CEREBRAL CONFIGURATIONS?

Those writers who take the position that man's neural system must necessarily have evolved structurally in a progressive fashion since Neanderthal man and who admit that no such progression can be substantiated on the basis of increase in size or weight are inclined to seek for modern "superiority" in some more subtle alteration. Weidenreich (1946), for example, sought such superiority in shape. He says, "The height of the Neanderthalian brain is, in all cases, clearly inferior to that of modern man." "Superiority," for Weidenreich, means an increase in prominence of the dorsal convexity above the locus of the junction of parietal and occipital lobes. Because this increase in dorsoventral diameter of the brain occurs in a structure the

[*] This apparently self-evident consideration is not necessarily deictic. There is, for example, a gradual decrease with age in the number of cells per unit volume of cerebral cortex, as Conel (1939, 1951, 1947, 1951, 1955) has shown, and it seems reasonable to assume that a smaller number of strategically situated cells, provided with elaborate synapses, may be more significant than a larger number of inconsequential elements. It is even conceivable that greater metabolic efficiency on the part of a few cells would more than compensate for the potential advantage of number in a more abundant population.

over-all size of which is not increased, it must be achieved by a reduction in the rostrocaudal diameter. Just why Weidenreich thought such a shift constituted an advance or "superiority" is far from clear. His reasoning devolves from the observation that the development of a more rounded form of the brain is a relatively late development, but Weidenreich must have been aware that the dorsoventral diameter of the human brain is not equally increased in all racial types and that it reaches its greatest natural prominence among plano-occipitals such as the Armenoids and Tyrolese (the Vedas also had a relatively higher cerebrum, as Sarasin has shown), but he did not discuss this situation. Instead he saw in dorsoventral enlargement the possibility that "association" areas might have been selectively enlarged (the fact that they had to be simultaneously rostrocaudally compressed is glossed over), and a highly theoretical speculation of G. Elliot Smith is quoted (somewhat irrelevantly) to provide substance to Weidenreich's hypothesis.

Flechsig was the first to emphasize the supposed relationship between intelligence and what he called "association areas," a term applied to those portions of the brain that are tardy in myelinating and that do not receive any primary afferent system or emit any long motor projection. That such regions perform associative functions is more than probable. That they perform such functions to a greater extent than other portions of the brain is open to question. There is no reason at all to suppose that what are called intellectual functions are specifically dependent upon them.

Weidenreich included in his figures (his fig. 79) endocranial casts from a gorilla, Pithecanthropus erectus, Neanderthal man, and modern man, but if he had used the endocranial cast of a chimpanzee it would have been apparent that this animal has a relatively greater dorsoventral cerebral diameter than does modern man. The difference in the relative magnitude of the dorsoventral diameters of the brain of the gorilla and chimpanzee would seem to be explicable on the basis of difference in the craniocervical angle of these two anthropoids, for the head of the gorilla is carried more decidedly forward than that of the chimpanzee. It is by no means impossible, judging from the pelvic and femoral configuration of early hominids, that they also carried their heads on a wider craniocervical angle than does modern man, and all reconstructions of these forms, such as Coon's (1954) of Sinanthropus, show very wide craniocervical angles. Weidenreich did recognize the possibility that brachycephalization was due to adjustment of the head to the erect posture, but his emphasis was on the contention that broadheadedness is an advanced state of development which is still progressing and not on the purely mechanical aspects of the relationship.

While the proportion of short and broad to long and narrow skulls seems to have increased from Neolithic times, it does not seem that this is a universal, irreversible, forward trend that is completely gene-controlled, or that it is correlated with a superior degree of intelligence.

With regard to the tendency towards broad-headedness, it may be pointed out that among modern male Scots short, narrow crania are becoming more numerous (Scott, 1953). In view of the high incidence of anatomic variations (especially those due to modifying influences which operate in the genic environmental sphere or on peristatic fetal-maternal relationships; Fischer, 1952) more work like that of Lasker (1953) and of Otto (1953) needs to be done. May brachycephalization be one of the alterations in body form and size due to a shift in human reproductive habits or to changes in ecological conditions, such as Bartholomew and Birdsell (1953) have emphasized?

Even if we grant that brachycephalization has become an established, progressive feature of contemporary man, we must admit that many groups of earlier men also exhibited this feature. It is easy enough to point out that cultural growth was most rapid among the round-headed peoples of the Mediterranean, but this is merely an *ad hoc propter hoc* argument, and it is chastening to recall that a few decades ago the economically prosperous and supposedly dolichocephalic north Europeans were arguing that long-headedness was positively correlated with intellectual superiority.

In any case, for the original argument to have real weight, the condition of brachycephalization itself still would require to be correlated with superior intelligence. Thus far no data have been brought forward establishing such a correlation. Ordinarily, the basis for the argument in favor of brachycephalization is shifted to some intermediate ground as by Weidenreich's assumption that spherical-brainedness is positively correlated with an increase in the "association" regions of the brain and that these are particularly concerned with intellectual functions. As an example of an "association" region the rostral portion of the frontal lobe has been most frequently cited. There are no easily accessible data to prove that such an increase has occurred with a differential in favor of that region, but even if there were we would still be faced with the difficulty of validating the assumption that these regions are the substrate of intelligence.

Within the past decade a mass of data have accumulated which throw considerable doubt on that assumption. Towards the end of the nineteenth century Gottlieb Burckhardt had the idea that if psychotic persons are bothered by auditory hallucinations one way to get rid of these would be to remove that portion of the cortex in which he thought auditory sensation ended. Burckhardt's (1890–1891) results were not very conclusive, but in 1935 Egas Moñiz (1936) revised the surgical treatment of psychoses in accordance with the hypothesis that it might be profitable to disconnect those portions of the brain most intimately related with complex mental activity. Moñiz chose the frontal lobe, and by 1951 more than 18,600 persons had undergone one or another type of frontal lobe operations. We have had, therefore, considerable oportunity to examine the validity of the belief that intelligence is situated in the frontal lobe. Because this subject was approached with notable bias in favor of the long-accepted supposition that it does, it is not surprising that all the psychologic studies have not been in agreement. This in itself indicates that we are not dealing with the clear-cut correlation everyone supposed existed and expected to find substantiated. It is not necessary to go into the details of the recent findings, but enough is now known to make it clear that an individual lacking both frontal lobes can function quite satisfactorily in our society and that many of what we regard as intellectual traits are not notably impaired in such individuals. Consequently, it would appear that the frontal lobe, as such, is not the physical substrate of what our psychological tests of intelligence measure.

Here again it is interesting to enquire how this erroneous concept achieved currency. I have previously explored this curious question (F. A. Mettler, 1949), as follows:

The attribution of changes in personality to frontal lobe damage is not so old as might be supposed. Although some psychic disorders were attributed to cerebral dysfunction even in the early post-Galenic period (C. C. Mettler, 1947) it was not until the second half of the nineteenth century that any evidence was brought forward to suggest that the frontal lobe is specifically concerned with psychic processes. There is nothing in Greisinger's (1867) book to this effect and the suggestion that Harlow's (1848) patient, Phineas Gage, of the so-called "crow-bar case," owed his personality changes (the phrase that he was "no longer Gage," appears in the record; Harlow, 1869, p. 14) to frontal lobe damage was an afterthought on the part of Ferrier. (For Harlow and most of his contemporaries the most significant feature of the case was the survival of the patient, and others, overzealous to defeat the phrenologists, were almost willing to argue that the brain was practically useless in order to achieve their purpose. It is interesting to observe, in passing, that one of the first cases in which a personality change was observed to follow a brain injury was a psychotic case in which the psychosis disappeared after attempted suicide by shooting through the head; Nobele, 1835.)

Welt's (1888) case of Franz Binz of Zürich was probably the first verified example of serious alteration of character and moral behavior due to a frontal lesion, the extent of which was established at autopsy. Franz Binz, like Phineas Gage, changed from a peaceful, gay, polite, and cleanly person to a violently quarrelsome sloven. Goltz, Hitzig, and Ferrier had previously described similar changes. Ferrier (1890) believed that removal of cortex rostral to the electrically excitable area produced "a form of mental degradation which appears to me to depend on the loss of the faculty of attention, and my hypothesis is that the power of attention is intimately related to the volitional movements of the head and eyes," Ferrier attributed the opinion that intellectual degradation may follow lesion of the rostral part of the brain to a number of previous authors, including Brissaud. Welt had been unable to demonstrate any true degradation of intellectual capacity in the case of Binz. Hitzig (1884) also thought that intelligence is impaired by injury of the frontal lobe in the dog, a belief controverted by Loeb (1902), and Bruns could find no evidence of impairment of intellect in one extensive tumor case of his own.

An unpleasant, nasty character was one of the triad of symptoms of release which Goltz felt succeeded frontal lobe changes. [The full triad was (1) general excitement (the capstone of the theory that injury of the cortex brought about a phenomenon of "release" was laid by Charcot, 1876–1880), (2) lack of self-control, (3) violence of spinal and bulbar activity.]

Clownish behavior (*Witzelsucht, mania bel espirit, lazzi, moria*) as a symptom of rostral frontal lobe damage appeared in Jastrowitz's articles of 1888 (Jastrowitz, 1888; see also Leyden and Jastrowitz, 1888; and Bruns, 1892) and formed a part of Bruns' (1897) table of frontal lobe symptomatology. Jastrowitz referred to the condition as *moria*.

Difficulties in the associational process entered the symptomatology of the frontal lobe through the work of Flechsig, who argued that two (originally he said three) "association" centers existed in the brain (a large parieto-occipito-temporal and a smaller frontal one) which gave rise to no projections but only associational fibers, for the purpose of interrelating afferent impulses. Flechsig felt that the frontal association field was primarily concerned with the association of impulses of bodily sense, as contrasted with vision and audition as special senses (he thought of the frontal lobe as containing sensory as well as motor capacities, as indeed its caudal part does), and that injury of it produced defects in personality and self-awareness. Association fibers from it were supposed to deal especially with memory images (Flechsig, 1896). Flechsig's theory was not widely accepted (Oppenheim, 1900) but the theory that psychiatric disorders depend upon an essential difficulty in the associational process long endured in the literature. Thus Bolton (1911) divided psychotic processes into two categories: (1) those in which there is defective control of the processes of lower association, and (2) those in which there is independent activity of the "centers of lower association." He placed apathetic, hebephrenic, and manic syndromes in the first category and illusory and hallucinatory states in the second.

Loss of initiative or apathy as symptoms of frontal lobe disease appeared in Bruns' tabulation and loss of complex emotional behavior probably should also be included here together with defective recognition, due to a degradation in perceptual ability. In contrast to simple apathy, ambulatory hyperkinesia was attributed by Baraduc (1876) as, much earlier, by Magendie, to frontal lobe lesion—specifically by Baraduc to atrophy of the left inferior frontal convolution.

Persistence of fear and the occurrence of panic reactions have been described as signs of frontal damage, and apparently, in cases of thrombosis of the arteries supplying the frontal region, may be so severe as to amount to delirium tremens. Perhaps these phenomena are to be related with Goltz's listing of release phenomena, though this is far from clear.

Memory defects for the past without impairment of the ability to learn and lack of planning for the future (deterioration of insight) are also listed as results of frontal lobe damage.

It may be justifiably said that these so-called "higher" functions discussed in the foregoing paragraphs are so ill-defined as to be scarcely worth scientific consideration. This depends upon one's point of view. One common criticism of the scientific method as applied to the present sphere is that it has not yielded quantitative support of phenomena which anyone, using merely observation, can easily perceive. Since scientific tests answer only the questions they have been designed to ask, it is, of course, possible that the proper tests have not been devised. On the other hand, it is perfectly possible that these "higher" functions are not functions of the frontal lobe at all or, at best, require damage of very large parts of the frontal lobe in such a way as to compound simple functional deficits into complex patterns of deficit.

The premier question which must receive an affirmative answer in order to conclude that the "higher" functions under discussion are frontal lobe functions, is, Do such deficits invariably appear if the frontal lobe is quite dysfunctional? Under such scrutiny the allocation of most of the preceding phenomena (slovenliness is an exception) fails to be substantiated. We must therefore conclude either that special circumstances, beyond the factor of frontal lobe damage, must be present for their appearance or that they are not true functions.

It becomes clear then that behind the notion that damage of the frontal cortex produces intellectual damage and personality change is a body of data which must be interpreted in a somewhat different light than that which has been employed in the past. We may consider several possibilities. "Intelligence" may be a generalized function of the neural system, or, alternatively, it may be situated in some special locus which has thus far escaped notice. Finally, it is possible that it may not easily be correlated with structural characteristics at all. For example, intelligence must certainly depend on a variety of factors just as does excellence in sports, and excellence in sports depends on the conjunction of the fitness of the individual with the requirements of the sport chosen. Intelligence presumably also involves not merely an aspect of fitness but the utilization of such fitness in a situation for which it is appropriate. One may question whether there is such a condition as intelligence without specifying the circumstances under which the intellectual skill is to become manifest. Because these external circumstances are obviously very variable, the search for a particular structural substrate would have to be abandoned in favor of a search for a variety of substrata to match the conceivable spectrum of requirements. We may approach the consideration of the possibility that intelligence may be a generalized cerebral function by asking whether Parker's (1922) emphasis on the neurocyte provides us with a useful clue.

IS·INTELLECTUAL CAPACITY DIRECTLY CORRELATED WITH THE NUMBER OF NEUROCYTES IN THE CEREBRAL CORTEX?

Still another approach to the problem of wherein the supposed superiority of the modern brain may lie is the assumption, already referred to above, that the functional elements of the cerebral cortex, notably its cells, and their functional capacities have increased in number as a result of an increased complexity of folding of cortical surface rather than as the result of an increase in mass. In other words, the free surface of the brain is said to have increased as the result of greater infolding without any increase in the spherical diameter of the cerebrum. Such a situation is certainly possible, and there is a difference among cerebra with regard to degree of convolutional complexity. It is further true that there is a difference between normal brains and the small cerebra of idiots (which are often relatively smooth), but, as in the case of weight or volume, no correlation can be established between degree of gyrencephaly and condition of sanity or intellectual proficiency.

There are two aspects to the problem of whether increased complexity of internal cerebral organization is of possible evolutionary significance. In the first place the fact of such increasing complexity must be established, and in the second place its relation to survival value must be demonstrated. Quantitative estimates of cortical complexity may be expressed in surface area measurements, which are very unreliable, or in terms of the relation of total volume of nerve cells to volume of cerebral cortex (gray cell coefficient; von Economo, 1926, 1929), or some equivalent of number, such as von Economo's photographic technique or a scanning densitometer measurement (Campbell, 1954). Simplified estimates of the gray cell coefficient can also be worked out on the basis of number, as well as volume, of cells in some arbitrary cubic unit of cortical tissue. Thus the argument that intelligence is related to number of nerve cells can be explored on a localized as well as generalized basis. Such volumetric work is still in its infancy and, I have already noticed, in connection with the discussion of total cerebral volume, some of the difficulties which have beset past computations involving volumetric units. Further, we have no information at all about earlier man and can argue only by comparison of what we find in the brains of different races of modern man and in animals. Obviously there is always a very real danger that superiority will be attributed to some causally unrelated but real concomitant difference which may be disclosed.

The psychologic correlates of the hypothesis that intelligence is a generalized brain function are the theories of vicarious cortical functioning and of mass action. Pavlov took the position that loss of one or another portion of the neural system, and especially of the cerebral cortex, could be compensated for by the extraordinary activity of other portions, the potentialities of which extended beyond their usual function. This principle is demonstrable, but it has limits. Extension of it to the proposition that any portion of the neuraxis (or cortex) can take over the functions of any other portion of the neuraxis (or cortex) is quite unwarranted. Moreover, when such a situation develops, the vicariously mediated activity is likely to be an obvious and, often, poor substitute for the original.

A similar criticism applies to the principle of mass action which is supportable to the extent that neural activity occurs in a frame of reference of totality of function which is distorted by truncation, often in seemingly inconsequential ways. The mass actionists have, however, been less interested in interaction than in the fact that much neural tissue is dispensable. Such a consideration of their work brings us close to the problem in hand. Unfortunately the fact that much neural tissue may be dispensed with does not demonstrate that the function of what has been removed exists elsewhere, as well as in what has been ablated. It may merely mean that the experimental enterprise is in irrelevant one.

Many persons in the United States not only have been subjected to psychosurgical operations that have removed more or less of the frontal lobe and therefore a considerable proportion of the "association" areas, but these operative procedures have also rendered enough brain non-functional to reduce these individuals to a functioning brain weight not greatly in excess of that of *Pithecanthropus,* depending on what the operated person's brain originally weighed. Nevertheless, as indicated above, such operations may not be followed by any alterations easily detected by psychologic tests. It is true that some patients give very poor performances after operations, but such a situation might be due to the progress of the original disorder for which the operation was done. It is much more significant that many mature patients show no such changes in our society as it is presently organized. The literature contains many impressionistic reports to the effect that such "psychosurgical" operations have adverse effects. Unfortunately we cannot rely on this type of report, but it is true that psychologic tests leave much to be desired by way of conclusiveness. There are limits to what psychologic testing can do, and many patients who refuse to cooperate in a psychologic test situation and cannot be included in statistical evaluations may easily provide the clue to what those portions of the brain that have been removed may "be good for." In social situations, such as those in which we customarily function, the shortcomings of the individual are often compensated for by the social conscience of his fellows. The simple fact that many rather deficient and essentially parasitic individuals move freely and in an undistinguished manner through our protective social structure should not be overlooked in any attempt to explain why persons who have little or no frontal lobe are not merely able to function in our society but are often able to earn very considerable salaries. In a truly competitive and less genteel society the individual who does not or cannot "pull his own weight" or whose wits are less than nimble is likely to succumb fairly early, and this is even more true of persons who do not bestir themselves in existences of a solitary nature. We cannot put this kind of pressure on individuals in psychologic test situations, and our tests consequently lack a certain depth and are devoid of the vitality which must be of importance to the student of survival values. Nevertheless, the lessons of psychosurgery are clear, and they are to the effect that we have overrated the importance of the frontal cerebral cortex in intellectual function. While it is likely that any one of us could ill afford to part with any cerebral substance if we were transported back to a situation in which we had to retrace the necessity of developing our culture all over again, our modern social system is so arranged that most of us can function at a very low level of efficiency most of the time. The "psychosurgical" data contain another clue of considerable importance and that is that we can more easily dispense with cortical gray matter than with subcortical cellular accumulations. I wish to return to this point farther along.

For the present then we may say that those authors who look for the progress of evolution in the direction of some generalized augmentation of cerebral function, such as might accompany an increase of nerve cells, may be correct, but there is no evidence at all to justify the assumptions that modern man has more such cells in fact than Cro-Magnon, Neanderthal, or even Swanscombe man, and it remains to be demonstrated that there is a positive correlation between number of neurocytes and what passes for intelligence. The position may be granted that a high degree of intelligence is a total function, but it is quite impossible for all or any portion of the cerebral cortex to subserve the function of all other parts.

A high degree of intelligence is certainly not localized in one particular portion of the neural system. It is, or should be, the sum of perfect functioning not merely of the neuraxis but of all other parts of the body. If it is true then that the future of our race depends on the most complete utilization of intelligence, we shall have to look for the most nearly perfect physical individual in order to find the most intelligent.

We all know that matters do not work out this way. We are all aware that the handsome matinee idol may be an unusually vapid individual and that beautiful blondes are often intolerable for protracted periods. The difficulty is, of course, not merely that a physical disability can be readily offset by a cultural advantage but that a disability may actually turn out to be an asset by virtue of its psychological activating quality. We cannot therefore look for survival of the race in over-all physical perfection. Moreover, as physical defects, such as myopia or a missing extremity, are very easily offset by technological devices, we must search for uncompensable limitations if we are to discover any areas wherein our development will be blocked in a progressive civilization.

CAN MAN SATISFACTORILY MAINTAIN A "LARGE" BRAIN?

Proponents of the theory that man's brain has been consistently enlarging have directed very little attention to the anatomic circumstances that are required for the maintenance of such a brain as modern man possesses or to what changes would be required if that brain were to undergo a future progressive increase in size.

OBSTETRICAL DIFFICULTIES

Obviously, at the very outset of independent existence the head of an infant must, under ordinary circumstances, pass through a birth canal the dimensions of which are unalterably fixed by the size and shape of the maternal pelvis. A not inconsiderable degree of obstetrical difficulty consists in the mismating of genotypically large males with females having a pelvic outlet too restricted for the uncomplicated delivery of the product of such a mating. The margin of obstetrical safety is not so great but that any appreciable increase in the size of the head of the infant would immediately influence the paranatal death rate adversely and markedly raise the incidence of brain injury among neonates. It is quite possible that increased head size and increased pelvic dimensions would occur together. This has been the course of events in the past (fig. 4), but pelvic size is an important selective factor with regard to magnitude of head size in any race and operates in favor of small-headedness.

The oxygen requirements of the neural system of neonates are different from those of adults. Newborn animals can endure a surprising reduction in oxygen, as anyone who has ever tried to drown kittens can testify. Nevertheless, there are specific limits to such endurance, and it would be interesting to know whether, as seems reasonable, such limits become progressively lower for neural systems of larger size. I am unaware of any studies on this subject, but we do possess an impressive mass of data which demonstrates that a very considerable proportion of brain-injured children have been damaged because of failure to get oxygen to all portions of the brain during intra-uterine existence, as well as at birth or immediately afterward.

It was long believed that most brain-injured children, the so-called cerebral palsy cases, were damaged during birth, but older doubts have been fortified in recent years by increasing evidence that a great many such children have been born without any notable difficulty in labor. Protracted and complicated labors do result in brain injuries and even deaths, as noted above, but much brain injury occurs before birth as well as during or afterward and as the result of processes the nature of which has only recently been elucidated. Two very important principles have emerged. These are, first, that gross malformations of the neural system almost always have their origin in the very earliest period of pregnancy (often before the mother is aware of her condition) and, second, that alterations in oxygen supply occurring in any part of pregnancy have very drastic effects. Almost any noxious influence that reaches the fetus in its very early, relatively undifferentiated period (especially during the first two weeks after conception) will result in a malformation but after the second month of pregnancy the neural system can withstand many insults, with the exception of oxygen deprivation, which would previously have done irreparable damage.

One possible reason for the precarious condition of the neural system with regard to variations in oxygen supply is probably to be sought in the manner in which blood is carried to the brain.

The brains of all primates are supplied with blood from two principal arterial reservoirs—the internal carotid and vertebral arteries. The ultimate branches of these two principal supplies anastomose at the base of the brain in a circulus arteriosus from which a crown of vessels penetrates and also embraces the brain itself. In very low forms, such as Amphibia, which have quite simple brains, the brain is supplied not only by vessels from a greater variety of sources, but the individual vessels of the brain itself exhibit many intercommunications (Herrick, 1948).

In herbivores and carnivores the situation is not so free as in *Ambystoma* nor so restricted as in the primates. The vascular net of the amphibian cerebrum has been replaced by the terminal vascular design seen in primates, but at the base of the brain the anastomotic pattern has been retained in

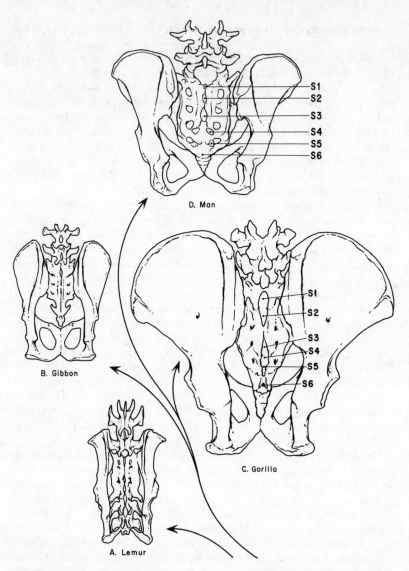

S1
S2
S3
S4
S5
S6

D. Man

B. Gibbon

S1
S2
S3
S4
S5
S6

C. Gorilla

A. Lemur

Fig. 4 Progressive widening of the sacrum and pelvis in primates (from Gregory, 1951, vol. 2).

what is called a rete mirabile, and this is supplied not merely from the vertebral and internal carotid arteries but also receives an abundant supply of blood from the external carotid through ophthalmic and meningeal branches which, in the human adult, do not ordinarily maintain any notable connection with the extracranial vascular arrangements.

In the human embryo an early, freely vascularized stage exists very briefly. During this period all the blood reaching the brain arrives via the internal and external carotid arteries, for no vertebral arteries exist until the end of the second month, at which time the arterial reservoir for the lower (infratentorial) part of the brain is shifted from the carotid to vertebral arteries and the external carotid contribution is gradually cut off.

Thus the arterial plan of the brain of the human infant passes through a series of changes which recapitulate those of lower phyla and, at the end of the second month, the embryo has already been committed to the primate pattern of supply. A very considerable number of developmental errors can occur in this process of recapitulation, but once it has been completed the pattern settled upon must prove adequate for all subsequent purposes, and it is not a pattern into which any considerable margin of safety has been built. From this time onward the brain enlarges and removes its internal substance farther and farther from its all important supply of blood and thus of oxygen. At the same time the tracery of vessels on the surface of the brain is progressively stretched out, and ultimately a rigid encasement for the entire brain develops in which, with little room to spare, any considerable increase in intracranial pressure will serve to prevent blood from entering the skull.

We now know that the brain of the fetus cannot withstand pronounced drops in maternal blood pressure which are not fatal to the mother. The effect of such a drop is to reduce the oxygen exchange through the placenta to a point where the oxygen concentration in the fetal blood is inadequate to maintain nerve tissue situated in those regions where the physiologic factor of safety is small. Such regions are those in the interior of the brain and in the white matter where the vessels are few and thin. Ultimately, if the child does not perish during the period of deprivation, the neural tissues in these regions break down, the vessels traversing them rupture, and a true apoplexy occurs in the fetus.

Phenomena of this type are probably more common today than ever before. Such circumstances can and do occur when pregnant women undergo surgical operation by modern techniques and could conceivably happen in high speed transport. Other sources of difficulty are infectious processes which impair placental circulation, drugs, and an improper regulation of the atmosphere such as occurs in combustion failures in tight modern houses, or automobiles, or during the breakdown of refrigeration or air-conditioning apparatus.

The problem of cerebral oxygen supply is also a serious one for adults and can be a limiting factor in our further evolution. Many of us are unaware to what extent the necessities of earning a living expose a significant proportion of the working population to neural damage through oxygen lack.

The neural system is very vulnerable to a number of chemical substances. Some of these substances, such as lead and carbon monoxide, are constantly about us, and great vigilance is required to avoid being poisoned by them. Others, such as DFP (diisopropyl fluorophosphate), the still unused "nerve" gas of the Germans of World War II, are unusual compounds which probably are more destructive as military threats to morale than as practical hazards. In an intermediate position are substances such as carbon tetrachloride, methyl alcohol, ergot, and manganese which are potentially dangerous but the use of which is reasonably well controlled.

Approximately a million and a half Americans are chronically exposed to carbon monoxide as an *industrial* chemical hazard. It may be assumed that the number of individuals exposed to this substance, and hazards such as lead compounds, organic solvents, and several of the other chemicals and

DEATH RATES AND NEUROPSYCHIATRIC PATHOLOGY

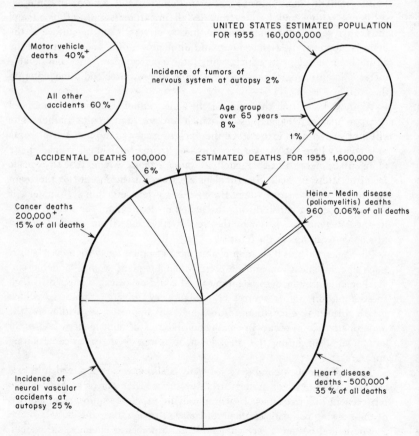

Fig. 5 Relative frequency of different causes of death and also of neuropathology.

compounds, is at least twice as great as industrial figures indicate. Moreover, it is probably not without significance that the neural effect of substances like carbon monoxide seems to be due entirely to anoxemia rather than to any special neurotropic action. Even in lead poisoning the initial reaction of the toxic chemical is with inorganic phosphates, a combination that has a very serious effect on the erythrocytes. Primary pathology of the neural system, in lead poisoning, is practically unknown.

The problem of supplying the brain with oxygen is not, however, restricted to the very young or to industrial workers. The third principal cause of death in the United States is major brain stroke. Murphy (1954) has pointed out that "one-half million persons in this country sustain strokes each year, and . . . one and one-fourth million hemiplegic patients are surviving in the hospital or at home."

Study of figure 5 will reveal (incidence of neural vascular accidents) that the number of persons who have vascular lesions in the neural system is appreciably larger than those who show evidence of such lesions, for such lesions are found in every fourth person who dies. In other words, many persons who will die of other causes and who will show no signs of nervous system damage before they die have substantial damage of the vessels of the nervous system. Had these individuals lived longer they would unquestionably have gone on to show failure of the nervous system.

As our population grows older, an increasing proportion of individuals will inevitably come to a situation in which the vascular supply of the neural system will break down.

All of these considerations point to the possibility that a large brain may not necessarily be a desirable endowment. Indeed, it is possible to experience a certain amount of uneasiness about such a prospect for it is not at all inconceivable that if man's brain were to increase without substantial modifications, both in his structure and culture, he might be moving in the direction of extinction.

CULTURE AND "INTELLIGENCE"

It is not often that scientists expend great labor to correlate two variables when the second of these is known to show marked variation in terms of a third, unconsidered variable. Nevertheless, this is exactly what we do when we search for a direct correlation between brain structures and "intelligence," for it is a truism that what we call intelligence is at least as dependent upon nurture as upon nature.

When all the available data have been examined we are forced to admit that no evidence exists to support the contention that man's cultural advance has been due to, or has even been paralleled by, structural changes in his nervous system. The assumptions that the cerebral cortex has become more convoluted or more efficiently organized, by virtue of an increase in the number of nerve cells in it, or because of increased synaptic contacts, are unsupported conjectures, and the belief that human intracranial capacity has undergone steady enlargement is at variance with the actual facts. Since the beginning of the Eolithic period, mankind's neural system has displayed a number of variations on a central structural theme, but no clear trend has become established. Many modern persons seem not to be more abundantly supplied with cerebral substance than any of the Eolithic or Neolithic variants, and indeed most of us have less in the way of brain mass than did Cro-Magnon man who seems not to have been especially successful in the business of survival.

On the other hand it is quite clear that since the Eolithic period mankind has literally inherited the earth. That he owes this inheritance to his culture no one will question, but there has been a tendency to regard culture and structure as essentially separate and antithetical. We speak of physical and social anthropologists, of anatomists, physiologists, psychologists, and sociologists—a literal army of departmentalized scholars, each viewing man from the point of view of his own individual discipline and each insisting upon parcellation.

What in fact do we mean when we admit that, of course, man's progress has been due to his culture? We may agree (as many have) that this is due to the assumption of the "erect posture, his free-moving arms and hands, his sharp-focusing eyes, a brain capable of fine judgment and decision as well as of keen perception, and the power of speech," as Coon (1954), among others, has pointed out, but all these things were man's in the Eolithic. Man is where he is today not because he has evolved new structural attributes but because he has used the capacities he possessed to provide himself with the means to develop beyond those capacities.

The development of clothing, of tools, of improved means of locomotion, of ways to produce and store food must be looked upon as intellectual accomplishments of the first magnitude. They are especially important in that they came into being at a time when the patterns and mechanisms for intellectual activity so familiar to us were still unknown, when man was still beset by great dangers, could not move far from water, was at the mercy of the sun and snow, and had no accurate records of the past nor clear confidence in the future.

By taking these first steps man had passed beyond the necessity for personal change. He had embarked upon the process of supplementing his evolutionary progress by developing outside himself what other species must attain by personal structure change.

CULTURAL DEVELOPMENT NULLIFIES THE SELECTIVE
INFLUENCE OF NATURAL ENVIRONMENT, BY PROTECTION FROM IT

Man's forward progress has been characterized by what have been called conquests. In terms of the sciences the implication of such a word is that, whereas man has previously had to come to terms with a physical or biological phenomenon, he has now managed to make himself more or less independent of the influence of such phenomena by virtue of his ability to manipulate the circumstances on which such phenomena depend or that he is at least able to escape from their undesirable effects. In terms of survival, man's knowledge and culture have, consequently, removed him one step farther from the compulsion of his original environment. He is not, of course, freed from obedience to natural law, but he is no longer the inevitable victim of the simple inexorable phenomenon he has learned to manipulate or circumvent. Such a cultural acquisition is the equivalent of an effective structural modification, but it has the disadvantage that a higher degree of vigilance is required for its effective maintenance.

The cultural acquisitions that free man from dependency on his natural environment are those that protect him from it and that widen his course of action. Science and technological advances operate in this dual manner, and it is to these substitutes for, or supplements to, structural evolutionary change that I now wish to direct attention. Before doing so it is necessary to point out that when cultural continuity is maintained such cultural acquisitions act to all intents and purposes in a society just as though they were genetically determined.

Charles Galton Darwin, the British physicist, has touched upon the biologic equivalence of culture in a rather restricted manner in connection with what he calls "creeds" or what we might call established beliefs (whether rational or not) which result in habit patterns. "A creed," says Darwin (1953), "may have the quality, possessed by the genes of mankind, of being able to produce a permanent effect upon humanity."

Thus it is not merely that aspect of culture that produces science and technologic advances and that removes man from dependency on a restricted environment which may be the equivalent of, or a substitute for, a genetically determined trait, but so also is *any* established course of action, whether rational or irrational. It is obvious that instead of freeing man from the exigencies of his natural environment and increasing his scope of action such an evolutionary change supplement might substitute any kind of abnormal restrictive environment and greatly limit man's scope of behavior.

EVOLUTIONARY CHANGE SUPPLEMENT

It may be advisable to define more precisely what is meant here by the term evolutionary change supplement and to give some examples. The essential point to bear in mind is that, by virtue of their survival value, human cultural alterations, whether things or thoughts, have come to serve as equivalents or substitutes for structural evolutionary changes, that these cultural alterations, when of a positive nature, protect man from his environment and increase his functional scope, but that they can, from a negative point of view, constitute an adverse artificial environment and severely upset man's structural evolutionary process.

One of the difficulties in dealing with evolutionary changes of any type is encountered in an attempt to separate genetically determined factors from those due to environmental influences. We are all aware that not only are botanical forms severely affected by the climate and soil in which they grow but that the size of animals' bodies and the magnitude of egg clutches are directly influenced by latitude. It is clear that both constitution and environment are active in such variation and that the genetic factors can be operative over a wide, though still definitely limited, range. The nonhereditary influence can be viewed as an evolutionary change supplement.

An important and presently threadbare example of the difficulty in separating genetic and environmental factors is the supposed inverse relation between fertility and level of intelligence. Solution of this problem has been obstructed not merely by a lack of satisfactory methods of measuring intelligence but also by the absence of a clear definition of what is meant by fertility. Are we to understand by fertility the capacity to produce offspring or rather their actual production, i.e., the birth rate? The use of a term such as fertility rate suggests that we are dealing with a genetically determined trait, for that is the meaning of the term in animal husbandry. A moment's reflection soon discloses, however, that local variations in the human birth rate involve cultural, environmental, or, in other words, non-genetic influences to as great an extent as, if not greater than, the actual capacity to produce offspring. Moreover, even the capacity to produce offspring may be influenced by such environmental factors as diet or radiation.

We come therefore to the realization that not only can we not say that what we measure by intelligence tests is entirely genetically determined but that even the birth rate is notably influenced by environment. Viewed in such a light we become aware that what at first sight seemed an interesting correlation between two genetic traits turns out to be no more profound an expression than the simple statement that ignorant persons display their ignorance in reproductive habits as well as in other ways.

Another difficulty in distinguishing between nature and nurture arises when we deal with such behavioral phenomena as become manifest in the interaction of the individual and its milieu. Are these the result of heredity or environment, or do they occupy an ambivalent and intermediary position? Not all evolutionary changes are obviously structural, although probably all depend on some type of structural change. As an example of what is meant by saying that not all evolutionary changes are obviously structural, it may be pointed out that the migratory habits of birds are not directly structurally self-evident. Nevertheless such habits, like all physiologic behavior, depend on a morphologic substrate and are therefore genetically determined, to some degree at least. In some behavorial patterns of birds, as in the tumbling of pigeons, both hereditary and what might be termed cultural factors are involved. For practical purposes newly emergent behavioral phenomena (having survival value and appearing relatively constantly in a population) whether of a simple physiologic or complex and apparently social nature may be considered solely genotypically determined evolutionary changes if they manifest themselves in their essentially important character in individuals of the species which have been reared in isolation.

More interesting is the position occupied by non-transmissible behavior patterns. These form, of course, a large part of the material of social behavior and, in man, reach the complexity of a definite culture. Social anthropologists have made it clear that culture is itself a product of evolution and undergoes all the usual aspects of evolutionary development. More recently attention has been directed to the fact that the culture produced by man constitutes an artificial environment which exerts a selective factor upon its creator. In other words it becomes itself a selective determinant. Many examples of such a situation might be cited. Man has created many machines on which his present culture is dependent. These machines call for certain behavioral traits in their operators. Operators failing to exhibit these traits or exhibiting them in common with other inconsistent traits not only fail to derive any benefit from the machines (and therefore fall behind in the socio-economic struggle for supremacy) but may in fact injure themselves (and often other persons near them). Again, individuals residing in areas that have long served as emigration sources and never as attractions to immigrants display, as the result of progressive personality selection, psychologic traits essentially different from those seen in newly opened frontier or prospecting communities.

It is not necessary to belabor the point that culture is at once a product and a determinant of selection, and it certainly has been adequately emphasized that the culture of a species may protect individuals who would otherwise be unfit for survival. I am not so sure that the broader aspect of this principle, notably that it shifts the emphasis for selection from the structural to the cultural level, has been sufficiently emphasized among morphologically minded individuals. (The shift to a culturally determined environment tends to result in differential reproduction in selected genetical systems as a result of weighting cultural adaptation more heavily in the struggle for survival than physical adaptation.) The fact that the physical unfit have had increasing opportunity to survive has been a cause of concern to many writers, but the fact that even greater opportunities for survival have been provided for the culturally adept seem not to have been recognized.

A species that can enhance its sensory capacity by instrumentation and its motor capabilities by technology is under no selective stress at the structural level, and structural modifications in such directions will have little survival, and therefore selective, value. On the other hand the individual who fails correctly to interpret the indicators of our technological civilization will soon be eliminated from this in one way or another.

Not all cultural variants have survival value any more than do all structural variants, but to those cultural elaborations that transcend the selective effect of organic (or important genetically determined behavioral) changes I have chosen to apply the term evolutionary change supplements. Behavioral patterns, not genetically transmissible, that have definite survival significance for the species are evolutionary change supplements. Various names could be applied to such developments, and it could be said that they are merely culture. They certainly are cultural alterations, but it would not be sufficient to characterize them in such a way solely, for not all culture, as has just been pointed out, has positive or negative survival value for the species or even acts as a selective force. Moreover, such a name would obscure the fact that these particular aspects of culture tend to encourage structural variation and protect the total species from specialized evolution. Neither would it be correct to consider particular cultural features simple supplements of evolutionary structural changes, for they also supplement behavior patterns. To call them evolutionary supplements would be to ignore the fact that they are also determinants of evolutionary processes. The phrase evolutionary change supplements does not entirely satisfy me, and I am sure additional objections, beyond those I have pointed out, can be raised by others.

One of the most interesting aspects of evolutionary change supplements is that they not only free a species from the forces that result in structural evolution but, by tremendously increasing intraspecies variability, they make it possible to develop very great potentialities for structural evolution. This is the result of a variety of influences, among which preservation of many more mutations than would otherwise survive is only one. Another is, of course, the tendency for cross breeding which is seen in most protective and permissive environments. These two factors are mutually reënforcing, because with the genetic reservoir greatly expanded as the result of mutation, cross breeding will result in further intraspecies variation.

There has been an almost uniform tendency to look towards the most highly developed examples of *Homo sapiens* as holding the hope for the future of our species, and it is certainly true that, as our culture is presently organized, the ability to develop evolutionary change supplements seems to be the only requirement for progress. The more we can control our environment and devise new ways to manipulate it and make it work for us the less we shall have to do with our own soma. Nevertheless, I can conceive of a situation in the brightly burnished and explosive future in which the capacity to survive in a very primitive environment might be the most import characteristic *Homo sapiens* could display, and the most valuable members of the species may prove to be those who are presently far down the scale in social acceptability.

To list all the supplements that have been developed for the neural system would constitute a complete catalogue of our cultural necessities and conveniences, but it is worth paying some attention to the areas in which such supplementation has been maximal and minimal.

It is customary to divide neural function into various types of categories which more or less overlap. Thus we can speak of autonomic and central neural functions, of spinal and cranial nerve functions, or of sensory, internuncial, and motor activities.

One might suppose that the greatest cultural developments would be in those spheres characterized by the capacities for nicety of sensory discrimination or degree of motor performance. It is certainly true that little or no cultural sophistication exists in areas such as olfaction, gustation, or vestibular function or in pedal dexterity, as contrasted with manual, but the great mass of cultural developments seem to be primarily directed towards supplementing the autonomic functions of the body and to the avoidance of actual discomforts. Mankind appears to be more interested in homeostasis at the social as well as the biologic level than hustling, and in ease than exertion.

Another generality which emerges in connection with what types of neural system supplements have and what have not been developed is that relatively little development has occurred in those areas in which the race as a whole is not naturally proficient. Thus there is great variation in the ability of persons to discriminate between gustatory sensations, and gustatory or olfactory sensory experiences would make very poor communications media. As a consequence, such experiences play an almost completely non-objective role in our culture. The implication seems clear that culture tends to develop around average natural attributes, which is in line with what we know about the tendency for social organizations to level off the hills of exceptional ability and fill up the valleys of deficiency.

THE DEMANDS OF THE FUTURE

There have been many guesses advanced as to what the world of the future will be like (Shapiro, 1933). We can be sure of little in this regard except that we can confidently expect more of what we are already aware. This being the case, it is safe to say that the world of the future will be full of technological advances, toxic hazards, high velocities, synthetic foods, and radiation dangers, all of which sum up to what man regards as improved material advantages and which result, in fact, in increased isolation from the natural environment of the physical world. It is an interesting observation that the nervous system is relatively resistant to many of these technological alterations. Notable exceptions exist with regard to oxygen deprivation, which we have already noticed, and with regard to nutrition.

THE NEURAL SYSTEM HAS NO CAPACITY TO STORE APPRECIABLE
QUANTITIES OF FOOD SUBSTANCES, ENZYMES, AND MINERALS,
DEFICIENCIES OF WHICH PRODUCE NOT ONLY PRONOUNCED REVERSIBLE
FUNCTIONAL CHANGES BUT ACTUAL STRUCTURAL DETERIORATION WHICH
MAY NOT BE ENTIRELY REVERSIBLE

Man has been remarkably adaptable in connection with his diet, being exceeded, from the point of view of omniverousness, by the hog alone. It might be expected that quite low forms would exhibit a greater versatility in ability to absorb nutriment and therefore to survive than does man, but the case seems to be quite otherwise, for it is enough to place some insects upon an unfamiliar though satisfactory type of food in order to starve them to death. Still, man's very omniverousness seems to have been achieved at the cost of a loss in the ability to discriminate between good and bad, or even poisonous, food. It is very difficult to fool felines or canines about their food in spite of their domestication, and it is even more difficult to fool an ape, but man possesses little ability to select what is good, and reject what is bad, from natural sources. This ability is more notable in the very young than in older individuals. Taste and olfaction are both of rudimentary significance in man and deteriorate quite rapidly with age. Tests on primitive peoples and groups, such as the Lapps, who are located away from the central streams of culture do not support the notion that the olfactory or gustatory senses of these people are any more acute than those of people with more advanced and centralized cultures. Among all groups of modern man there is great individual variability in olfactory and gustatory sensitivity. In general about one-third of any population sample is practically anosmic and ageustic, but even those individuals who exhibit a good sense of smell and taste show little ability to live off an unfamiliar terrain. Modern man's nutrition provides an interesting example of the manner in which evolutionary change supplements function and is affected by a wide range of cultural and economic factors which will probably exert increasing degrees of pressure as the pressure of population density continues to increase. The essentially irrational role that culture plays in food habits and preferences has been explained by many serious and competent writers, and the extent to which processed, "substitute," and "supplementary" food products have supplanted natural foods has clearly been demonstrated to be dependent on the disinclination of people to expend the time and trouble in bringing the latter to the table. Psychiatrists have also shown the extent to which eating and eating habits have become substitutive functions unrelated to the actual bodily need for food as nutritive material. All these circumstances suggest areas requiring attention in the future in order to make certain that the neural system man has is adequately provided with the material it needs in order to function at peak capacity.

ANOTHER DIFFICULTY ARISING FROM FOODS, FROM THE POINT OF VIEW
OF THE NEURAL SYSTEM, IS THE NOT INCONSIDERABLE DANGER OF
ACTUAL POISONING

Here again the economic factors involved are especially· compelling. Tremendous quantities of insecticides, fungicides, dye products, and hygroscopic
agents are carried forward in food products brought to the table. It is rather
pointless to inveigh against the possibility of poisoning ourselves, when our
society is organized in such a manner as to force the producer to use dangerous materials in order to maintain the small margin of profit that keeps him
in business, when we beat Federal, state, and county budgets down to such
a level that no really efficient job of inspection can be done, and when the
consumer himself (or shall I say herself) shows a strong disinclination to
select safer food products which require time and labor in bringing them to
the table.

The opportunity for modern mankind to poison himself does not begin
with food and end with war. It covers a wide variety of possibilities encom-
passing practically all circumstances in which modern man comes in contact,
from the cradle to the grave, in his technical environment.

THE MODERN WORLD IS FULL OF ACCIDENT AND TECHNICAL HAZARDS

As the individual grows older and becomes ambulatory, his neural system
runs the risk of new conflicts with our culture. Although the death rate of
children in the first decade of life has been greatly lowered, this lowering has
been due to a reduction in the mortality from disease, not because of more
satisfactory safeguards against accidents. One might suppose that the children
of well-educated, solicitous, and careful parents would have a lower death rate
than the children of parents with little or no education, but what little information we have on this subject (and it is old) does not bear out that
common assumption (Lennox, 1924). There is, of course, a higher death
rate in slum areas, but many factors other than the lack of protection of
children are involved in such communities. There can be little doubt but that
the pattern of development of the nervous system (the insatiable and direct
curiosity and lack of care and foresight as well as of understanding, all
directly related to the manner in which the human neural system develops
ontogenetically) is responsible for the high death rate from accidents.

INFECTION

The period about 10 years of age is one at which neurological infections
are especially likely to occur. At that time the individual has attained, in
most modern cultures, full adult mobility but only partial immunity. It is,
moreover, an age at which intracranial neoplasms, which may have been

present from birth, now begin to become manifest. The brain reaches its maximum volume about the tenth year of life, but the cranium does not acquire its fullest size with the end of the second decade at which time the brain occupies about two-thirds of the endocranial volume. There is therefore a critical period of maximum endocranial filling at about the end of the first decade.

BEHAVIORAL DISORDERS

With the advent of adolescence, psychiatric disorders become distressingly more frequent and, for those who see in such conditions overt manifestations of biochemical disturbances, the metabolic shifts attendant upon a changing hormonal situation are conceived to provide the basis for this rise in incidence. While it is probable that the origin of severe psychiatric disturbances begins long before adolescence, it does seem to be true that in many endocrine disorders, such as myxedema, which begin with birth the more serious aspects of intellectual deficit are cumulative. Thus, the myxedematous child who has not received thyroid medication prior to the second decade of life usually has a permanently damaged neural system.

THE WITLESSNESS OF CHILDHOOD
PASSES INTO THE RISKINESS OF ADOLESCENCE

It takes the human being a long while to develop a sense of caution and to achieve a respect and understanding for, and of, destructive machinery. The primary killer of the first decade of our race continues as the principal cause of death throughout the second decade. If childhood is the age of simple curiosity and exploration, adolescence is the period of experiment and manipulation. It is at this latter age that the neural system is exposed to a new and serious though still fortunately minor peril—habituation to drugs. All such habituations (whether heroin addiction, alcoholism, barbiturates, or phenanthrene habituation—the smoking or coffee habits) are all essentially neural habituations, and the only real difference between the coffee drinker and morphine addict lies in the urgency and nature of his dependency, both dependencies being dictated through and by the nervous system.

WITH THE DEVELOPMENT OF ADULTHOOD AND THE ACQUISITION OF FULL
MUSCULAR POWER CERTAIN INADEQUACIES OF OUR EVOLUTIONARY STATE
BECOME APPARENT

Sensory acuity has already begun to fail before the individual has gone far into the third decade, and there is a marked degree of deterioration in the condition of the teeth which, if it were not offset by cultural skill, would soon exert a marked limiting influence upon many individuals.

Sensory deterioration, though perceptible, is not yet incapacitating, but the active physical life of the second and third decade soon discloses that man's assumption of the upright posture has been achieved at the risk of an essentially unstable vertebral column. In quadrupedal infraprimate species the vertebral column forms a rather simple horizontal arch of the classical type in which the highest point is in the center and the central vertebrae behave much like keystones. In the lower primates such as the fossil lemur, *Notharctus,* or recent baboon the vertebral column has not become organized in such a way as to introduce any appreciable risk into its stability. In man, however, the situation is greatly altered, and a double or sigmoid curvature has replaced the original arch. Where this curvature is free, as in the cervical and lumbar regions, anteroposterior displacements in the elements of the column are not uncommon, with the result that the contained spinal cord and nerves may be damaged. Sudden compressive forces, such as may occur in directional change in high speed travel, greatly increase the probability of such structural failures. It may be asked why this feature of human structure should be a greater hazard at the present time than it was in an equestrian society. There is no doubt that ruptured or herniated nucleus pulposus, as this condition is called, was a common cause of trouble for our carriage-riding predecessors, but a torso well-splinted by abdominal and back muscles properly developed by horseback riding is not particularly vulnerable to this disability. We are not, however, making comparisons here between the twentieth and nineteenth centuries but between the quadrupedal, semi-quadrupedal, and erect postures. Sciatica, the name by which this condition was known to our forbears, has been a familiar feature of the literature of medicine from earliest times, and there is every indication that the unstable dynamics of our vertebral column, although long known, constitute a definite contemporary hazard to the safety of the neural system in view of the demands of high speed travel and the lack of opportunity to maintain a properly exercised axial musculature.

RADIATION

While it is probable that all of the population of the future will be subjected to more or less potentially dangerous radiation, it seems likely that adults will be subjected to more intense and prolonged exposure than the young or aged. Fortunately the neural system is peculiarly resistant to the effects of radiation, and it is only by radiation during early intra-uterine life that any notable effect would be produced.

WARFARE

There seems to be no particular reason to suppose that the neural system would be particularly vulnerable to bacterial or biologic warfare. We are not well prepared from the point of view of public defense against biologic attack, but (with the exception of certain improbable parasitic infections, such as by trypanosomes or cysticerci) most populations are naturally well protected, as the result of natural, or easily acquired, immunity against infections of the neural system. The case is quite otherwise with regard to chemical warfare.

PHYSICAL DISTURBANCES

One might suppose that physical disturbances would adversely affect the neural system, and they do but not preferentially and, in the case of some agents (such as vibration caused by pneumatic drills), to a lesser extent than joint surfaces, tendon sheaths, and bony structures. Some physical disturbances, notably decompression and the thermal extremes of runaway industrial processes, may disturb the neural system extensively though in an indirect manner. Heat stroke and freezing occur only after there has been a breakdown in the heat-regulating mechanism, such as sweatgland fatigue or failure of the metabolic processes to cope with a reduction in environmental temperature. Aviation black-out is due either to lack of oxygen or to gravitational or centrifugal force manifesting itself differentially with regard to the body and its circulating blood, and in such a way as to result in regional anemia.

CHARACTER OF THE NERVE CELL

Although the neural system is the physical substrate for many delicate perceptual and adaptive processes, it is not a fragile and precarious tissue but a tough apparatus. Nevertheless it must have the means to maintain itself by food and oxygen in a minimum condition. In respect to the need for food and oxygen, we have not advanced far in 500 million years. Our nerve cells still require to be bathed in an aqueous, nutrient, oxygen-containing medium much like their Cambrian progenitors required, and this would appear to continue as a definite limitation upon the future.

Until quite recently we were of the opinion that mature nerve cells of the central neural system could not regenerate. We knew that the distal processes of neurocytes could and did regenerate, but it seemed as though the fibers inside the spinal cord and brain were devoid of this property. Moreover, when cells situated there were seriously damaged they seemed to be unable to recuperate and usually perished.

Such a situation now appears to be due to factors outside the nerve cell itself. Probably it is caused by the overenthusiastic activity of elements associated with the more sedately behaving nerve cells which are as frequently thwarted by the reparative activity of these associated elements as by the original traumatic situation. Anyone who is blessed with well-meaning but meddlesome relatives will appreciate the predicament of the neurocytes!

We now know that neurocytes will survive in tissue culture when removed not only from the body of embryos but even from that of adult humans. Moreover, such cells regenerate their broken processes and attempt to establish a kind of communal relationship. In my own laboratory we have found that such cells do not merely survive but are capable of being excited by electrical stimulation. Electrodes so small their tips cannot be seen under the microscope can be constructed and inserted within the cell in order to study its internal behavior! The study of the electrophysiology of single nerve cells grown outside the body has therefore become an actuality, and we have a tool with which to study the metabolism of the various elements of the nervous system *in vitro*. In this way the effect of drugs, vitamins, and other chemicals on such cells can be investigated directly. The possibility of the isolation of individual cell types is also within our grasp, and the construction of an artificial nervous system from real, living neural elements is a very definite possibility of the future.

HOW THE NERVOUS SYSTEM BREAKS DOWN

There is another way in which we can approach the problem of what the future has in store for the nervous system. Instead of attempting to identify the substances and conditions that place definite limits on its ability to function, we can try to determine what the most common types and causes of neural disintegration have in common. We have three major sources of information on this subject—mortality and morbidity statistics and autopsy findings. The figures on morbidity statistics can be profitably augmented by data on industrial hazards, absenteeism, the incidence of accidents, and the manner in which medical (and dental) services are utilized.

Necropsy statistics (fig.5) lead us to believe that of the persons who will presumably die this year one-third will have notable damage of the nervous system. Mortality statistics are misleading, because the actual cause of death in a case of apoplexy may be pneumonia. It is for this reason that the autopsy findings on unselected cases are more informative as to the true extent of neural damage. By far the largest number of these neural lesions are the result of failures of blood supply to the nervous system. One-quarter of all dead persons show notable damage of this nature. Of such cases one-third have had actual hemorrhages, whereas the remainder exhibit softening and death of neural tissue as a result of inadequacy of blood flow.

Of the 33 per cent of autopsy cases with neural lesions, about 25 per cent is therefore accounted for on the above basis and the remaining 8 per cent is accounted for by approximately equal proportions (2%) of tumors, trauma, malformations, and infections of the neural system.

Six per cent of all deaths are due to accidents each year, and a large proportion of these must be considered due (in more than one sense) to neural failure or inadequate function from the point of view of natural selection.

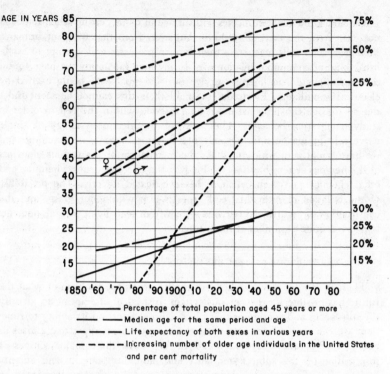

Fig. 6 Composite of three more or less independent graphs (data obtained from Joseph Zubin from Dublin, Lotka, and Spiegelman, 1949; and from Statistical Bulletin of the Metropolitan Life Insurance Co., 1949, vol. 30, no. 10, pp. 1–3; 1952, vol. 33, no. 3, pp. 1–3; 1953, vol. 34, no. 4, pp. 1–2). Lowermost line on lowermost graph shows percentage of total population aged 45 or more from 1850 through the present; median age for same period shown in upper left line in same area. Life expectancy for individuals of both sexes and born in various years shown by two dashed lines in center of graph. In upper right quadrant, three dotted lines show times at which generations born in various years from 1900 through the present exhibited a 25, 50, and 75 per cent mortality. Thus, of the generation born in 1900, 25 per cent were dead at age 25 (or 1925), and half are dead now. By 1972 three-quarters of that generation presumably will have died.

In summary then, although trauma of the neural system is especially lethal and although a surprisingly high percentage of tumors and malformations are found in the neural system and it is rather susceptible to infection, the overwhelming cause of destruction of neural tissue is failure in blood supply.

Morbidity statistics reveal a much higher percentage of persons to be affected by neuropsychiatric disorders than are found to contain evidence of neuropathology at death. This is not due to such a simple matter as the fact that not all neuropsychiatric disorders depend on obvious organic substrate, for there are many lesions demonstrable after death that are not accompanied by obvious interference with function. This is because the nervous system, like other bodily tissues, contains a certain amount of spare material.

About 3 per cent of the population of the United States suffers from neuropsychiatric disorders which are ongoing and serious (table 9), other than deafness, blindness, and old age. Of this number of persons by far the largest proportion suffer from psychiatric or convulsive disorders.

Although advanced age is not in itself a disease, in the common sense of the word, there are few persons who have passed the age of 65 who do not exhibit a certain amount of psychomotor deterioration. At the present time about 8 per cent of the population is 65 years or older (fig. 5).

A figure of 10 per cent would therefore be a very conservative one for persons exhibiting impaired neural function. If one included persons who are deaf, mute, and or blind, or who are suffering from some temporary neuropsychiatric impairment, an estimate of 20 per cent would not be too high for that proportion of the population which at any moment must be considered unable to participate in the true type of activity on which survival would depend if the protective mechanisms of society were to break down. If, because of military urgency, such protective mechanisms were ineffectual for a protracted period, this entire segment of the population might very well succumb.

While the effect of morbidity due to neuropsychiatric disorder is non-adaptive behavior, it is not easy to explain what the most important cause or causes for such disorders may be, because when we speak of a psychiatric disease we really are only applying the term to non-adaptive behavior and

TABLE 9

PREVALENCE OF ONGOING SERIOUS NEUROPSYCHIATRIC DISORDERS IN THE UNITED STATES

Demyelinizing diseases		
Total	8,000	5/100,000
In northern latitudes	6,000	10/100,000
Cerebral palsy (major congenital defects)	500,000	300/100,000
Born annually	11,000	
Expected mortality in infancy	1,500	
Expected life institutionalization	3,000	
Remaining in society	6,500	
Convulsive disorders (epilepsy)	750,000+	500/100,000
Serious psychiatric disorders	2,800,000	1,750/100,000

the term must necessarily be relative. It is sometimes said that complexity in civilization "causes more mental breakdowns." This is probably not true, but it is certainly true that non-adaptive behavior has less social significance in less complex societies and that what Coon has called the paleolithic organization of social life can tolerate such behavior more easily than a highly specialized urban culture. The incidence of psychiatric morbidity rises in urban communities not because such communities contain or produce more "breakdowns" but because they extrude non-adaptive individuals more vigorously than do agricultural communities and because such individuals succumb in non-supportive environments. This is just another way of saying that culture exerts its own selective effect, and we have therefore come again upon the ubiquitous manner in which evolutionary change supplements operate. In very primitive, unorganized societies psychiatrically ill individuals soon perish. In simple, organized societies they may not only survive but may be treated as privileged persons. In highly competitive societies they are protected but extruded if they possess no useful skill or creative ability. It is surprising to what extent society is able to absorb aberrant behavioral patterns which are not merely non-contributory but frankly aberrant, providing the individual exhibiting the pattern has something useful to offer the community.

Ordinarily an environmental situation admits of only one directional developmental tendency. There is only one "ideal." In a regulated, variable environment a number of different ideals may be tolerable and the individual traits which go towards the development of such different ideals may be mutually contradictory or even antagonistic or destructive.

A scientifically organized, mechanistic society must necessarily depend on the creative ability of its reflective minds, and these must operate in the relatively free and unhurried milieu which is itself destroyed by the very machine and increased productivity which the reflective mind creates. We all know creative engineering geniuses whose preoccupations with generalities and principles result on the one hand in constant and almost daily scientific and mechanical advances and whose preoccupations, on the other hand, also make them practically unfit to drive a simple automobile. Traits such as rapid reaction time and the ability to develop generalities, both of great value to our society, are not necessarily present in the same individual, nor does the same individual necessarily exhibit one of these traits throughout his lifetime.

In a rigid and obligatory environment individuals departing from the requirements of the environment are ultimately obliterated. In our social organization the accident-prone driver can travel in public conveyances, obtain a chauffeur, stay at home, move to an isolated community, or even obtain repeated respite from obliteration through the technical skills of the medical profession.

Not only does the manipulation of environment lead to great intraspecies variation by the preservation of variants and mutants and provision for these to procreate, but interbreeding among all the members of the species is facilitated.

For the individual who considers himself the prototype of the future and the fittest human this is a dismal prospect indeed. For the biologist such shuffling about constitutes no real alteration in the species, because the moment such an elaborated species is brought into direct contact with a compulsive environment all the irrelevant variants are promptly eliminated.

It would appear that while man's cultural development has tended on the one hand to preserve variants that will ultimately prove to have been useless it will also have the effect of guarding the species by having protected it from the commitment of specific evolutionary specialization. Not only has average man remained unspecialized but he has, in the process of domestication, become a result as well as a manipulating factor of that process and now presents a bewildering degree of variation not merely at the structural but also at the behavioral level, to the consternation of obstetricians and delight of psychologists.

CONCLUSION

Attention has been drawn to the fact that there is no good evidence to support the assumption that man's neural system has undergone any progressive alteration in the direction of greater size or complexity since the middle of the Pleistocene. It was at this period that cultural development became manifest, and the hypothesis is advanced that, with the advent of culture, man achieved a degree of independence from his environment and was therefore no longer under the necessity of developing structural modifications to survive. Consideration is drawn to the fact that the culture man has created has itself become a selective factor in his development and has resulted in great variation in the species.

It is pointed out that man's nervous system has some definite structural and functional limitations and that structural evolution in the direction of a larger or more complex neural system would require the movement of the species form into a direction in which the factors of structural and physiologic safety are already very narrow. Evolution of the species, in the sense of improvement in living conditions and extended and continued manipulation of the environment, would consequently appear to have to occur at a cultural rather than structural level. The specific structural limitations placed on man's neural system appear to be those that animal forms have inherited from the earliest Paleozoic, notably the necessity of a cell living in an aqueous medium to obtain oxygen and food.

In its broadest sense structural evolution may be regarded as a process that really gathered momentum and significance when unicellular organisms became combined into complex bodies in which the component cells assumed specialized functions. In so far as later forms are concerned, this process appears to have been extended by the cooperation of complex individuals in social systems. There is nothing novel about a comparison of the social order in which individuals are the subsidiary units to biologic bodies in which cells are the units, but, within the culture man has developed, there seems to be no clear, general recognition of the fact that a social order implies that individuals must accept the principle of specialization and cooperation and that neither the individual nor the system can achieve maximum efficiency if the subsidiary elements of the system insist that they can accomplish any and all tasks in the social order. Certainly, if there is to be any considerable evolution in which the neural system is to participate, it is quite clear that individual neural systems must draw upon the cultural reserves of the order, and this implies specialization on the part of particular individuals.

Before putting down the subject in hand, I should like to call attention to the fact that a recognition of the cooperative function of the individual involves a radical revision on the part of the individual in the concept of the "I" and "not I." A high degree of cooperative activity cannot be achieved in the presence of a strong sense of distinction between what is the concern of the individual and what is not. On the other hand a marked weakening in the ability to distinguish between the "I" and "not I" can have serious psychiatric consequences.*

How does the neural system determine what is a part of the self and what is not? It is not possible to develop this consideration to any extent at this place, but it is not difficult to demonstrate that identification of the self with substance involves to a very large extent the degree of personal satisfaction the individual can obtain from such substance. Under such circumstances my glasses are much more significant to me than the last toe of my left foot. Our cultural development has progressed therefore to the point where we can easily place a higher evaluation on an item of technological achievement than on a part of our own body. This would seem to be a rather interesting way of raising the question whether evolutionary progress may not be moving not only faster but more significantly in the area of culture than structure.

REFERENCES

Baraduc 1876 Troubles cérébraux analogues a ceux de la paralysie générale. Bull. Soc. Anat. Paris, pp. 277–279.
Bartholomew, G. A., and J. B. Birdsell 1953 Ecology and the protohominids. Amer. Anthrop., vol. 55, pp. 481–498.
Blomquist, H. E. 1953 Über die aus dem 5–6 Jahrhundert n. Chr. stammenden Knochenfunde von Kjeldamäki (im Kirschspiel Wöra, Süd-Ostbothnien, Finnland). Ann. Acad. Sci. Fennica, vol. 36, pp. 5–37.
Bolton, J. S. 1911 A contribution to the localization of cerebral function based upon the clinico-pathological study of mental disease. Brain, vol. 33, pp. 26–148.
Bonin, G. von 1934 On the size of man's brain as indicated by skull capacity. Jour. Comp. Neurol., vol. 59, pp. 1–28.
Broca, P. 1862 Sur la capacité des crânes parisiens des divers époques. Bull. Soc. d'Anthrop. Paris, ser. 1, vol. 3, pp. 102–116.

* This subject has been considered further by Professor Mettler in Fundamentals of psychology: psychology of the self. Ann. N. Y. Acad. Sci., 1961.

Bruns, L.   1892   Ueber Störungen des Gleichgewichtes bei Stirnhirntumoren. Deutsche med. Wochenschr., vol. 18, pp. 138–140.

——   1897   Die Geschwülste des Nervensystems. Berlin.

Burckhardt, G.   1890–1891   Ueber Rindenexcisionen. Allg. Zeitschr. f. Psychiat., vol. 47, pp. 463–548.

Campbell, B.   1954   The organization of the cerebral cortex. Jour. Neuropathol. Exp. Neurol., vol. 13, pp. 407–416.

Charcot, J. M.   1876–1880   Leçons sur les localisations dans les maladies du cerveau et de la moelle épinière faites à la faculté de médecine de Paris. Paris, 2 vols.

Cobb, W. M.   1955   The age incidence of suture closure. Anat. Rec., vol. 121, p. 277.

Conel, J. LeR.   1939–1955   The postnatal development of the human cerebral cortex. Cambridge, Massachusetts, Harvard University Press, 5 vols.

Coon, C. A.   1954   The story of man. New York, Alfred A. Knopf.

Craik, K. J. W.   1952   The nature of explanation. Cambridge, Cambridge University Press.

Darwin, C .G.   1953   The next million years. Garden City, New York, Doubleday and Co., Inc.

Donaldson, H. H.   1895   The growth of the brain. London, Walter Scott, Ltd.

Dublin, L. I., A. J. Lotka, and M. Spiegelman   1949   Length of life. Revised edition. New York, Ronald Press Co.

Dubois, E.   1914   Die gesetzmässige Beziehung von Gehirnmasse zu Körpergrösse bei den Wirbeltieren. Zeitschr. f. Morphol. u. Anthrop., vol. 18, pp. 323–350.

Economo, C. von   1926   Ein Koeffizient für die Organisationshöhe der Grosshirnrinde. Klin. Wochenschr., no. 14.

——   1929   Wie sollen wir Elitegehirne verarbeiten? Zeitschr. f. d. g. Neurol. u. Psychiat., vol. 121, pp. 324–409.

Ferrier, D.   1890   The Croonian lectures on cerebral localization. London, Smith, Elder and Co., p. 151.

Fischer, E.   1952   Über das Wesen der anatomischen Varietäten. Zeitschr. f. menschliche Vererbungs- u. Konstitutionslehre, vol. 31, pp. 217–242.

Flechsig, P.   1896   Gehirn und Seele. Auflage 2. Leipzig.

——   1896   Die Localisation der geistigen Vorgänge, insbesondere der Sinnesempfindungen des Menschen. Leipzig.

Gregory, W. K.   1951   Evolution emerging. A survey of changing patterns from primeval life to man. New York, The Macmillan Co., 2 vols.

Greisinger, W.   1867   Mental pathology and therapeutics. Translation by C. L. Robertson and J. Rutherford. London, The New Sydenham Society.

Harlow, J. M.   1848   Passage of an iron rod through the head. Boston Med. and Surg. Jour., vol. 39, pp. 389–393.

——   1869   Recovery from the passage of an iron bar through the head. Boston, D. Clapp and Son, p. 20.

Herrick, C. J.   1948   The brain of Amblystoma punctatum. Chicago, The University of Chicago Press.

Hitzig, E.   1884   Zur Physiologie des Grosshirns, Wandervers. d. Südwestd. Neurol. u. Irrenärzte in Baden, 17 Juni, 1883. Arch. f. Psychiat., vol. 15, pp. 270–275.

Jastrowitz, M.   1888   Beiträge zur Localisation im Grosshirn und über deren praktische Verwerthung. Deutsche med. Wochenschr., vol. 14, pp. 81–83, 108–112, 125–128, 151–153, 172–175, 188–192, 209–211 (see especially p 111).

Keith, A.   1925   The antiquity of man. London.

LASKER, G. W.   1953   Environmental growth factors and selective migration. Human Biol., vol. 24, pp. 262–289.

LE GROS CLARK, W. E.   1954   The fossil evidence for human evolution. Chicago, The University of Chicago Press.

LENNOX, W. G.   1924   Child mortality with reference to the higher education of parents. Amer. Jour. Hygiene, vol. 4, pp. 52–61.

LEYDEN, E., and M. JASTROWITZ   1888   Beiträge zur Lehre von der Localisation im Gehirn. Leipzig, Thieme, p. 82.

LOEB, J.   1902   Comparative physiology of the brain and comparative psychology. New York, G. P. Putnam Sons.

LULL, R. S., H. B. FERRIS, G. H. PARKER, J. R. ANGELL, A. G. KELLER, and E. G. CONKLIN   1922   The evolution of man. New Haven, Yale University Press.

MARTIN, R.   1928   Lehrbuch der Anthropologie. Auflage 2. Jena, G. Fischer, 3 vols.

METTLER, C. C.   1947   History of medicine. Philadelphia, The Blakiston Co.

METTLER, FRED A. (ED.)   1949   Selective partial ablation of the frontal cortex. New York, Paul B. Hoeber, Inc.

MOÑIZ, EGAS   1936   Les premières tentatives opératoires dans le traitement de certaines psychoses. Encéphale, vol. 31, no. 2, pp. 1–29.

MURPHY, J. P.   1954   Cerebrovascular disease. Chicago, The Year Book Publishers, Inc.

NOBELE   1835   Ann. Med. Belge, Fevrier, Compte Rendu. Cited by Haeser, H., 1836, Fall einer bedeutenden Gehirnverletzung. Schmidt's Jahrbücher, vol. 9, pp. 321–322.

OPPENHEIM, H.   1900   Diseases of the nervous system. Translated by E. E. Mayer. Philadelphia, J. B. Lippincott, p. 399.

OTTO, W.   1953   Über Geburtenverteilung der verschiedenen Wuchsformen. Zeitschr. f. Altersforschung, vol. 7, pp. 130–139.

PARKER, G. H.   1922   The evolution of the nervous system of man. In Lull, R. S., and others, The evolution of man. New Haven, Yale University Press, pp. 80–102.

RETZIUS, G.   1915   Wächst noch die Grösse des menschlichen Gehirns? Zeitschr. f. Morphol. u. Anthrop., vol. 18, pp. 49–64.

ROCHE, A. F.   1953   Increase in cranial thickness during growth. Human Biol., vol. 25, pp. 81–92.

ROWLAND, LEWIS P., and FRED A. METTLER   1949   Cell concentration and laminar thickness in the frontal cortex of psychotic patients. Jour. Comp. Neurol., vol. 90, pp. 255–280.

SCOTT, J. H.   1953   The variability of cranial and facial dimensions in modern skulls. Brit. Dental Jour., vol. 94, pp. 27–31.

SHAPIRO, H. L.   1933   Man—500,000 years from now. Nat. Hist., vol. 33, pp. 582–595.

SKERLJ, B., and Z. DOLINAR   1950   Staroslovanska okostja z Bleda. Monogr. Slovene Acad. Sci. Arts, Ljubljana, cl. 1, no. 2, pp. 67–104.

STRAUS, W. L., JR.   1954   Some problems of human evolution. Anat. Rec., vol. 121, p. 371.

TILNEY, FREDERICK, and H. A. RILEY   1928   The brain from ape to man. New York, Paul B. Hoeber.

TORGERSEN, J., B. GETZ, U. HAFSTEN, and H. OLSEN   1953   Steinaldersmannen fra Bleivik, Skåre, Rogaland. Årbok Univ. Bergen, Naturvitenskap. Rekke, no. 6, pp. 1–53.

VIERORDT, H.   1893   Anatomische physiologische und physikalische Daten und Tabellen. Jena, Gustav Fischer.

WEIDENREICH, FRANZ 1924 Die Sonderform des-Menschenschädels als Anpassung an den aufrechten Gang. Zeitschr. f. Morphol. u. Anthrop., vol. 22, pp. 51–282.
———— 1946 Form and qualities of the human brain and skull in the light of evolution. In his Apes, giants and man. Chicago, The University of Chicago Press.
WELT, L. 1888 Ueber Charakterveränderungen des Menschen infolge von Läsionen des Stirnhirns. Deutsches Arch. f. klin. Med., vol. 42, pp. 339–390.

THE SPEARMAN AND THE ARCHER—

AN ESSAY ON SELECTION IN BODY BUILD

ALICE BRUES

INTRODUCTION

Body build presents many interesting aspects to the student of selection in man. Various local and minor groups have become specialized in body size or body shape, though most tend to cluster about a general average for the species, with a considerable degree of variation within each group. As between major races, or populations on a continental scale, the differences are unclear; any attempt to characterize a major race by a typical physique can be countered by the citing of exceptions. In addition, body build has a fairly apparent relation to the environment and man's energy exchanges with it, though the very degree of polymorphism which it exhibits leads us to suspect that its survival value involves numerous elements, some of which are rather obscure. Recent clinically slanted studies of body build have in fact emphasized the durable quality of physiques which are not considered strong in the muscular sense. These findings can explain in part the retention by most populations of considerable genetic variability with respect to body build. If, as is probable, the implications of body build for health and longevity are more complex than has yet been demonstrated, the polymorphism of body build may prove to be influenced by a balance between physiological factors which work at cross purposes. Such a balance could be unrelated to specific environment; or it could be profoundly affected by it, as in relation to temperature, nature of available foodstuffs, or the presence of specific transmissible diseases or occupational hazards.

A further possible element in selection, with which this paper proposes to deal specifically, is the relation of body build to the efficiency with which different activities can be carried out, particularly those activities which vary with culture and means of subsistence. In our recent civilization we may justify the maintenance of polymorphism in body build as suitable to the carrying out of a variety of occupations; but this explanation cannot be projected to ancient and primitive peoples who lack such a degree of occupational specialization. In such groups we would expect that the characteristic tools and techniques of each economy and cultural stage would establish an optimum type of body build toward which selective trends would aim during

Reprinted from *American Anthropologist*, 61: (1960), 457–69.

that period. The present essay will attempt to explore the implications of this thesis with respect to the evolution and distribution of the varieties of body build.

If any doubt remains in regard to the potentialities of selection in body build, it may be resolved by consideration of changes wrought in domestic animals. Smaller species such as the chicken and rabbit have been brought to body weights commonly three or more times that of the wild progenitors. Dwarf or pygmy strains have also been bred out from time to time, the most recent being a minuscule pig intended as a laboratory animal. Body build selection in the Sheldonian sense is also apparent—as the development of ectomorphy in the race horse as opposed to mesomorphy in the draft horse. Among cattle the beef breeds have been selected for mesomorphy in order to increase the bulk of edible muscle, and a generation ago the domestic pig could have been put forth as the epitome of endomorphy. However, with the increase in use of vegetable oils and the declining price of lard, hog breeders have rapidly faced about, and the endomorphic lard hog has been replaced by a more mesomorphic type which produces better chops. Here body build has been shown susceptible to selection even to the extent that the trend is readily reversible. There is no reason for supposing that the potentialities of selection for body build in man have been any less, though natural selection even under cultural conditions will probably not be as rigorous or rapid as artificial selection, particularly as practiced by the genetically sophisticated breeders of the present time.

Various possible selective influences on body build have been studied in many animals, some in fact being suggested and demonstrated (as well as one can demonstrate the progress of evolution) by comparison of the build of various species with their capabilities and habits. One of the most obvious and first to be noted is the advantage of slender build with long limb segments in the attainment of speed of movement. Another factor is "strength," usually a rather poorly defined term, with respect to the self-defense of an individual who stands his ground instead of fleeing. It is notable that carnivores, which must generally reach their prey by speed and dispatch it by direct force, tend to remain average in build. The predatees, however, are prone to reject this compromise and choose a policy either of flight, with specialization for speed, or of static defense, with a tendency to increased body size. In fact, one of the most insidious of evolutionary traps is the sacrifice of mobility for indestructible size, as seen in our closest kin the gorilla. As we shall see later in the analysis of factors of strength, lateral build also is favorable to static defense, and is developed concomitantly with increasing size in many cases. Large size and comparatively lateral build are also favored by cold environment, since they tend to retard heat loss by reduction of relative surface area. Small body size may be an advantage if an animal can slip into crevices not large enough for others to pass; it has been suggested that the development and survival of pygmy types of man in dense jungle environments has been favored by selection on this basis. Endomorphy presents advantages in a cold climate because of the favorable insulating effects of the subcutaneous fat layer. Endomorphy has also been suggested as an asset where food supplies vary greatly from season to season, since the endomorph presumably stores excess aliment more readily (Coon, Garn, and Birdsell 1950).

In evaluating physical efficiency from the complete biological standpoint, we must also take into consideration the dietary requirements of different sized individuals. In the rigors of primitive culture a large body may be very costly to maintain. Body bulk must be used efficiently in terms of its food-getting capacity; for it will little profit a primitive hunter if his hunting proceeds increase 10 percent while his appetite goes up 11 percent. For this reason the nicest adjustment of body to activity will be by change of shape rather than size. In the course of this study the author had occasion to examine anthropometric data on modern athletes distinguished in various sports. It revealed little except that they were all fine, large individuals compared with the general population—in fact, veritable giants compared with most peoples in a primitive population. One suspects that if their athletic accomplishments were strictly weighted according to the amount of food it took to keep them going, they might yield their world's records to their smaller competitors. Most of them would undoubtedly be expensive ornaments in a primitive society. Certain data on stature in relatively modern populations, in fact, suggest that there is a tendency for the larger individual (and race) not to work, but instead to bully others into working for him.

WORK, FORCE AND ENERGY

In order to understand the potentialities of various body types for various cultural techniques, we need to analyze the concept of "strength" in physical activities. The word "strength" is not found in the physicist's vocabulary; it is a lay term which inextricably confuses the physical concepts of work, force, and energy. Force is the simplest of this constellation of concepts; it is measured in pounds, and in its simplest form is that influence which a heavy object exerts by resting on something; force can also be exerted in various directions and by various means other than the collaboration of mass and gravity. The concept of force leads to that of pressure, measured in pounds per square inch, which depends on the area through which a force is exerted on a surface; pressure, so defined, is important in overcoming the resistance of an object which is to be broken or altered in shape. Force and pressure are measures of a momentary state only. When force acts so as to move something for a distance, we say that work has been performed. That which can produce work, when properly directed or released, is known as energy. Energy may be electrical, chemical, or of other forms; at present we are mainly concerned with mechanical energy, which may be potential, if embodied in a configuration of matter under tension, as in a drawn bow; or kinetic, if embodied in motion, as in a flying spear. Kinetic energy is the most readily measurable of energy forms, being expressed by the product of the mass and the velocity of a moving object, and from it we infer the amount of energy that was necessary to set the object in motion. Energy is conserved through various transmutations between potential and kinetic energy and work performed; in the case of energy manifested by the animal body, it is ultimately derived from the chemical energy present in foodstuffs, and mediated by the action of muscle.

The peculiar role of muscle tissue in energy exchange is its capacity to shorten against resistance. This may produce free motion in a part of the body or something grasped by it; more exactly, it accelerates the mass of a portion of the body and attached object and causes it to attain a velocity, thus transforming chemical into kinetic energy. If the motion produced is resisted by some elastic structure, or in other analogous ways, much of the energy is stored as potential energy. A muscle, contracting, exerts a certain amount of force; and the force which it can exert under maximum effort depends on what is called its physiological cross-section. The latter, except where certain special arrangements of muscle fibers exist, is equivalent to the cross-section area of the muscle itself. This force of contraction, it should be noted, is the pull in pounds as exerted at the point on the skeleton where the muscle inserts. The length of a muscle does not affect the force of the pull which it exerts, but, since muscle fibers can only contract a certain fraction of their length, does determine the distance over which motion at the insertion of the muscle can be produced. A short stout muscle will exert greater force over a less distance, and a long thin muscle less force over a greater distance; if their total bulk (cross-section $\times$ length) is the same, their capacity for work (force $\times$ distance) is the same, although their exact properties and capacities will differ because of their shapes (Bowen 1949:33–34).

In nearly all cases the force exerted by the contracting muscle is not applied directly to the outside environment, but is mediated by certain lever arrangements within the skeleton. One of the simplest examples which can be given—as well as one applicable to many work operations—is the contraction of the biceps muscle producing bending of the elbow. The muscle inserts into the radius below the elbow joint, and the ultimate force against the environment is generally exerted by the hand. In this arrangement the hand always moves through a much larger arc than does the point of muscle insertion, and by simple mechanical law the movement of the hand while greater in distance is less in force. The exact ratio of reduction of force in this arrangement depends on the relative lengths of the segment of the skeleton lying between the joint axis and the muscle attachment, and the length of the segment between the muscle attachment and the part of the hand with which the force is finally applied. If the total length of the forearm is reduced, with the muscle attachment remaining in the same place, the force of the hand movement is increased and the distance of movement decreased. Given the same force, as measured at the muscle attachment, and the same rate of contraction, there is an inverse ratio between the force of pull of the hand, as it would be measured by a tension dynamometer, and the speed with which the hand can be moved in a flailing or throwing action. The power leverage is accomplished by a short forearm, the speed leverage by a long forearm. Since a long thin muscle, as we have seen above, exerts less force, but over a greater distance, than a short thick one, increasing length of the proximal as well as the distal segment of the limb accentuates speed and lessens force. Conversely, the shorter proximal muscle as well as the shorter distal limb segment increases force. It is easy to see then why the stocky individual is thought of as "strong" in terms of the force which he can exert momentarily in lifting a weight or crushing a resistant object, a common lay concept of strength. (Tappen even found an achondroplastic dwarf among his champion weight lifters.) This is in spite of the fact that a tall slender individual of the same weight will have approximately the same work capacity (dependent on total muscle bulk) though his muscular system, due to shape of muscles and skeletal leverages, cannot at any moment exert as many pounds of force on a resistant object (Jones 1947). The apparent paradox that the physically "strong" individual is not always constitutionally strong appears in this light to be based on an oddity of definition. This individual is "strong" not because he is made of different material but simply because he is of a different shape.

MECHANICS OF ESSENTIAL ACTIVITIES

The most primitive of the mechanical actions in which body form is selective is locomotion. The striking variations in limb size associated with brachiation versus terrestrial progression have been exhaustively discussed in relation to the evolution of the higher primates. It should be pointed out, however, that terrestrial progression is not precisely the same thing in all environments. Running is the most rigorous of bipedal acts and the one requiring the highest specialization for bipedal progression; yet there are many environments in which running can be performed only intermittently, and only in fairly open country can running speed alone be relied on for either pursuit or flight. Elsewhere one must have the ability to pass obstacles by leaping, climbing, or in the case of light brush, crashing through. Of these activities, only leaping is consistent with the type of build which is optimum for running. It appears likely that the original specialization of the human leg took place with *Australopithecus* and related forms, in an open prairie country where continuous running and leaping were possible. Such an environment is conducive to running specializations in all animals, and generally results not only in leg lengthening but in overall slender build. This effect would hardly be expected in a terrestrial animal dwelling in a tropical forest where progression among underbrush and vines is slow and crooked, except for the animal which has sufficient bulk to tear through obstacles by sheer weight. This environmental difference probably determined the divergence in build between the gorilla and the progressive terrestrial hominids.

An environment which offers special problems for terrestrial locomotion is that of the northern forest. Here large tree-trunks, not subject to decay as in warm climates, lie fallen and sometimes piled up two and three deep, so that walking, let alone running, cannot be performed for more than a few yards continuously; in fact, the technique of choice often is to traverse the tops of the barricades and avoid descent to the ground. Travel in such an environment involves as much or more climbing than walking, so that although terrestrial in the technical sense, it requires some of the talents of an arboreal animal. Probably the evolutionary lag in the limb skeleton of Neanderthal man is related to the fact that he remained close to the edge of the continental glacier in a zone which produced this type of forest (Weckler 1954).

Under primitive conditions a critical operation for survival is the use of weapons, particularly against larger animals and man. Their use against a human enemy is relatively rare, but particularly critical when conflict occurs. In killing animals for food, especially the larger ones, much is at stake in a single motion both as regards the safety of the hunter and the amount of food represented by the victim. It should be remembered also that earlier hominids and men, with their less developed armamentarium, were not dealing with animals which had acquired a "fear of man," and were in real danger of attack upon themselves. Hence efficiency of weapon use, if related to body build, makes the latter a selective factor of considerable importance.

The aggressive and defensive techniques of a terrestrial hominid in the pre-weapon stage would probably have to follow the pattern of the gorilla, whose destructiveness is in proportion to the amount of squeezing or crushing force exerted momentarily on the fragile parts of the victim. Such a technique places a premium on large muscle bulk combined with power leverages in the skeletal and muscular arrangements. The end result of selection under such circumstances is large size with lateral build and limb segments short relative to muscle bulk. This physique in a pronounced form drastically reduces speed of locomtion, and such an animal finally becomes a herbivore, since, though he could kill anything he could catch, he cannot catch anything.

The first presumed hominid weapons are the ungulate femora described by Dart (1949) as the weapons of *Australopithecus*. These fall into the general class of "blunt instruments" and are associated with a besticidal (and homicidal) technique which we shall refer to as "bludgeoning." In this technique the typical weapon is designed to crush some part, most effectively the skull, rather than to penetrate deeply, and hence does not have a sharp point. Such a weapon is not generally thrown, since its crudity makes it advisable to retain it in the hand for repeated blows as needed. It seems reasonable to assume that as long as artifacts are blunt or axe-like and not apparently adapted to tipping a projectile, some form of the bludgeoning technique was in use.

Bludgeoning does not require any very specialized application of energy. Within reasonable limits, the destruction wrought on the victim will depend on the total amount of energy absorbed; that is to say, a four-pound club moving at the rate of ten feet per second will probably smash as much skull as a two-pound club moving at the rate of twenty feet per second, and so on, unless the velocity is so low that the blow simply pushes. Thus the effectiveness of the bludgeon can remain the same with two factors reciprocally varying, namely, the weight of the object accelerated and the velocity which it attains. In this case neither momentary force nor speed of action need be at a maximum; rather, the total amount of energy embodied in the moving weapon, and therefore the total amount of muscular work performed, determines the effectiveness. Thus the determining factor in terms of body structure will be the aggressor's total bulk of muscle, rather than specific proportions or leverages. Equal matching of opponents under these circumstances could be adequately brought about by weight classes as in modern boxing. A reasonable amount of variation as between linear build with speed leverages and lateral build with power leverages, would not affect efficiency. Therefore, during the stage when bludgeoning was the typical weapon technique, large body size would be a favorable selective factor without particular favor to any extreme of build, though probably at first laterality of build would be carried over as a concomitant of some continued use of wrestling or crushing behavior.

The invention of projectile weapons introduces selective factors other than total muscle bulk. It has been a general trend in the development of projectile weapons, from spear to bullet, that the size of the projectile has decreased and the velocity increased. There are sound reasons for this. The amount of kinetic energy embodied in the projectile, and consequently the amount of destruction that it can produce in the object which brings it to a stop, is, as in the case of the bludgeon, a product of the mass of the projectile and its velocity. Hence the size of the weapon can profitably be decreased if its velocity increases. There are definite advantages to this change. The moving projectile is always subject to the force of gravity, which draws it off course and eventually brings it to the ground. In the case of the light but rapidly moving projectile, the influence of gravity is far less in proportion to the momentum carrying it in the direction of its aim. Hence the range and accuracy of a projectile can be greatly increased by trading weight for speed, while its destructive power remains the same. As a result, the history of projectile weapons is a succession of inventions for increasing the speed at which the projectile flies. (A secondary effect, due to aerodynamic considerations, is increase in the specific gravity of the projectile.)

In the case of the spear, the first of man's projectile weapons, maximum efficiency will be attained by increasing to a maximum the velocity of the spear as it leaves the hand. There were probably intermediate stages from the bludgeon, through some instrument used as a pike, to the spear thrown first crudely over a short distance (as the bludgeon or club might be sometimes thrown) to the true spear designed to be propelled at high speed from a considerable distance. There is a critical point in this process which is related to the form of the tip of the weapon. In bludgeoning, where more than one blow is generally struck, it is desirable that the weapon shall not penetrate; if it does, it is difficult to withdraw for successive blows. In the fully developed spear, the point is made sharp and small, so as to give a maximum pressure at the point of contact and penetrate deeply, preferably to some vital spot. It cannot then be withdrawn readily, and if a second try is made a spare weapon may be needed. As soon as a sharp point is placed on a weapon, the user is committed to a technique of maximum penetration with accurate aim. He not only can operate at a distance but operates better so, since if actual bodily contact with the victim occurs, aim is difficult and the inability to withdraw the weapon becomes dangerous. This is probably why the pike has never been popular as a weapon except for purposes such as boar-hunting, where danger is construed as sport—a concept foreign to the primitive, in most cases.

We may assume, then, that as soon as we find weapon points designed for penetrating ability, a course has been set for the development of maximum projectile velocity in the hunting technique. (How much earlier this may have taken place we cannot know, since it is likely that the first weapons designed for throwing were merely sharpened and that the adaptation of stone work to a narrow spear point was rather later than the first use of the sharp-pointed weapon.) The importance of velocity in the use of the projectile immediately places a premium on speed leverages in the body. We should expect, then, that concomitant with refinement in shape and increased penetrating power in stone artifacts, a situation is arising in which linear body build is becoming the most efficient type for weapon manipulation. This raises several interesting questions with regard to the spear as a typical weapon. The physique of a group might influence its likelihood of adopting the spear as a standard weapon after it had become known to them, even though it was potentially a superior weapon to the bludgeon. This would produce a kind of group selection in which more linear races would have an advantage because of their ability to exploit the newer weapon; we might imagine, for instance, that one of the weaknesses of the Neanderthals in their final conflict with *Homo sapiens* was not simply that the latter had superior weapons of projectile nature, but that the Neanderthals could not have used these weapons to advantage even after attaining knowledge of them, because of their heavy build and adaptation to power rather than speed. (We might call them "muscle-bound"; this term is the derogatory synonym of "strong" and denotes the loss of speed and agility which accompanies specialization in the direction of force.) Later, within a group in which the spear had become a standard weapon, there would be selection in favor of the individuals who, because of linearity of build, were able to attain the maximum in range and accuracy with it, and thereby enjoy a better food supply. (It should be noted that any improvement in hunting technique thins out the supply of game and increases its wariness, so that the less well equipped group or individual can no longer survive with a technique that was formerly adequate.) In either case, whether competition was within the group or between groups, the change-over from bludgeon to spear would eventually cause the proportion of linear individuals within the species to increase, by creating a new standard for optimum body build. The heavy physiques which had been most efficient in the use of the bludgeon would now be selectively discriminated against, while individuals of linear build would multiply. An actual decrease of body weight would be an asset since it would decrease food requirements.

A second stage in the use of the spear involves development of a throwing-stick which artificially extends the length of the limb and so increases the velocity of the spear. Within limits this extension of the throwing arm appears not to decrease accuracy appreciably. This affords a means of compensating for the disadvantage of a short arm in the use of the spear. Possibly it was devised as a means of adapting the spear to the use of peoples of more lateral build, who would not have been apt to have developed the spear themselves but might have received it from others. The possibility that the throwing-stick represents a compromise with body build finds confirmation in the fact that the very linear spear-users of Africa generally throw the spear with the bare hand; apparently the throwing-stick has little to offer to a physique with maximum built-in speed leverages.

The next major invention in weapons was the bow, which offered a means of further increasing velocity and allowing reduction in mass of the projectile. The mechanics of the bow are totally different from those of the spear and must be carefully considered in relation to body build. As we have seen, the determining factor in the efficiency of the spear is the velocity with which the weapon leaves the hand, and it is favored by linear build and bodily leverages conducive to speed. High velocity is the desideratum of the arrow also; but the velocity of the arrow is not dependent on speed of motion of the hand. The energy imparted to the arrow, which, making due allowance for the mass of the arrow, determines its velocity, is stored as potential energy in the drawn bow and is in no way affected by the speed with which the bow was drawn. (In fact, some late and powerful types of crossbow were wound up with cranks.) The amount of energy stored in a given bow varies with the length of the draw; and since the pull becomes harder the further the bow is drawn, the critical factor is the maximum absolute pulling force which the drawing arm can exert just before the arrow is released.

(More exactly, perhaps, the force which can be exerted with sufficient ease that aim is not impaired.) Since the possible length of draw is limited by the individual's arm length, best results are obtained if the stiffness of the bow is adapted to the individual archer's pulling ability so that he is exerting his maximum pull at the optimum length of draw. The importance of momentary force in efficiency of use of the bow entirely alters the selective advantage of body build. The archer requires a power leverage in the arm, which is favored by short limb segments and relatively short and thick muscles; the exact opposite of the most favorable structure for throwing a spear. We must imagine, then, that any selective effects of weapon use on body build were reversed when the bow supplanted the spear. The incomplete distribution of the bow and its failure to become the dominant weapon among some peoples who knew it shows that for some groups it was not worth while to make the transition, in spite of the theoretical superiority of the bow. The bow probably developed and spread most rapidly among peoples who were of short stature and relatively mesomorphic, and by the process of selection made them more consistently so over the course of time. Insofar as selection could be even more specific, we would expect the use of the bow to favor the increase of individuals whose laterality of build was particularly well expressed in the shoulder and upper extremity ("omomorphy": Howells 1952: Factor 2). Our present esthetic standards for the male physique seem still to reflect the influence of an age of archery.

The ectomorph's adaptation of the bow is to increase its length, as in the famous English long bow. Here the distance between the position of the string at rest and when drawn is increased. In this arrangement less force, multiplied by greater distance of draw, can store the same amount of energy. This, however, involves very considerable loss of efficiency. When the length of the bow is increased, the thickness must be increased also, to prevent the draw becoming too easy. This markedly increases the total mass of the bow, and as a result much of the energy stored in the bow is expended in accelerating the free ends of the bow itself. In order to transmit a greater proportion of the stored energy to the arrow, the mass of the arrow must be increased. This change—greater mass and less velocity—is a backward step as far as efficiency of a projectile weapon is concerned. It is for this reason that the short Turkish bows attain a greater maximum performance than heavier bows (Klopsteg 1955).

Influences of physique may perhaps be seen in other aspects of the hunting technique associated with various weapons. Neanderthal man is often and probably correctly pictured as capturing game by traps or surrounds in which the animals were dispatched by bludgeons. This is a plausible picture, since Neanderthal man's skeleton is not that of a swift runner. Inability to outrun the game, and a need to approach close to kill it, would require some special devices. (In justice to the species, it should be noted that such a type of hunting would require a greater degree of intelligent planning and cooperation than was needed by their fleeter contemporaries.) If Dart's suppositions are correct, the picture we have of the hunting Australopithecines is anomalous. These hominids apparently ran down game with their new-found bipedal celerity and then clubbed it to death. A light running and leaping animal should not have to carry a heavy club in his hand, and furthermore he cannot use it as efficiently as a larger and heavier individual. Perhaps we may see two ways of solving this dilemma, as shown by two types: the Neanderthal type, who kept the bludgeon and developed a heavier physique to go with it; and the sapiens type, who invented the spear and was then directed by selection toward a linear build, with further improvement of running ability. It is interesting to note that recent recrudescences of the bludgeon principle, the clubs and maces of medieval Europe and Polynesia, have appeared among peoples of comparatively large stature and balanced physique. The typical association of the spear with approach to game by running, and the bow with approach by stalking, is interesting. This is undoubtedly due in part to the fact that throwing of the spear can more readily be combined with running in one continuous movement, while aiming of a bow requires a stationary moment during which already alerted game can increase its distance. However, it would appear that the habitual spear-thrower, because of his linear build, would as a rule be a swifter runner than the typical archer.

With the coming of the Neolithic economy there are new instruments of culture and changed emphases on old ones. The hunting technique becomes less important as hunting itself becomes a sideline; and Neolithic man becomes more and more a wielder of the hoe or other soil-stirring apparatus. The mechanical principles involved in the use of projectile weapons are no longer pertinent. Destroying the cohesion of the soil is work, in the physicist's as well as the layman's sense, and the amount accomplished is in proportion to the amount of muscular energy applied. The hoe is in effect a bludgeon, which requires neither speed of action nor necessarily great momentary force but rather an uninspiring, back-breaking combination of both. The wood-cutting axe of the Neolithic is also a bludgeon with respect to its manner of use and demands on physique. The optimum food-getter of the Neolithic economy is not the long-limbed spearman or the broad-shouldered archer, but a sturdy peasant of medium build. Of course, beginning in the Neolithic and continuing into modern times, there has been an increasing development of means for the individual or the group to escape work in the sense that is represented by the hoe and the axe. Herding, cultivation of vine and tree crops, and finally special trades, have been outlets for groups or individuals of less work capacity. However, well into the 16th century, human power harnessed by the treadmill or galley was a simple commodity of industry in which each individual was roughly worth his weight in muscle (Ubbelohde 1955:54–55). It is interesting to speculate whether the lead taken by North European groups in the development of an agricultural-mechanical civilization may have resulted from their having been retarded by their marginal position in receiving specialized weapons, and consequently having passed, with a minimum interval, from the bludgeon stage of hunting to the threshold of the Iron Age (Coon 1939). Thus, bypassing the stage of linearity which would have resulted from a long spear-using period, or the wide-shouldered specialization of a period of archery, they approached the heavy toil of an early civilization with a physique preadapted to it. If Coon is correct, there may have been appreciable continuity of Neanderthal blood as well.

CONCLUSIONS

Since this paper is presented as an essay and not as a finished study, the term "conclusions" is used with some hesitancy. Perhaps only one conclusion should be drawn: that the customary concept of man as physically unspecialized should be regarded with doubt. In contrast to animals whose way of life is rigidly determined by their physical bodies, we are impressed with the physical versatility of man. However, it is interesting to speculate that even within our own species there has been some correlation between physique and habitual activity, resulting in a reciprocal influence between culture and body build. This influence may take several forms: a dominant weapon or tool may alter the average physique of a race using it over the course of time by giving a selective advantage to individuals of a body build best adapted to its use. It may also alter the numerical proportions of conflicting races of which one is physically better adapted to the use of a valuable implement —this better adaptation perhaps being itself the result of a long intra-group selection. And differences in physical type between races may retard the transmission from one group to another of a new tool or weapon, and with it a whole new way of life.

A series of slightly disconnected suggestions is made on the basis of this hypothesis. *Australopithecus* is pictured as imperfectly adapted physically to his way of life, having a light linear build appropriate to his running habits and open plains habitat, but resorting to a bludgeon-like weapon which would be more effectively used by a heavily built individual. Neanderthal man was physically well adapted to his weapons, having the heavy muscle-bound physique best adapted to the use of blunt crushing implements. In contrast technically and physically were the precursors of Homo sapiens, who developed the spear as the first projectile weapon and were then selectively directed toward greater linearity of build, at the same time developing and enhancing the bipedal skill of *Australopithecus* more rapidly than did *Homo neanderthalensis*. This "linear" stage in the evolution of physique has been preserved, possibly even exaggerated, in the contemporary Australian, who is still a spearman. Most of the peoples of Africa reflect this stage to a greater or lesser degree. It is suggested that the submergence of *Homo neanderthalensis* resulted from the unequal contest between the newer projectile weapon and the older bludgeon, to which Neanderthal man was bound because of his physical adaptation to it perhaps as much as by ignorance or conservatism. Soon the more refined projectile weapon, the bow, appeared, and though its exact origin may be doubtful, there is no doubt that it reached its highest development among the central Mongoloids, who show in lateral build and strong shoulders the highest adaptation to its use. The bow became widely known but in spite of its technical advantages was not everywhere adopted as the principal weapon; and in the case at least of the extremely linear peoples of East Africa, the reason for its rejection appears to be that the prevailing physique was so preferentially adapted to the use of the spear.

At the time of the beginning of agriculture a new selective trend appeared, in the direction of a generally heavy build, capable of sustained labor. The physical types most highly specialized for the bow and the spear were poorly adapted for agricultural pursuits, the very linear spearmen being the least effective, though the idealized archer, with light hips appended to his broad shoulders, will also be somewhat inadequate for heavy labor. Where ecological conditions were favorable, herding became the high culture of the most linear Africans and the most lateral Mongoloids. Other groups of these same races compromised with agriculture, probably with a slow subsequent modification of body build. Since body build is difficult to judge from the skeleton, it is interesting to note that body proportions are to some extent reflected in the cranium, so that in the marginal position and decline of dolichocephaly, both in the Old and New Worlds, we may see reflected the overwhelming of the spearman by the archer and finally by the agriculturist.

All of these suggestions are speculative and should be critically questioned in principle, as well as with respect to those details which are found to have been misrepresented as a result of overgeneralization. It is hoped, however, that these ideas will illuminate the complex problem of selection in man. Any selective effects suggested here must be considered jointly with other types of selection; to mention only one of particular prominence, selection in relation to climate (Coon 1954). And finally, adequate evaluation of all hypotheses concerning selection in man will require the cooperation and interest of ethnologic field workers who are able to observe at first hand the interactions of man with his natural and cultural environment.

REFERENCES

Bowen, W. P. 1949 Applied anatomy and kinesiology, 6th ed. H. A. Stone ed. Philadelphia, Lea and Febiger.

Coon, C. S. 1939 The races of Europe. New York, Macmillan and Company.
———— 1954 Climate and race. Smithsonian Report for 1953, 277-298.

Coon, C. S., S. M. Garn, and J. B. Birdsell 1950 Races: a study of the problems of race formation in man. Springfield, Ill., Charles C. Thomas.

Dart, Raymond A. 1949 The predatory implemental technique of Australopithecus. Amer. Jour. Phys. Anth. 7:1-38.

HOWELLS, W. W. 1952 A factorial study of constitutional type. Amer. Jour. Phys. Anth. 10:91–118.

JONES, H. E. 1947 The relationship of strength to physique. Amer. Jour. Phys. Anth. 5:29–40.

KLOPSTEG, P. E. 1955 Archery. Encyclopedia Britannica, Vol. 2, 265–269.

TAPPEN, N. C. 1950 An anthropometric and constitutional study of championship weight lifters. Amer. Jour. Phys. Anth. 8:49–64.

UBBELOHDE, A. R. 1955 Man and energy. New York, George Braziller, Inc.

WECKLER, J. E. 1954 The relationship between Neanderthal man and Homo sapiens. American Anthropologist 56:1003–1025.

CULTURE, PERSONALITY,

AND EVOLUTION

JULES HENRY

The purpose of this paper [1] is to attempt to show the relationship between environmental stress, physiological change, and human evolution. With this in mind I shall start from two relatively well-established empirical findings on the differences between lower animals and *Homo sapiens*.

1. Man differs from lower animals in the great variability of his genetically determined mechanisms for governing intraspecific interaction. Stated another way, man differs from lower animals in his enormous reduction of genetically determined innate response mechanisms. In fact, whatever genetically determined mechanisms man has for governing intraspecific relations are so obscured by cultural and idiosyncratic factors that it is at present almost impossible to describe rigorously any stable interpersonal response pattern that is valid for the species. Here, of course, as in all other aspects of his life, man is approached by the higher primates (Riesen 1954; Yerkes and Yerkes 1929).

2. Man differs from lower animals in the enormous increase in the variability of his capacity to discharge impulse over substitute pathways. This follows logically from the first generalization. Though this capacity—called "displacement" (Tinbergen 1951) in the lower vertebrates—appeared early in the phylum, it reaches unparalleled development in man.

The great variability in *Homo sapiens* of the genetic basis for intraspecific response has brought it about that man has everywhere created different social structures in conformity with the varying conditions of life. One purpose—though not always the consequence—of these social structures is the same as in lower animals, to make intraspecific interaction predictable. From this point of view kinship systems are meant to serve in man the purpose that genetically based innate response mechanisms serve in the lower animals. However, the lack of specificity of man's genetic mechanisms has placed him in the situation of constantly having to revise his social structures because of their frequent failure to guide interpersonal relations without tensions felt as burdensome even in the society in which they originate. Stated another way: because man's genetically determined mechanisms for governing interpersonal relations lack the specificity and predictability found in lower animals,

Reprinted from *American Anthropologist*, 61:2 (1959), 221–26.

man, in constructing society, frequently makes choices that create interpersonal situations heavily laden with stress. Meanwhile, given the necessity of constantly revising his social structures, and given his enormous variability, *Homo sapiens* gropes with his massive cerebral cortex toward the solution of the variety of interpersonal problems peculiar to the species and arising under the varying conditions of human life. Thus man has been presented with a unique evolutionary task: because his mechanisms for determining interpersonal relations lack specificity, he must attempt to maximize social adaptation through constant conscious and unconscious revision and experimentation, searching constantly for social structures, patterns of interpersonal relations, that will be more adaptive, as he feels them. Man's evolutionary path is thus set for him by his constant tendency to alter his modes of social adaptation. Put somewhat in value terms, man tries constantly to make a better society, i.e., one in which he can feel more comfortable. When he makes a "mistake," he tries to change. This is one way in which he evolves (cf. Simpson 1955).

In the process of social adaptation, stresses arise within human society that have serious somatic consequences. The fundamental discovery of psychosomatic medicine is that individual stress, originating in the social process, may have destructive consequences—the so-called diseases of adaptation (Selye 1956)—in every organic system of the human body, depending on the nature of the stress and the individual constitution. It is therefore apparent that in constructing interpersonal systems, man may create one in which social tensions are so severe that serious organic consequences ensue. If it can be shown that these affect reproduction, the psychosomatic problem becomes an evolutionary one; and since the determining stresses are cultural in origin the problem becomes a cultural anthropological one also.

The relationship between sociocultural stress and reproduction is one of the best documented in psychosomatic medicine (Bass 1947; Benedek et al. 1953; Berle and Javert 1954; Kelly et al. 1954; Kroger 1952; Whitacre and Barrera 1944). Amenorrhea, spontaneous abortion, and infertility have been shown repeatedly to be associated with personality disorder originating in sociocultural stress. These voluminous materials meanwhile do not take account of the large number of men and women who simply withdraw from reproduction by not marrying. If now we accept the assumption current in psychosomatic medicine that a specific disorder will not occur in the presence of stress unless a genetically determined constitutional factor related to that disorder is present, it can then be urged that sociocultural stress acting on the reproductive mechanism of women with the specific constitutional factor will reduce or destroy fertility. It would then follow that persons carrying constitutional susceptibility would fail to reproduce that susceptibility and it would not be perpetuated. In this way, stresses generated by culture would act selectively through personality on certain gene-determined constitutions.

As yet no constitutional determinant has been discovered in females with disturbances of reproductive function. However, a recent paper by Pilot et al. (1957) on duodenal ulcer indicates the general direction in which the search for genetic factors in all psychosomatic illness is moving. In a study of identical adult male twins having similar personalities, and also the hypersecretion of pepsin characteristic of patients with duodenal ulcer, it was discovered that the twin with ulcer had an extremely stressful life situation, while the other did not. Thus the discovery of one genetic component that brings about selective reaction to stress encourages us to believe that others will be discovered for other of the diseases of adaptation. In a recent study of coronary artery disease in 46 young men, it was hypothesized that in addition to the stressful life situation of the patients, "some intrinsic metabolic fault, probably inherited" played an important role in establishing the disease because of the resulting inadequate metabolization of cholesterol (Miles et al. 1954).

Meanwhile, much suggestive evidence comes from the field of animal psychology, where Scott (1950, 1957) and Ginsburg (1954) have demonstrated the differential reactions of different genetic strains of the same species (dogs and mice) to identical stress, and Abood and Gerard (1954) have shown that the susceptibility of the DBA strain of mice to audiogenic seizures is related to its deficiency in two substances necessary to normal brain function.

In view of the data from humans and animals, it would therefore appear that organic dysfunction generated by sociocultural stress acting on a genetic factor must, in the long run, exert a selective effect on the population by direct action on the reproductive mechanism. Meanwhile, it is necessary to take account of indirect influences also. For example, Stephenson and Grace (1954) and Bacon et al. (1952) have urged the importance of psychogenic (i.e., stress) components in cancer of the cervix and breast, thus suggesting that whenever there is a hereditary predisposition to cancer (Cowdry 1955) such a person under sociocultural stress is more likely to die from the disease than one who is not under stress.

Since in all these cases of psychosomatic disturbance, stress may act selectively on the population to eliminate individuals with genetically determined vulnerabilities to stress, the evolutionary course of Homo sapiens as a biosocial being becomes an issue for cultural and physical anthropology.

In this view the evolution of man becomes an expression of individual human genetic capacities for adaptive radiation (Simpson 1955) within a social organization; and the problem of culture change becomes one in the biochemical study of human response to social stress in a changing milieu. Specifically, the question is: in any situation of culture change, what is the total human response in physiological as well as in social anthropological terms? In this view, it is just as important to know, for example, that a people resists culture change because it raises their blood pressure as because it increases the hours they must work.

Increased variability, in Homo sapiens, of the genetic basis for intraspecies interaction has gone hand in hand with an increase in his capacity to discharge impulse in displacement activities. When these two processes became associated in man with his dependence on social life, the stage was set for the elimination from human society of all members unable to displace activity and feeling in socially tolerable ways. What social life did, then, was to put human displacement activity precisely in the center of biosocial adaptation, making it the veritable pivot of society as well as an important determinant of individual survival. We can see then that from the biological point of view, culture is the product of a patterned displacement and modification of response release guided by symbolic processes. Freud called this sub-limation.

All of this enables us to understand better the role of unconscious processes in human society, for their function has been to provide the *Anlage* on which man could develop a variety of transformations of impulse into cultural forms which he has then been able to use to achieve predictability and solidarity. Many ceremonials and much of kinship observance derive from this source. The initiation rites of the Murngin (Warner 1937), to give but one example, are dramatizations of mythical events having their origin in Murngin phantasy. Meanwhile, the rites serve important organizing functions in Murngin society, providing the supernatural sanction for age, sex, and kinship behavior.

The unique biosocial condition of man imposed upon his organism the necessity for adapting to an entirely new phase of physiologic existence; adaptation to stresses emanating from symbolic stimuli. The task of bringing this symbolico-adjustive system into more precise relationship with the phylogenetically older homeostatic mechanisms of the body therefore became a central evolutionary task for *Homo sapiens*. For example, he no longer had only the relatively simple problem of avoiding noxious material agents in order to keep his alimentary tract sound; he had now, under the new conditions, to bring the kind of order into his sociosymbolic life that would prevent the development of functional disorders of the gut.

Taking sociosymbolic stress, then, as a key factor, and attempting to formulate the evolutionary problem in a general way, we can construct the following model:

$$1. \quad E \rightarrow S_s, O$$

which states the probability that the evolution of *Homo sapiens* is related to sociosymbolic stress (S_s) as it interacts with certain organ processes (O) of individuals. If we now consider the relation of the adaptive capacities of individuals in the same way, we get the model

$$2. \quad N \rightarrow e(R_s, C_{da})$$

which states the hypothesis that natural selection in man (N) is related (among other things) to genetically determined individual variability in reaction to stress (R_s) (Lacey and VanLehm 1952) and to genetically determined individual variability in capacities to displace activity (C_{da}),[2] but that both are affected by life-experience (e).

We may now substitute the right hand member of 2 for O in the first model on the grounds that organ processes (O), as considered here, are closely related to the individual's genetically determined reactions to stress and to his capacities for displacement. Substituting, we get

$$3. \quad E \rightarrow S_s, \ e(R_s, \ C_{da})$$

which states the hypothesis that the evolution of *Homo sapiens* is in close relation to sociosymbolic stress (S_s) as this interacts with life-experience-conditioned genetically based variability in reactions to stress (eR_s) and with life-experience-conditioned genetically based capacities for displacement (eC_{da}).

Models 2 and 3 illustrate the circularity of the genetic-life-stress problem as it exists in man, for it points up the fact that because sociosymbolic stresses (S_s), individual life experiences (e), and genetic factors are in constant interaction and mutually affect one another, the constitution versus environmental determinant problem is extremely difficult to solve in human beings. With laboratory animals it is a different story because of the possibility of establishing experimental conditions. In man the problem will be solved eventually through long-term sociobiological studies of individuals from birth —or before.

In view of the preceding paragraphs it would seem that the union of physical and cultural anthropology in a common enterprise is inevitable. In this, cultural anthropology would study the sources of sociosymbolic stress and its consequences for personality function, and physical anthropology would examine the consequences of stress or lack of it in terms of the genetic components of physiological change. Since the physical anthropologist is already no longer a "stones and bones man" but is becoming concerned with more detailed study of the total organic problem of *Homo sapiens,* and since students of personality and culture are already dealing with problems of sociosymbolic stress (Caudill 1955; Henry 1949; Mead 1947; Wallace 1956), the pathways of the two sub-disciplines of anthropology must soon merge.

NOTES

[1] I am most grateful to Viktor Hamburger of the Washington University Department of Zoology for his thoughtful discussion of this paper, particularly with respect to the first section.

[2] The only work I know that suggests this probability is Scott's (1950) on dogs. Tinbergen (1951) has summarized much of the data on displacement activities in lower vertebrates, but there is no study of individual variability in displacement in the same species under controlled conditions.

REFERENCES

ABOOD, L. G., and R. W. GERARD 1954 A phosphorylation defect in the brains of mice susceptible to audiogenic seizures. *In* Biochemistry of the developing nervous system. New York, Academic Press.

BACON, C. L., R. RENNEKER, and M. CUTLER 1952 A psychosomatic survey of cancer of the breast. Psychosomatic Medicine 14:453–460.

BASS, F. 1947 L'amenorrhée au camp de concentration de Térézin (Theresienstadt). Gynecologia 123.

BENEDEK, T., GEORGE HAM, F. P. ROBBINS, and M. D. RUBINSTEIN 1953 Some emotional factors in infertility. Psychosomatic Medicine 15:486–498.

BERLE, B. B., and C. T. JAVERT 1954 Stress and habitual abortion: their relation and the effect of therapy. Obstetrics and Gynecology 3:298–306.

CAUDILL, W. C. 1955 Some effects of social and cultural systems in reaction to stress. M.S.

COWDRY, E. V. 1955 Cancer cells. Philadelphia, W. B. Saunders.

GINSBURG, B. 1954 Genetics and the physiology of the nervous system. Proceedings of the Association for Research in Nervous and Mental Diseases, Vol. 33.

HENRY, J. 1949 Anthropology and psychosomatics. Psychosomatic Medicine 11:216–222.

KELLEY, K., G. E. DANIELS, J. POE, R. EASSER, and R. MARRE 1954 Psychologic correlations with a secondary amenorrhea. Psychosomatic Medicine 16:129–147.

KROGER, W. S. 1952 Evaluation of personality factors in the treatment of infertility. Fertility and Sterility 3:542–553.

LACEY, J. I., and R. VANLEHM 1952 Differential emphasis in somatic response to stress. Psychosomatic Medicine 14:71–81.

MEAD, M. 1947 The concept of culture and the psychosomatic approach. Psychiatry 10:57–76.

MILES, H. W., S. WALDFOGEL, E. L. BARABEE, and S. COBB 1954 Psychosomatic study of 46 young men with coronary artery disease. Psychosomatic Medicine 16:455–477.

PILOT, M. L., L. D. LENKOSKI, H. M. SPIRO, and R. SCHAEFER 1957 Duodenal ulcer in one of identical twins. Psychosomatic Medicine 19:221–227.

RIESEN, AUSTIN H. 1954 Chimpanzee society and social behavior. Paper presented to the Committee on the Behavioral Sciences. University of Chicago, M.S.

SCOTT, J. P. 1950 The relative importance of social and hereditary factors in producing disturbances in life adjustment during periods of stress in laboratory animals. *In* Life stress and bodily disease. Proceedings of the Association for Research in Nervous and Mental Diseases, Research Publications, Vol. 29. Baltimore, Williams and Wilkins, pp. 61–71.

—— 1957 The genetic and environmental differentiation of behavior. *In* The concept of development, Dale B. Harris ed. Minneapolis, University of Minnesota Press, pp. 1001–1122.

SELYE, HANS 1956 The stress of life. New York, McGraw-Hill.

SIMPSON, GEORGE G. 1955 The meaning of evolution. New York, Mentor Books.

STEPHENSON, J. H., and W. J. GRACE 1954 Life stress and cancer of the cervix. Psychosomatic Medicine 16:287–294.

TINBERGEN, N. 1951 The study of instinct. Oxford, Clarendon.

WALLACE, ANTHONY F. C. 1956 Mazeway resynthesis: a biocultural theory of religious inspiration. Transactions of the New York Academy of Sciences, Ser. 11, Vol. 18.

WARNER, W. L.   1937   A black civilization. New York, Harper and Bros.

WHITACRE, F. E., and B. BARRERA   1944   War amenorrhea. Journal of the American Medical Association 124:399–403.

YERKES, R. M., and A. W.   1929   The great apes. New Haven, Yale University Press.

THE STRUCTURAL

AND FUNCTIONAL DIMENSIONS

OF A HUMAN EXISTENCE

A. IRVING HALLOWELL

In view of the tremendous acceleration in our knowledge of man during the present century—biological, psychological, anthropological—it might be supposed a silly question to ask: What are the structural and functional dimensions of a human existence? Yet the late E. A. Hooton, in the introductory paper to a symposium presented in 1953 on *The Non-Human Primates and Human Evolution* (Hooton, 1955) began by saying, "Anthropology is the study of man, but difficulties have been encountered in formulating a scientific definition of man." At the same symposium C. R. Carpenter made the provocative statement that the assumption, although acceptable "either implicitly or explicitly" to many of his colleagues, that the phenomena known as "mind," language, society, culture and "values" exist exclusively on the level of human evolution was untenable for him. What, then, *are* the distinguishing features of a human existence?

PROBLEMS OF CHARACTERIZING MAN

Two years prior to that symposium, K. P. Oakley, reflecting on the problem presented by the Australopithecines, published an essay entitled "A Definition of Man" (1951). He characterized attempts "to distinguish man from the rest of brute creation [by labeling him] the reasoning animal, the talking animal, the tool-making animal [as being] for the most part . . . philosophical exercises." In the end, however, he settled on man as the tool-maker as the best working definition. The persistence of this characterization ever since the pre-evolutionary days of the eighteenth century probably deserves independent investigation. It has been attributed to Benjamin Franklin, although no one seems to have cited an explicit reference in his voluminous writings (see note in White, 1942). In the twentieth century, Bergson's concept of *Homo faber* promoted the characterization in intellectual circles far beyond anthropology. Dr. Glass has called my attention to a reference in Sherrington and to the implications in Korzybski's "time-binding" concept in regard to the idea that a tool-making animal is one who anticipates the future (for an exposition of Korzybski's ideas, see Montagu, 1953). Among contemporary

Reprinted by permission from the *Quarterly Review of Biology*, 31: (1956), 88–101.

anthropologists the remarks of Le Gros Clark (1953) and Straus (1953b; 1955) are sufficiently representative of the use of this characterization.

But Oakley did not imply by his definition what others who have used the same label before him have implied. While he asserted tool-making to be a *human* trait, it is not characteristic of the family Hominidae as a whole, but only of later members of this family, in particular, of the genus *Homo*. Oakley has elaborated this point elsewhere (1953b) by remarking that "in the discussion on the evolution of man, one should keep quite clear these distinctions between the Hominidae and man. . . . The ancestors of early Pleistocene man, such as *Pithecanthropus,* were below the level which we take to be human from the point of view of brain size or from the point of view of function, that is, tool-making, and yet one would not say, 'Well, now, those are another family, those are Pongidae.' Whether one should have some subgeneric subfamilial name such as 'Prehominidae,' I do not know, but it seems to me it is very important to keep that idea in mind." All this is reminiscent of French anthropological writing, where we often find a "rigid line of specific distinction between *Homo faber,* that catchall of presumably soulless though manually dexterous super-anthropoids or 'prehominiens,' and *Homo sapiens* who is man" (Briggs, 1949). In this connection it is interesting to note that J. Huxley (1953) has used the term "proto-men" to distinguish early hominid types such as Java man and Peking man from "man in the proper sense of the word," that is, *Homo sapiens,* representing the "fully human phase." W. W. Howells has also pointed out (1950) that "we have reached the point where such terms, especially 'human,' 'ape,' 'anthropoid' and 'man-ape,' are actually embarrassing, except as applied to living forms, or in the case of the last, to the South African australopiths. When we talk about anthropoid and human history, the word 'ape' keeps changing its meaning." Even more recently Le Gros Clark (1955) has warned us against the colloquial usage of such terms as "man" and "human," since they are not synonymous with "the zoological terms Homo and Hominidae or to the adjectival form hominid." There is no doubt about the ambiguity of our English terminology.

The problem that has arisen seems to focus upon the difficulty, when dealing with possible transitional organic forms, of coordinating structural and functional data in a unified evolutionary picture. Some investigators, like Zuckerman (1954), have used both structural and functional criteria as a matter of course. According to him, "there is no difficulty about defining the major overt features in which man differs from all other Old World or catarrhine Primates. Man is a big-brained Primate with the power of articulate speech. He walks erect and uses his hands—emancipated from the task of carrying his body—to work with artificially fashioned tools. His teeth, and correspondingly his face, are small relative to those of the apes, and he is omnivorous as opposed to being predominantly frugivorous. These are the essential physical qualities [sic] which distinguish him from the ape, whose capacity for speech is confined to the utterance of sounds the connotation of which is purely emotive and whose very limited ability to use 'permanent tools' as demonstrated in experimental studies, is probably never manifested in the wild." Perhaps Zuckerman has less difficulty in distinguishing man from other.Primates because he is one of those who have concluded "that the Australopithecines were predominantly ape-like and not man-like creatures."

It is interesting, then, to note the emphasis given in current discussion to functional rather than structural criteria. [For a contrasting non-functional emphasis see Dobzhansky (1944) and Mayr (1950).] With respect to the question whether the Australopithecines should be grouped with the Hominidae or the Pongidae, Le Gros Clark (1950) says, "Taxonomic difficulties of this sort, of course, are bound to arise as discoveries are made of fossils of a seemingly transitional type, and with the increasing perfection of the fossil record, probably the differentiation of man from ape will ultimately have to rest on a functional rather than an anatomic basis, the criterion of humanity being the ability to speak and make tools." And in a recent review of the evolutionary question Father Koppers (1952) asserts, "It is of course for the historians (prehistorians, social historians and ethnologists) to decide whether the Australopithecines are to be reckoned as human beings or not. Only when *culture elements,* objects produced by humanly intelligent activity, have been irrefutably established can the existing doubts and uncertainties be dispelled."

A similar stress on functional criteria is likewise reflected in the broad-gauged treatment of man's position in the evolutionary hierarchy presented by Julian Huxley and G. G. Simpson. Both of them have rigorously rejected the concept of man espoused by what Huxley has called the "nothing-but school"—"because man is an animal, a primate, and so on, he is *nothing but* an animal or *nothing but* an ape with a few extra tricks" (see Simpson, 1949). Simpson comments (1949), "It is important to realize that man is an animal, but it is even more important to realize that the essence of his unique nature lies precisely in those characteristics that are not shared with any other animal. His place in nature and its supreme significance to man are not defined by his animality but by his humanity." And Huxley (1953) says, "A greater flexibility of behavior, and a higher organization of awareness, enabled living substance to become capable of conceptual thought and symbolic language; and these . . . are the two distinguishing marks of man, and the basis of the latest deployment of life." What Simpson and Huxley are stressing are behavioral criteria that far transcend man's purely taxonomic status in the world of living things.

FUNCTIONAL AND STRUCTURAL EVOLUTION AND CULTURE

The use of behavioral or functional criteria such as speech or tools represents, of course, a piecemeal approximation to a categorical distinction which has been current in general anthropology for a long time. It is that man is unique among the Primates, and stands apart from all other animals as well, in possessing culture. In fact, the concept of culture and the identification of a human level of existence with a cultural mode of adaptation seems to have become a commonplace not only among cultural anthropologists but among archeologists and physical anthropologists, to say nothing of sociologists and others. Not so long ago, Kroeber (1950), said that "the most significant accomplishment of anthropology in the first half of the twentieth century has been the extension and clarification of the concept of culture."

There are some indications, however, that it is not quite so easy to apply the generic concept of culture as the differential criterion of a human status, as was once thought to be the case. I have already pointed out that Carpenter, whose field researches among infra-human primate groups remain unparalleled, is not convinced that culture is a unique human phenomenon. The recent reactions of Straus to the application of the culture concept illustrate another facet of the same problem. In his remarks at the Wenner-Gren Symposium, Straus (1953) defined man as a primate possessing culture, and touched upon key points that cultural anthropologists have stressed for a long time. However, later when referring to his remarks at the Wenner-Gren conference, Straus (1955) said, "Subsequently, it has been amply demonstrated that the term 'culture,' even in its application to present-day human groups, is used inconsistently by anthropologists and without general agreement as to its precise meaning. . . . The term 'culture' remains particularly 'vague' and 'virtually undefinable' when applied to the comparative study of behavior within the order Primates." What Straus almost suddenly seemed to become aware of was the more acute and sophisticated analyses of the meaning and conception of culture which have recently come to the fore in anthropology; in particular, the monograph by Kroeber and Kluckhohn (1952), which offered 164 definitions of culture systematically culled from the literature of Europe and the United States. Straus referred, among other items, to a review of this monograph by Leslie White (1954) in which the latter wrote, "Thirty years ago most anthropologists—in the United States at least—knew what they meant by culture, and most of them meant, I believe, what Tylor meant in 1871 when he formulated his 'classic' definition. ['Culture or Civilization, taken in its wide ethnographic sense, is that complex whole which includes knowledge, belief, art, morals, law, custom, and any other capabilities and habits acquired by man as a member of society.'] But who knows what Mr. X means by culture today? Culture is 'learned behavior'; it is not behavior at all but 'an abstraction from behavior'; it is 'intangible,' a 'logical construct'; it is a 'psychic defense system'; a 'precipitate of social interaction,' a stream of ideas; it 'consists of n different social signals that are correlated with m social responses,' etc. One anthropologist at least has gone so far as to question the 'reality' of culture."

To anyone who has not lived through some of these discussions the situation may well seem more chaotic than it actually is. Where, then, do we stand with respect to "culture" as the primary differential between man and other Primates? Rather than seek directly for a formal definition, I prefer to phrase the question as, What can be said about the necessary and sufficient conditions that distinguish a human level of existence?

In the first place, I would note that culture as dealt with by cultural anthropologists has been observed, analyzed, conceptualized, and defined exclusively on the basis of data derived from ethnography and history. In the second place, direct observations and historical records apply to only one species of man—*Homo sapiens*. For other members of the genus *Homo*, behavior must be inferred from archeological material. In other words, culture in its richest and, to the cultural anthropologist, most typical forms—running the gamut from speech through technological equipment and its material products, to social and economic organization, music, and world view—is associated with *Homo sapiens* alone, so far as reliable observations go. Indeed, it has been the common denominators of culture and the over-all similarities in basic pattern which, together with species identity, have provided the best argument for the world-wide comparability of cultural data as well as the generic concept of culture.

Consequently, it is only by inference that we can possibly extend this whole complex to other groups of the Hominidae, a zoological family which was certainly not differentiated in the first place by the possession of culture. For those who include the Australopithecines as a subfamily, bipedal locomotion becomes the unifying trait of the whole taxonomic group. It is easy to see the pertinence of Oakley's comment (1953) that "when you try to translate 'man' and 'human' into scientific terms you get into difficulties." Thus if the Australopithecines are classified as Hominidae on structural grounds, this does not make them "human." And since it is not yet established to the satisfaction of everyone that the australopiths made tools, and no one has seriously argued that they possessed speech, the old equation man = human = culture cannot be correlated with the zoological category Hominidae without further analysis. Then there is the general theory, now widely current, that modification in posture was the first and most important step in human evolution which preceded the later expansion of the brain in the Pleistocene and was necessary in order to free the hands for tool-using (see, e.g., Mayr, 1950, and particularly Washburn, 1950).

If there were differential structural lines of development taking place during the Pleistocene, how are we to conceive the accompanying behavioral stages with reference to culture? The structural changes that made possible erect posture and bipedalism provided the initial foundation for a novel behavioral plateau. But, however the behavioral patterns of this stage in hominid development may be conceived, it is surely impossible to identify them with those that must have developed later as a consequence of an expanded cortex. Our concept of culture, it seems to me, must now take account of differential behavioral plateaus which, in turn, are related to structural changes.

Are we to assume that the early Pleistocene hominids Coon (1954) has labeled "half-brained men" possessed culture in the same sense as *Homo sapiens*? Is a fully developed human brain structure irrelevant as a prerequisite for a fully developed cultural mode of adaptation? Is a "half brain" as good an instrument as a whole brain for the development and functioning of human speech, music, the graphic and plastic arts, abstract thinking, and religion?

This leads to a third observation. Along with their rejection of the notion of unilinear stages in cultural evolution, twentieth century anthropologists have implicitly, if not explicitly, conceived of culture as some kind of whole with a relatively constant categorical content, in so far as it constituted a human differential. Disparate chronological relations between various cultural traits—such as fire in relation to tools, speech in relation to fire—have, for the most part, been avoided. This has led to a somewhat paradoxical situation: whereas opponents of human evolution in the nineteenth century were those who naturally stressed evidence that implied discontinuity between man and his primate precursors, anthropologists in the twentieth century, while still giving lip service to morphological evolution, have, by the special emphasis laid upon culture as the prime human differential, implied what is, in effect, an unbridged behavioral gap between ourselves and our closest relatives. The possession of culture has tended to become an all-or-none proposition.

The principal theory which exemplifies this point of view in American anthropology is the one advanced by Wissler in *Man and Culture* (1923). Wissler projected a "universal pattern" of culture full-fledged from properties he conceived the human germ plasm to possess. He said, "the pattern for culture is just as deeply buried in the germ plasm of man as the bee pattern in the bee," so that "a human being comes into the world with a set, or bias, to socialization, according to a definite pattern . . . by reason of which a man is a human being and not a termite, a bee or even a monkey. The human pattern, therefore, is a part, if not the whole, of man's inborn behavior . . . man builds cultures because he cannot help it, there is a *drive* in his protoplasm that carries him forward even against his will." This is psycho-biological determinism with a vengeance. Actually, the content categories of Wissler's universal pattern paralleled very closely the chapter headings of any standard ethnographic monograph: technology, social organization, myths and tales, religion, and so on. But Wissler did not elaborate his hypothesis for the different genera and species of fossil Hominidae. He did not say whether the universal pattern for culture was embedded in the germ plasm of *Pithecanthropus* as well as *Homo,* and *Australopithecus* had not yet been discovered. Even later writers, like Murdock (1945), who, following Wissler, have made use of the idea of a "universal pattern" which "links all human cultures, simple and complex, ancient and modern" and whose origin must therefore be sought "in the fundamental biological and psychological nature of man and in the universal conditions of human existence," do not specify what "human" refers to in a biological frame of reference. As a matter of fact, it has always remained an open question whether the generalizations that have been made about "man" apply only to the genus *Homo* or more widely; but the lack of empirical data, linguistic as well as cultural, has left the answer moldering in limbo.

We have become more critical, too, particularly of various possible inferences from structure to function. It was not so long ago, for example, that deductions regarding capacities for learning, manual skill, and talking inferred from the endocranial casts of early genera of the Hominidae, were taken more seriously than now (Le Gros Clark, 1955). In these latter days, however, one hears repeated Weidenreich's classic statement that the interpretation in detail of an endocranial cast is "no more reliable than any other form of phrenology." Speech was one of the major items in Wissler's universal culture pattern, but can we now assert with any confidence that speech was characteristic of all the Hominidae? If the Australopithecines are included in this family, the unequivocal answer would be No! And even if we don't, there is now no unanimity of opinion.

It is sometimes worth while to recall past speculation when considering contemporary problems, and in connection with the question of speech as a generic "human" trait, it will be remembered that Lord Monboddo and others in the eighteenth century thought that speech was *not* typical of the earliest stages of human development. Within the past few years, two English biologists, R. J. Pumphrey and J. B. S. Haldane, have also argued that human language is a very, *very* recent development. While communication is not denied—since varying forms of animal communication have been described—what Haldane (1955) calls "descriptive language" only appeared "with the technological revolution of the Upper Paleolithic." Pumphrey (1953) says that "on the grounds that the use of tools and the use of speech imply intellectual processes of the same order which are characteristically human, some authorities have inclined to refer the origin of speech to the lower Pleistocene or even to the Pliocene." The author attempts to refute this idea. Whatever we may think of his arguments, it is a striking fact that he is not alone in depriving several early types of man of a capacity most anthropologists were once inclined to attribute to them. Following this line of reasoning, there would have been "culture" long before speech (in the sense in which we are familiar with it in *Homo sapiens*) developed.

There is likewise a logical parallel between the way in which culture, in the generic sense, has been conceived as a constant pattern of categorized items, typical of man from the very beginning, and the assemblage of physical traits (erect posture, big brain, reduced canines, and so on) which biologists have used so often to characterize a human status. Both sets of patterned traits could be fitted together with little difficulty so long as the temporal aspects of the chronological picture remained somewhat vague, the actual gaps in man's ancestry remained unfilled, and so long as fossil forms that might suggest transitional structural and behavioral stages did not turn up. Until this happened, a fair-sized brain and erect posture, with speech inferred, could remain associated as indications of an unequivocal human status; and if tools and the use of fire could be demonstrated besides, this behavioral evidence clinched the matter because "culture" could then be inferred. Lip service could be given to evolution but many of the complexities of the process could be sidestepped, such as the evolution of different physical characters at different rates, as well as different behavioral patterns and culture traits. As Howells (1950) has pointed out, "Heretofore we have been given to talking about 'the appearance of man'—the tyranny of terminology—as if he had suddenly been promoted from colonel to brigadier general, and had a date of rank. It is now evident that the first hominids were small-brained, newly bipedal, protoaustralopith hominoids, and that what we have always meant by 'man' represents later forms of this group with secondary adaptations in the direction of large brains and modified skeletons of the same form." Analogically, it is equally doubtful whether we should any longer talk in terms of the "appearance of culture," as if culture, too, along with man had almost suddenly leaped into existence. For if we do, we may unwittingly find ourselves in the *anti-evolutionist* camp. Only recently Father Koppers (1952) has forcibly asserted: "The ethnologist when surveying his field, no matter how far removed in space or in time, finds only man complete with understanding and freewill and no trace of wholly or half-animal pre-human beings. In the face of ethnological data, it is impossible to uphold the extreme principle of evolution. We call it an extreme point of view, in so far as it has not confined itself to organic matter but has sought from time to time—and still frequently seeks—to include the field of mental development within its orbit."

But once we have adopted an evolutionary frame of reference, how is it possible to draw an arbitrary line between morphological evolution and behavioral evolution, between structure and function? On the functional side, even though not open to direct observation, we must assume a social and psychological dimension. The infra-human primates maintain a social existence, and the later level of adaptation we have called cultural cannot be considered apart from a psychological dimension in evolution except by *deliberately* excluding it. As a matter of fact, comparative psychology has made it its business to deal with the psychological dimension of evolution, starting far below the primate level. And learning theory as applied to man has been developed to a considerable degree through experimental observations on rats!

The problem of human evolution, then, is inherently complex, since variables other than organic ones must be taken into account. We are compelled to recognize a novel adaptive plateau where the actual determinants of behavior are less and less relevant to innately acquired structures. Once we begin to consider all these complex variables in relation to one another, to weigh them and order them chronologically as best we can, the nearer we shall be able to approach an answer to the basic question: What are the necessary and sufficient conditions that have made a human existence possible?

PROTOCULTURE AND CULTURE

I believe it can be shown that among the necessary, but not sufficient, conditions prerequisite for the development of a cultural mode of adaptation are those which must have linked the early Hominidae with their precursors and with other primate forms as well. Furthermore, I think we need a term to characterize an intermediate phase or plateau of behavioral evolution which carries some, but not all, of the connotations with which the concept of culture has been invested. The term I suggest is *protocultural*.

Data on infra-human primates observed in their natural habitat or under laboratory conditions suggest some lineaments of this phrase. For deductions from comparative behavior are as methodologically legitimate as those from comparative anatomy. It seems to me, too, that the concept of protoculture may prove useful in resolving the question: Do the infra-human primates have culture? The answer to this question too often has depended upon a formal definition of culture that takes no account of the evolutionary process. At the same time the concept of protoculture should lend support to the traditional view that culture in its fully developed form *came to be* a unique "human" attribute, if human is not identified with hominid. Yet it does not leave this characteristic feature of human adaptation rootless when viewed in the perspective of behavioral evolution.

Let us now consider some of the key points involved in the differentiation I am proposing between a protocultural and a cultural level of adaptation.

1. The term culture, however defined, cannot be dissociated from the learning process. From the time of Tylor—who used the word "acquired"— culture has always been conceived as referring to learned behavior or the products of learned behavior.

2. While culture could only have emerged in a species capable of learning, the latter mode of adaptation is, of course, not a unique human phenomenon. It can be assumed as a capacity of most animals, whether primate or not. The more important question turns upon the role which learning plays, both quantitatively and qualitatively, in the total life history of the organism. In the evolution of the Hominidae in particular, there is the basic question, What is the relation between learning in the most advanced type of *Homo* and the expansion of the cerebral cortex?

3. Culture always has a locus in social groups—communities, societies—

that are organized or structured units. The functioning of these groups is dependent upon social learning, i.e., upon influences mediated in social interaction. The individual has to be groomed to become an integral unit in an on-going social system.

Infra-human primates live in structured social groups and learning is likewise one of the conditions relevant to the operation of these at a protocultural level. Bartholomew and Birdsell (1953) make the point that "even on the non-human level, population density may be controlled by behavioral factors, either genetic or learned," and that "territoriality and dominance relations, which are dependent on learned behavior, contribute to the determination of group relations and population density." Carpenter (1942) has explicitly stressed the necessity of socialization as a condition for the integrative functioning of such groups: "A given number of monkeys and apes does not make or equal what I have been calling a group. . . . Suppose we try this experiment; Raise in isolation animals of the species, but of the right sex and age to compose a group which meets the requirements of the formula for the average group characteristic of a species. These individuals will then be released together. What will happen? Some may so fear others that they flee. Some will be antagonistic and fight. Others will form into groups and remain together, as had been hoped or predicted, into a single organization. Why? Even though social drives are operative and social incentives are present, the monkeys have not been conditioned to each other. They have not been socialized—i.e. they have not learned to make fitting responses to each other as complexes of stimuli. What is lacking is what I have called *integration*.

"Social integration is conceived to begin with birth and to involve definable processes of social learning and adjustment. These processes are organic and involve the expressions and satisfactions of physiological drives. From one viewpoint, effective social integration of an individual conditions it in a manner to make it responsive to the communicative acts, motor expressions, including gestures, and vocalizations. These communicative acts, involving specific stimuli patterns and fitting responses, constitute the core of group coordination. Let it be remembered that the stimulus aspects of communicative acts cannot be operative except on a background of social integrations —i.e. animals which are conditioned to each other."

Tylor in 1871 defined culture as the "capabilities and habits acquired by man as a member of society." Hart (1938) has expressed the opinion that this definition "more than any other single sentence [is] responsible for the present gap between the biological and social studies. . . . Is there any real evidence [he asks] that man is the only species which can possibly profit by living in a society and thus acquiring capabilities and habits which aid his survival as a species? That methods of behavior learned after birth from the fellow members of the same species do not exist at all at any other level of culture, except the human level? If such evidence did exist, it would destroy entirely the view of nature as one continuous chain; the gap between organic and superorganic evolution would be as great as that between inorganic and organic, and astronomy would be as relevant to anthropological studies as biology." Hart goes on to say that in his opinion observations such as those reported by Zuckerman (1932) in *The Social Life of Monkeys and Apes* are "strongly indicative of the fact that in social life, as in morphology, the gap between the higher apes and man is small if not smaller than Huxley suspected and as few writers since Huxley have been willing to admit." The absence of references in the anthropological literature to Hart's article is itself indicative of a failure to come to grips with evolutionary theory in socio-cultural and psychological, as well as morphological, terms. Today we can say that at the infra-human level the monkey or ape also acquires habits as a member of society. Besides this, the functioning of these subhuman societies as integral units appears to be dependent to a large degree upon learning.

This relation between learning and social structure is continuously operative from a protocultural level up through a cultural level of adaptation. Besides sharing a gregarious existence with the infra-human primates, man also shares one of the basic mechanisms through which social life is structured at a lower level no less than at a higher one. Thus one of the basic conditions necessary for the expansion and elaboration of social behavior and group organization at a cultural level was established prior to the morphological changes that led to both erect posture and the expansion of the cortex. We can generalize even further and say that among the higher primates, even in the absence of speech, various habits may become socialized and transmitted as group attributes. For example, when the primate colony at Orange Park was established "the pioneer chimpanzees were shown how to work the drinking fountain, and through the years ape has aped ape and no further instruction of new generations has been necessary" (Howells, 1954). Another example would be nest-building among chimpanzees. Nissen (1955) has pointed out that there is good evidence that nest-building is not instinctive like grooming, "but is rather transmitted by imitation or tuition from one generation to the next: "it is, therefore, one of the very few items of behavior seen in these animals which may be classified as cultural." It might better be called *protocultural*. Culture involves much more than the social transmission through imitative learning of acquired habits (that is, the "social heredity" concept). Together with learning, however, and in the absence of speech, it may be considered one of the prerequisites of culture, perhaps the most important earmark of a protocultural level and a necessary condition for a cultural mode of life.

Eiseley (1955a, b) has called our attention to a most important fact in the course of man's development: so far as organic inheritance is concerned, man's gut is not that of a true meat-eater, nevertheless at a very early stage he became carnivorous. In other words, as a bipedal ground-dweller of the grasslands he underwent "a transition in food habits which is unique on the planet" (1955a). Linked with the discovery and the use of fire, the development of these new food habits in the Hominidae could only have become socialized and perpetuated through learning. If it be assumed that this occurred because these dietary habits had a high adaptive value and that in the beginning they were acquired and socially transmitted without speech, this would be an example of one of the earliest stages in man's protocultural development.

James Boswell thought Franklin's definition of man as a tool-making animal was excellent because "no animal but man makes a thing, by means of which he can make another thing." But he ventures to offer a definition of his own: "Man is a 'cooking animal.' The beasts have memory, judgment, and all the faculties and passions of our mind, in a certain degree, but no beast is a cook." (Hill, ed., 1950.)

4. Beach (1949) has stressed the fact that the new feature of mating behavior in the primates is the "emancipation" of the female from the cyclic control of the oestrous hormones. "In no other mammalian group does such continuous mating provocation occur, for all other combinations of reproductive features lead to the limitation of mating behavior to certain physiologically defined periods, even when the animals come together in groups" (Chance and Mead, 1953). This suggests one of the underlying conditions that has led to the widespread occurrence of the biparental family among the infra-human primates, as contrasted with uniparental family groups among the lower mammals. Males, that is, became permanent members of a social unit consisting of the females with which they mate and their offspring. This over-all pattern of association seems to remain constant irrespective of variant forms (monogamous, polygynous, or sexually communistic as among the howlers).

In addition, infra-human primate societies are relatively small in numbers; only two generations are associated. Furthermore, individuals of the younger generation may leave at puberty and form other groups. This very limited temporal association between generations, combined with the absence of symbolic communication, imposes an inherent limitation upon the possibility that the transmission and accumulation of whatever learned behavior may exist—even the simplest habits—can affect the behavior of subsequent generations in any but very limited ways. Furthermore, two of the tentative generalizations which Carpenter (1955) has formulated on grouping behavior among non-human primates emphasize (a) that such groups "tend strongly to be autonomous, self-maintaining and regulating" and "express resistance and hostility to other organized groups of the same . . . species"; and (b) that "organized groups of a population of the same species in a limited region do not have super-group social mechanisms." There is thus nothing comparable with communities or tribes on the human level, and Carpenter adds, "Kinship relations are not operative, and inbreeding is the rule rather than the exception. . . ." Biparental family patterns are, then, another identifiable trait of a protocultural level which link the Hominidae with lower primate forms.

A cultural level is reached only when the biparental unit is *transcended* as the sole matrix of the social relations of individuals, and when the expanding dimensions of the social order to which individuals must adjust functions as a *moral order* as well. This development, in turn, is contingent upon the emergence of a novel psychological structure. [For a further elaboration of these points see Hallowell (1955), particularly Chap. 1, "Personality Structure and the Evolution of Man," and Chap. 4, "The Self and Its Behavioral Environment."] Sexual behavior now is evaluated in relation to traditionally recognized norms of conduct in a non-familial as well as a familial context. Social sanctions reinforce culturally constituted values and standards of conduct. The introception of moral values, unconsciously as well as consciously, has become a major determinant in the behavior of individuals with a *human* psyche.

5. Although so complex a topic is beyond the scope of this paper, it is necessary to say something about the study of communication in animals compared to man. As Hebb and Thompson (1954) observe, "One essential key to social organization is the means of communication, in the broad sense of the way in which the behavior of one animal induces cooperative behavior in another." These writers believe that "too much attention . . . has been given to man's special vocal behavior." In their broadly gauged conception of communication they include "reflexive" or nonpurposive communication as contrasted with phenomena of a psychologically higher order. In a recent bibliographical survey, Schneirla (1952) concludes, "An adequately comparative program of study of such phenomena is long overdue, particularly to clarify the relationships of concepts such as 'sign,' 'signal,' and 'symbol,' as well as the criteria of 'language,' all of which appear to suffer from a heavy load of speculation and a minimum of systematic research. Research on questions concerning levels of phenotypic relationships through successive generations of lower animal groups, certainly basic to a needed re-evaluation of the broad problem of 'culture,' should enlist the active attention of social psychologists, sociologists and anthropologists alike." Since we do not have the results of such a program available, it is necessary to get along as best we can.

In the first place, I would assume that in all social animals some kind of communication takes place, although the sensory modalities involved may differ greatly. I would also assume that communication has a common generic function whether in animals or man: it is one means by which the coordination of behavior may be facilitated.

We know, of course, that infra-human primates lack speech, although they live in structured societies. We also know that a system of orally produced signs or signals is important in one group of New World monkeys that has been closely observed and in the Old World gibbons. Are the dozen distinguishable sounds produced by the howlers and almost as many produced by the gibbons identical throughout the species and innately determined? Or is learning involved?

If, in any non-human primate species, oral *signals* were learned and transmitted, and showed intraspecific variability, this would be a protocultural fact of great significance. As against this possibility, in the case of the howlers on Barro Colorado Island, Carpenter stresses group autonomy and hostility, but a common series of oral signals. This suggests that learning is not involved. In any event, these particular sounds seem to be clearly in the category of signals. Their utterance calls for action in some particular situation. They have no representative functions. They are not vehicles for the conception of objects or events (Langer, 1942). Even the chimpanzee who has been tested in the laboratory has not convinced observers that he has much capacity for symbolization, to say nothing of symbolic communication (Yerkes, 1943). And the observations on the homebred Viki (C. Hayes, 1951) make it more evident than ever before that a chimpanzee, whatever its other accomplishments, cannot be taught to speak even with maximum encouragement. On the other hand, the Hayes seemed to experience no difficulty in communicating with Viki at a sublinguistic level. This was essential to the mutual social adjustment of Dr. and Mrs. Hayes and Viki, whose role was that of a child in their home. While Viki made relatively "little use of gestures with the hand alone, without contacting an object or person," she often pointed to things she wanted, and sometimes she made use of what the Hayes called "iconic signs." An example of the latter is when "she moved her empty hand back and forth above the ironing board, apparently to show what she wanted." Personally I should call this a gestural symbol, but this only shows the terminological difficulty *we* sometimes experience in communicating about communication. The Hayes go on to report that Viki could convert such signs into "symbols" (in the narrow sense), that is, could convey a meaning through a representative act that bore an essentially arbitrary relationship to its physical character. "When Viki was very young, we never took her for a ride in the car without taking some spare diapers along. As a result, she invented the device of asking for a ride by bringing us a handful of diapers from the bathroom. Later, she no longer wore diapers, but there were still some in the bathroom, and she still brought them out when she wanted a ride. When we eventually disposed of the non-functional diaper supply, Viki asked for a ride by running into the bathroom and coming out with a handful of Kleenex tissues—which only bore a faint resemblance to diapers. These tissues had never had any direct connection with rides, and by this time Viki had quite likely forgotten how the whole thing started. Except for its history, this would now appear to be communication by means of an arbitrary convention developed by the chimpanzee."

I mention this case because, in principle, this kind of symbolization developed further is exactly what we find in human speech where there is no ostensible connection between the sounds used and the object, concept, or event represented. If a mode of *gestural* communication based on such a principle had been observed functioning in a chimpanzee social group I would call it protocultural. But the only observation we have is on a single home-bred animal. Yet it is worth noting that we have here the *invention* of an arbitrary symbol motivated by the need to communicate. To become socially useful any non-iconic or arbitrary representation, whether vocal or not, must be learned by a series of individuals. This is one of the peculiar and distinctive features of human speech.

So far as communication in man is concerned, we know that the possession of speech presumes the capacity to invent and make use of extrinsic symbolic systems, that is, representation of objects and events that can be responded to not only by the organism itself but by other organisms to whom the socially significant symbol is communicated and is the vehicle of meanings. Thus skill in the manipulation of symbols is directly involved with the development of man's rational capacities. But symbolization is likewise involved with all other psychic functions—attention, perception, memory, dreams, imagination, and so on. Representative processes, both intrinsic and extrinsic, are at the root of man's ability to deal with the abstract qualities of objects and events, the ideal as well as the actual, the intangible along with the tangible, the absent as well as the present object or event, with fantasy and with reality. A negative feature of the protocultural phase is the absence of any evidence that suggests the transformation of individual experience into any kind of socially significant symbols.

6. Finally, a word about man as the tool-maker and the status of tools at archeological horizons as an index to "culture." In recent years, with the emphasis given to the priority of erect posture over cortical expansion in human evolution, the use and making of tools in the Hominidae have been put in a new perspective. Bartholomew and Birdsell (1953) have gone so far as to suggest that "protohominids were dependent on the use of tools for survival." If this be true, then of course *tool-using* would long antedate speech, to say nothing of a cultural level of adaptation. But at a subcultural level quite a few animals use tools. This has been observed in birds (Darwin's finch); in infra-human primates, in particular, various species have shown considerable facility in implementation. The Pongidae do not appear to be especially superior.

Animal psychologists, however, have not found it easy to say exactly what constitutes tool-using. Liberally interpreted, it might well include the piling up of boxes in order to secure food, the use of sticks to achieve the same end, or pole vaulting. Nissen (1946) says, "Perhaps it should refer to performances such as the breaking off of a branch of a tree or the freeing of an iron bar, as described by Köhler for chimpanzees, in order to obtain an instrument for further purposes. The nearest thing to the manufacture of tools in the ordinary sense seen in primates, is the observation by Köhler of a chimpanzee fitting together two short sticks in order to make a long one." But this observation has not been repeated.

We may assume, then, that the chimpanzee and other infra-human primates have innate capacities that enable them to make occasional use of tools, and perhaps when highly motivated even to make them. But there is no evidence that would suggest more than this. We can, therefore, scarcely deny an equivalent capacity to the Hominidae. Possibly adaptation in a new environmental corridor made tool-using and fire, along with the acquisition of new food habits, of special survival value. However this may be, it seems possible that a protocultural stage in tool-using might have been reached rather early, even before the development of speech. This is suggested by the evidence of nest-building in chimpanzees. Thus, in greatly lengthening the perspective in which tool-using should be viewed, Bartholomew and Birdsell (1953) may be right: ". . . in contrast to all other mammals, the larger arboreal primates are, in a sense, tool-users in their locomotion. As they move through the maze of the tree tops, their use of branches anticipates the use of tools in that they routinely employ levers and angular momentum. The grasping hands on which the locomotion and feeding of primates depends are, of course, obviously preadapted for tool use. Rather than to say that man is unique in being the 'tool-using' animal, it is more accurate to say that *man is the only mammal which is continuously dependent on tools for survival* [my italics]. This dependence on the learned use of tools indicates a movement into a previously unexplored dimension of behavior, and this movement accompanied the advent of bipedalism. With the assumption of erect posture, regular use of tools became obligatory; the ability occasionally to use tools must have preceded this in time." Oakley's statement (1954) that "though man's Pliocene ancestors were not tool-makers, they were tool-users," appears to support this view. As empirical evidence Oakley refers to the baboon skulls at Taung, which presumably were pierced by artifacts in the hands of the Australopithecines.

Oakley goes on to say, "What is in doubt is when and why in their evolutionary career the Hominidae became tool-makers." Reflecting on this problem, he opens several interesting lines of speculation. He does not think it necessary to assume that the earliest hominid tool-users, or even tool-makers, possessed speech: "There are indications that speech, as we know it, though not necessarily language, was invented only at a comparatively late stage of cultural development." (The use of the term "cultural" in this statement is an example of the need for a more discriminating terminology and the recognition of developmental levels.) Oakley speculates further that "man's earliest means of communicating ideas was by gestures with the hands . . . [and that perhaps] an increasing preoccupation of the hands with the making and using of tools could have led to the change of manual to oral gesturing as a means of communication." I am not concerned here with the plausibility of this theory; but since speech has always been considered an integral part of culture, any gestural stage in the development of communication in the Hominidae would clearly be at the level I have called protocultural.

On the basis of the empirical evidence now available, Oakley, in the same paper, presented a tabulation of six stages in the development of tool-using and tool-making in the Hominidae. The first stage is labeled "occasional use of improvised tools and weapons," and refers specifically to *Australopithecus* and Pliocene hominids. The second stage is that of "occasional tool-making" and the "dawn of Early or Lower Paleolithic." (It should be recalled here that it may be no accident of discovery that the remains of *Pithecanthropus* with which tools have been found associated [Peking Man] are of Middle Pleistocene dating.) "Regular tool-making with marked standardization" does not appear until the fourth stage, at which point the precursors of *Homo sapiens* are definitely involved. The tabulation is captioned: "Six Levels of Culture on the Basis of the Use and Making of Tools." Now it is interesting to observe that although Oakley has defined man as the tool-maker, yet he does not identify man with the Hominidae and denies to the early Hominidae the capacity for speech; nevertheless he converts "culture" into an umbrella term which, when fully expanded, he uses to cover every manifestation of tool-using and tool-making throughout the family *Hominidae*. It seems to me that without drawing too fine a line, the first two stages of Oakley's scheme would be clarified by calling them *protocultural* stages.

That some such line needs to be drawn is clearly indicated ·in the earlier part of his article by Oakley himself. There he stresses the wide psychological gap between *tool-using* by primates and *tool-making* by man. Referring to the chimpanzee Sultan who *made* a tool, Oakley points out that this feat was accomplished with a visible reward as incentive: "There is no indication that apes can conceive the usefulness of shaping an object for use in an imagined eventuality." He then goes on to cite a famous passage in Köhler's *Mentality of Apes* in which Köhler stresses the temporal limits, past and future, of the world of the chimpanzee. It seems to me also necessary to stress the enormous difference between the unique events in the life of Sultan that led him to make the famous tool and the human situation in which the material used for making tools, the forms they take, and the techniques of manufacture, are all part of a tool-making tradition which, in turn, is part of a more inclusive cultural whole. Sultan's feat, though remarkable, is at a subcultural level because he could not learn either tool-using or tool-making from his fellow-apes. On the other hand, so far as the early Hominidae are concerned, it seems possible, as I have said, that a tradition of *tool-using* for limited purposes and on certain occasions could have arisen before the development of speech. However, if the tools found associated with some of the early Hominidae are interpreted in this way, the level would be protocultural rather than cultural. I would assume that one of the criteria of this protocultural level might be the absence of standardization or functional differentiation in tool forms and little, if any, evidence of inventiveness and technological progress. The opposite would be the case where a full-blown cultural level had been reached.

A number of years ago Leslie White (1942) published a paper, "On the Use of Tools by Primates" (1942). The point he made has been overlooked in recent discussions of man as the tool-*maker*. His conclusion was that "on the material and mechanical side, as well as upon the intellectual and social, culture is dependent upon the use of symbols." Tool-making at the human level implies an act performed in the present which cannot be dissociated from a purposeful use of the object at some future time. In the absence, then, of some traditional means of symbolically mediated temporal orientation, how would such behavior be possible for an ape (or perhaps an early hominid)? Tool-making is *psychologically* much more complicated than tool-using. Among other things, we would have to assume that the ape possessed a capacity for "self-awareness," and that he could somehow represent himself in some future time to himself. Thus, even though Sultan made a tool, the psychological field in which he acted was qualitatively different from that in which man acts in his tool-making. The goal toward which Sultan's needs were directed was in his immediate perceptual field, and the reward he claimed was not long delayed. But a far more important point of difference is that a man does not just make a tool: quite apart from any technological knowledge involved, he *shapes* it, and for this he must have some image in mind which necessitates intrinsic representative processes. Besides, the shape image he has is not usually idiosyncratic: it is related to the shape of the tools in his cultural tradition in the same way that the material used and the technological knowledge involved are related. It is difficult to see, then, how these factors could be integrated or transmitted without speech. Yet in Pumphrey's discussion of the relation of speech to tools he remarks that there is "no valid reason for assigning intellect to a maker of implements."

Thirty years ago Grace A. de Laguna (1927) argued that tool-making is integral with man's capacity for dealing indirectly with things through the functioning of analytical discrimination of their objective properties not only in relation to himself, but to other things. The tool-maker must be able to distinguish clearly among properties relative to the ends he has in view. This kind of perception transcends the infra-human primate level: it necessitates conceptual thought. Thus, "it is scarcely credible, even aside from the more theoretical psychological considerations, that the art of chipping stone implements could have been developed by men who had not yet learned to speak." Furthermore, to have undergone any great development, since "the evolution of tools is essentially a social evolution"—or as we would now say, cultural—a primary condition was "the permanent organization of the social group, bound together by language." In a later, unpublished manuscript de Laguna has succinctly expressed her thought by saying, "*Homer faber is Homo cogitans.*"

Pumphrey seems to think that the spider's web and tools actually belong to the same category. If "man" be defined as a tool-maker rather than a tool-user, and artefacts in archeological horizons be interpreted as evidence of a "human" status, this characterization remains restricted, if not arbitrary, in significance unless the socio-psychological implications of tool-making as an integral part of the problem are fully clarified. A scientific definition of man, to be really inclusive in scope, is contingent upon the integration of all relevant data and upon an analysis that gives full weight to all the socio-psychological factors involved in a human existence.

My purpose in suggesting that we need to discriminate between different levels of adaptation in the behavioral evolution of man is based on the fact that structural criteria alone do not seem sufficient to define a human level of existence. The recognition of a protocultural stage takes cognizance of behavior linkages between the Hominidae and other primates which, although they may be difficult to deal with, are of no less theoretical importance than the more precisely determinable morphological facts.

SUMMARY

1. Many definitions of Man have been proposed, but due to limited knowledge or a unilateral disciplinary approach they have been restricted in scope and have not met with unqualified acceptance.

2. The problem has persisted even into a period when reliable knowledge about the chronological aspects of man's development has been accumulating at an unprecedented rate in archaeology and physical anthropology; when novel behavioral observations on infra-human primates have become available; when the data of cultural anthropology have increased immensely, and psychologists have gained new insights into the determinants and mechanisms of behavior.

3. A human level of existence needs definition in more than structural terms, and the behavioral levels of adaptation observed in living primates are as legitimate a basis for reconstructing behavioral evolution as are deductions from comparative anatomy.

4. The term *protoculture* is introduced as a convenient term for conceptualizing a behavioral plateau that links the Hominidae with other primates. At this stage we have in rudimentary and unintegrated form many of the indispensable conditions for the development of culture in its unique form at the human level: learned behavior, biparental families, structured social groups, some form of communication, tool-using if not tool-making.

5. A further exploration of the distinction between a protocultural and cultural level of adaptation, giving full weight to the socio-psychological factors involved in a human existence, should make possible a more adequate and scientific definition of man.

REFERENCES

BARTHOLOMEW, G. A., JR., and J. B. BIRDSELL 1953 Ecology and the proto-hominids. Amer. Anthrop., 55:481–498.

BEACH, F. A. 1947 Evolutionary changes in the physiological control of mating behavior in mammals. Psychol. Rev., 54:297–315.

BRIGGS, L. C. 1949 The meaning of the term *Homo sapiens* as it is used by French anthropologists. Amer. J. phys. Anthropol., n.s., 7:128–129.

CARPENTER, C. R. 1942 Characteristics of social behavior in non-human primates. Trans. N. Y. Acad. Sci., Ser. II, 4:256–257.

——— 1952 Social behavior of non-human primates. Structure et physiologie des sociétés animals, Colloq. int. Cent. nat. Rech. sci., 34:227–246.

——— 1954 Tentative generalizations on the grouping behavior of non-human primates. Hum. Biol., 26:269–276. Also *in* The Non-Human Primates and Human Evolution (J. A. Gavan, ed.), pp. 91–98. Wayne University Press, Detroit. 1955. (Summary of the more extensive 1952 paper.)

CHANCE, M. R. A., and A. P. MEAD. 1953 Social behavior and primate evolution. Symp. Soc. exp. Biol., 7 (Evolution): 395–439.

COON, C. S. 1954 The Story of Man: From the First Human to Primitive Culture and Beyond. Alfred A. Knopf, New York.

DE LAGUNA, GRACE A. 1927 Speech: Its Function and Development. Yale University Press, New Haven.

DOBZHANSKY, T. 1944 On species and races of living and fossil man. Amer. J. phys. Anthropol. n.s., 2:251–265.

EISELEY, L. C. 1955a Fossil man and human evolution. Yearbook of Anthropology, I (W. L. Thomas, Jr., ed), pp. 61–78. Wenner Gren Foundation for Anthropol. Research, New York.

——— 1955b The Paleo Indians: their survival and diffusion. *In* New Interpretations of Aboriginal American Culture History, 75th Anniversary Vol., Anthrop. Soc. Wash., Washington, D. C.

ETKIN, W. 1954 Social behavior and the evolution of man's mental faculties. Amer. Nat., 88:129–142.

GAVAN, J. A. (ed.) 1955 The Non-Human Primates and Human Evolution. Wayne University Press, Detroit. (First published *in* Hum. Biol., 26, No. 3, 1954.)

HALDANE, J. B. S. 1955 Animal communication and the origin of human language. Sci. Progr. (Lond.), 43:385–401.

HALLOWELL, A. I. 1955 Culture and Experience. Univ. Pennsylvania Press, Philadelphia.

HARING, D. C. 1949 Is culture definable? Amer. soc. Rev., 14:26–32.

HART, C. W. M. 1938 Social evolution and modern anthropology. *In* Essays in Political Economy in Honour of E. J. Urwick (H. A. Innes, ed.), pp. 99–116. Univ. of Toronto Press, Toronto.

HAYES, CATHERINE. 1951 The Ape in Our House. Harper & Bros., New York.

HAYES, K. J., and CATHERINE HAYES. 1954 The cultural capacity of chimpanzee. Hum. Biol., 26:288–303. Also *in* The Non-Human Primates and Human Evolution (J. A. Gavan, ed.), pp. 110–125. Wayne University Press, Detroit. 1955.

HEBB, D. O., and W. R. THOMPSON. 1954 The social significance of animal studies. *In* Handbook of Social Psychology, Vol. I (G. Lindzey, ed.), pp. 532–561. Addison-Wesley Pub. Co., Cambridge.

HILL, G. B. (ed.) 1950 Boswell's Life of Johnson. Vol. V. The Tour to the Hebrides. 6 vols. Oxford University Press, Oxford.

HOOTON, E. A. 1954 The importance of primate studies in anthropology.

Hum. Biol., 26:179–188. Also *in* The Non-Human Primates and Human Evolution (J. A. Gaven, ed.), pp. 1–10. Wayne University Press, Detroit. 1955.

HOWELLS, W. W. 1950 Origin of the human stock: concluding remarks of the chairman. Cold Spr. Harb. Symp. quant. Biol., 15:79–86.

———— 1954 Back of History: The Story of Our Own Origins. Doubleday & Co., Garden City, New York.

HUXLEY, J. 1953 Evolution in Action. Harper & Bros., New York.

KOPPERS, W. 1952 Primitive Man and His World Picture. (Edith Raybould, trans.) Sheed & Ward, London and New York.

KROEBER, A. L. 1950 Anthropology. Sci. Amer., 183:87–94.

———— and C. KLUCKHOHN. 1952 Culture: A Critical Review of Concepts and Definitions. Pap. Peabody Mus., 47:1–223.

———— and OTHERS (EDS.) 1953 Anthropology Today. Univ. of Chicago Press, Chicago.

LANGER, SUSANNE K. 1942 Philosophy in a New Key. Harvard University Press, Cambridge.

LE GROS CLARK, W. E. 1950 History of the Primates: An Introduction to the Study of Fossil Man. Second edition. The British Museum (Nat. Hist.), London.

———— 1955 The Fossil Evidence for Human Evolution. Univ. of Chicago Press, Chicago.

MAYR, E. 1950 Taxonomic categories in fossil hominids. Cold Spr. Harb. Symp. quant. Biol., 15:109–118.

MONTAGU, M. F. A. 1953 Time-binding and the concept of culture. Sci. Mon. Wash., 77:148–155.

MURDOCK, G. P. 1945 The common denominator of cultures. *In* The Science of Man in the World Crisis (R. Linton, ed.), pp. 123–142. Columbia University Press, New York.

NISSEN, H. W. 1946 Primate psychology. Encyclopedia of Psychology (P. L. Harriman, ed.), pp. 546–570. Citadel Press, New York.

———— 1951a Social behavior in primates. *In* Comparative Psychology (C. P. Stone, ed.), Third edition, pp. 423–457. Prentice-Hall, New York.

———— 1951b Phylogenetic comparison. *In* Handbook of Experimental Psychology (S. S. Stevens, ed.), pp. 347–386. John Wiley & Sons, New York.

———— 1954 Problems of mental evolution in the primate. Hum. Biol., 26:277–287. Also *in* The Non-Human Primates and Human Evolution (J. A. Gavan, ed.), pp. 99–109. Wayne University Press, Detroit. 1955.

OAKLEY, K. P. 1951 A definition of man. Sci. News, 20:69–81.

———— 1953a Dating fossil human remains. *In* Anthropology Today (S. Tax and others, eds.), pp. 43–56. Univ. of Chicago Press, Chicago.

———— 1953b [Discussion of papers on "Physical anthropology and the biological basis of human behavior," Chap. 15.] *In* An Appraisal of Anthropology Today (S. Tax and others, eds.), pp. 259–260. Univ. of Chicago Press, Chicago.

———— 1954 Skill as a human possession. *In* History of Technology, Vol. I (C. J. Singer and others, eds.), pp. 1–37. Oxford University Press, Oxford.

PUMPHREY, R. J. 1953 The origin of language. Acta Psychol., 9:219–239.

RÉVÉSZ, G. 1944 The language of animals. J. gen. Psychol., 30:117–147.

SCHNEIRLA, T. C. 1952 A consideration of some conceptual trends in comparative psychology. Psychol. Bull., 49:559–597.

SCHULTZ, A. H. 1950 The physical distinctions of man. Proc. Amer. phil. Soc., 94:428–449.

SHERRINGTON, C. 1953 Man on His Nature. Anchor Books, Doubleday & Co., Garden City, New York.

SIMPSON, G. G. 1949 The Meaning of Evolution. Yale University Press, New Haven.

STRAUS, W. L., JR. 1949 The riddle of man's ancestry. Quart. Rev. Biol., 24: 200–223.

—— 1953a Primates. *In* Anthropology Today (A. L. Kroeber and others, eds.), pp. 77–92. Univ. of Chicago Press, Chicago.

—— 1953b [Discussion of papers on "Physical anthropology and the biological basis of human behavior," Chap. 15]. *In* Appraisal of Anthropology Today (S. Tax and others, eds.), pp. 262–264. Univ. of Chicago Press, Chicago.

—— 1954 Closing remarks. Hum. Biol., 26:304–312. Also *in* The Non-Human Primates and Human Evolution (J. A. Gavan, ed.), pp. 126–134. Wayne University Press, Detroit. 1955.

TAX, S., and OTHERS (EDS.) 1953 An Appraisal of Anthropology Today. Univ. of Chicago Press, Chicago.

WASHBURN, S. L. 1950 The analysis of primate evolution with particular reference to the origin of man. Cold Spr. Harb. Symp. quant. Biol., 15:67–78.

WHITE, L. A. 1942 On the use of tools by primates. J. comp. Psychol., 34: 369–374.

—— 1954 Review of A. L. Kroeber and C. Kluckhohn, Culture: A Critical Review of Concepts and Definitions. Amer. Anthrop., 56:461–468.

WISSLER, C. 1923 Man and Culture, Thos. Y. Crowell, New York.

YERKES, R. M. 1943 Chimpanzees: A Laboratory Colony. Yale University Press, New Haven.

ZUCKERMAN, S. 1954 Correlation of change in the evolution of higher Primates. *In* Evolution as a Process (J. Huxley, A. C. Hardy, and E. B. Ford, eds.), pp. 300–352. George Allen & Unwin, London.

PERSONALITY STRUCTURE

AND THE EVOLUTION OF MAN

A. IRVING HALLOWELL

The rejection of any theory of unilinear cultural evolution seems to have led to a declining interest in all problems of cultural evolution as well as in any *inclusive* approach to what was once considered a central problem of anthropology—the evolution of man. It almost appears as if, in recent years, we had tagged the problem of human evolution as an exclusively biological problem. Or, perhaps more accurately, a problem that centers around the morphology of the primates in relation to the emergence of creatures that can be identified as true hominids. Other orders of continuity and differentiation that human evolution implies have dropped out of the picture, although in the nineteenth century they were the focus of considerable interest. We have even tended to leave the definition of man in the hands of the physical anthropologist. Does this mean that we are all agreed that the only criteria of human status are morphological criteria? Are there no others of any importance? Is even the question of human evolution in its inclusive aspects of no interest to those of us who are not physical anthropologists?

It is paradoxical, I think, that whereas opponents of human evolution in the nineteenth century were those who naturally stressed evidence that implied discontinuity between man and his primate precursors, anthropologists of the twentieth century, while giving lip service to organic evolution have, by the special emphasis laid upon culture as the prime human differential, once again implied an unbridged gap between ourselves and our animal forebears. Yet continuity as well as differentiation is of the essence of any evolutionary process. So where, may we ask, do the roots of culture lie at the pre-human level? Even the concept of human nature in the minds of some has become relativistic—relativistic, that is, to the particular cultural form through which it is empirically manifest. But if this is so, what is the emergence of a cultural mode of adaptation a function of? Surely not of a subhuman nature, since other primates, whatever their distinctive natures, did not evolve a cultural mode of existence.

What has happened, of course, is the human paleontologist, expert in biology, has concentrated on the morphology, locus and succession of early

First delivered as the Presidential address before the American Anthropological Association in New York City on 18 November 1949, this article is reprinted from *American Anthropologist*, 52:2 (1950), 159–73.

hominids and related forms. And in recent years new discoveries have kept him extremely busy. The prehistoric archeologist, on the other hand, has concentrated on the forms, distribution and succession of the objects from which the early cultures of man can be inferred. Neither has been directly concerned with *behavioral evolution,* an area which lies somewhere between the morphological facts and the material cultural evidence of man's existence. In other words, human evolution has been mainly approached thorugh two lines of evidence: (1) skeletal remains, fragments of an organic structure which is only one of the material *conditions* of behavior; (2) the material products of human activity. Consequently, it is easy to understand how it has come about that man's human status has so often been characterized in terms of one or more criteria derived from these sources alone: the structure of the brain case, teeth, pelvis, foot, for instance, or the use of tools.

But there is an obvious difference between these two indicative categories of a human status when viewed evolutionally. The material evidence of organic structure can be related to the morphological traits of other primates, including those of an earlier temporal period, and facts about both continuity and differentiation can be stated. The contrary is true of the material cultural remains. *Their* only connections can be traced *forward,* not backward. So while they may be an index to the presence of man, tools tell us little about the steps in his evolution. If we wish to get behind the tool, as it were, we have to ask questions which neither the archeologist nor the physical anthropologist can answer by a direct appeal to his data. Tool-making is a specific product of behavior and what we have to know in order to explain the making and using of tools by one creature and not another is the kind of psychobiological structure that is a necessary condition of tool-making.[1] In this particular case we know that while, under certain conditions, individual chimpanzees have been observed to construct tools, tool-making and using is not an attribute of chimpanzee society. Neither is it traditional in any other infrahuman primate society. The problem becomes perplexing from the standpoint of human evolution since what we would like to know is whether there is any inner continuity between the processes which make it possible for an infrahuman primate to make and use tools and tools as a characteristic feature of human cultural adaptation. In order to gain any understanding of this problem a deeper question must be faced. It was propounded in the nineteenth century as the evolution of mind, the emergence of the human mind being conceived as the flowering of a long process.

No wonder some of those who reflected on this question, but who had chiefly the facts of comparative anatomy as their data, sincerely felt like St. George Mivart that such facts "re-echo the truth of long ago proclaimed by Buffon, that material structure and physical forces can never alone account for the presence of mind." [2] In this, of course, they were essentially right. In fact Mivart, a prolific and widely read writer, stated the problem very well in 1874. He says, "Man being, as the mind of each man may tell him, an existence not only conscious, but conscious of his own consciousness; one not only acting on inference, but capable of analyzing the process of inference, a creature not only capable of acting well or ill, but of understanding the ideas 'virtue' and 'moral obligation,' with their correlatives freedom of choice and responsibility—man being all this, it is at once obvious that the principal part of his being is his mental power.

> In nature there is nothing great but man,
> In man there is nothing great but mind.

We must entirely dismiss, then, the conception that mere anatomy by itself can have any decisive bearing on the question as to *man's nature and being as a whole*. To solve this question, recourse must be had to other studies; that is to say, to philosophy, and especially to that branch of it which occupies itself with mental phenomena—psychology.

"But if man's being as a whole is excluded from our present investigation," he goes on to say, "man's body considered by itself, his mere 'massa corporea,' may fairly be compared with the bodies of other species of his zoological order, and his corporeal affinities thus established." [3]

It is clear from this quotation that to Mivart an inclusive approach to the evolution of man required that some consideration be given man's psychological evolution. Nevertheless he himself felt impelled to adopt a more exclusive approach: he kept to the material evidence. In the background of Mivart's thinking as well as of others who reflected upon problems of human evolution in the post-Darwinian period and long thereafter, there persisted the old metaphysical dualism of Descartes, the mind-body dichotomy. Psychologists and philosophers were almost forced to wrestle with the mind-body problem in some form, while anthropologists of the same period were content to deal with the material evidence of evolution and leave them to labor undisturbed.[4] But, however phrased, the problem of "mental" evolution still remains: [5] for neither the facts of organic structure in themselves, nor any reconstruction of behavioral evolution exposes the differential factors that ultimately led to the transformation of a subhuman society into a human society with an expanding cultural mode of adaptation. Consequently, some reconceptualization of the whole problem seems in order and I think we already have moved in that direction. It is no longer adequate, for example, to identify mind with mental traits such as consciousness, reason, intelligence, or, even more vaguely, with some sort of quantitative variable such as "mental power," which one then attempts to trace up or down the phylogenetic scale. Yet in the recent discussions of the Australopithecines one well-known authority on primate morphology employs both "mental power" and "intelligence" as conceptual indices for inferring the superior capacities of the Australopithecine over the chimpanzee and gorilla. It is even suggested that the superior "mental power" of the former accounts for the fact that they were able to hunt and kill baboons. Since these creatures were reportedly evolving in the human direction one may seriously ask whether such an index of mental power involves much more in principle than the mental equipment of cats for killing rats! [6]

As K. S. Lashley has recently pointed out, "The interest of early students of comparative psychology was in finding the origin of human mental *traits*. Darwin and Romanes could point out behavior of animals which suggested similarity of emotional character, memory, and intelligence to that of man, and could show the similarity increased with increasing bodily similarity to man. They could not specify what was changing in evolution or the nature of the steps between different levels of behavior. We are in a scarcely better position today. It is not possible to classify unit factors in behavior and to trace the development of distinct entities, as one may trace the evolution of the heart, the gill arches, or the limbs. For such a classification it is necessary to know the mechanisms by which the behavior is produced and to trace the evolution of these mechanisms." [7]

Recent developments in personality psychology incline me to believe that we can be more optimistic than Lashley implies. For in man we must not only consider intrinsic mechanisms, but a structural basis of behavior which is also rooted in the gregarious nature of the primates and the potentialities offered for the socialization of individual experience. In recent years the concept of personality structure, whose genesis lies in social interaction, offers the beginnings of a conceptual resolution of the old mind-body dichotomy while, at the same time, it relates the individual to his social setting. The assumption is that the individual functions as a psychobiological whole, as a total personality. Behavior has a structural basis, but this structuralization has arisen in experience and cannot, therefore, be reduced to an inherited organic structure. "Intelligence," "reason," or other mental traits then become specific functions of the personality structure. Thus, the distinctive psychological organization of the human being, whether described as mind or personality structure, is just as much a function of his membership in a social group as it is a function of his inherited organic equipment.[8]

From the standpoint of human evolution, then, both a social matrix of conduct *and* the expansion of the cortex are among the necessary conditions for the emergence of a *human* mind or a human personality structure. Just as bodily evolution and mental evolution cannot be separated, neither can psychological structuralization and the social evolution of mankind. To behave humanly as an adult the individual must become psychologically organized in a socialization process. His biological equipment is only *one* of the conditions necessary for this. Social or sensory isolation is a fatal handicap. Hence, it seems reasonable to suppose that the emergence of culture as a prime attribute of *human* societies must be somehow connected with a novel psychological structure rooted in the social behavior of the gregarious primate that gave rise to man. It is at this point that organic evolution, behavioral evolution and the old problem of mental evolution come to a common focus.

Consequently, the achievement of a human status in the evolutionary process, when taken inclusively, is not to be conceived as a simple function of the possession of specific organic traits—brain size, foot structure, or some specific psychological traits such as intelligence, but as a total *psychobiological* adjustment that implies an overlaid psychological structure functionally integrated with organic structure. And just as in biology it is axiomatic that new structures give rise to new forms of behavior, the same principle applies here. The question is not what kind of biological structure makes a hominid, but what kind of psychobiological structure not only makes a man but at the same time accounts for human society and culture. In other words, human evolution is not just a biological problem, or a problem of cultural origins, or a problem that involves the development of a human mind. It is one of the central problems that must be grappled with if we are fully to understand man's uniqueness, the total conditions underlying his evolution and his capacities for cultural achievement.

But can we in our present state of knowledge make any inferences regarding the generic characteristics of man's novel personality structure? It seems to me that what we already know about the personality structures of human beings, whether considered in their individual or group aspects, suggests that they may be regarded as specific forms of a *generic* psychic structure in man that clearly differentiates him from related primates, as well as from other animals. This structure is the foundation of man's specialized form of adaptation as a species as well as the basis of his personal adjustment as an individual. Consequently, it is just as important a factor in determining his human status as is the structure of his teeth or his feet. It is, in fact, the key to his human nature and the psychodynamics of his adjustment to life, just as his feet are a key to the biodynamics of his terrestrial adaptation. And just as we may say that in terms of morphological taxonomy man belongs to a zoological family, in terms of a taxonomy of levels of psychodynamic adjustment man is characterized by a unique psychic structure the generic form of which we have only begun to discern in the common features that underlie the range and variation of personality structures that have been empirically investigated in recent years.

To begin with, from all our observations of man after he has reached a fully human estate, we must infer that the psychobiological structure underlying this new level of adjustment is one which, while permitting the transcendence of an infrahuman level, by no means cuts man off from his animal heritage. On the contrary, the psychological evolution of man conforms to the principle of continuity and differentiation that we find in all organic evolution. Man functions on two levels at once, and, under certain conditions tends to regress. Indeed, this possibility is intrinsic to the nature of man since from the standpoint of psychodynamics his adjustment is not a simple function of organic structure but of personal experience and behavioral environment as well.

The cognitive aspects of man's transcendence of his animal heritage always has proved impressive and gave rise to the over-simplified characterization of man as a "rational" animal. But as far back as the eighteenth century Swift writing to Pope (1725) said, "I have got material towards a treatise proving the falsity of that definition *animal rationale* and to show it would be only *rationis capax*," [9] i.e., capable of reason. Today we are able to discern more clearly than before that whatever "rationality" man may possess it is not a unitary mental trait; nor a function that can be contrasted with, or divorced from, other aspects of man's personality organization such as feeling and emotion. From an evolutionary point of view, however, it is one of the major indices to man's capacity for the transcendence of the immediate, local, time and space bound world of the other primates who lack the capacity for dealing effectively with objects and events outside the field of direct perception. Man, too, deals with present objects and events but, in addition, he is capable of adjusting his behavior to past and future objects and events. In a more technical psychological sense this means that the psychobiological structure that the hominid evolved is one in which intervening variables which mediate between immediate stimuli and overt behavior came to play a more primary role. Such intervening variables include unconscious processes such as dreams, as well as conscious operations like thinking and reasoning "whereby the remote as well as the immediate consequences of an impending overt action are brought into the psychological present, in full force, so to say, and balanced and compared." [10]

The common denominator of these intervening variables that so intimately link his "inner world" with his adjustment to the outer world and his fellow man is the symbolic or representative principle. This simply means that at the level of human adjustment the *representations* of objects and events of all kinds play as characteristic a role in man's total behavior as does the direct *presentation* of objects and events in perception. Thus skill in the manipulation of symbols is directly involved with the development of man's rational capacities. But symbolization is likewise involved with all other psychic functions—attention, perception, interest, memory, dreams, imagination, etc. Representative processes are at the root of man's capacity to deal with the abstract qualities of objects and events, his ability to deal with the possible or conceivable, the ideal as well as the actual, the intangible along with the tangible, the absent as well as the present object or event, with fantasy and with reality. Every culture as well as the personal adjustment of each individual gives evidence of this, both at the level of unconscious as well as conscious processes. Then, too, symbolic forms and processes color man's motivations, goals, and his affective life in a characteristic way. They are as relevant to an understanding of his psychopathological as to his normal behavior. If man's ancestors had remained *literal* realists like other animals, the hominid as we know him would never have evolved. Consequently one of the basic questions which a consideration of the generic aspects of man's psychobiological structure involves is the root of man's capacity for the symbolic transformation of experience.[11] I do not intend to go into this difficult question here but, among other things, it would appear to involve the transition from capacities for *intrinsic* representative processes in animals below man, to the creation when we reach the human level of *extrinsic* symbolic systems. An animal for whom intrinsic symbolization is possible "is capable of carrying away with it from a situation . . . some inner change or state which 'stands for' the response which it will later make when it reencounters the same situation." [12] In other words, a central process is involved which functions as a substitute for actual sensory cues. Imagery would be a concrete example. But there is no way of directly projecting or communicating intrinsic symbolic processes. For this to occur some media that can be externalized by the organism must be employed. Extrinsic symbolization, then, involves the operation of the representative principle on a higher and more complex level since socially communicable media may take on conventionalized representative functions. Thus symbols of this category can be responded to not only by the organism itself but by other organisms to whom the socially significant symbol is communicated. By means of a drawing, vocalization or, perhaps even by gestures, I can make you acquainted with *my* dream. Consequently in the case of man extrinsic symbolic systems functioning through vocal, graphic, plastic, gestural or other media, made it possible for groups of human beings to share a common meaningful world. A meaningful world in man being, in part, symbolically mediated implies a *cultural* milieu which becomes inextricably meshed with the world as biologically and physically constituted.

While the expansion of the cortex was undoubtedly *one* of the necessary conditions that made possible the increasing importance of intervening variables, and while the social transmission of extrinsic forms of symbolization implies learning, these conditional factors alone do not explain the evolution of extrinsic symbolization itself, nor the diversity of the systems that eventually arose. But I think it is quite clear that culture is unthinkable without extrinsic symbolization as a prime condition, speech, of course, being only one of the prime symbolic forms. However, since man's ancestors were a gregarious species, the matrix of such a step and the expansion and elaboration of its manifold possibilities must be conceived as a social matrix. From this the psychobiological structure that evolved cannot be dissociated. Thus at the human level of adjustment intervening variables became the integrative focus of intrinsic representative processes *and* socially transmissible extrinsic symbolic systems, at both conscious and unconscious levels.

Turning now to this social setting of the behavioral evolution of man, what reasonable deductions can be made with respect to the question of continuity and differentiation in this frame of reference that is relevant to our central problem? The socialization process, I think, gives us an important lead. For at both the human and subhuman levels we not only have parents and their offspring in continuous social interaction, we have single births and a considerable period during which the young are dependent. Now such dependence not only implies the need for care on the part of infants, it implies a power of life and death over the infant. There is also a common requirement at both levels—each new individual added to the group as a dependent infant must undergo a process of socialization under the direct influence of adults and subject to their demands. Carpenter has emphasized the essential experience of socialization as an indispensable condition for the social functioning of such groups.[13]

We may assume, therefore, that the socialization process and the adjustment through learning that it implies links man with his primate forebears. But, even if it should turn out that we are able to ascertain that certain common habits in the subhuman primate are not only learned but socially transmitted, I do not think this fact alone would change the psychobiological status of the primates.[14] It would only be a small step in the human direction, a necessary but not a sufficient condition for the advance to the human level. For it seems quite apparent from the empirical evidence that inter-individual adjustment in the infrahuman primates is confined to responses to signs and signals. So far as symbolic processes are involved at all they are confined to the intrinsic type, the type of representative process that under adequate conditions of motivation enable a chimpanzee to make a tool or solve other problems. The young primate responds to tutelage, or discipline if you will, that is mediated from outside himself, and while he forms habit patterns on this basis that enable him to play the simple roles demanded of him in the group, there is no higher level of psychobiological integration. For example, he could never be trained to abhor incest.

The shift that occurred from this simple level of adjustment to one in which, through the mediation of extrinsic symbols, a higher level of integration could be reached is the crux of the problem of psychobiological evolution in the case of the hominid. Nevertheless, we must not lose sight of the continuity that was maintained from the ape level to man. For at the human level, too, and particularly in the earliest stages of the socialization of the individual relatively simple conditioning processes are likewise operative along with more complex levels of learning. What, then, are the special features of this higher level of integration that make it possible for man to function differently from any other animal, to act in ways denied to them? In a highly epitomized form it seems to me that these are:

First, the emergence of a dominant integrative center of the personality and consequently the development of ego-centered processes which permit man to become an object to himself. Associated with this new level of organization we have such universal characteristics of the human being as self-consciousness, self-identification and reference, self-evaluation, self-stimulation, self-control, the possibility of relating one's contemplated or actual conduct to traditional ideals and values, etc. The fact that every human social order operates as a moral order is, among other things, contingent upon man's becoming an object to himself. Together with man's capacity for self-direction and self-control the foundation is laid for holding the adult individual in all societies morally responsible for his overt actions and, in some societies, even for conduct that occurs in dreams, that is, at the level of intrinsic symbolization.

As a result of self-objectification human societies become social orders of conscious selves, in contrast with the societies of other primates where the development of ego-centered processes as part of the psychobiological structure of the individual do not become salient. In fact, when viewed from the standpoint of this peculiarity of man, cultures may be said to be elaborated systems of meaning which, in an animal capable of self-awareness, implement a type of adaptation which makes the role of the human being intelligible to himself, both with reference to an articulated universe and to his fellow men.

Secondly, what is perhaps even more significant and interesting is that, in addition to man's capacity for consciously evaluating his own acts and directing his own conduct we now know that impulses and fantasies of which he is not unaware are unconsciously evaluated for him. That is to say, his emotional nature becomes structuralized in such a way that anxiety, guilt and depression become indices to the integrative level reached by the personal adjustment of the individual in relation to the symbolically expressed and mediated norms of his society. This peculiarity of man involves, of course, the Freudian concept of the superego as part of the personality structure of man.

What I should like to stress here without going into the moot points of a complex matter is the positive theoretical value of such a construct. It permits a deeper insight into one of the psychological mechanisms involved in the direct transmission of culture values while, at the same time, it helps to explain how an enhancement of ego development in man, who has remained so closely bound to his animal heritage through biologically rooted impulses, has been able to create and maintain effective social orders geared to highly diverse institutions and value systems. For, while on the one hand the superego functions as a kind of brake upon the ego, on the other, it facilitates the positive relations of the individual to socially sanctioned ideals and even the creation of new values. Without this ontogenetically rooted and largely unconscious aspect of the personality structure of man it is difficult to explain a great many things in the operation of human society and culture.

Going back once again to the seventeenth and eighteenth century thinkers who speculated about the nature of man and society we can well appreciate one of their major difficulties. They understood quite well the egotistical impulses of man, but they also had to account for a functioning social order. Hence they were driven to postulate certain *innate* moral qualities in man— whether good or bad. On the other hand, they had to invoke some form of "social contract" to bring men together and governmental institutions with coercive powers to influence man from outside himself. Even today we are apt to get into difficulties if we *only* conceptualize the transmission of culture in terms of socially acquired habits, or stress too much the outward coercive power of institutions as the mainstays of an effective social order. The concept of the superego as an intrinsic part of the psychobiological structure of man bridges the gap between the "inner" man, the social order and cultural tradition.

That both the ego and the superego are structuralized in the socialization process is now a general assumption. How this takes place would divert us into the complications of the theory of personality genesis. But there is no doubt that both intrinsic and extrinsic symbolizations enter into this very intricate process. Man could hardly have become an object to himself without the use of symbolic means, particularly in view of the fact that the ego has to be built up from a level of crude, unorganized needs and desires. This is what Freud implied when he wrote, "Where id was, there shall ego be."[15] To what extent we have ego development in animals below man is a question that needs further examination. If we assume a complete break from lower primate to man we open another gap and another "mystery."[16] Symbolization also enters into the concomitant development of a superego in man. When Freud, referring to this facet of the personality structure says that the long dependence of children upon parents "leaves behind it a precipitate, which forms within his ego a special agency in which this parental influence is prolonged,"[17] he is, of course, speaking metaphorically. What is meant in a more literal sense is that by some central symbolic process in the organism attitudes, qualities or other aspects of the parents become represented in a parental "imago." But as Freud himself clearly points out this is only the beginning of superego structuralization in the individual. In time, he says, the superego "takes over contributions from later successors and substitutes of his parents, such as teachers, admired figures in public life, or high social ideals."[18] "Takes over" implies identification with such personages and integration of their qualities or what they stand for into the personality through the operation of symbolic processes. And the further taking over of "high social ideals" points to the possibility of the development of a superego which transcends identifications with actual or ideal personalities, one that is identified wtih unmediated abstract ideals.

I need not point out, I think, that in the early stages of the child's development in every society conflicts arise between the impulses of the individual and the demands of parents or cultural surrogates.[19] These conflicts have to be resolved. The significant human fact is that instead of these conflicts becoming externalized and resolved on that basis they may be resolved for better or for worse, by unconscious repression. That is to say, certain impulses may never reach ego-awareness because the symbolic representations of them are excluded. Consequently the individual cannot deal with them through any external mode of adjustment because he is unaware of such impulses.

Thus, such processes as symbolization, identification, conflict, repression, etc., are some of the major mechanisms through which man becomes psychobiologically structured in the socialization process. They are intrinsic to the psychodynamics of human adjustment. Indeed, they are far more characteristic processes than learning which is, of course, a mode of adaptation not only shared with other primates, but with animals far lower on the phylogenetic scale. Consequently, there is nothing particularly human about learning *per se*. The "Law of Effect" does not apply to man alone. What *is* unique is the role which symbolization plays in the learning process and the contingence of the other mechanisms we have mentioned upon it. All of these together permit a higher order of integration and flexibility in human behavior. As Mowrer says,[20] "Living organisms which are unable to employ symbols versatilely are doomed to relative fixity of response, which, in the case of responses which have both remote and immediate consequences, is almost certain to result in a failure of 'integration.'" It has also been pointed out that loss of flexibility in personal adjustment is one of the key problems in the psychopathological aspects of human behavior.[21] Thus the transmission of culture, if realistically viewed, must be thought of not as the acquisition through a simple conditioning process, of habits or cultural traits as they appear in our descriptive ethnographic accounts, but as part of a very complicated and symbolically mediated learning process in which mechanism like conflict and repression play their role in the total integrative structure that we call the human personality.

Traditional terms like the "psychic unity" of man, or "human nature" which have been somewhat emptied of their original meaning become genuinely significant again if we mean a primate whose level of adjustment implies such processes and mechanisms. As Roheim once remarked, "The most basic of all basic personalities is the one connected with the fact that we are all human."[22]

The generic psychobiological structure of man I have attempted to outline here is one that does not require any particular systems of *extrinsic* symbolization as its medium. Just as biological structures once evolved in a rudimentary form possess potentialities for development and differentiation, so did the fundamental pattern of human psychological organization. Cultures could arise in which the significance of objects and events in the surrounding world, man's relation to man and the potential range of personal experience could be given a different valence. Man's world became one that was not simply given. It was constantly moulded by his interaction with it. Through the manner in which he represented it to himself it further became meaningful to him. But once a particular cultural system became established, a mode of life to which future generations had to adjust became perpetuated. The individual was forced to make his personal adjustment to life by means of the symbolic system provided by his society. But no culture frees the infant from the fundamental conflict arising from the biologically rooted impulses on the one hand, and the demands of parents or parent surrogates on the other, nor the need for some internal resolution of such conflicts. But the demands of the parents and the manner in which children are handled are not identical in all societies; hence the crucial importance of the socialization process in relation to the differential strains and stresses that account for the personality structure under one set of conditions as compared with another. What personality and culture studies have done is to demonstrate how important such differences are. When we have more knowledge of the range and variation in the human personality structure in relation to major provincial determinants we shall be able to state with more precision what is common to man everywhere. By that time we may be able to construct a better picture of the psychobiological structure of man as an evolving primate.

NOTES

[1] Leslie A. White drew attention to this problem a number of years ago in an article entitled "On the Use of Tools by Primates," 1942. He wrote (p. 371) "Tool-using among men is a different kind of activity, fundamentally and qualitatively different in a psychological sense, from tool-using among apes. Among apes the use of tools is a sensory, neuro-muscular conceptual process. Among men it is a sensory neuro-muscular conceptual and symbolic process. It is the ability to use symbols which has transformed anthropoid tool behavior into human tool behavior."

[2] St. George Mivart, 1874, p. 251. I am indebted to Mr. J. Gruber for calling my attention to this reference.

[3] *Ibid.*, pp. 188–189; italics inserted. Mivart was a Roman Catholic and he and G. J. Romanes, a close follower of Darwin, locked horns in a famous controversy. See St. G. Mivart, *The Origin of Human Reason*, 1889 and C. J. Romanes, *Mental Evolution in Man*, 1889.

[4] More recently Leslie A. White discussed the mind-body question, from a behavioristic point of view, in a short article, "Mind is Minding," 1939, p. 169, and three phyletic levels of mental organization in "The Mentality of Primates," 1932, pp. 69–72, in which he maintains that the difference between man and ape "is one of kind, not of degree." In 1935, John M. Cooper in "The Scientific Evidence Bearing upon Human Evolution," reviewed the problems of both organic and mental evolution. So far as the former is concerned he says that the evidence is in favor of the theory, but he maintains paradoxically that evidence for the latter has weakened since the days of Darwin "with the progress of cultural and linguistic anthropology and seemingly with the progress of comparative psychology and of the experimental psychology of the higher human mental processes." So he concludes that "the chasm between the brute mind and the human mind is at present unspanned, and we can see no way in which it could have been spanned in the past" (p. 52). It should be noted that Cooper's *a priori* assumptions about the nature of the human mind are closely related to both his conceptualization of the problem and the conclusion to which he comes.

[5] For a recent authoritative summation based on animal experimentation see T. C. Schneirla, 1949, "Levels in the Psychological Capacities of Animals."

[6] See Wilton M. Krogman, 1948, p. 18, quoting W. E. Le Gros Clark.

[7] K. S. Lashley, "Persistent Problems in the Evolution of Mind," 1949, pp. 29–30. Italics inserted.

[8] Many years ago John Dewey emphasized this fundamental point ("The Need for a Social Psychology," 1917). Although it has become much more familiar since that time, his statement is worth repeating. He wrote that "What we call 'mind' means essentially the working of certain beliefs and desires, and that these in the concrete,—in the only sense in which mind may be said to *exist*,—

are functions of associated behavior varying with the structure and operation of social groups." Thus instead of being viewed as "an antecedent and ready-made thing," mind "represents a reorganization of original activities through their operation in a given environment. It is a formation, not a datum, a product and a cause only after it has been produced. Now theoretically it is possible that the reorganization of native activities which constitute mind may occur through their exercise within a purely physical medium. Empirically, however, this is highly improbable. A consideration of the dependence in infancy of the organization of the native activities into intelligence upon the presence of others, upon sharing in joint activities and upon language, makes it obvious that the sort of mind capable of development through the operation of native endowment in a non-social environment is of the moron order, and is practically, if not theoretically, negligible." Cf. also George H. Mead, *Mind, Self and Society*, 1934.

[9] Quoted by Roger P. McCutcheon, 1949, p. 34.

[10] O. H. Mowrer and A. A. Ullman, 1945, p. 79.

[11] *See* e.g., Susanne K. Langer, 1942, Chap. 2 and 3; Ernst Cassirer, 1944, Chap. 2 and 3.

[12] Mowrer and Ullman, *op. cit.*, p. 78.

[13] C. R. Carpenter, 1912, pp. 256–257.

[14] David Bidney, 1947, p. 376, maintains that "all animals which are capable of learning and teaching one another are capable of acquiring culture. Hence *not culture in general but human culture,* as manifested in systems of artifacts, social institutions and symbolic forms of expression, *is peculiar to man.*" By conceptualizing culture from a broad "genetic and functional point of view," Bidney avoids drawing an absolute categorical distinction between the mode of adaptation in man and other animals. At the same time he stresses the distinctive character of "anthropoculture." In terms of Bidney's distinction I am concerned with the psychobiological structure that makes anthropoculture possible.

[15] Sigmund Freud, 1933, p. 112.

[16] O. H. Mowrer, 1946, pp. 321–322, is of the opinion that it is "desirable to speak of ego processes rather than egos. By so doing one is in a much better position to set up operational criteria for determining the precise extent to which such processes may be said to be in operation in any given organism and at any given stage of development. My own understanding of what ego processes are suggests that they are gradually elaborated both as the human child develops and as one ascends the phylogenetic scale."

[17] Sigmund Freud, 1949, p. 16.

[18] Ibid., p. 17.

[19] Cf. T. H. Huxley and Julian Huxley, *Touchstone for Ethics, 1893–1943*, 1947. Julian Huxley maintains (p. 4) "That man is inevitably (and alone among all organisms) subject to mental conflict as a normal factor in his life, and that the existence of this conflict is the necessary basis or ground on which conscience, the moral sense, and our systems of ethics grow and develop."

[20] Mowrer and Ullman, *op. cit.*, p. 81.

[21] For explicit references, *see* Mowrer and Ullman, *op. cit.*

[22] Quoted in George Devereux, 1945, "The Logical Foundations of Culture and Personality Studies," p. 122.

REFERENCES

BIDNEY, DAVID 1947 Human nature and the cultural process. American Anthropologist, Vol. 49, p. 367.

CARPENTER, C. R. 1942 Characteristics of social behavior in non-human primates. Trans. of the New York Academy of Sciences, Series II, Vol. 4, No. 8, pp. 256–257.

CASSIRER, ERNST 1944 An Essay on Man. New Haven.

COOPER, JOHN M. 1935 The scientific evidence bearing upon human evolution. Primitive Man, Vol. 8, pp. 1–56.

DEVEREUX, GEORGE 1945 The logical foundations of culture and personaltity studies, Trans. of the New York Academy of Sciences, Series II, Vol. 7, No. 5, p. 122.

DEWEY, JOHN 1917 The need for a social psychology, Psychological Review, Vol. 24.

FREUD, SIGMUND 1933 New Introductory Lectures on Psychoanalysis. New York.

——— 1949 An Outline of Psychoanalysis. New York.

HUXLEY, T. H., and JULIAN HUXLEY 1947 Touchstone for Ethics, 1893–1943. New York and London.

KROGMAN, WILTON M. 1948 The man apes of South Africa. Scientific American, May, p. 18.

LANGER, SUSANNE K. 1942 Philosophy in a New Key. Cambridge.

LASHLEY, K. E. 1949 Persistent problems in the evolution of mind. Quarterly Review of Biology, Vol. 24, pp. 29–30.

McCUTCHEON, ROGER P. 1949 Eighteenth Century Literature. New York, p. 34.

MEAD, GEORGE HERBERT 1934 Mind, Self and Society. Chicago.

MIVART, ST. GEORGE 1874 Man and Apes, An Exposition of Structural Resemblances and Differences bearing upon Questions of Affinity and Origin. New York.

——— 1899 The Origin of Human Reason. London.

MOWRER, O. H. 1946 The law of effect and ego psychology. Psychological Review, Vol. 53, pp. 321–322.

MOWRER, O.H., and A. A. ULLMAN 1945 Time as a determinant in integrative learning. Psychological Review, Vol. 52, p. 79.

ROMANES, G. J. 1889 Mental Evolution in Man. New York.

SCHNEIRLA, T. C. 1949 Levels in the psychological capacities of animals, in Philosophy for the Future, edited by Roy Wood Sellars, V. J. McGill, Marvin Farber. New York.

WHITE, LESLIE A. 1932 The mentality of primates. Scientific Monthly, Vol. 34, pp. 69–72.

——— 1939 Mind is minding. Scientific Monthly, Vol. 48, p. 169.

——— 1940 The symbol: the origin and basis of human behavior. Philosophy of Science, Vol. 7, pp. 451–463.

——— 1942 On the use of tools by primates. Journal of Comparative Psychology. Vol. 34, pp. 369–374.

CLIMATE, CULTURE,

AND EVOLUTION

PAUL T. BAKER

In the almost ninety years since Darwin published "The Descent of Man and Selection in Relation to Sex" (1871) many aspects of our knowledge about human evolution have changed. So much so that Darwin would probably find considerable study necessary to understand a symposium on culture or fossil man. However, if he were to join a discussion on climate and human evolution, he would be perfectly at home with his 1870 concepts.

In his famous book, he wrote that a naturalist not familiar with the races "would be deeply impressed with the fact . . . that the different races of men are distributed over the world in the same zoological provinces, as those inhabited by undoubtedly distinct species and genera of mammals." Darwin later discussed the possibility that variations in solar radiation in different parts of the world were responsible for the variations in the skin colors of races and came to the conclusion: "Although with our present knowledge we cannot account for the differences of color in the races of man, through any advantage thus gained, or from the direct action of climate; yet we must not quite ignore the latter agency, for there is good reason to believe that some inherited effect is thus produced."

Despite Darwin's feeling that climate was somehow involved in human evolution, he could not believe that climate or any other aspect of the physical environment had produced the racial variations in our species. As so many others he was impressed with the unique potentials of human culture to modify the human form. He stressed the role of varying concepts of human beauty in determining our form and finally concluded: ". . . of all the causes which have led to the differences in external appearance between the races of man and to a certain extent between man and the lower animals, sexual selection has been the most efficient."

Using statistical tools and data not available in Darwin's time, recent studies have shown that there is a high degree of relationship between climatic variables and some of the morphological variables in the human species (Roberts, 1953; and Newman, 1953 and 1956). Experimental studies have demonstrated that certain of these characteristics provide adaptive advantage to the individuals endowed with them.

Reprinted by permission from *Human Biology*, 32:1 (1960), 3–16.

Individuals who have a small amount of body fat, great body linearity and brunette skin can probably march for substantially longer distances in a hot desert that their morphological counterparts (Baker, 1955). Individuals with a stocky body build and large deposits of subcutaneous fat can sit nude for considerably longer periods in a cool temperature with less loss of body heat and less metabolic disturbance than the desert-adapted thin man (Baker and Daniels, 1956; LeBlanc, 1954). Experimental evidence has even shown us that the American Negro who has his extremities exposed to below freezing temperatures is much more likely to suffer from frostbite than the American White who is exposed to the same condition. On the other hand, American Negroes show less deviation from normal core temperature when they perform work under hot wet conditions than do American Whites, even though matched for the body linearity and fat, factors which might affect strain levels (Baker, 1959). Australian aborigines who sleep nude under cold conditions apparently have mechanisms of vaso-constriction which permit them to conserve body heat and sleep peacefully in a situation where European Whites would burn up great quantities of food shivering, while totally unable to sleep (Scholander, 1958).

These are but a few of the newly documented biological adaptations of different racial groups to their climatic environment. These examples have been selected because they represent those where specific genetic inheritance is most clearly indicated. Since this line of investigation has become popular in only the last ten years, there is every reason to believe that examples of human genetic adaptation to climatic environment will multiply rapidly.

It thus seems that Darwin's belief about the possible role of climate in race formation has been verified. However, it is not enough to find evidence of climatic adaptation. There remains the much larger question of how climatic selection would operate on man's genetic structure to produce these adaptations.

First, there must be the genetic potential and although mutations make anything possible, the overlapping of most racial characteristics in the various groups of Homo sapiens makes it seem probable that climatic selection has worked primarily on the polymorphism of the human genetic structure.

Second, climatic selection must have operated either by modifying the fertility of the individuals involved or by the actual death of carriers of certain genes before or during their reproductive life span. As of now, most evidence points to the latter probability. It is easy to visualize the tall skinny Yahgan freezing to death while out in a canoe in a snow storm but more probably the family died around a fire suffering from malnutrition and consequent disease while their short fat counterparts comfortably collected shellfish in the cold water.

Admittedly this example is speculative. It is so because it relies upon placing climatic selection in a cultural context. Yet it is almost impossible to imagine climatic selection outside the cultural media. Paleontological and archaeological evidence clearly indicates that man had already acquired tools and fire before *Homo sapiens* evolved as a species (Washburn, 1959). Most racial characteristics, therefore, evolved in groups who had well-developed cultures. Unless the culture form was an interactive part of the selective process, climatic selection would not have operated as it did on *Homo sapiens*. Going back to one bit of experimental evidence: the Australian aborigine seems to have a genetic adaptation to sleeping nude in the cold. This trait could not have been selected in a different cultural context. Given clothes, use of the brush shelter which he knew how to build, or even lacking the fire which was on either side of him during sleep, it is doubtful that the aborigine would have been genetically selected for this particular form of vaso-constriction.

To completely reject the concept of climatic selection without cultural involvement would be premature, but from anthropology's present theoretical framework it is more accurate always to consider the role of culture when trying to formulate a human evolutionary process related to climate. At least racial differences in climatic adaptation would seem to depend in part on cultural factors.

Since culture usually forms an essential link in "climatic selection," it is important to understand the ways in which climate and culture may interact to produce selection. There is, of course, the direct action of climate on culture and perhaps the reciprocal, but this belongs more properly to cultural evolution and archaeology. Based on the known examples of climatic adaptation in man, there appear to be five patterns of climate-culture interaction which determine the specific form of selection.

These five are: (1) Primary climate-culture interaction in any "climatic selection"; (2) "Cultural selection" reinforcing "climatic selection"; (3) "Cultural selection" opposing "climatic selection"; (4) Cultural blocks to "climatic selection"; (5) Cultural mediation in "climatic selection."

Rather than define these five categories in detail, it may be more enlightening to choose a single body characteristic and show how the interaction forms are required to explain the species-wide variation in the trait.

THE SURFACE-AREA/WEIGHT RATIO

Many of the recent studies relating body morphology to climate have emphasized the surface-area to weight ratio as an important trait in climatic adaptation. Coon, Garn and Birdsell (1950) pointed out that larger surface area per unit of weight might result in a greater loss of heat from the body to the surrounding environment. They, therefore, felt that the attenuation of the Nilotic Negro formed a body adaptation to hot desert conditions. This form was contrasted to the short square body build of the Eskimo, who was presumably cold adapted. Roberts (1953) later presented quantified data on the relationship between the separate entities of weight and stature to climate, but it remained for Schreider (1950 and 1951) actually to combine this data into a surface-area over weight ratio and correlate it to the climatic environment of different populations.

Despite reasonably conclusive evidence of a human SA/W relationship to climate it cannot be, thereby, concluded that this is a racial variation which has developed as a climatic adaptation. First it must be experimentally shown that variations in this trait confer specific climatic adaptation. Second, it must be shown that the degree of racial variation found for this ratio is at least in part indicative of group differences in genetic structure.

EVIDENCE FOR ADAPTATION

In contradiction to the original hypothesis put forth by Coon, Garn and Birdsell, experimental work has thus far failed to show that a high SA/W ratio provides any great physiological advantage to hot-desert dwellers (Baker, 1955; and Adolph, 1947). Beyond lowering water requirements because of a small body size, a high ratio has no appreciable effect on man's desert heat tolerance. Actually this could have been anticipated from a detailed knowledge of human physiology. The human body depends primarily upon the cooling derived from sweat evaporation for maintaining thermal homeostasis in a hot desert. The hot dry air of the desert has enormous evaporative power and is apparently capable of evaporating sweat much more rapidly than the human body can produce it. Since the sweat production of the active man is related more closely to his fat-free body mass than it is to his surface area, the total cooling per unit of weight would be predicted to be very similar for men of quite different surface areas.

Continuing on a theoretical basis, a high SA/W ratio may provide decided advantage to the man who must do physical exercise under hot wet climatic conditions. When the air has a high moisture content combined with high temperatures, such as that in tropical forest regions, it no longer has the capacity to evaporate all the sweat produced by an active man. Under these conditions a significant proportion of the sweat will form water droplets and run off the man, providing no body cooling. Thus in the hot wet climate, the total surface area over which a given sweat production is spread will govern the amount of cooling derived. Since the amount of sweat produced by a man is governed by his weight of fat-free mass then, with activity held constant, increases in SA/W ratio should lower the heat strain on a man in the tropics.

Unfortunately this theoretical prediction is without experimental verification simply because no one has yet performed the experiment. The only direct evidence which can be offered at this time is the common observation that large men, who have low SA/W ratio, appear to produce a greater proportion of unevaporated sweat when they work hard in a hot wet environment.

Only in the cold is Coon, Garn and Birdsell's hypothesis fully substantiated by both the theoretical and experimental evidence. If the vaso-constriction of different groups of men is the same, and if the amount of subcutaneous fat is the same, it is a thermodynamic law that heat loss is in direct relation to surface area. This rather dogmatic statement may be made because man's heat loss in the cold is a simple process of conductance and radiation. The shape factor may have some slight effect but it seems safe to assume that the morphological characteristics of men with low SA/W ratios would not be in the direction of more pointed or angular surfaces. Since the surface area controls the heat loss, and fat-free body weight (with other factors held constant) controls the heat production, it becomes *axiomatic* to state that for nude men, the lower the SA/W ratio the lower the heat loss per unit weight.

Experimental studies have shown that, for American Whites, variation in subcutaneous fat is probably a more significant factor in cool climate homeostasis than SA/W ratio variations (Baker and Daniels, 1956; Baker, 1959; LeBlanc, 1954). However, when subcutaneous fat was held constant, individuals with lower ratios maintained higher core temperatures at lower weight-adjusted metabolic rates (Baker and Daniels, 1956; Baker, 1959).

From the present theoretical and experimental evidence it appears that at least under hot, wet and cold conditions, the first requirement has been fulfilled and the correlations of SA/W to climate mean some kind of functional advantage to the groups involved.

GENETIC INVOLVEMENT

The second requirement was a genotypic involvement in the previously mentioned variations in SA/W ratio. Before questions of genotype can be discussed, the rather complex SA/W ratio or index must be broken down into its parts and morphological determinants. Surface-area to weight ratios as reported by almost all investigators are no more than a special function of height and weight. Since actual surface area is an extremely time-consuming measurement, most students rely on DuBois' (1936) original study of 8 men or perhaps the later mathematical refinements (Sendroy and Cecchini, 1954). These formulae are reasonably efficient when applied to White Europeans, and Rhodal (1952) reports that they also apply to Eskimos. Despite these studies it is hard to believe that the simple measurement of height and weight will provide equally accurate estimates of surface area for the short-bodied, long-legged Nilotic and long-bodied, short-legged Mongoloid. It seems to me quite probable that the Nilotic has a greater surface area than estimated from his height and weight while the Mongoloid's is lower than estimated.

The most direct factor involved in the ratio is weight. Without becoming too deeply involved in the reasons, one can point out that as body weight goes up the SA/W ratio goes down. Simple solid geometry shows that going from a one-inch cube of wood to a two-inch cube increases its weight eight-fold but increases its surface area only fourfold. While human weight to surface area does not progress in such a simple manner, surface area does not proportionally increase with weight. This means that a 160 lb. man always has a lower SA/W ratio than a 120 lb. man, provided his stature or body proportions are not pathologically aberrant.

The genetic involvement of the ratio may therefore be judged primarily by the extent to which body weight is genetically determined, secondarily by the genetic determination of stature, and to some unknown extent by the genetic involvement in body-trunk to leg-length ratios.

Quite obviously both the weight and stature of groups of men are variable depending on the action of the physical and cultural environment in which the phenotype develops. In the terms Hulse has used with reference to this matter, height and weight are among the most plastic of human characteristics. Nevertheless, no one has shown or suggested that a group of African Pygmies living in American culture, even for several generations, would acquire the height and weight of European-derived Americans. Although there may also be some changes in trunk to leg ratios, the American Negro still has a longer leg in relation to trunk than the American White (Hooton, 1959). The exact proportion of plasticity vs. polymorphism in the racial distribution of the SA/W ratio cannot be quantified. But it seems safe to state that at least part of the group variation in this ratio is related to differences in gene frequencies.

MODES OF SELECTION

Our ratio has now fulfilled the two essential criteria and appears to be an example of a body characteristic which has been climatically selected. This brings up the much more difficult question of how the selection took place. It is in the potential modes of selection that it becomes obvious culture can never be discounted.

To begin with basic assumptions: it is assumed that all of the recorded group genetic variation in the SA/W ratio is the result of plasticity and polymorphism. That is, given the time and selective pressure, which existed during past epochs, Pygmies would have acquired the stature of Europeans or Europeans the stature of Pygmies, had their roles been reversed. This assumption obviates the necessity for reconstructing the size and shape of a proto-Pygmy or proto-Nilot since, whatever the size and shape of the ancestral group, if it had a *Homo sapiens* type of size polymorphism, the group would have (with appropriate selection) evolved to its present SA/W ratio.

In the previous section, the potential advantage of a low or high SA/W ratio was noted in relationship to very particular situations. Thus, in the hot wet tropics an advantage might accrue to an active individual if he had a high ratio. The actual degree of advantage would increase as the activity increased. For two men playing checkers in the shade of a tree, it is extremely doubtful that any difference in their core temperature or performance could be found, whatever the individual difference in SA/W ratio. On the other hand, if their culture demanded hard work, the men with a low ratio would probably suffer from a substantially higher core temperature, might therefore have a lower performance potential (Fine and Gaydos, 1959) and, if the work was hard enough, would either quit or die of heatstroke. When the culture requires high metabolic output many modes of selection are possible —social selection or inability to obtain enough food or even death of the "unfit." However, the important point is that culture must be involved and unless the culture form required considerable activity, "climatic selection" could not operate.

The accompanying illustration is an attempt to indicate the primary selective process. Since SA/W is believed to be normally distributed, it has been depicted by the normal curve (figure 1). As the combined climatic and

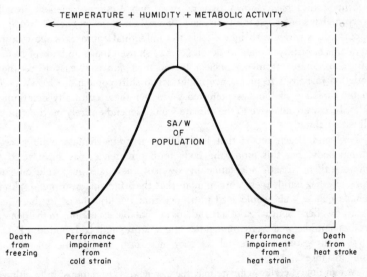

TEMPERATURE + HUMIDITY + METABOLIC ACTIVITY

SA/W
OF
POPULATION

Death
from
freezing

Performance
impairment
from
cold strain

Performance
impairment
from
heat strain

Death
from
heat stroke

Fig. I Graphic depiction of the climatic selection process: climatic and behavioral factors on the top line determine the position of a given population distribution of surface area per unit of weight (SA/W) in relation to the selective phenomena shown below.

cultural factors shown at the top act to bring a population into heat or cold stress areas the individuals at one extreme of the distribution will be more frequently and drastically stressed than those at the opposite end. However, other factors distributed by chance probably make the individual SA/W selection group another normal curve with its mean near the extreme being stressed.

Although this figure may not be necessary to explain the process, depicting the selection for normally distributed traits in this manner leads to some interesting questions. For example, it suggests that groups living in hot wet areas may have SA/W ratio distributions which are skewed to the left while those in cold stress areas show skewness to the right. To the author's knowledge, no one has investigated the problem.

CLIMATE-FREE
CULTURAL FACTORS WHICH HELP DETERMINE SA/W RATIOS

The low correlations between SA/W ratios and climatic characteristics demonstrate quite conclusively that climatic selection does not alone determine the ratio of any given group. A number of other factors of the physical environment are undoubtedly involved, but the problem also remains whether any purely cultural factors may be operative.

One of the more obvious cultural factors is the standard for mate selection. Recent studies have shown that in most non-Western societies virtually everyone has some opportunity to mate. Nevertheless, the frequency of mating opportunities varies with how closely the individual approaches the cultural standards of beauty. Ford and Beach (1952) showed that standards of beauty vary considerably from one society to the next and it is easy to see how variation in body size preference might act to shift population SA/W ratios in the direction of the size preferred. Whether these culturally determined ratio shifts were adaptive to the climate would depend entirely on the group's climatic habitat.

Ford and Beach report that the Chukchee prefer females who have a plump body. For this group the body form preference may have acted to improve their climatic adaptation by lowering their ratio in a cold climate. On the other hand, these authors note that the Maricopa also prefer plump female mates. This would lead to a poor climatic adjustment in these hot-desert dwellers. Southwest desert Indians are notable exceptions to the general relationship between environmental temperature and body build (Baker, 1958), suggesting that sexual selection may override climatic selection in some instances.

As mentioned earlier, climate may have some direct relationship to cultural traits but if ignored these examples show how climate-free cultural factors may act to augment or detract from the morphological adaptation of man to his climatic niche.

FAILURE OF THE CULTURAL LINK

It might be thought that the cultural component of some climatic selections could be ignored on all but a theoretical level since most cultures demand outdoor activity of their people. The major exceptions are obviously the very recent "Westernized" cultures which provide sedentary indoor activity.

Although statistical evidence is lacking, it is doubtful whether anyone would suggest that Americans in Montana or Southern Arizona are now being climatically selected at a genetic level. However, there are other earlier culture forms where at least some segments of the population were culturally shielded from climatic selection. Any society which has class or caste, and this includes almost all agricultural societies, reduces the climatic exposure of the upper strata. Inbreeding upper classes have been reported larger in body size for almost all societies (Coon, Garn and Birdsell, 1950). This difference is usually ascribed to better nutrition, and diet is undoubtedly important. However, there are other factors involved. In places like India and central Africa, the larger body size of the upper class is ascribed to the social dominance of an invading large-size race (Risley, 1915). If this formed a complete explanation, it is peculiar that the reverse case of small upper-class people has not been reported somewhere in the world.

It is probable that there is no climatic selection for larger body size in the upper class but neither is there climatic selection against this large size. In hot climates the lack of essential high activity for most upper-strata members breaks the hypothetical selection process. Whatever their SA/W ratios, these individuals have equal opportunity of reproducing and will not be subject to death or reduced nutrition because of their heat tolerance. It may be that much of the class or caste difference in the SA/W ratios is simply the result of phenotypic plasticity, but if any of it is polymorphism this difference may be partially the end result of a failure in the cultural selection link. Again, without any clear evidence to support the hypothesis, it might be suggested that the high SA/W ratios in tropical populations may be maintained in a manner similar to the high incidence of sicklemia in the African malarial areas. That is, as long as climatic selection for heat tolerance is continuing, there is a high ratio, but when the selective process is disrupted, other selective phenomena produce a rapid rise to a larger body size and consequently lower SA/W ratio. If there were evidence showing a smaller body size for the upper strata of cold-area societies a stronger argument could be provided for this hypothesis.

CULTURAL MODIFICATION OF CLIMATIC SELECTION

Failure of the culture link can, therefore, block many forms of climatic selection, but in doing so it may also start a new climate-linked selective process in operation. As long as men had no clothing they could not survive in climates which had temperatures below freezing. With the acquisition of clothing, the selection for SA/W was greatly reduced since man could now utilize the much more effective adaptive trait of his fellow mammals —their fur. With fur clothing man penetrated far into the zones of the world with below freezing temperatures. Although clothing effectively helps to maintain core temperatures, it fails adequately to protect man's extremities at very low temperatures. Thus a new type of selection came into operation and morphological plus functional mechanisms which would reduce susceptibility to frostbite were now selected.

When large differences in the incidence of frostbite occurred between Negro and White soldiers in the two World Wars, they were attributed to cultural differences. However, during the Korean conflict a large and very careful epidemiological study was performed. In this study all the potential cultural factors in frostbite, down to the number of changes of socks were studied. Even with all the training and behavioral factors controlled, American Negroes had a much higher incidence of frostbite. Orr and Fanier (1951) estimated that, with all other known factors controlled, American Negroes born in the North had five times the incidence of frostbite of American Whites also born in the North. In fact, the racial difference was about the most important etiological factor found.

These results prompted climatic physiologists to search for a genetic factor which would account for the difference. On the basis of earlier Japanese work (Yoshimura and Iida, 1950 and 1952), Meehan (1955) studied the temperature changes of the finger when men otherwise thermally équilibrated put their fingers in ice water. In a large group of Negro and White soldiers he found the Whites responded by temperature cycling much more frequently than the Negroes. A small group of Eskimos showed an even stronger cycling response than Whites. Since a pair of identical twins in the study had virtually identical responses, he concluded that the differences were probably genetic.

Two subsequent studies by other investigators have reconfirmed the Negro-Whites differences found by Meehan. Rennie and Adams (1957) cite evidence to the effect that these differences would be related to frostbite susceptibility. In the most recent study Iampietro et al. (1959) show that in a group of 17 White admixed American Negroes and 18 Whites the lowest 25% of responders were all Negroes while the top 25% were all Whites.

Even though additional study of the temperature "hunting" response is indicated for other racial groups, there is enough evidence to indicate a genetic adaptation. Yet, we know that without well made clothing men could not have survived in an environment where frostbite could have occurred.

Thus, the development of a technology which reduced or perhaps stopped the selection of low SA/W ratios created a new environment where culture and climate acted together to produce a new and effective selective force.

SUMMARY AND CONCLUSIONS

When Darwin tried to explain the morphological variations in man he noted that although there were some obvious correlates between climatic zones and human morphology it was equally obvious that cultural differences could have produced great variation. We have continued to separate climate and culture when considering the factors in racial evolution. A close examination of the problem suggests that both climate and culture are involved in any form of climatic selection. Thus, it becomes important to understand the ways in which climate and culture can interact to effect genetic selection.

Five forms of interaction have been suggested, but more may become apparent as new knowledge on the adaptive value of racial differences is attained. These five forms treat climate and culture as independent variables and ignore the possible direct relationship between these divisions of man's environment. This discussion does not stress the role of other physical environmental factors in determining race differences, but it should be remembered that probably most racial differences are the product of multiple selective factors and even climate and culture together will not explain the total interracial variability in morphological traits.

To demonstrate the modes of selection created by the five forms of climate-culture interaction, group variations in surface area over weight are analyzed in the interaction framework. An examination of this morphological trait shows: (1) a relationship to climatic zones; (2) that the group variations have adaptive value; (3) that some of the variation reflects genetic polymorphism. From this evidence it is concluded that "climatic selection" has acted to produce some of the racial differences in this ratio. Consideration of the selective modes shows how the selection might have occurred and also some of the reasons why there is not a perfect relationship between climatic zone and the surface area over weight ratio.

REFERENCES

ADOLPH, E. F. 1947 Physiology of Man in the Desert. Interscience Publishers, Inc., New York.

BAKER, P. T. 1955 Relationship of Heat Stress to Gross Morphology. Env. Prot. Div. Technical Rept. EP-7, QM R&D Center.

―――― 1958a Racial differences in heat tolerance. Am. J. Phys. Anthrop., 16:287–305.

―――― 1958b The biological adaptation of man to hot deserts. Am. Naturalist, 42:337–357.

―――― 1959 American Negro-White differences in the thermal insulative aspects of body fat. Human Biol., 31:316–324.

BAKER, P. T., and F. DANIELS, JR. 1956 Relationship between skinfold thickness and body cooling for two hours at 15°C. J. Applied Physiol., 8:409–416.

COON, C. S., S. M. GARN, and J. B. BIRDSELL 1950 Races: A Study of the Problems of Race Formation in Man. Charles C. Thomas, Springfield, Ill.

DARWIN, CHARLES 1871 The Descent of Man and Selection in Relation to Sex. Murray, London.

DUBOIS, D. 1936 Basal Metabolism in Health and Disease. Lea and Febiger, Philadelphia.

FINE, B. J., and H. F. GAYDOS 1959 The relationship between individual personality variables and body temperature response patterns in the cold. Env. Prot. Res. Div. Technical Rept. EP-106, QM R&E Command.

FORD, C. S., and F. A. BEACH 1952 Patterns of Sexual Behavior. Harper & Brothers, New York.

HOOTON, E. A.   1959   Body build in a sample of the United States Army. Env.
· Prot. Res. Div. Technical Report EP-102. QM R&E Command.

HULSE, F. S.   1960   Adaptation, selection, and plasticity in ongoing human
evolution. Hum. Biol. 32:63–79.

IAMPIETRO, P. F., R. F. GOODMAN, E. R. BUSKIRK, and D. E. BASS   1959   Response of Negro and White males to cold. J. Applied Physiol., 14:798–800.

LEBLANC, J.   1954   Subcutaneous fat and skin temperature. Canad. J. Biol. and
Physiol. 32:407–417.

MEEHAN, J. P.   1955   Individual and racial variations in a vascular response to
a cold stimulus. Military Medicine, 116:330–334.

NEWMAN, M. T.   1953   The application of ecological rules to the racial anthropology of the aboriginal New World. Am. Anthrop., 55:311–327.

―――   1956   Adaptation of man to cold climates. Evolution, 10:101–105.

ORR, K. D., and D. C. FANIER   1951   Cold Injuries in Korea during the Winter
of 1950–1951. Army Medical Research Laboratory, Fort Knox, Ky.

RENNIE, D. W., and T. ADAMS   1957   Comparative thermoregulatory responses
of Negroes and White persons to acute cold stress. J. Applied Physiol., 11:
201–204.

RISLEY, H.   1915   The People of India. W. Thacker & Co., London.

ROBERTS, D. F.   1953   Body weight, race and climate. Am. J. Phys. Anthrop.,
11:533–558.

RODAHL, K.   1952   The body surface area of Eskimos as determined by the
linear and the height-weight formulas. Am. J. Phys. Anthrop., 10:419–426.

SCHOLANDER, P. F., H. T. HAMMEL, J. S. HART, D. H. LEMESSURIER, and J.
STEM   1958   Cold adaptation in Australian Aborigines. J. Applied Physiol.,
13:211–218.

SCHREIDER, E.   1950   Geographical distribution of the body-weight/body-surface
ratio. Nature, 165:286.

―――   1951   Anatomical factors of body-heat regulation. Nature, 167:823–824.

SENDROY, J., and L. P. CECCHINI   1954   Determination of human body surface
area from height and weight. J. Applied. Physiol., 7:1–12.

WASHBURN, S. L.   1959   Speculations on the interrelations of the history of
tools and biological evolution. Human Biol., 31:21–31.

YOSHIMURA, H., and T. IIDA   1950   Studies on the reactivity of skin vessels to
extreme cold. Part I. A point test of the resistance against frostbite. Japanese
J. Physiol., 1:147–159.

―――   1952   Studies on the reactivity of skin vessels to extreme cold. Part II.
Factors governing the individual differences of the reactivity or the resistance
against frostbite. Japanese J. Physiol., 2:177–185.

ANTHROPOLOGICAL IMPLICATIONS

OF SICKLE CELL GENE DISTRIBUTION

IN WEST AFRICA

FRANK B. LIVINGSTONE

During the past fifteen years, data on the frequency of the sickle cell gene have accumulated to such an extent that its world distribution can now be outlined in considerable detail. Frequencies of more than 20 percent of the sickle cell trait have been found in populations across a broad belt of tropical Africa from the Gambia to Mozambique. Similar high frequencies have been found in Greece, South Turkey, and India. At first it appeared that there were isolated "pockets" of high frequencies in India and Greece, but more recently the sickle cell gene has been found to be widely distributed in both countries (Choremis and Zannos 1956; Sukumaran, Sanghvi, and Vyas (1956). Moreover, between these countries where high frequencies are found, there are intermediate frequencies, in Sicily, Algeria, Tunisia, Yemen, Palestine, and Kuwait. Thus, the sickle cell gene is found in a large and rather continuous region of the Old World and in populations which have recently emigrated from this region, while it is almost completely absent from an even larger region of the Old World which stretches from Northern Europe to Australia.

When the broad outlines of the distribution of the sickle cell gene first began to emerge, several investigators attempted to explain various aspects of this distribution by migration and mixture. Lehmann and Raper (1949) attempted to show that the differences in the frequency of the sickle cell gene among the Bantu tribes of Uganda were due to varying degrees of Hamitic admixture; Brain (1953) and Lehmann (1954) postulated migrations from Asia to account for the distribution of the sickle cell gene in Africa; and Singer (1953), using an age-area type of argument, postulated that the sickle cell gene arose by mutation near Mt. Ruwenzori and diffused from there. However, it was recognized early in the development of the sickle cell problem that regardless of the extent to which migration and mixture explained the distribution pattern of the sickle cell gene, its high frequencies in various widely scattered areas raised some additional and striking problems in human population genetics.

Since persons who are homozygous for the sickle cell gene very rarely reproduce, there is a constant loss of sickle cell genes in each generation. In

Reprinted from *American Anthropologist*, 60:3 (1958), 533–62.

order for the gene to attain frequencies of .1 to .2, which are equivalent to about 20 to 40 percent of the sickle cell trait, there must be some mechanism which is compensating for this loss. In other words, there must be some factor which is tending to increase the number of sickle cell genes in the population. Neel (1951) first pointed out that there are two outstanding possibilities; either the sickle cell gene is arising frequently by mutation, or the heterozygote for the sickle cell gene possesses a selective advantage over the normal homozygote which offsets the selective disadvantage of the sickle cell homozygote (balanced polymorphism). Since the evidence (Vandepitte et al. 1955) indicated that the mutation rate was not sufficient to maintain the high frequencies, selection in favor of individuals with the sickle cell trait seemed to be implicated as the factor which was maintaining them.

When Allison (1954a; 1954b; 1954c) advanced the hypothesis that the heterozygote for the sickle cell gene possessed a relative immunity to falciparum malaria, he marshalled the first clear evidence for the mechanism by which selection maintained the observed high frequencies. In addition to experiments on sicklers and nonsicklers which seemed to show that the sicklers could cope more easily with a malarial infection, Allison (1954b) also showed that the tribal frequencies of the sickle cell gene in Uganda and other parts of East Africa could be explained as well by his malaria hypothesis as by varying degrees of Hamitic admixture. Thus, Allison's work showed that selection must be taken into consideration in any attempt to explain the distribution of the sickle cell gene.

Although selection has undoubtedly played a major role in determining the frequencies of the sickle cell gene in the populations of the world, in many areas other factors in addition to selection may well be involved. Allison (1954b) has shown that most of the tribes of East Africa seem to have frequencies of the sickle cell trait which are in approximate equilibrium with the amount of malaria present, but there appear to be many populations in West Africa and elsewhere for which this is not so. It will be the purpose of this paper to show how the distribution of the sickle cell gene in West Africa is the result of the interaction of two factors, selection and gene flow. Gene flow will be used here to include both migration and mixture; the term migration is used where the gene flow involves the movement of breeding populations or large segments of them, and mixture where the breeding populations remain rather stationary and the gene flow involves the exchange of individuals between them. Of course, any actual situation is usually a combination of these two "polar" concepts.

According to modern genetic theory as developed by Wright and others, there are five factors which can contribute to gene frequency change: selection, mutation, gene drift, gene flow, and selective mating. Strictly speaking, an attempt to explain the distribution of any gene must take into consideration all five. However, three of these factors—mutation, gene drift, and selective mating—are thought to have had relatively little effect on the features of the distribution of the sickle cell gene in West Africa which this paper will attempt to explain, and thus will not be discussed at any length in this paper.

The general plan of the paper will be as follows. First, the distribution of the sickle cell gene in West Africa will be plotted; then an attempt will be made to correlate this distribution with that of falciparum malaria in West Africa. It will be assumed that the high frequencies of the sickle cell gene are in equilibrium with the particular endemicity of malaria in which they are found. Thus, by comparing these two distributions we can determine where the frequencies of the sickle cell gene appear to be explained by selection (i.e. are in equilibrium), and we can also determine where the frequencies appear to be very far from equilibrium and hence where other factors in addition to selection appear to be involved. The rest of the paper will then be concerned with the populations which do not appear to be in equilibrium. In order to explain why the frequencies of the sickle cell gene in these populations are not in equilibrium with the present-day endemicity of malaria, it is necessary to have some idea of the ethnic and culture history of West Africa. The literature on the culture history of West Africa is rather sparse, so the major part of this paper will be an attempt to infer its broad outlines from the distribution of language and of certain domesticated plants in West Africa.

THE DISTRIBUTION OF THE SICKLE CELL GENE IN WEST AFRICA

In the following compilation of data on the distribution of the sickle cell gene in West Africa, several early publications of surveys have been omitted. In all of these reports, the tribe of the persons tested is not given, and the reports could thus contain subjects from several breeding populations with very different frequencies of the sickle cell gene. Data by tribe are available for the areas covered by these surveys, except for part of Evans' (1944) survey. His sample from the Cameroons has been included since there are no other data from this area.

Where the same tribe has been tested by different investigators, differences in the frequency of the sickle cell trait have been tested by a chi-square test. If the differences were not significant, the results have been combined. However, for several large tribes which extend over considerable distances and into several different countries, the samples have been kept separate when they were obtained in different countries.

For the surveys in which paper electrophoresis or other biochemical tests were done on the bloods, all individuals who would have been positive for the sickle cell test were counted as positive without regard to whether they appeared to be homozygous or heterozygous for the sickle cell gene. Thus, the frequency of the sickle cell trait, as used in this paper, includes both heterozygotes and any living homozygotes for the sickle cell gene. However, recent studies (Lehmann and Raper 1956) indicate that homozygotes for the sickle cell gene rarely survive the first years of life, so that most likely very few homozygotes are included in the tribal samples. Throughout the discussion, sickle cell trait frequencies will be used instead of gene frequencies, since the trait frequencies are used by most investigators and hence their significance is more easily comprehended. Since very few homozygotes are included in the samples, the gene frequency would be close to one-half the trait frequency in all cases.

Except for the Ivory Coast, Dahomey, and the Cameroons, the compilation is by tribe. The Dahomey and Cameroons samples have been included in an effort to fill up large gaps in the distribution in areas where tribal investigations are nonexistent. These samples have combined several tribes and thus have probably combined data from isolates which differ significantly from one another in the frequency of the sickle cell trait. Since they are also quite small samples, this paper will not consider them in detail.

Due to the lack of investigations, and also to the multiplicity of small tribes which inhabit the Ivory Coast, the tribal samples from there are all rather small. Since the frequency of the sickle cell trait is o percent in Liberia to the west of the Ivory Coast and greater than 20 percent in Ghana to the east, the Ivory Coast is an area of crucial concern to this study. For this reason, the tribal samples have been combined into larger linguistic units to increase the sample sizes and thus give them more reliability. The tribes which have been combined are very closely related, since in most cases they speak the same language with only dialectic differences between them.

TABLE I

THE FREQUENCIES OF THE SICKLE CELL TRAIT IN THE TRIBES OF WEST AFRICA

Country Tribe	Investigations *	Number Examined	Number Positive	Sickle Cell Trait (%)
Senegal				
Wolof (Ouolof)	16, 18	2277	151	6.63
Lebu (Lebou)	16, 18	522	31	5.94
Serer	16, 18	1515	50	3.30
Soce	16	70	11	15.71
Fulani (Peul)	16, 18	299	27	9.03
Tukulor (Toucouleur)	16, 18	634	60	9.46
Dyola	18, 19	39	2	5.13
Mandiago	16, 18, 19	101	1	0.99
Gambia				
Mandingo-Western Division	2	167	18	10.78
Mandingo-Keneba	2	240	15	6.25
Mandingo-Jali	2	115	7	6.09
Mandingo-Manduar	2	59	10	16.95
Mandingo-Tankular	2	132	32	24.24
Fulani (Fula)	2	127	24	18.90
Dyola (Jola)	2	312	53	16.99
Wolof (Jolloff)	2	104	18	17.31
Saracole (Serahuli)	2	96	8	8.33
Bainunka	2	90	15	16.67

THE FREQUENCIES OF THE SICKLE CELL TRAIT IN THE TRIBES OF WEST AFRICA (CONTINUED)

Country Tribe	Investigations *	Number Examined	Positive Number	Sickle Cell
Portuguese Guinea				
Papel	24	500	15	3.00
Mandiago (Mandjaca)	15	500	16	3.20
Balante (Balanta)	15	500	25	5.00
Feloop (Felupe)	15	466	6	1.72
Baiote	15	473	6	1.27
Nalu	15	501	14	2.79
Saracole	15	286	24	8.39
Mandingo (Mandinga)	15	500	75	15.00
Biafada (Beafada)	15	505	77	15.25
Pajadinca	15	358	66	18.44
Fulani (Fula-Foro)	15	500	115	23.00
Fulani (Fula-Preto)	15	430	108	25.12
French Guinea				
Fulani (Foula)	15, 16, 18	682	109	15.98
Susu	5, 18, 19	48	15	31.25
Kissi	19	18	4	22.22
Loma-Kpelle (Toma-Guerze)	19	40	8	20.00
Sierra Leone				
Creole	2	42	10	23.81
Timne	2	52	15	28.95
Mende	2, 23	1124	330	29.36
Liberia				
Kissi	17	298	58	19.46
Mende	17	77	13	16.88
Gbandi	17	352	54	15.34
Vai	17	93	13	13.98
Kpelle	17	982	128	13.03
Loma	17	511	65	12.72
Gola	17	183	22	12.02
Belle	17	29	3	10.34
Bassa	17	811	58	7.15
Dei	17	53	2	3.77
Mano	17	709	15	2.12
Gio	17	428	9	2.10
Grebo	17	69	1	1.45
Krahn	17	154	1	0.65
Kru	17	148	1	0.68
Webbo	17	77	0	0.00
French Sudan				
Moor (Maure)	18, 19	70	4	5.71
Saracole	16, 18	196	16	9.18
Bambara	16, 18	262	27	10.31
Mandingo (Malinke)	18, 19	50	8	16.00
Fulani (Peul)	20	152	22	14.47
Songhai	20	100	11	11.00
Ivory Coast				
Senufo	5, 19	33	8	24.24
Agni-Baule	5, 19	53	7	13.21
Dan-Gouro	5, 19	30	0	0.00
Lagoon	5, 19	48	2	4.17
Bete	5, 19	53	1	.89
Bakwe	5, 19	63	1	1.59

Country Tribe	Investigations *	Number Examined	Positive Number	Sickle Cell Trait (%)
Upper Volta				
Samogo	20	120	8	6.67
Bobofing	5, 19, 22	232	57	24.57
Lobi	5, 19	15	3	20.00
Mossi	5, 19, 20	207	24	11.59
Gurma	5, 19, 20	34	3	8.82
Gurunsi	5, 19	14	1	7.14
Ghana				
Mossi (Moshie)	10, 11	121	5	4.13
Dagarti	11	97	11	11.34
Dagomba	11	71	3	4.23
Ewe	2, 10, 11	232	54	23.28
Fanti	2, 10, 11	204	48	23.53
Ga	2, 10, 11	367	67	18.26
Twi	2, 10	111	24	21.62
Frafra	9	680	66	9.71
Ashanti	2	102	23	22.55
French Togoland				
Kabre	4	1104	109	9.87
Dahomey				
Dahomeans	5, 19	55	5	9.09
Niger				
Djerma (Zabrama)	2, 19	69	15	21.74
Tuareg	3	93	5	5.38
Nigeria				
Yoruba	7, 13, 25	3477	853	24.53
Igalla	25	155	28	18.06
Ibo	2	51	11	21.57
Cameroons	12	138	21	15.22
Kerikeri	14	159	17	10.69
Fulani	14	184	31	16.85
Hausa	1, 6, 14	611	107	17.51
Lake Chad				
Mobur (Mobeur)	21	273	49	17.95
Kanembu (Kanembou)	21	76	17	22.37
Mangawa	21	58	12	20.69
Sugurti (Sougourti)	21	37	6	16.22

* References are as follows:

1—Adamson (1951)
2—Allison (1956)
3—Barnicot, Ikin, and Mourant 1954)
4—Bezon (1955)
5—Binson, Neel, and Zuelzer (unpublished)
6—Bruce-Chwatt (unpublished)
7—Charles and Archibald (unpublished)
8—Colbourne, Edington, and Hughes (1950)
9—Colbourne and Edington (1956)
10—Edington and Lehmann (1954)
11—Edington and Lehmann (1956)
12—Evans (1944)
13—Jelliffe and Humphreys (1952)
14—Jelliffe (1954)

15—Leite and Ré (1955)
16—Linhard (1952)
17—Livingstone (1958)
18—Neel, Hiernaux, Linhard, Robinson Zuelzer, and Livingstone (1956)
19—Pales and Linhard (1951)
20—Pales and Serere (1953)
21—Pales, Galais, Gert ,and Fourquet (1955)
22—Raoult (unpublished)
23—Rose and Suliman (1955)
24—Trincao, Pinto, Almeida, and Gouveia (1950)
25—Walters and Lehmann (1956)

Although the individual tribal samples are small, there is no indication that this procedure has combined tribes which have very different frequencies of the sickle cell trait.

Table 1 shows the frequency of the sickle cell trait for West Africa by tribe and also by country. For the purposes of further discussion, the spelling of all tribal names has been standardized. On Table 1 the names used by the original investigators are shown in parentheses after the standardized name.

The distribution of the frequency of the sickle cell trait in West Africa is shown on Figure 1. In order to make the general configuration of the distribution more easily visualized, the frequencies have been grouped into five categories: 0–2, 2–8, 8–15, 15–22, and greater than 22 percent. The frequency of the sickle cell trait can be seen to exhibit extreme variability, sometimes over very short distances. In many cases there are significant differences in the frequency of the trait even within the same tribe. For example, the Fulani have frequencies ranging from 8 to 25 percent, and the Mandingo in the Gambia vary from 6 to 28 percent. Although this great variability impedes generalizing about the distribution, some significant generalizations can nevertheless be made.

Generally, the higher frequencies tend to be toward the south, and, despite many exceptions, there is some indication of a north-south gradient in the frequency of the sickle cell trait. The distribution of falciparum malaria follows a similar gradient, and, in addition, all the populations which have sickle cell trait frequencies greater than 15 percent inhabit areas where malaria is either hyperendemic or holoendemic.

In an environment in which malaria is hyperendemic or holoendemic, the disease is transmitted throughout most of the year, so that the individuals are continually being reinfected. The average number of infective bites per person per year is always greater than about 5, and in some areas ranges up to 100 or more. Thus, infants are infected with malaria shortly after birth, and for about the first five years of life every child is engaged in a mortal struggle with the parasite. During these years the parasite rate (i.e., the percentage of individuals harboring malaria parasites) is close to 100 percent and there is a considerable mortality from the disease. Those individuals who survive this struggle have a solid immunity to malaria. In later years they are being continually reinfected with malaria but are able to keep their infection at a sub-clinical level. The parasite rate then decreases among older children and is lowest in adults. In holoendemic malaria the adult parasite rate will be about 20 percent and the adults will almost never have any clinical symptoms of malaria, while in hyperendemic malaria the adult parasite rate will be somewhat higher and the adults will sometimes have clinical symptoms, usually chills and fever. However, in both these conditions there is seldom any adult mortality from malaria.

It is in an environment in which malaria is either hyperendemic or holoendemic that the heterozygote for the sickle cell gene has been postulated to

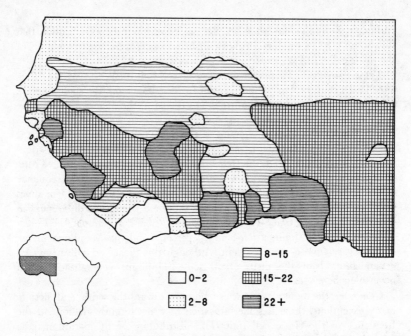

Fig. I   The distribution of the frequency of the sickle cell trait in West Africa.

have a selective advantage over the normal homozygote. Allison (1954a) and Raper (1955) have shown that, although sicklers are infected with falciparum malaria almost as readily as nonsicklers, in the younger age groups the very high densities of parasites are not found as often among sicklers. In addition, Raper (1956) has shown that the sicklers do not suffer from cerebral malaria and blackwater fever as much as nonsicklers. Since these are the complications of falciparum malaria which result in death, the sicklers had a lower mortality rate from falciparum malaria. In addition, I have postulated (1957a) that if the sickling females did not have as heavy falciparum infections of the placenta as did normal females, they would have a higher net reproduction rate and hence this could be another mechanism by which malaria was maintaining the high frequencies of the sickle cell gene. Although the evidence is not conclusive, it seems for the most part favorable to this hypothesis. When the evidence for both these mechanisms is considered as a whole, it seems to be conclusive that malaria is the major cause of the high frequencies of the sickle cell gene. One would therefore expect to find high frequencies of the sickle cell trait in areas in which malaria is either hyperendemic or holoendemic.

From about the latitude of the Gambia south, West Africa is almost entirely characterized by hyperendemic or holoendemic malaria; hence, high frequencies of the sickle cell trait would be expected. However, there are many populations in this region with very low frequencies of the trait. The majority of them are found in three areas: (1) Coastal Portuguese Guinea, (2) Eastern Liberia and the Western Ivory Coast, (3) Northern Ghana. The low frequency populations which are found in Northern Ghana differ from those in the other two areas by having high frequencies of the gene which is responsible for Hemoglobin C. This gene is an allele of the sickle cell gene (Ranney 1954), so that in Northern Ghana the sickle cell locus is a tri-allelic system. Since the selective values associated with the various phenotypes of this system are not known at present, the equilibrium frequencies for these populations cannot be ascertained (see Allison 1957 for further discussion of this problem). Thus, one cannot say whether or not these populations are in equilibrium for this locus. The rest of this paper will therefore be concerned with the two areas, Coastal Portuguese Guinea and Eastern Liberia-Western Ivory Coast, where the Hemoglobin C gene is almost completely absent (Neel et al. 1956).

Cambournac (1950) in Coastal Portuguese Guinea and Young and Johnson (1949) in Eastern Liberia found malaria to be either hyperendemic or holoendemic in these areas where low frequencies of the sickle cell trait are found. Thus, these frequencies appear to be very far from equilibrium, and hence do not seem to be explained by the factor of selection alone. An attempt will now be made to show how the explanation involves the two factors, selection and gene flow. More specifically, two hypotheses will be advanced to explain these low frequencies:

(1) The sickle cell gene has been present in some parts of West Africa for a considerable time, but, due to the comparative isolation of the low frequency populations in Portuguese Guinea and Eastern Liberia, is only now being introduced to them.

(2) The environmental conditions responsible for the high frequencies of the sickle cell gene have been present for a relatively short time among these populations, so that the spread of the sickle cell gene is only now following the spread of the selective advantage of the gene.

In order to demonstrate these propositions, two general types of evidence will now be considered; first, the distribution of language in West Africa, from which an attempt will be made to ascertain the general outlines of the migrations which have occurred there; then, the archeological evidence and the distributions of certain domesticated plants in West Africa, from which an attempt will be made to determine the broad outlines of the culture history of the area. From a consideration of the culture history of West Africa and the relationship between culture patterns and the endemicity of malaria, the spread of the selective advantage of the sickle cell gene will be inferred.

THE DISTRIBUTION OF LANGUAGE IN WEST AFRICA

In the following discussion Greenberg's (1955) classification of African languages will be used, since it is the most recent and also the most widely accepted. In addition, Greenberg is attempting to make a "genetic" classification of African languages. Languages are said to be genetically related when their similarities are due to their development from a common ancestral language. It is this type of linguistic relationship which is most likely to have biological significance, since the ancestors of the speakers of genetically related languages were probably once members of the same breeding population and thus biologically related. Greenberg's classification is concerned with the larger linguistic families of Africa and the larger subgroupings within these families. Since it will be necessary at times to separate the languages into smaller subgroups, other sources will be used, but only when these agree with Greenberg's overall classification.

Except for the Songhai, Hausa, Kerikeri, Tuareg, Moor, and the tribes around Lake Chad, all the tribes listed on Table 1 speak languages belonging to the Niger-Congo family. The exceptions noted above speak either Songhai, Central Saharan, or Afro-Asiatic languages. These tribes are in the northern and eastern parts of West Africa and a considerable distance from the two low frequency areas of the sickle cell trait with which we are concerned. Therefore, this discussion will be concerned only with the Niger-Congo languages.

Figure 2 shows the language distribution in West Africa, both by family and by subfamily within Niger-Congo. The Niger-Congo family contains seven subfamilies: (1) West Atlantic, (2) Mande, (3) Gur, (4) Kwa, (5) Ijo, (6) Central Group, (7) Adamawa-Eastern. All of these subfamilies have some member languages in West Africa, but, with the exception of the Adamawa-Eastern speakers in northern Central Africa, the Niger-Congo languages in Central, East, and South Africa all belong to a single subfamily (Central Group) and even to a single subgroup (Bantu) within that subfamily.

Because of the great linguistic diversity in West Africa, this area appears to have been inhabited for a relatively long time by speakers of Niger-Congo. On the other hand, because of the similarity of language in the area inhabited by the Bantu peoples, this area has undoubtedly been peopled by a relatively recent spread of those peoples. As Greenberg (1955:40) states:

If the view of the position of the Bantu languages presented here is accepted, there are certain historical conclusions of considerable significance which follow. When Sapir demonstrated that the Algonkian languages were related to the Wiyot and Yurok languages of California, it was clear that, if this demonstration was accepted, it constituted a powerful argument for the movement of the Algonkian-speaking peoples from the west to the east. Here we have not two languages, but twenty-three separate stocks all in the same general area of Nigeria and the Cameroons. The evidence thus becomes strong for the movement of the Bantu-speaking peoples from this area southeastwards. The usual assumption has been a movement directly south from the great lake region of East Africa. It will also follow that this is a relatively recent movement, a conclusion which has generally been accepted on the basis of the wide extension of the Bantu languages and the relatively small differentiation among them.

In discussing the archeological and ethnological evidence, an attempt will be made to give reasons for the relatively recent spread of the Bantu from Nigeria, as well as to show that this other evidence seems to support the linguistic evidence.

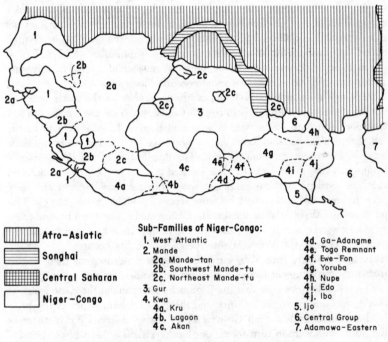

		Sub-Families of Niger-Congo:	
▦	Afro–Asiatic	1. West Atlantic	4d. Ga-Adangme
▤	Songhai	2. Mande	4e. Togo Remnant
		2a. Mande–tan	4f. Ewe-Fon
▦	Central Saharan	2b. Southwest Mande-fu	4g. Yoruba
		2c. Northeast Mande-fu	4h. Nupe
▢	Niger–Congo	3. Gur	4i. Edo
		4. Kwa	4j. Ibo
		4a. Kru	5. Ijo
		4b. Lagoon	6. Central Group
		4c. Akan	7. Adamawa-Eastern

Fig. 2 The distribution of language in West Africa

In West Africa west of Nigeria, there are four subfamilies of Niger-Congo: West Atlantic, Mande, Gur, and Kwa. With the exception of the rather recent movement of the Fulani pastoralists across the entire length of West Africa, the West Atlantic languages are all located along the coastal fringe of West Africa. The Kwa languages are distributed along the Guinea Coast from Liberia to Central Nigeria, with the great majority of them located in the tropical rain forest. In the central part of West Africa, in two large blocks, are the Mande languages on the west and the Gur languages on the east. These languages are for the most part located in the sudan, although several Mande groups have penetrated the tropical rain forest in Sierra Leone, Liberia, and the Ivory Coast.

The tribes with low frequencies of the sickle cell trait in Portuguese Guinea speak West Atlantic languages, but some Mandingo groups in the Gambia, who speak a Mande language, also have relatively low frequencies. In Eastern Liberia and the Western Ivory Coast, the tribes with low sickling frequencies include speakers of Kwa and Mande languages. Thus, with the exception of Gur, all these subfamilies include some languages whose speakers are far from equilibrium with respect to the sickle cell gene. Since these subfamilies also include some languages whose speakers have high frequencies of the sickle cell trait and seem to be close to equilibrium, the frequency of the trait is not correlated with language. This seems to indicate that the gene has been introduced into this part of West Africa since these subfamilies of Niger-Congo began to separate. However, since there is considerable linguistic diversity within the subfamilies, their separation occurred long ago.

Although there is no correlation of the frequency of the sickle cell trait with the linguistic subfamilies in this part of West Africa, the tribes with low frequencies in both Portuguese Guinea and Eastern Liberia seem to be the indigenous inhabitants of West Africa who have been forced back into these areas by later migrants from the east. The distribution of the West Atlantic languages along the coast with some isolated pockets in the interior indicates that the speakers of these languages were once more widespread and have been forced back to the coast by more recent invaders (Forde 1953). This retreat of the West Atlantic speakers is documented to some extent, and there is general agreement that the general trend of migration has been toward the west. Of course, the West Atlantic peoples probably occupied the coastal regions at an early time also, but their present concentration there results from their displacement from a wider area by invaders from the east.

Several authorities state that the Baga, who now inhabit the coastal regions of French Guinea, originally inhabited the Futa Djallon, which is the highland area of Central French Guinea. The Baga were forced out of there by the Susu, who were in turn forced out by the Fulani (Houis 1950; Demougeot 1944; Joire 1952). This forcing back of the West Atlantic speakers was also noted by Beranger-Ferand (1879:285) in the Casamance River area of the French Senegal. He divides the populations of this region into three groups:

A. Peuplades primitives (Feloupes, Bagnouns).

B. Peuplades envahissantes (Balantes, Mandingues, Peuls).

C. Peuplades adventives (Ouolofs, Saracoles, Toucouleur, Mandiagos, Machouins, Taumas, Vachelons).

He then states that A are the indigenous inhabitants; B are the fighters who conquered; and C are the traders or farmers who infiltrated in small groups. In Gambia the same migrations have been noted by Southorn (1952) and Reeve (1912). Reeve (1912:17) states:

The only relics that are to be found today of the primitive negro race which originally occupied the forest belt between the Senegal and the Rio Grande are the Serreres on the coast, north of the Saloum River, who are pagans and were cannibals; the Feloops, Floops, or Flups, as called by early voyagers, but now, in the valley of the Gambia, known as the Jolahs, occupying the territory between the seacoast and the headwaters of the Vintang Creek, about one hundred miles inland; the Patcharis or Pakaris in the Middle Valley, and the Bassaris including the Kunyadis, in the Upper Valley. These will be again referred to, and it is evident, from the chronicles of the different writers on the subject of slavery in this part of West Africa, that it was these Arcadians and forest dwellers, with their simple manners and customs of sustaining life from the products of the forest, field, and streams, who supplied the bulk of the trade, under the pretext that they worshipped idols, and therefore were considered to be outside the pale of humanity by the races that had adopted the Koran.

Thus, it can be seen that these writers agree that the Feloops, who have one of the lowest frequencies of the sickle cell trait, are one of the indigenous tribes. In addition, Reeve states that the Serer, who also have a low frequency of the trait, are the indigenous inhabitants in the north and in the past were hunters and gatherers and not agriculturalists. It should also be noted that Leite and Ré (1955), who tested the tribes of the Portuguese Guinea for sickling, give a similar explanation for the differences in the frequency of the sickle cell trait which they found.

The tribes with low sickling frequencies in Eastern Liberia and the Western Ivory Coast include speakers of Mande languages and of Kwa languages. All of the speakers of Kru and Lagoon languages, which belong to the Kwa subfamily, have very low frequencies of the sickle cell trait, and the positives for the trait who do occur among these peoples are in the eastern tribes where they are in contact with the Agni, Baoule, and other Akan speakers. On the other hand, the Kwa speakers who are to the east of the Kru and Lagoon peoples all have relatively high frequencies of the sickle cell trait. Viard (1934) states that the Guere, who speak a Kru language, came from the east, and Yenou (1954) makes a similar statement for the Alladians, who speak a Lagoon language. Since the linguistic relationships point to the east, these statements are probably true. Much has been written about the migrations of the Akan, Ewe, Ga, and other Kwa speakers who are to the east of the Kru and Lagoon speakers, and most authorities agree that the general direction of migration of these tribes has been to the southwest. Since the Lagoon languages are quite similar to the Togo Remnant languages (Bertho 1950), it seems that the speakers of these languages were forced back into peripheral areas by the Akan peoples (i.e., Ashanti, Fanti, Agni, Baoule), when they migrated to Southern Ghana. The movement of the Agni and Baoule into the Ivory Coast is quite recent—17th century according to most authorities. Thus, it seems that some Kwa speakers were more widespread through the tropical rain forest when the later Kwa migrants entered it and were then forced back by these later migrants. Since the later migrants have high frequencies of the sickle cell trait, it appears that they introduced the sickle cell gene into this part of West Africa.

In addition to the Kru and Lagoon-speaking peoples, there are several tribes with low sickling frequencies who speak Mande languages in Eastern Liberia and the western Ivory Coast. These are the Mano, Gio, Dan, Gouro, and other smaller groups. At the border between the Mano and the Kpelle, the frequency of the sickle cell trait increases sharply. Although these peoples both speak Mande languages, they belong to different subgroups of the Mande subfamily (Prost 1953). Kpelle is related to Mende and Susu to the northwest in Sierra Leone, and this tribe has undoubtedly come into Liberia from that direction. However, Mano and the other Mande languages whose speakers have low frequencies of the sickle cell trait are related to several Mande languages in the Upper Volta Province of French West Africa and also to a Mande language in Nigeria. Vendeix (1924) states that the Dan, and Tauxier (1924) that the Gouro, came into their present habitats from the northeast. Donner (1939) states that the Dan came from the north into the forest and forced the Kru peoples ahead of them. It would thus appear that these Mande tribes with low sickling frequencies came into their present location by a different route than that of their Mande neighbors to the northwest in Liberia and Sierra Leone. The Bobofing, who speak a language related to these Mande languages whose speakers have low sickling frequencies, have 25 percent of the sickle cell trait and are some distance to the northeast of the Dan and Gouro; so that it seems that the sickle cell gene was introduced after the separation of these languages. The Mandingo are to the north of the Mano, Dan, and Gouro, and between them and the Bobofing. From the 12th to 15th centuries A.D. when the Mali Empire, which was ruled by the Mandingos, was at its height, these people are known to have expanded out from their original homeland. It would appear that this expansion of the Mandingo forced the Mano, Dan, and Gouro into the forest and separated them from their relatives to the northeast.

The two areas of low frequencies of the sickle cell trait thus seem to be inhabited by peoples who have been forced back into these peripheral areas by later migrants from the east and northeast. However, this does not mean to imply that all the later migrants had the sickle cell gene. It is possible that the Kwa migrants to Southern Ghana introduced the gene into this part of West Africa by migration; but along the West Atlantic coastal fringe, the sickle cell gene seems to have spread in the past by mixture, and is still spreading in this manner today.

In the Central Ivory Coast on the border of the Kru and Lagoon peoples on the west and the Akan peoples on the east, there is a sharp increase in the frequency of the sickle cell trait. Since all the Kwa peoples from the Akan east to the Ibo in Nigeria have very high frequencies of the trait, it seems that these peoples possessed the sickle cell gene when they migrated into these regions from the east and northeast. However, along the Atlantic Coast of West Africa from the Senegal to Central Liberia, the gene does not seem to have been introduced by large-scale migration. The highest frequencies of the sickle cell trait in this region are found in the Gambia and in Sierra Leone, which are also the two places where Mande peoples have penetrated to the seacoast in large numbers. Since the Mande peoples were the migrants from the east, it would appear that they introduced the sickle cell gene into this part of Africa. However, the smooth gradient in the frequency of the trait in Sierra Leone and Liberia seems to indicate that the gene was introduced after the original Mande migrations. Starting with the Susu in northwest Sierra Leone who have a sickling frequency of 31 percent and proceeding southeastward, there is a smooth gradient in frequency which is not correlated with language. The speakers of Southwest Mande-fu languages, the Mende in Sierra Leone, the Mende in Liberia, the Gbandi, Loma, and Kpelle, have 29, 17, 15, 13, and 13 percent, respectively, while the West Atlantic speakers, the Timne, Kissi, and Gola, have 29, 19, and 12 percent respectively. The Vai, who speak a Mande-tan language and are the latest immigrants from the interior (McCulloch 1950), have a frequency of 14 percent, which is also in agreement with this gradient. In Portuguese Guinea, where the Mande peoples have not penetrated in great numbers, there is also a smooth gradient in the frequency of the sickle cell trait. Starting on a small section of the seacoast between the Casamance River and the Rio Cacheu where the Feloop and Baiote have 1 to 2 percent, the frequency increases going inland to 5 percent among the Mandjak, and then to 15 percent among the Biafada and Mandingo. It thus seems that along the West Atlantic coastal fringe of West Africa the sickle cell gene has spread and is still spreading by mixture and not by large scale migration, while the gene appears to have spread through the tropical rain forest along the Guinea Coast by the migration of the Akan and other Kwa-speaking migrants from the east. The archeology and culture history of West Africa will now be examined in an attempt to provide some explanation for the manner by which the sickle cell gene has spread there.

THE ARCHEOLOGY OF WEST AFRICA
AND ORIGIN OF THE WEST AFRICAN NEGRO

Although there has been less archeological excavation in West Africa than elsewhere in Africa, it is now beginning to appear that West Africa was inhabited during most of man's cultural development, as was most of the continent. Lower Paleolithic hand axes and Middle Paleolithic Levallois flakes have been found in scattered places throughout West Africa (Alimen 1955). However, no rich sites comparable to those in East and South Africa have been excavated for these stages. Nevertheless, the scattered finds indicate the presence of man in West Africa during these periods, which lasted up to the end of the Pleistocene. Following these periods in time, microlithic sites are documented for Ghana (Shaw 1951), French Guinea (Joire 1952), Nigeria (Fagg 1951), and other places in West Africa. Some of these microlithic cultures seem fairly recent and perhaps attributable to the ancestors of the present Negro inhabitants. However, little skeletal material has been found.

The earliest skeletal material which is found close to West Africa is a skull from Singa in the Sudan. This find has been dated by Arkell (1952) as Upper Pleistocene and is associated with a Levallois culture. The skull is stated to be archaic Bushman and related to the Boskop skull from South Africa. From this find it appears that the Bushman was once much more widespread than today and in Upper Pleistocene times Bushman-like peoples were in the Sudan. This statement is supported by the presence of Bushman-like rock paintings and archeological cultures similar to that of the present day Bushman over most of the southern half of the African continent. The presence today in Tanganyika of the Hatsa, who speak a Kahoisan language and still have a predominantly Stone Age culture (Fosbrooke 1956), also supports it.

The first appearance of skeletal material which has Negroid affinities is in this same area of the Sudan, but apparently much later. At Esh Shaheinab, which is on the Nile near Khartoum, several skeletons with Negroid affinities have been found in association with a microlithic hunting and gathering culture, which also had pottery. Around the fringes of the Sahara there are other finds of Negroid skeletal material, all of which seem to belong to this general period. The famous Asselar skull from north of Timbuktu, which is considered to be Negro, is from this general period, and Alimen (1955) also indicates that some of the skeletal material associated with the Capsian culture in Tunisia has Negroid affinities. In addition to this skeletal material, many of the early rock paintings in the Sahara seem to depict Negroid peoples.

The Esh Shaheinab site has been dated by radiocarbon as 5200 years ago, or shortly after the beginnings of agriculture in Egypt. The radiocarbon dates on the Capsian culture are about 7500 years ago. Alimen (1955) indicates that the Neolithic of Capsian tradition is found in French Guinea, but this is probably much later than the Capsian sites which have been dated by radiocarbon. It should also be noted that in this context Neolithic does not mean food-producing, but only that the culture had polished stone artifacts.

The first archeological evidence of the Bantu in South and Central Africa is much later than the evidence from northern West Africa, and appears to be after the beginning of the Christian era. Alimen (1955:304) states: "Iron entered the Congo very late, by means of the Bantu invasion, which later spread to the Rhodesias in only 900 A.D." Further, Alimen states (1955:370) that iron working came to the upper valley of the Orange River in the 13th century A.D. and here too is associated with the arrival of the Bantu. Previous to the expansion of the Bantu, East and South Africa were inhabited by Bushman-like peoples.

The archeological evidence thus seems to indicate that at about the time of the introduction of agriculture into Africa, Negro peoples with a microlithic culture were living around the fringes and even in the middle of the Sahara, while most of South and East Africa was inhabited by Bushman-like peoples. Since the Pygmies would seem to be indigenous to Central Africa, they were perhaps responsible for the microlithic cultures found there. For West Africa there are numerous legends of Pygmies (summary in Schnell 1948), so it is possible that at this time Pygmies also inhabited West Africa. However, Joire (1952) thinks there is no evidence for Pygmies in West Africa and assigns the microlithic sites in French Guinea to the Baga tribe. The diffusion of agriculture through Africa, and its effect on the preceding distribution of peoples will now be considered.

THE INTRODUCTION OF AGRICULTURE AND IRON WORKING INTO AFRICA

The first evidence of a farming economy in Africa occurs in Egypt at Fayum, which dates about 4000 B.C. Because of the domesticated plants and animals associated with this culture, it is thought to be derived from Asia Minor (Ailmen 1955). Seligman (1939:52) shows instances of Egyptian contact with Negroes in the late predynastic period, which he dates at about 3000 B.C., and Negroes are also known to have been living in the Sudan at Esh Shaheinab at about the same time. The inhabitants of Jebel Moya in the Sudan are also stated to be Negroes, who were forced westward by the Arabs around 700 B.C. (Mukherjee, Rao, and Trevor 1955). Thus, agriculture seems to have spread from Egypt to the Negro peoples who have since been forced south and west by the Arabs and by Berber peoples such as the Tuareg.

Iron working was also introduced into Africa from Asia Minor via Egypt (Forde 1934; Arkell 1955). There was a considerable iron industry flourishing at Meroe in the Sudan in 600 B.C., about which Arkell (1955:147) states: "Indeed there is little doubt that it was through Meroe that knowledge of iron working spread south and west throughout Negro Africa." The next evidence for the spread of iron southwest of the Sudan is in Northern Nigeria where Fagg (1956) has discovered the Nok culture, which is dated in the second half of the first millennium B.C. by geological methods. Assuming that iron working spread here from Meroe, this is about the date which would be expected. This culture contains both iron and stone axes; but since the iron axes have the same shape as the stone ones, this appears to be a transitional culture which had only recently adopted iron working. Since Mukherjee, Rao, and Trevor (1955) found the inhabitants of Jebel Moya to be most similar in physical type to the West African Negro, the westward migration of these people in the first millennium B.C. could very likely have been the method by which iron working was introduced to West Africa. In any case, this appears to be one route by which iron working was introduced into West Africa.

In the western part of West Africa, iron working seems to be somewhat later, and the evidence seems to indicate that it was not introduced via Meroe. Corbeil, Mauny, and Charbonnier (1948) think that iron working was introduced into the Cape Verde region around Dakar by Berbers who arrived there from the north about 300 B.C. Later, Mauny (1952) states that iron

287

working was introduced into this region by the Phoenicians in the first century A.D., since the words for iron in many of the languages of this region seem to be derived from Phoenician. Although it is possible that some peoples along the coast obtained iron from the Phoenicians, it would seem more likely that iron working was brought across the Sahara, since contact with the Phoenician ships would not seem to have been close enough for the transference of all the techniques which iron working requires. Cline (1937) states: "Within the bend of the Niger lies the only large area where iron remains have been found associated with stone-using cultures." However, Nok culture in Northern Nigeria had not been discovered at the time Cline was writing, so that there appear to be two areas with these transitional cultures. In the same area Cline (1937) describes another type of iron working site which has copper and a much richer assemblage altogether. These sites he associates with the Ghana Empire. This empire was founded about 300–400 A.D. (Fage 1955), at about the time the camel was introduced into the western Sahara, and its rise to eminence is associated with increasing trade with Mediterranean civilizations. It thus appears that iron working was introduced into the western part of West Africa shortly before this empire was founded and probably was introduced from the north across the desert.

The preceding evidence indicates that both agriculture and iron working were introduced into West Africa from Asia Minor via Egypt, although both were no doubt diffused along several different routes. Agriculture was present in Egypt centuries before iron working and probably began to spread through Africa before iron working was introduced from Asia Minor. However, this early spread of agriculture seems to have been mostly by stimulus diffusion, since the basic crops of Egypt, wheat and barley, did not spread to the Sudan. Even today, millet and sorghum are the basic crops throughout the Sudan. Both millet and sorghum, or at least some species of them, are considered to have been domesticated in Africa (Miege 1951; Viguier 1945) and to have been cultivated there "since antiquity" (Miege 1951). Viguier (1945:165) states: "Aug. Chevalier considers the western sudan and its saharan border as one of the centers of the origin of domesticated sorghum." Since the agricultural methods used for them are similar to those for wheat and barley, and in addition the crops are all grains, it would seem reasonable to postulate that an early spread of agriculture from Egypt involved these crops. The techniques involved in the cultivation of these grains did not entail any considerable technological change from that of a microlithic hunting and gathering culture. The tool assemblage at Fayum in Egypt is not very different from that of the Natufian in Palestine or that of the Capsian. As this early agricultural economy spread, it either drove the hunting cultures before it or perhaps was adopted by these peoples. However, one of the hypotheses of this paper is that this economy could not spread throughout tropical Africa.

Although a Neolithic millet and sorghum economy could spread through the Sudan, it was not until the introduction of iron working and/or better yielding tropical crops that the Negro agriculturalists could exploit the tropical rain forest. Thus, the forest remained the home of primitive hunters until quite recently. In West Africa these hunters appear to have been Negroes whose descendants can be seen today in the low sickling frequency areas of Portuguese Guinea and Eastern Liberia; and in Central Africa they were Pygmies, whose descendants are the low sickling frequency "true" Pygmies, the Babinga of French Equatorial Africa (Hiernaux 1955).

A combination of three factors prevented the spread of this agricultural economy through the tropical rain forest: (1) the poor quality of the soils, which wear out after a few crops; (2) the difficulty of clearing the forest with stone tools; and (3) the low yields of millet and sorghum.

In Northern Ghana and Northern Nigeria, where millet and sorghum are still the basic crops today, in many places the same fields are cultivated year after year (Manoukian 1952; Gourou 1950). On the other hand, in Sierra Leone a new field is cleared every year (McCulloch 1950), and in the forest regions of Nigeria, Gourou (1950) states that it takes 30 years for the soil to recover after one crop, while Forde (1951) indicates that the fields are cultivated for three or four years before being left fallow. Some comparison of the relative yields of the various crops can be obtained from Gourou's (1950:39) figures of yields in the French Sudan, although this is not tropical rain forest. Millet yields 5 cwt. per acre; yams, 15 cwt. per acre; and cassava, 32 cwt. per acre. However, from a nutritional standpoint the important yield is the number of calories per unit of land. Combining data from several African countries, Brock and Autret (1952) give the following figures for the yields of various crops in thousands of calories per hectare: millet yields 1,530; sorghum, 1,854; yams, 3,554; and cassava, 7,090. Thus, when these three factors are considered together, it would seem to be difficult for a Neolithic millet and sorghum economy to exist in a tropical rain forest environment. It should be emphasized, however, that this hypothesis does not mean to imply that there were no agriculturalists in the tropical rain forest prior to the introduction of iron working and tropical root crops. There was undoubtedly some agiculture and "whittling away" at the tropical rain forest in the areas which border on the Sudan. However, these innovations were a necessary prerequisite for the great explosion of the Bantu peoples out of Nigeria, which filled up half a continent in a relatively short time.

Together with iron working, the domestication of two indigenous crops opened the tropical rain forest as a habitat exploitable by the Negro agriculturalists. Chevalier (1952:16) states that the yam, *Dioscorea latifolia*, was domesticated in West Africa. Today the most widespread species of yam in Africa is *D. cayenensis*, which is derived from *D. latifolia* (Chevalier 1946). From its distribution it would seem most probable that these yams were domesticated in Nigeria. With the yam and iron working, the Bantu peoples then spread throughout the Central African tropical rain forest from their original homeland, which Greenberg (1955:116) places in the central Benue

River valley in Nigeria. In many places today the Bantu do not have the yam as a staple crop, but this theory only attempts to explain the original rapid spread of the Bantu. This theory is supported by linguistic evidence, by the fact that transitional iron working cultures are known in Northern Nigeria and also by the fact that the spread of iron working in Central and South Africa is associated with the spread of the Bantu. In addition, in several areas where yams are no longer the Bantu staple there is still ritual associated with this crop, which seems to indicate that it was previously more important. For example, among the Kpe in the Cameroons, where cocoyams are now the staple crop, Ardener (1956:46) states: "Although subsidiary in Kpe agriculture, this crop [i.e. yam] is remarkable for the fact that it is the only one to which some degree of ritual is attached. . . . The ritual elements in the cultivation of the yam, the present economic importance of which is quite small, suggests that this crop . . . may have been a staple food in the past history of the Kpe."

Also from Nigeria, some of the Kwa peoples spread in similar fashion through the West African tropical rain forest to the Ivory Coast and forced other Kwa peoples, the Kru and Lagoon speakers, westward into the Ivory Coast and Liberia. The Kru and Lagoon peoples were probably in the tropical rain forest as hunters and gatherers prior to this spread of agriculture. Agriculture has since been introduced to most of the Kru and Lagoon peoples, but it usually has rice as the basic crop, which comes from a different center of dispersal, or manioc, which was introduced into West Africa from the New World. Even today in the Ivory Coast, as several botanists (Miege 1953; Chevalier 1952) have remarked, there is a sharp boundary of yam cultivation on the Bandama River, which is also the border between the Baoule and Kru peoples. In addition, the yam cultivators, such as the Agni, have an elaborate ritual associated with the yam harvest (Rahm 1953; Miege 1953), which indicates great reliance on this crop. Although the Kru peoples have for the most part adopted agriculture, there is still more reliance on hunting in the Kru area (Kerharo and Bouquet 1949), and there are some groups who are still mainly hunters. In Eastern Liberia, Schwab (1947:79) states: ". . . there is one clan or small tribe . . . living to the north of the Tchien near the Nipwe River who have a reputation as elephant hunters, like the pigmies of the southeastern Cameroun."

The cline in the frequency of the sickle cell trait coincides with this spread of yam cultivation. The Kru and Lagoon peoples have almost o percent of the sickle cell trait, except where they come in contact with the yam cultivators, while the yam cultivators in the Eastern Ivory Coast, Southern Ghana, and Nigeria all have high frequencies of the trait. Thus, it seems that the sickle cell gene was brought into this part of Africa by the migrations of the yam cultivators westward from Nigeria, and at present both agriculture and the sickle cell gene are spreading to the hunting populations, which were in the forest prior to the spread of yam cultivation.

Perhaps a little later than this spread of yam cultivation, there was another spread of agriculture through the West African tropical rain forest. Porteres (1949) has shown that somewhere around the Middle Niger River Valley, a wild African species of rice, *Oryza glaberrima,* was domesticated. He dates this domestication at about 1500 B.C. (ibid.:560), but the spread of this crop through the tropical forest seems to be much later than the postulated date, and even later than the introduction of iron. There is evidence (Little 1951: 26) that the first Mande peoples to enter the tropical rain forest were hunters. Little dates this migration at least 400 years ago. However, the most plausible date seems to be about 1300 A.D., when the Susu appear to have migrated to French Guinea from the Middle Niger region (Joire 1952). Thus, it would seem that the Mande and West Atlantic peoples in the tropical forest were still hunters about 600 years ago, and that rice agriculture has since been introduced to them. Joire (1952) assigns the microlithic archeological sites which are known in French Guinea to the Baga people, who speak a West Atlantic language. These people thus were in the tropical forest prior to the immigration of the Mande peoples and to the later spread of rice agriculture.

The spread of iron working and rice cultivation through this part of the West African tropical rain forest, after the original Mande migration, does not seem to be associated with any large scale migration; it probably occurred by diffusion, since the Mande peoples who have now adopted rice cultivation were in the same location as hunters. Thus, according to the evidence, the spread of rice agriculture by diffusion seems to coincide with the spread of the sickle cell gene by mixture. In addition, the spread of rice cultivation appears to be later than the original Mande migration, as does the spread of the sickle cell gene. Rice cultivation also diffused to the West Atlantic-speaking peoples, as did the sickle cell gene. Thus, the type of gene flow—in one case migration and in the other mixture—which was responsible for the spread of the gene in West Africa seems to be related to the manner of the spread of agriculture. However, agriculture seems to have spread farther than the gene. The Kru peoples in Eastern Liberia, and the West Atlantic peoples in coastal Portuguese Guinea, are today rice cultivators. The reason for this lag in the spread of the sickle cell gene is due first of all to the fact that it takes several generations for the gene to build up to appreciable frequencies, but it also seems to be due to the relationship of the selective advantage of the sickle cell gene to slash and burn agriculture. This relationship is due in turn to the complex epidemiology of malaria in West Africa, which we will now consider.

MAN, MALARIA, AND MOSQUITO IN WEST AFRICA

In West Africa the relationship between man, malaria, and mosquito is very highly evolved, due largely to the habits of the major vector of malaria, *Anopheles gambiae.* This mosquito is attracted to human habitations and usually rests in the thatched roofs of an African village. It bites man regularly, and breeds in a variety of places. Wilson (1949) has estimated that 75 percent of the malaria in Africa is due to *A. gambiae*. Its breeding places are so diverse that, when attempting to delimit them, entomologists usually state where it cannot breed. *A. gambiae* cannot breed in (1) very shaded water, (2) water with a strong current, (3) brackish water, (4) very alkaline or polluted water (Holstein 1953).

If we now consider the types of water which would be found in the tropical rain forest, it can be seen that there would be few places for *A. gambiae* to breed in unbroken tropical rain forest. The high emergent shade trees and the trees of the middle "story" of the forest so effectively shade the ground that there would be few, if any, areas that were unshaded. In addition, the layer of humus on the forest floor is very absorbent, so there would be few stagnant pools. It is only when man cuts down the forest that breeding places for *A. gambiae* become almost infinite (De Meillon 1949). First, with continued cutting of the forest, the soil loses all of its humus and becomes laterized. At this stage it is practically impervious to water; puddles are constantly renewed by the frequent tropical rains and so persist indefinitely. Second, man's refuse and his villages provide more abundant breeding places for the mosquito. Third, the swamps become open and hence possible breeding places.

In a hunting population, which does not destroy the forest, malaria would thus not develop this complex relation with man. Malaria could still be present, but not the holoendemic malaria which characterizes most of Africa today. Hunters do not build the type of permanent habitation in which *A. gambiae* lives, and since a hunting population moves frequently the mosquito could not keep up with the human population, so to speak. Also, in the epidemiology of any disease there is a critical size for the population below which the disease cannot persist. Since hunting populations are small, they would be closer to this critical size and perhaps even below it.

The Pygmies provide an example of such a hunting population, but unfortunately no malaria surveys of hunting Pygmies are available. Schwetz, Baumann, Peel, and Droeshant (1933) did examine three groups of Pygmies for malaria and found that they had less than the surrounding Negroes, but these Pygmies were building houses and farming, and so cannot be considered a hunting population. Putnam (1948), who lived with the hunting Pygmies for 20 years, states that they do not suffer from malaria. His account also shows that the Pygmies do not cut down the forest and do not build their rude huts in a clearing but in the middle of the forest. These customs would appear to be the reasons for the absence of malaria among them.

If this complex relationship between parasite, host, and vector which is characteristic of holoendemic malaria could not have developed in hunting populations, then the selective advantage of the sickle cell gene would not be present in these populations. If, as has been postulated, the Feloop and other peoples in Portuguese Guinea and the Kru peoples of Eastern Liberia and the Western Ivory Coast were the last remnants of hunting populations which once were spread through the tropical forest, then the absence of the selective advantage of the sickle cell gene in these populations would have prevented it from becoming established, even if there had been some gene flow from neighboring Sudanic peoples. Although considerable areas of tropical rain forest are shown on any vegetation map of West Africa, these are greatly broken up by agricultural settlements and fields. Nevertheless, the last northern remnants of the forest are located in Portuguese Guinea near one area of low sickling frequencies, and the other area in Eastern Liberia is in the center of the largest remaining block of tropical rain forest.

The frequencies of the sickle cell trait among the Pygmies also support this theory, although the comments of several authorities might seem to contradict it. Regarding the Pygmies and Pygmoids, Hiernaux (1955:463) states; "They generally show a lower frequency of sicklemia than the surrounding populations, as shown in Table 2. In all cases but one, the frequency is lower in the Pygmoids. The most striking difference is between the Bondjo and Babinga, who are true Pygmies." Since most Pygmy groups have formed symbiotic relationships with their Negro neighbors, the frequencies among them can easily be explained by mixture, which is known to be occurring (Putnam 1948).

There is other evidence that *A. gambiae* has spread rather recently through the West African tropical rain forest. In the area around the Firestone Plantation in Liberia, shortly after the forest had been cut down, Barber, Rice, and Brown (1932) found that *A. gambiae* accounted for 46 percent of the mosquito population found in the native huts, while *A. funestus* accounted for 51 percent, and *A. nili* for 3 percent. However, at the present time in this same area, *A. gambiae* accounts for almost 100 percent of the mosquito population (Max J. Miller, personal communication). Barber, Rice, and Brown (1932) found holoendemic malaria, which is not present today; however, this change is due to malaria control and not to changes in the mosquito population. These figures thus indicate a significant increase in *A. gambiae* when the forest is cut down. Even more significant are Barber, Rice, and Brown's comments on the effects of reforestation on the mosquito population. They state (1933:629):

We felt that it would be interesting to know what would be the condition of things when the rubber trees had grown and the unplanted ravines and swamps had become "rejunglized." We surveyed Mt. Barclay Plantation where the stream borders have grown up with brush or long grass. After a long search in the streams we found only two or three larvae, *A. mauritianius* and *A. obscurus*. In a pool near a village *A. costalis* was plentiful.

It can thus be seen that *A. gambiae* (the authors call the species *A. costalis*) was not present in natural water but only near a village. The authors also discuss "rejunglization" as a means of malaria control, but state that it would not be feasible due to the breeding places which would persist around the villages. In the absence of these villages, which are not built by hunting populations, and in the presence of unbroken tropical forest, the intensity of malaria would be much less. This seems to have been the situation in West Africa prior to the spread of slash and burn agriculture. Therefore, the spread of this agriculture is responsible for the spread of the selective advantage of the sickle cell gene, and hence for the spread of the gene itself.

SICKLE CELLS, DISEASE, AND HUMAN EVOLUTION

The preceding explanation of the distribution of the sickle cell gene and its relation to the culture history of West Africa has broad implications for the role of disease in human evolution. In considering the epidemiology of the sickle cell gene, Neel (1957:167) suggested that either the mutation which resulted in the sickle cell gene was very rare or else the spread of the gene was at present favored by special circumstances of relatively recent origin. The detailed arguments of this paper would seem to show that there are indeed special circumstances of recent origin, while at the same time not excluding the possibility that the mutation is quite rare. The special circumstances are considered to be the conditions necessary to maintain holoendemic malaria due to *Plasmodium falciparum*. This parasite is in fact regarded as evolutionally the most recent species of malaria to parasitize man (Boyd 1949). If, as has been proposed, a mobile hunting population in the tropical rain forest could not develop holoendemic malaria, then this high endemicity would perhaps be even later than the adaptation of the parasite to man as its host. Since the agricultural revolution occurred only about 7000 years ago and spread much later to Africa, it appears that the development of the environmental conditions which are responsible for the spread of the sickle cell gene are relatively recent, as Neel postulated they should be.

The agricultural revolution has always been considered an important event in man's cultural evolution, but it also seems to have been an important event in man's biological evolution. Prior to this revolution, the size of the human population was controlled to a large extent by the size of its food supply, and man's ecological niche was comparable to that of the large carnivores, or more closely perhaps to that of a large omnivore such as the bear. With the advent of the agricultural revolution, the food supply was no longer the major factor controlling the size of human populations. Man broke out of his ecological confinement and there was a tremendous increase in the size of the human population, an increase which was limited only by the available land. Haldane (1949, 1956) has stated that disease became the major factor controlling the size of human populations at this time, and his statement seems to be supported in one case by the spread of holoendemic malaria.

Two results of the agricultural revolution seem to account for this change in the role of disease in human evolution: (1) the great changes in the environment, and (2) the huge increase in the human population. Both of these seem to be involved in the development of holoendemic malaria. First, when man disrupts the vegetation of any area, he severely disrupts the fauna and often causes the extinction of many mammals, particularly the larger ones. When this happens, there are many known instances of the parasites of these animals adapting to man as the new host (Heisch 1956). It is thus possible that the parasitization of man by P. *falciparum* is due to man's blundering on the scene and causing the extinction of the original host. Second, concomitant with the huge increase in the human population, this population became more sedentary and man also became the most widespread large animal. Thus, he became the most available blood meal for mosquitoes and the most available host for parasites. This change resulted in the adaptation of several species of the Anopheline mosquito to human habitations and the adaptation of many parasites to man as their host. Under these conditions, holoendemic malaria and probably many other diseases developed and became important factors determining human evolution. It should be noted, however, that through domestication man has created large populations of other animals and these have influenced the epidemiology of several human diseases including malaria (for malaria examples, see Hackett 1949; Draper and Smith 1957). The sickle cell gene thus seems to be an evolutionary response to this changed disease environment. Hence, this gene is the first known genetic response to a very important event in man's evolution when disease became a major factor determining the direction of that evolution.

REFERENCES

ADAMSON, P. B. 1951 Haematological and biochemical findings in Hausa males. Jour. of Tropical Medicine and Hygiene 54:73–77.

ALIMEN, H. 1955 Préhistoire de l'Afrique. N. Bourbée, Paris.

ALLISON, A. C. 1954a Protection afforded by sickle-cell trait against subtertian malarial infection. British Medical Journal 1:290–294.

———— 1954b The distribution of the sickle-cell trait in East Africa and elsewhere, and its apparent relationship to the incidence of subtertian malaria. Transactions of the Royal Society of Tropical Medicine and Hygiene 48:312–318.

———— 1954c Notes on sickle-cell polymorphism. Annals of Human Genetics 19:39–57.

———— 1956 The sickle-cell and haemoglobin C genes in some African populations. Annals of Human Genetics 21:67–89.

———— 1957 Population genetics of abnormal human haemoglobins. Proceedings of the First International Congress of Human Genetics 430–434. New York, S. Karger.

ARDENER, E. 1956 Coastal Bantu of the Cameroons. London, International African Institute.

ARKELL, A. J. 1952 Egypte et Soudan. Comptes rendus, XIX Congrès Géologique International 5:276–278. Algers.

———— 1955 A history of the Sudan. London, The Athlone Press.

BARBER, M. A., J. B. RICE, and J. Y. BROWN 1932 Malaria studies on the Firestone Rubber Plantation in Liberia, West Africa. American Journal of Hygiene 15:601–633.

BARNICOT, N. A., E. W. IKIN, and A. E. MOURANT 1954 Les groupes sanguins ABO, MNS et Rh des Touareg de l'Air. L'Anthropologie 58:231–240.

BERENGER-FERAND, L. J. B. 1879 Les Peuplades de la Sénégambie. Paris, Ernest Leroux.

BERTHO, J. 1950 La place du dialecte adiukru par rapport aux autres dialectes de la Cote d'Ivoire. Bulletin de l'Institut Français d'Afrique Noire, Dakar 12:1075-1094.

BEZON, A. 1955 Proportion de sicklémiques observée en pays Kabré (Togo). Médecine Tropicale 15:419-422.

BINSON, J., J. V. NEEL, and W. W. ZUELZER N.D. Unpublished data.

BOYD, M. F. 1949 Historical review. In: Malariology: a comprehensive survey of all aspects of this group of diseases from a global standpoint, M. F. Boyd ed. Vol. 1:3-25. Philadelphia, W. B. Saunders.

BRAIN, P. 1953 The sickle-cell trait: a possible mode of introduction into Africa. Man 53:154.

BROCK, J. F., and M. AUTRET 1952 Kwashiorkor in Africa. World Health Organization Monograph Series, No. 8. Geneva.

BRUCE-CHWATT, L. J. N.D. Unpublished data.

CAMBOURNAC, F. J. C. 1959 Rapport sur le paludisme en Afrique Equatoriale. WHO/MAL/58, Afr./Mal/Conf/14.

CHARLES, L. J., and H. M. ARCHIBALD N.D. Unpublished data.

CHEVALIER, A. 1946 Nouvelles recherches sur les ignames cultivées. Revue de Botanique Appliqué et Agriculture Tropicale 26:26-31.

——— 1952 De quelques Dioscorea d'Afrique Equatoriale toxiques dont plusieurs variétés sont alimentaires. Revue de Botanique Appliqué et Agriculture Tropicale 32:14-19.

CHOREMIS, C., and L. ZANNOS 1957 Microdrepanocytic disease in Greece. Blood 12:454-460.

CLINE, W. 1937 Mining and metallurgy in Negro Africa. General Series in Anthropology, No. 5. Menasha, George Banta Company.

COLBOURNE, M. J., G. M. EDINGTON 1956 Sickling and malaria in the Gold Coast. British Medical Journal 1:784-786.

COLBOURNE, M. J., G. M. EDINGTON, and M. H. HUGHES 1950 A medical survey in a Gold Coast village. Transactions of the Royal Society of Tropical Medicine and Hygiene 44:271-290.

CORBEIL, R., R. MAUNY, and J. CHARBONNIER 1948 Préhistoire et proto-histoire de la presqu'ile du Cap Vert et de l'extrème ouest sénégalais. Bulletin de l'Institut Français d'Afrique Noire, Dakar 10:378-460.

DE LAVERGNE DE TRESSAN, M. 1954 Inventaire linguistic de l'Afrique Occidentale Français et du Togo. Mémoires de l'Institut Français d'Afrique Noire, No. 30, Dakar.

DE MEILLON, B. 1949 Anophelines of the Ethiopian Region. In Malarialogy: a comprehensive survey of all aspects of this group of diseases from the global standpoint, M. F. Boyd ed. Vol. 1:443-482, Philadelphia, W. B. Saunders.

DEMOUGEOT, A. 1944 Notes sur l'organisation politique et administrative du Labe avant et dupuis l'occupation française. Mémoires de l'Institut Français d'Afrique Noire, No. 6, Dakar.

DONNER, E. 1939 Hinterland Liberia. London, Blackie and Son.

DRAPER, C. C., and A. SMITH 1957 Malaria in the Pare area of N. E. Tanganyika. Transactions of the Royal Society of Tropical Medicine and Hygiene 51:137-151.

EDINGTON, G. M., and H. LEHMANN 1954 A case of sickle-cell haemoglobin C disease and a survey of haemoglobin C incidence in West Africa. Transactions of the Royal Society of Tropical Medicine and Hygiene 48:332-335.

——— 1956 The distribution of haemoglobin C in West Africa. Man 56:36.

EVANS, R. W. 1944 The sickling phenomenon in the blood of West African natives. Transactions of the Royal Society of Tropical Medicine and Hygiene 37:281–286.

FAGE, J. D. 1955 An introduction to the history of West Africa. Cambridge, Cambridge University Press.

FAGG, B. 1951 Preliminary report on a microlithic industry at Rap Rock Shelter (Northern Nigeria). Prèmiere Conférence Internationale des Africanistes de l'Ouest 2:439–440, Institut Français d'Afrique Noire, Dakar.

——— 1956 A life-size terra-cotta head from Nok. Man 56:89.

FORDE, C. D. 1934 Habitat, economy, and society. London, Methuen.

——— 1951 The Yoruba-speaking peoples of South-Western Nigeria. London, International African Institute.

——— 1953 The cultural map of West Africa: successive adaptations to tropical forests and grasslands. Transactions of the New York Academy of Science 15:206–219.

FOSBROOKE, H. E. 1956 A stone age tribe in Tanganyika. South African Archeological Bulletin 11:3–8.

GOUROU, P. 1953 The tropical world. New York, Longmans, Green and Co.

GREENBERG, J. H. 1955 Studies in African linguistic classification. New Haven, Compass Publishing Co.

HACKETT, L. W. 1949 Conspectus of malaria incidence in Northern Europe, the Mediterranean Region, and the Near East. In Malariology: a comprehensive survey of all aspects of this group of diseases from a global standpoint, M. F. Boyd ed. Vol. 2:788–799, Philadelphia, W. B. Saunders.

HALDANE, J. B. S. 1949 Disease and evolution. Supplement to La Ricerca Scientifica 19:3–10.

——— 1956 The argument from animals to men, an examination of its validity for anthropology. Journal of the Royal Anthropological Institute 86:1–14.

HEISCH, R. B. 1956 Zoonoses as a study in ecology. British Medical Journal 1:669–673.

HIERNAUX, J. 1955 Physical anthropology and the frequency of genes with a selective value: the sickle cell gene. American Journal of Physical Anthropology 13:455–472.

HOLSTEIN, M. H. 1952 Biologie d'Anopheles gambiae; Recherche en Afrique-Occidentale Française. World Health Organization, Geneva.

HOUIS, M. 1950 Les minorités de la Guinée cotière, situation linguistic. Études Guinéennes 4:25–48, Institut Français d'Afrique Noire, Conakry.

JELLIFFE, D. B., and J. HUMPHREYS 1952 The sickle-cell trait in Western Nigeria. British Medical Journal 1:405.

JELLIFFE, R. S. 1954 The sickle-cell trait in three Northern Nigerian tribes. West African Medical Journal 3:26–28.

JOIRE, J. 1952 La préhistoire de Guinée Française (Inventaire et mise au point de nos connaissances). Conferencia International Africanistas Occidentais 4:295–365, Lisboa.

KERHARO, J., and A. BOUQUET 1949 La chasse en Côte d'Ivoire et en Haute Volta. Acta Tropica 6:193–220.

LEHMANN, H. 1954 Distribution of the sickle-cell gene: a new light on the origin of the East Africans. Eugenics Review 46:1–23.

LEHMANN, H., and A. B. RAPER 1949 Distribution of the sickle-cell trait in Uganda and its ethnological significance. Nature 164:494.

——— 1956 Maintenance of high sickling rate in an African community. British Medical Journal 2:333–336.

LEITÉ, A. S., and L. RÉ Contribution a l'étude ethnologique des populations africaines. Archives de l'Institut Pasteur d'Algérie 33:344–349.

LINHARD, J. 1952 Note complémentaire sur la sicklémie dans la région de Dakar. Revue d'Hematologie 7:561-566.

LITTLE, K. 1951 The Mende of Sierra Leone. London, Routledge and Kegan Paul.

LIVINGSTONE, F. B. 1957a Sickling and malaria. British Medical Journal 1: 762-763.

——— 1958 The distribution of the sickle cell gene in Liberia. American Journal of Human Genetics 10:33-41.

MANOUKIAN, M. 1952 Tribes of the Northern Territories of the Gold Coast. London, International African Institute.

MAUNY, R. 1952 Essai sur l'histoire des métaux en Afrique occidentale. Bulletin de l'Institut François d'Afrique Noire, Dakar 14:545-595.

McCULLOCH, M. 1950 Peoples of Sierra Leone Protectorate. London, International African Institute.

MIEGE, E. 1951 Les céréales en Afrique du Nord, le maïs et le sorgho. Revue de Botanique. Appliqué et Agriculture Tropicale 31:137-158.

MIEGE, J. 1952 L'importance économique des ignames en Côte d'Ivoire. Revue de Botanique Appliqué et Agriculture Tropicale 32:144-155.

MILLER, M. N.D. Personal communication.

MUKHERJEE, R., C. R. RAO, and J. C. TREVOR 1955 The ancient inhabitants of Jebel Moya (Sudan). Occasional Publications of the Cambridge University Museum of Archaeology and Ethnology, No. 3, Cambridge.

NEEL, J. V. 1951 The population genetics of two inherited blood dyscrasias in man. Cold Spring Harbor Symposiums on Quantitative Biology 15:141-158.

——— 1957 Human hemoglobin types, their epidemiologic implications. New England Journal of Medicine 256:161-171.

NEEL, J. V., J. HIERNAUX, J. LINHARD, A. ROBINSON, W. W. ZUELZER, and F. B. LIVINGSTONE 1956 Data on the occurrence of Hemoglobin C and other abnormal hemoglobins in some African populations. American Journal of Human Genetics 8:138-150.

PALES, L., P. GALLAIS, J. BERT, and R. FOURQUET 1955 Le sicklémie (sickle cell trait) chez certaines populations Nigero-Tchadiennes de l'Afrique Occidentale Française. L'Anthropologie 58:472-479.

PALES, L., and J. LINHARD 1951 Sicklémie en A. O. F. Biologie Comparative des Populations de l'A. O. F. Publications Direction Générale de la Santé Publique, Dakar.

PALES, L., and A. SERERE 1953 La sicklémie en Afrique Occidentale Française (Haute Volta). L'Anthropologie 57:61-67.

PORTERES, R. 1949 Le système de riziculture par franges univariétales et l'occupation des fonds par le riz flottants dans l'Ouest-africain. Revue de Botanique Appliqué et Agriculture Tropicale 29:553-563.

PROST, R. P. A. 1953 Les langues Mandé-sud du groupe Mano-Busa. Mémoires de l'Institut Français d'Afrique Noire, No. 26, Dakar.

PUTNAM, P. 1948 The Pygmies of the Ituri Forest. In A Reader in General Anthropology, C. S. Coon, ed. New York, Henry Holt.

RAHM, V. 1954 La Côte d'Ivoire, centre de recherches tropicales. Acta Tropica 11:222-295.

RANNEY, H. M. 1954 Observations on the inheritance of sickle-cell hemoglobin and hemoglobin C. Journal of Clinical Investigations 33:1634-1641.

RAOULT, M. N.D. Unpublished data.

RAHM, V. 1954 La Côte d'Ivoire, centre de recherches tropicales. Acta Tropica 2:1186-1189.

——— 1956 Sickling in relation to morbidity from malaria and other diseases. British Medical Journal 1:965.

REEVE, H. F.   1912   The Gambia. London, Smith, Elder and Co.

ROSE, J. R., and J. K. SULIMAN   1955   The sickle-cell trait in the Mende tribe of Sierra Leone. West African Medical Journal 4:35–37.

SCHNELL, M. R.   1948   A propos de l'hypothèse d'un peuplement Négrille ancien de l'Afrique Occidentale. L'Anthropologie 52:229–242.

SCHWAB, G.   1947   Tribes of the Liberian hinterland. Papers of the Peabody Museum of American Archaeology and Ethnology, Vol. 31, Harvard University, Cambridge.

SCHWETZ, J., H. BAUMANN, PEEL, and DROESHANT   1933   Étude comparative de la malaria chez les pygmées et les indigenes de la forêt de l'Ituri (Congo Belge). Bulletin de la Societé de Pathologie Exotique 26:639–651.

SELIGMAN, C. G.   1939   The races of Africa. T. Butterworth, London.

SHAW, C. T.   1951   Archaeology in the Gold Coast. Première Conférence Internationale des Africanistes de l'Ouest 2:467–499, Institut Français d'Afrique Noire, Dakar.

SINGER, R.   1953   The sickle cell trait in Africa. American Anthropologist 55:634–648.

SOUTHORN, B.   1952   The Gambia. London, George Allen and Unwin.

SUKUMARAN, P. K., L. D. SANGHVI, and G. N. VYAS   1956   Sickle-cell trait in some tribes of Western India. Current Science 25:290–291.

TAUXIER, L.   1924   Nègres Gouro et Gagou. Paris, P. Geuthner.

TRINCAO, C., A. R. PINTO, C. L. ALMEIDA, and E. GOUVEIA   1950   A drepanocitemia entre a tribo papel da Guine Portuguesa. Anais do Instituto de Medicina Tropical, Lisboa 7:125–129.

VANDEPITTE, J. M., W. W. ZUELZER, J. V. NEEL, and J. COLAERT   1955   Evidence concerning the inadequacy of mutation as an explanation of the frequency of the sickle-cell gene in the Belgian Congo. Blood 10:341–350.

VENDEIX, M.   1924   Ethnographie du cercle de Man (Côte d'Ivoire). Revue d'Ethnographie et Traditions Populaires 5:149–169.

VIARD, R.   1934   Les Guerés, Peuple de la Forêt. Paris, Societe de Geographie.

VIGUIER, P.   1945   Les sorghos à grain et leur culture au Soudan Français. Revue de Botanique Appliqué et Agriculture Tropicale 25:163–230.

WALTERS, J. H., and H. LEHMANN   1956   Distribution of the S and C haemoglobin variants in two Nigerian communities. Transactions of the Royal Society of Tropical Medicine and Hygiene 50:204–208.

WESTERMANN, D., and M. A. BRYAN   1952   Languages of West Africa. London, International African Institute.

WILSON, D. B.   1949   Malaria incidence in Central and South Africa. In Malariology: a comprehensive survey of all aspects of this group of diseases from a global standpoint, M. F. Boyd ed. Vol. 2:800–809, W. B. Saunders, Philadelphia.

YENOU, A. D.   1954   Quelques notes historiques sur le pays Alladian (Basse-Côte d'Ivoire). Notes Africaines No. 63:83–88, Institut Français d'Afrique Noire, Dakar.

YOUNG, M. D., and T. H. JOHNSON   1949   A malaria survey of Liberia. Journal of the National Malaria Society 8:247–266.

FOSSIL MAN

AND HUMAN EVOLUTION

LOREN C. EISELEY

INTRODUCTION

In the sixties of the last century, two men examined the course of human prehistory, as it was then known, and proceeded to come to diametrically opposed conclusions. There would be nothing particularly remarkable about this observation except for one thing: both men had discovered the principle of Natural Selection independently and both were confirmed evolutionists. Their names were Charles Darwin and Alfred Russel Wallace—scholars destined to be remembered far beyond their century—yet, on the subject of man, they could not agree. Most people, if they have knowledge of this controversy at all, assume that Charles Darwin won the argument, but it has become ever more apparent in the last few years that, while the basis of the discussion may have shifted a little, the truth is that the argument is still before us, if anything more powerfully than ever, and the same contentions are still unresolved.

A little less than one hundred years after the publication of *The Origin of Species,* anthropologists are arrayed on the same battlegrounds. Insignia on their standards may be slightly altered, but they fight the same weary battle, the lines wavering now this way and now that as a new fossil is revealed. Perhaps it is time for a military assessment to be written—time to examine the nature of the struggle and to ask what it is that we are endeavoring to demonstrate. Some have been in the trenches so long that they may well have forgotten, and the suspicion grows that there are others among us who do not know how they came into the redoubts which they defend so valiantly. It will do no harm, therefore, to review a debate which, smoldering since the nineteenth century, has re-emerged once more with renewed vigor in the year just past.

Nearly one hundred years ago, Charles Darwin and a little band of intrepid followers were involved in a dramatic effort to convince their fellow men not alone that evolution had taken place in the animal and plant world about them, but that man himself had arisen by natural processes of the same order, according to gruff old Adam Sedgwick, as those producing the crust on a kettle. Another scholar pondering the change of doctrine sighs wistfully as

Reprinted by permission from *Current Anthropology* (1956), 61–78.

though loath to give up all hope, "The Creator is there but much farther off than we thought." Each of these remarks epitomizes in its own way the frightening shadow which passed over men's minds after the rise of the evolutionary philosophy. It is only now, after the passage of a century, that modern science is beginning to awaken to the fact that man, toppled unwillingly from his position of simple faith by the evolutionists, has in truth become one of the most unstudied and important enigmas in the whole realm of biology.

In their understandable eagerness to demonstrate the newly discovered principles governing the development of life, Darwin and his followers unconsciously minimized the distance stretching between man and his lowly cousins, the apes. The whole drama can be pretty well summed up in the clash between Darwin's pugnacious defender, Huxley, and Richard Owen, Britain's leading anatomist and wily defender of the established order. It was a battle that Owen fought unscrupulously and was destined to lose, yet Huxley's very triumph reveals the curious myopia which had descended upon nineteenth century science. It was a myopia which led to greater argumentative emphasis upon whether the brain of man resembled that of an ape physically rather than upon what might be contained in the two dissimilar heads mentally. "You may think," parodied Kingsley in *The Water-Babies,* "that there are other more important differences between you and an ape, such as being able to speak, and make machines and know right from wrong, and say your prayers, and other little matters: but that is just a child's fancy, my dear. Nothing is to be depended upon but the great hippopotamus test." *

It was perhaps inevitable, considering the time, place, and circumstances, that the attention of the Darwinists and their horrified audience should have been fixed upon the characters man shares with the animal world about him, or that enthusiastic converts should have striven to minimize and close up, to the extent possible, the gap which appeared to yawn between rational, thinking man and his remote relatives in the forest. The occupants of institutions for the feeble-minded, and even Lombrosian criminals, were being speculatively eyed as atavistic throwbacks to an earlier human stage; there is clear evidence in the writings of Darwin that early man was viewed as something akin to the gorilla. Science and theology both had become so immersed in their squabble over what physical resemblances did or did not demonstrate about man's origins, that the wonder and mystery of human achievement began to depart. It is to be said to the everlasting credit of Alfred Russel Wallace, therefore, that he raised a lonely voice of protest which scarcely would be heard until the passage of a hundred years. He has been called inconsistent and a romantic. He was all these things. But his inconsistency was sometimes the product of a formidable insight which could not rest comfortably with half-truths, either his own or those of anyone else. While his colleagues

* A play on words involving the hippocampus minor.

rested content with their laurels, he went on searching, pondering over "some fundamental law of development of which we have as yet no notion" (Marchant, 1916, p. 219). In the midst of giving Darwin sound advice on how to meet his critics, he was capable, in a kindly but direct fashion, of indicating his doubts that a particular argument had been either potent or satisfactory.

It was this restless, never-contented aspect of Wallace's personality which finally led him beyond the reach of his fellows. In his great age he grew opinionated and, for a scientist, some of his follies were conspicuous. Nevertheless, they were the inescapable accompaniment of that restless leaping mind which long ago in Ternate conceived the whole theory of Natural Selection in one lightning flash of feverish insight.

Longer and more intimately than any other of the great biologists Wallace had lived and sailed with savages. He had endured in small boats the sufferings of dangerous passages among the reefs and shoals of the Malay Archipelago. Somewhere out of these experiences had emerged a different conception of the savage brain than that entertained by the average Victorian scholar who was inclined to view natives as mental and moral fossils. By contrast, Wallace came to regard them as possessing minds little if in any degree inferior in natural endowment to civilized Westerners. This point of view marks him as diverging greatly from the orthodox outlook of his period. It also leads us directly to the contrasting paths taken by himself and Darwin over the question of human evolution. A summary will make the issue clear; furthermore, it is an issue which still confronts the student of human evolution today.

THE DARWIN-WALLACE CONTROVERSY

To analyze the precise attitude held toward fossil man and the existing races, or toward fossil man and the existing great apes, by Darwin and his followers during the decades immediately following the publication of *The Origin of Species* (1859) and *The Descent of Man* (1871) is not an easy task. There are inconsistencies and confusion produced by attempts to equate the creatures of the fossil past with the forms of the living primates, as when Darwin quoted evidence to show that the La Naulette jaw, that of a Neanderthalian, was supposed to have possessed "enormous" projecting canines (Darwin, C., n.d., p. 425); or that some of the skulls of Australian aborigines showed, in the males, traces of a gorilloid sagittal crest (*ibid.*, p. 868). After making statements of this kind, however, Darwin seemed afterwards to have been impressed with certain criticisms by the Duke of Argyll and to have expressed a contradictory speculation (*ibid.*, pp. 443–444) that a formidable and huge primate might not have become social. "Hence it might have been an immense advantage to man to have sprung from some comparatively weak creature" (*ibid.*, p. 444).

Placing as he did so much emphasis on the struggle for existence, Darwin once more found himself embarrassed with the "weak creature" he had been forced to postulate. "These ancestors," he protested defensively, "would not have been exposed to any special danger, even if far more helpless and defenseless than any existing savages, had they inhabited some warm continent or large island, such as Australia, New Guinea or Borneo, which is now the home of the orang." Even here, however, Darwin was forced to invoke the "competition of tribe with tribe" along with the "inherited effects of habit," to bring about man's ascent to a position far above that of his nearest living relatives. Here at last we come suddenly upon the key point which, so far as human evolution was concerned, arrayed Darwin and Wallace upon opposing platforms. In the Darwinian philosophy, natural selection was not a principle of self-growth. It could produce only a relative superiority sufficient to maintain a given species in active competition with its enemies or give it at best some slight advantage in the life-struggle. In a sense, therefore, it was a self-limiting principle. How then, challenged Darwin's colleague, Wallace, did the human brain develop so far beyond what was necessary to secure the bodily safety and primitive needs of its possessor? "Natural Selection," maintained Wallace, "could only have endowed the savage with a brain a little superior to that of an ape, whereas he actually possesses one but very little inferior to that of the average members of our learned societies" (Wallace, 1869, pp. 391–392).

Wallace had reached this position by degrees so that he must have taken his other evolutionary colleagues by surprise. In 1864, in the *Anthropological Review,* he had set forth the idea that with the rise of man, natural selection was ceasing to act upon the body and was coming to act almost solely upon the human intelligence. Man, he contended, was old and had attained the upright posture long before the final changes in the skull and brain which characterize our living species. Other animals had continued to change and modify under evolutionary pressures; in man, by contrast, all but mental evolution had largely ceased. Man, in other words, had transferred to his mechanical devices the *evolution of parts* which characterizes the rest of the world of life. Even racial differences, in Wallace's view, were essentially survivals from the time when man was still a cultureless animal.

Now at the time of this first treatise Wallace was still a firm believer in the part played by natural selection in this process. He saw competition between groups of men as promoting by slow degrees the rise of better brains and a higher ethic. Darwin had expressed no objection to this, in fact had confessed admiringly "the great leading idea is quite new to me . . . yet I had got as far as to see with you, that the struggle between the races of man depended entirely on intellectual and moral qualities" (Darwin, F., Vol. 3, p. 90). It was only later that the disagreement came. Wallace's estimates of human antiquity did not bother the Darwinists, nor did his study of the rise of the human brain. He had clung carefully to the basic Darwinian precepts; insensible variations, selection through the struggle for existence among competing human groups. Then in 1869 he drastically altered his opinions (Wallace, 1869, pp. 359–394). For the first time in his career the co-discoverer of the principle of Natural Selection abandoned the attempt to explain human evolution by that hypothesis. Man's brain, the "primitive" brain of the living savage, houses abilities for which in his present state he has no need and which therefore, could not possibly have arisen through competition with others of his kind. Even in language, argued Wallace:

This view is supported by the fact that, among the lowest savages with the least copious vocabularies, the capacity of uttering a variety of distinct articulate sounds, and of applying to them an almost infinite amount of modulation and inflection, is not in any way inferior to that of the higher races. An instrument has been developed in advance of the needs of its possessor (*ibid.*, p. 393).

Wallace, mincing words very little, intimated that he could only see in the rise of the human brain a directive spiritual force unaccounted for in purely mechanistic terms.

Darwin, with the great and generous tolerance which lighted the long life-pathway of the two men, wrote his kindly disagreement, saying half-humorously—half-wistfully, "I hope you have not murdered too completely your own and my child" (Marchant, 1916, p. 197). Thomas Huxley, by contrast, gave vent to a statement which today sounds strangely arrogant and anthropologically distorted. Wallace asked, said Huxley, "How were all or any of these faculties first developed, when they could have been of no possible use to man in his early stages of barbarism?" "Surely," Huxley responded, "the answer is not far to seek.

. . . The lowest savages are as devoid of any such conceptions as the brutes themselves. What sort of conceptions of space and time, of form and number, can be possessed by a savage who has not got so far as to be able to count beyond five or six, who does not know how to draw a triangle or a circle, and has not the remotest notion of separating the particular quality we call form from the other qualities of bodies? None of these capacities are exhibited by men, unless they form part of a tolerably advanced society."

Warming to the task of demonstrating that artistic talents are the inevitable product of the struggle for existence, Huxley continued:

The experience of our daily life shows that the conditions of our present social existence exercise the most extraordinarily powerful selective influence in favour of novelists, artists, and strong intellects of all kinds; and it seems unquestionable that all forms of social existence must have had the same tendency . . . (Huxley, 1871, pp. 471–473).

Coming in a time of ruthless industrial exploitation and grinding poverty among the English masses, these words have a strange ring. Huxley for once had been caught off-balance in a petulant and ill-tempered defense of his master—a defense which, so far as Wallace is concerned, was singularly inept, and lacking in the sort of facts and evidence which Huxley was fond of demanding from other people. Yet one must be fair. Huxley was writing in the same year in which Tylor introduced and defined the word "culture" in English anthropology. It is plain, as one examines the writings of practically all the Darwinian circle, that they often confused genetic endowment with cultural achievement, and that simple cultures constantly were being regarded as signs of inferior biological capacities. It is interesting to observe once more that, although Darwin and Huxley had *encountered* savages in the days of their voyages, Wallace alone had cast his lot and his fortunes for months and years among remote peoples and had sailed from island to island dependent upon their good will. Wallace had his peculiarities, but the kind of statement of which we have found Huxley guilty would never have been made by the old wanderer of the Malayan seas.

At this point we have arrived at an impasse. Darwin, wavering and uneasy about the true nature of the "struggle for existence" among men seemed hesitant as to whether to describe his fossil men as gorilloid or of some milder-tempered and weaker-bodied variety of primate. In spite of an occasional warning that the early human progenitor is not to be compared in exactitude with the living apes, he postulated that man must have achieved an upright posture from the semi-erect position of a chimpanzee or gorilla. These hesitations are of course perfectly understandable—the living primates are practically all that Darwin had with which to work. In the end, although he had earlier spoken disparagingly of Lamarck, he was forced to fall back upon the inherited effects of habit. His sole explanation for the rise of the human brain to its present exalted position lay in this vaguely Lamarckian statement and in the assumption of constant struggle between one group and another, in which the group with the greatest intelligence survived.

At first this latter interpretation appealed to Wallace. Later, as we have seen, it ceased to satisfy him but, in turning away from Natural Selection, he embraced a mysticism which he was never afterward to escape completely. As a consequence, the very genuine problem that he raised faded from men's minds with the full triumph of the Darwinian hypothesis, and his intimations of the possible great age of the human stock became an acceptable doctrine from which his name slowly disappeared.

Within the last year, however, in part stimulated by the discussions at the 1952 International Symposium on Anthropology supported by the Wenner-Gren Foundation, in part independently arrived at in the curiously expectant atmosphere which has hovered over the new Australopithecine discoveries, there has been a sudden renewal of the century-old question propounded by Wallace. Three times in a year's space the question of how man got his brain had been independently enunciated (Chance and Mead, 1953; Eiseley, 1953; Etkin, 1954). The query may be differently phrased and expressed in the technical jargon of a later and more specialized biology, but essentially it is the old question of 1869. This time it is being asked with a full recognition of the depths of our ignorance and with a realization that Wallace was right when he wrote in 1876 that

however great may have been the intellectual triumphs of the nineteenth century, we can hardly think so highly of its achievements as to imagine that, in somewhat less than twenty years, we have passed from complete ignorance to almost perfect knowledge on two such vast and complex subjects as the origin of species and the antiquity of man (Wallace, 1876, p. 72).

The fact that close on to another century we are only now beginning to bestir ourselves over this question of the curious uniqueness of the human brain shows how long we have been silenced with the idea that the step from an ape to a man is as simple as the first evolutionists imagined or even wished it to be.

THE PILTDOWN SKULL

In a recently published paper (Eiseley, 1954b), we have been at some pains to show that the archeological discoveries in Europe during the late decades of the nineteenth century were a considerable disappointment to the evolutionists. In the first flush of their enthusiasm, the Darwinists plainly had hoped to demonstrate that the human line descended in Ice Age times into some sort of small-brained ancestor of definitely anthropoid affinities. Instead, they had seen the archeologists turn up a succession of Upper Paleolithic big-brained Cro-Magnons or equally big-brained Neanderthals. Those opposed to the Darwinian theory of human development found considerable sources of comfort in this situation. They lost no time in pointing out that most of our upper Pleistocene ancestors did not appear as morphologically primitive as certain of the existing races. Today, of course, we know that the time scale of the Pleistocene was being underestimated and that, in addition, the significance of Neanderthal man was not fully appreciated: at the time of which we speak only one calvarium had been described; the face, unfortunately, was missing.

There is no doubt that this first failure to find the sort of ancestral remains demanded by the Darwinian theory played its part in Wallace's elaboration of his hypothesis that, amidst constant and omnipresent organic change, man alone had to a marked degree escaped that law by the development of mind. Man, once he had attained a truly human level, might well remain physically the only unchanging creature in the midst of the universal alterations wrought by on-flowing time. "This will enable us to understand," Wallace went on to point out, "how the fossil crania of Denise and Engis agree so closely with existing forms, although they undoubtedly existed in company with large mammalia now extinct" (Wallace, 1895, p. 180).

The discovery of the apparently dissimilar fossils of Pithecanthropus and Piltdown presented the scientific world with two ostensible choices. The Java discovery seemed to bear out Wallace's contention that the attainment

of upright bipedal progression had preceded the later skull changes consequent upon a slowly expanding brain. Moreover, Dubois' earlier estimate
that Pithecanthropus belonged on a late Tertiary time horizon would not
have clashed with Wallace's belief that

you must go to an enormous distance of time to bridge over the difference between
the crania of the lower animals and of man (Wallace, 1864, p. clxxxv).

Piltdown, on the other hand, with its *sapiens* brain-box and its anthropoi-
dal lower face, suggested the possibility that the development of the brain
had led the rest of the body in the course of evolution (Miller, 1928, p.
419). Pycraft (1917, p. 391) had even suggested that in spite of its well-
developed brain, it had not fully attained the upright position. Since in the
early years of its history, Piltdown had been given a dating almost as old as
the Java discovery, the only way that the disparity between the two forms
could be resolved was to assume that they represented two distinct lines of
human evolution. This, of course, presented the additional anomaly of practically suggesting two distinctly different evolutionary forces at work. It is
no wonder that the aged Wallace, who lived long enough to know of the
Piltdown discovery, wrote to a friend: "The Piltdown skull does not prove
much, if anything!" (Marchant, 1916, p. 347). Probably he was at least
partially activated by a feeling that the skull did not fit his theory of human
development, but in any case his doubts were to prove well-founded. In
November of 1953 the scientific world was rocked by the news that the long-
studied fragments of the Piltdown specimen, as well as the associated artifacts, represented a deliberate and unscrupulous hoax (Weiner, Oakley, and
Clark, 1953). Portions of a *sapiens* cranium had been combined with half of
the jaw of a recent orang in such a manner that key anatomical points which
might have settled the controversy had been carefully destroyed.

The amount of subjective speculation indulged in for years over the
Piltdown "fossil," and to which many leading authorities contributed, can
now be viewed historically as a remarkable case history in self-deception. It
should serve as an everlasting warning to science that it is not theologians
alone who may exhibit irrational bias or give allegiance to theories with only
the most tenuous basis in fact. That scientists in the early years of a new discipline should have been easily deceived is not nearly so embarrassing as the
rapidity with which they embraced the specimen solely because it fell in
with pre-conceived wishes and could be used to support all manner of convenient hypotheses. The enormous bibliography in several languages which
grew up around the skull is an ample indication, also, of how much breath
can be expended fruitlessly upon ambiguous or dubious materials. Remembering the *Mud Fog Papers,* one cannot but sigh with relief that there was
not a Dickens around to immortalize the Piltdown story. Perhaps, on second thought, and for the permanent reduction of the scientific ego, it would
have been a good thing had there been.

With the elimination of the Piltdown cranium as a valid fossil, a considerable re-organization of our thinking in regard to the nature of human evolution has become necessary. Nevertheless, it is a re-organization which still involves the two persistent questions raised by Wallace in the eighteen-sixties; namely, *how long did it take to turn an ape into a man?*, and secondly, *by what means were the enormous powers of the human mind evolved?*

Pithecanthropus had long since been elevated to a position in the somewhat ill-defined Middle Pleistocene of Java and all of the later discovered, big-browed, paleanthropic forms of man were apparently not greatly older, and some were much younger, than this. Moreover, in South Africa a constantly increasing array of primitive man-apes, possibly cultureless, and definitely sub-human in appearance, had been discovered stretching through the indefinite reaches of the lower Pleistocene. Were these creatures, or some group among them, the actual ancestors of men? Was true man, then, to be regarded as a very rapid emergent out of a lower Pleistocene array of ground-dwelling, bipedal apes?

Before attempting to review this situation, let us examine two statements of Wallace which will put the nature of the problem succinctly before us. Either, he said, man developing by natural selection into a specialized and unique organism must have arisen very early and "spread in dense waves of population over all suitable portions of the great continent—for this, on Mr. Darwin's hypothesis is essential to rapid developmental progress. . . ." or if, on the contrary, "continued researches in all parts of Europe and Asia fail to bring to light any proof of his presence [during the Tertiary period], it will be at least a presumption that he came into existence, at a much later date and by a more rapid process of development." In that case, Wallace continued, it will be a reasonable argument that man's origin "is due to distinct and higher agencies" (Wallace, 1876, pp. 64–65).

It should now be apparent, through these propositions of Wallace, where the rearrangement of our remaining human fossils is leading us. It is leading us straight toward Wallace's second proposition, though not necessarily to the acceptance of his idea of direct supernatural guidance in the evolution of man. If our briefly sketched confinement of the major rise of the human brain to the Pleistocene is even approximately correct, it would appear to demand some other evolutionary mechanism beyond that of the old Darwinian struggle of man with man or group with group. The movement would appear much too fast. It has something about it of the nature of a quantum step. Lest I seem to be favoring Wallace's point of view unduly, let me quote the words of three practical experimental scientists who find themselves concerned with the same problem. M. R. Chance and A. P. Mead say, "No adequate explanation has been put forward . . . to account for the development of so large a cerebrum as that found in man" (Chance and

Mead, 1953, p. 395).* Professor Etkin, although propounding a theory of his own about the early beginnings of man's mental faculties, admits with sincere humility that in his view "the origin of abstract thought, for example, mathematical reasoning, and of truly ethical behavior . . . are not explicable in the biological terms developed . . ." (Etkin, 1954, p. 140).

THE AUSTRALOPITHECINES

Considering these modernly expressed doubts of the experimental biologists, our re-examination of the human phylogeny in the light of the modern fossil evidence seems amply justified. Certainly the time appears past when simplistic assumptions about the competitive use of tools can be used to account for all aspects of the human mind. There is a sense of grinding inadequacy in this materialistic doctrine, particularly when, viewing the higher realms of man's endeavor in 1893, Robert Munro (1893, p. 505) in an opening address before the British Association for the Advancement of Science remarked sententiously, ". . . imagination, conception, idealisation, the moral faculties . . . may be compared to parasites which live at the expense of their neighbours." It is no wonder, surveying this uninspired remark, that Whitehead once observed that the last twenty years of the nineteenth century represented one of the dullest periods in human thought since the close of the First Crusade.

The idea that all of the qualities which make man such a unique and remarkable creature could have been dismissed as a mere "rattle in the machinery" of a creature evolved solely by the dextrous use of a flint ax is appalling, not because it was enunciated sixty years ago, but because it reappears in anthropological discussions even today. The archeologist, in particular, must be on guard, for there is an understandable temptation to see in the development and multiplcation of tools from their crude Pleistocene beginnings up to the present some kind of simulacrum or objectified representation of the state of the mind itself: simple brain, simple tools. The cumulative aspects of culture may be forgotten and the argument persuasively launched that a "tool" enables us to determine without any fancy metaphysical deduction the point at which a monkey has become a man.

Within limits this notion may have a certain degree of purely archeological validity, but it does not tell us very much about how the ancestral primate got into this tool-using activity, nor why, if he was so largely concentrated upon this aspect of life alone, he should not have gone merrily and independently along his own path to the present day, devoting his attention to the bashing out of his neighbors' brains instead of engaging in all that tremendous assortment of institutional activities which occupies most of his waking hours. Robert Munro, in dismissing the higher moral faculties of man as

* Reprinted in this Volume as revised by Chance, pp. 84–130.

309

pretty but unimportant, was unwittingly disavowing the very nature of the human psyche: the creature lives on dreams and is in that sense unique. It is not the ax in the hand but the symbols flowing through the time tracts in the head that are the real tools of this creature.

Before pursuing this aspect of the mind further, however, we must descend the time ladder and, in the skulls which are the castoff containers of the dream, strive to make out when, from the standpoint of Wallace's theory, the dream began. The evidence is not conclusive, but it may suffice to aid us in the resolution of a hundred-year-old controversy.

In the warm regions, theorized Wallace, "we may trace back the gradually decreasing brain of former races, till we come to a time when the body also begins materially to differ. There we should reach the starting point of the human family. Before that period he had not enough mind to preserve his body from change, and would, therefore, have been subject to the same comparatively rapid modifications of form as other mammals" (Wallace, 1864, p. xvii). Interestingly enough, this statement, written long before there was any fossil evidence to substantiate it, now appears for the first time to be corroborated at least in some degree by the increasingly disparate array of Australopithecine man-apes being turned up by the South African workers.

The later forms of paleanthropic man—now that *Eoanthropus* has been eliminated—vary little save in the degree of cranial advance throughout the latter half of Pleistocene times. They thoroughly justify Wallace's belief in the transformation of the skull as the enlarging brain promoted the last changes that man's body, according to the belief of the great evolutionist, was destined to undergo before it assumed its timeless aspect in the midst of universal change.

The newest cranium from the South African beaches is essentially merely another paleanthropic form on approximately the same level with *Homo rhodesiensis* or Solo Man (Drennan, 1954, pp. 879–884). *Atlanthropus mauritanicus* for the first time reported with Abbevillian cultural remains appears on the basis of preliminary reports to be probably another earlier big-brow ridged form of man (Hillaby, 1954). Only among the Australopithecines is a curious difference in size and appearance prevalent. We say this with full recognition of differences among authorities; differences even as to whether these creatures walked erect (Zuckerman, 1954), or whether (which is unlikely) they should be given so many generic appellations as have been applied to them. Still, when the number of species is reduced, when the likelihood that some at least are not human, even though perhaps bipedal, is duly considered, two things remain apparent: *they seem closer than any living apes to man even if relatives rather than on the direct line of ascent, and they show a surprising variety of physical form.* There are indications that some, at least, belong structurally at the Plio-Pleistocene border; one cannot escape the feeling that here at last we are approaching a confusing variety of ground apes who are disconcerting to our taxonomists for the very reason long ago intimated by Wallace. We have, in other words, stumbled into the world of essentially cultureless or almost cultureless proto-human types which are diverse in form because they represent evolution still at work *upon the parts of the body*, rather than upon the selection of mental patterns leading toward essential uniformity of other bodily characters.

We need not conclude, since most of these creatures appear to be Pleistocene (Peabody, 1954, p. 703), that we have reached the very bottom of the human ladder. Such forms as Heidelberg and *perhaps* the newly discovered *Atlanthropus* strongly suggest that more advanced and truly human forms were in existence in lower Ice Age times. Nevertheless, this in no way abrogates the significance of our main point; namely, that if living ground apes of a human cast were alive in the early and middle Pleistocene, it is unlikely that the rise of the true human stock can be assumed to be a great deal earlier. If such had been the case, one might assume that the competition on the world's open grasslands would have resulted in the earlier and more rapid extinction of the man-apes. It would thus appear that Wallace was right in his suggestion of 1876 that if man could not be shown to have dominated the Old World land mass in large numbers during the Tertiary, some other more rapid process of evolution than that envisaged in the Darwinian philosophy must have been at work in the production of man. This would appear to be equally true whether we assume modern man emerged directly from Neanderthaloid ancestors or whether, taking the mysterious and faceless crania of Swanscombe and Charente for evidence, we assume that the development of the *sapiens* brain lies somewhat farther back in time.

Having briefly examined the juxtaposition of the known human fossils, there is only one fact about human evolution which need deeply concern us, or draw our attention away from the spectacle of universal organic change, in order to trouble ourselves over the destiny of one solitary life form. It is the still-remaining puzzle posed by Wallace, as to what has brought the existing human races out synchronously upon so similar a mental platform, even though many have never competed with each other tool-wise. The nineteenth century, equating level of technology with level of biological ability, was never troubled by this question. It was sufficient for our grandfathers to say that we

> have got
> The Maxim gun
> and they have not.

We of this generation have witnessed vast social changes, seen such forgotten marginal people as the Eskimo fly airplanes, and the sons of forest peoples attend Cambridge or Oxford. Darwin, thinking of survival by natural selection, could speak of "Esquimaux, with whom the art of fishing and managing canoes is said to be hereditary" (Darwin, F., Vol. 3, p. 90); C. Carter Blake could say in 1864, "Psychical endowments of a lower grade than those characterizing the Andamaners cannot be conceived to exist; they stand next to brute benightedness" (Blake, p. cxlviii). The world of the last century seemed fixed, the native was dying of the white man's diseases, and the Darwinists spoke assuredly of the time when he would be gone as surely as the Tasmanians or the vanishing orang.

Today, by a curious twist, there are times when it appears that it is the White world that is contracting. How is it, then, that men, remote from where the scientific revolution arose, practice its arts in remote jungles and obscure wastes where its whisper never came and where there can have been no competitive biological differences based on such a struggle? How is it that Wallace's dictum has held true that man in these remote districts had latent capacities very similar to, if not the equal of those possessed in the civilized centers of the world? This Negro, in other words, who paddled a dugout canoe along dark and tree-hung water-ways, this Indian who gestured naked on a lonely pinnacle at ships bound through the freezing waters of the Horn, possessed somewhere beneath the tangle of his unkempt hair the same pulsing electric patterns that in other lands have measured stars, or weighed evidence in seats of judgment, or twinkled like fireflies as the lines of a great poem woke its strange sad memories in the brain of man. All over the world before the fundamental verities men feel, bleed, die in not very dissimilar ways. It is not surprising that Wallace stood abashed before this mystery; the surprising thing is how few Victorians understood it; perhaps, ironically, their conscious superiority made their feats of colonization possible.

THE BIOLOGICAL HYPOTHESES

Biologists in general have avoided grappling with the question that troubled Wallace. Or, if they have done so, it has often been ineffectively in terms of generalities, or marred by the surviving confusion over biological potentialities, as contrasted with social heredity. As Etkin has pointed out (1954, p. 130), most writers start with at least a crude level of symbolic communication as *assumed*. The pre-adaptation or other explanation of the shift over from the purely *signal* communication of the animal to the linguistic activities of men is left unexplained for the simple reason that no one adequately has come to grips with the problem. It is the recognition of this fact that has led to renewed speculation in the year just past.

Chance and Mead (1953) have contended that the immature primate male, often forced to inhibit his sexual desires in a society like that of the baboons, for example, where a dominant old male is overlord, would be selected in terms of his ability to control his impulses and thus protect himself. As a consequence, the role of the brain cortex involved in such conscious control of his instinctive functions would be enhanced, and the consequent pre-adaptation perhaps lead on to other intellectual advantages than those allowing survival in a ferocious pack of primates ridden with intense male competition for dominance. The young male, in other words, learned to inhibit his sexual drives and bide his time against stronger opponents. I am inclined, however, to share Etkin's view that, interesting and provocative though this speculation is, and certainly not without applicability in some primate societies, as an explanation it seems scarcely adequate to account for the first steps in the development of the human brain. One might almost observe that if similar behavior patterns involved in the familial activities of various modern primates were the sole forces at work in the creation of the human psyche, the experiment would have been launched more frequently by nature.

As it stands, baboons are still baboons and macaques, macaques. If we do not try to extract a single cause from its matrix and let it carry the whole burden of explanation, it may be, of course, that we will someday be able to postulate from these comparative studies of living primates just what additional factor in the case of man may, among several accessory causes, have turned the trick. But we are far from that point today. The genuine and forthright willingness of Chance and Mead, and Etkin to grapple specifically with the problem, as well as to face the limitations of their data, is a healthy sign for the future.

Atkin draws a picture rather different from that of Chance and Mead and, so far as man is concerned, develops it further. He accepts the cortical control of sexual behavior emphasized by Chance and Mead as contributing to the socialization of the primates, but points out that intense male competition for dominance in polygamous groups "is not universal among primates" (Etkin, 1954, p. 131). He further observes critically that

Perhaps a more fundamental defect of the theory is that it is nonadaptational, making the various aspects of human intelligence incidental to selection in respect to other characteristics which, it should be pointed out, operate in the male sex only (*ibid.*).

In the case of very early man, using the Australopithecines as a possible example, he contends that the absence of heavy canines in the males suggests less internal sexual competitiveness among males and, in addition, greater solicitude for the family. "The development of a hunting economy can occur, in an anthropoid," Etkin affirms (p. 136), "only if the male cooperates in feeding and caring for the young. The presupposition of monogamy for pre-cultural man which is here made is based on the impracticability of a single male operating successfully as protector and provider for many females." Etkin observes, therefore, that the "central feature of the social behavior of the 'hunter' anthropoid must be an integration of the male into the monogamous family unit in which he is the primary hunter."

The anthropoid baby could no longer be cared for by the mother alone as in the old frugivorous arboreal world. Once given this new environment promoting male cooperation in the family and among other males, a whole new series of selective forces conducive to the improvement of the brain would have come into play. Ideational behavior would have promoted the emergence of language under the new difficult hunting conditions and the desirability of permanent familial relationships between the sexes would, Etkin believes, not alone have promoted the growth of language but the loss of a distinct oestrus phase in favor of a diffuse and extended sexual interest which may have further reduced the typical male primate patterns of aggression and dominance. With the emergence of even rudimentary speech, the social bond would be further strengthened. Relaxation of selection pressure for rapid maturation would follow upon a greater degree of familial permanency and, in its turn, tend to reduce male jealousy. Increased opportunities for learning among the young would follow.

Etkin is frank to admit that his approach is in some degree speculative, but no more so than many of the inferences we are forced to draw from comparative anatomy. His treatment has, it appears to the present writer, one great advantage over many of the anthropological theories brought forth to date: it is complex, not simplistic. It does not seize upon a single factor such as tools and attempt to make that factor carry the full weight of human development. Etkin, instead, emphasizes a design of interwoven and related processes all operating at once.

Nevertheless, being something in the nature of a pioneering attempt, it may be said to falter somewhat in the elucidation of just what pre-adaptations may have promoted the survival of the ancestral primate when he first reached the ground, what brought him there, and what aspects of his mind at that stage may have promoted the rise of symbolic communication. Most of these are still very difficult questions, and Etkin is not to be blamed if he stumbles slightly on this transitional threshold which he has duly and correctly noted that the anthropologist tends to avoid. It is plain, however, even in Etkin's excellent paper that he himself prefers to begin with a proto-human family which has already successfully divided its labor and responsibilities and has pretty thoroughly mastered its ground environment. In our next and concluding section we shall examine some of these points and try, as well, to suggest an answer to Wallace's final question; namely, if men, with all their cultural diversity are, throughout the world, so intellectually similar, how did they attain this status and how, moreover, did they attain it so much more rapidly than Darwin's theory would explain? With what, in his solitary environment, is the primitive contending that makes it possible for his descendants a generation or two later to take their places satisfactorily in the great universities of the world? If natural selection is indeed at the root of this process, it is a natural selection that Darwin never visualized and that drove Wallace to have recourse to divine guidance. The gap between man and ape is not as the early Darwinians saw it—a slight step between a gorilla and a Papuan, or a chimpanzee and a gibbering Hottentot. Instead, it stretches broad and deep as time itself.

It is a fact long noted by philosophers that time, as discussed among men, is always treated in the language of space. Time is "behind" us and "before" us; it is a river and it "flows," or one remembers an episode "far off" in the past. Without wishing to make too much of the figurative expressions of modern tongues, it is not without interest that the arboreal world presents space to the primate, and particularly to the brachiating, upright primate, in a more dangerous multi-dimensional way than is true of any other creature. Leaving aside the question of language for the moment, the world of the tree-dweller demands a constant assessment of space in a way unknown to the pronograde creature on the ground. The steady following of the sense impressions from the nose becomes impossible, and must be replaced by reliance on sight—and sight of the keenest stereoscopic variety. Moreover, this space is presenting constantly, to the animal in the act of swinging through it, a panorama of dangers and opportunities which are less the steady succession of things observed by a moving ground animal than they are the ups and downs and sideways and befores of the multi-dimensional tree world. Objects demand, in terms of mental imagery, much more accurate visual reporting and an ability of the mind to twist its attention at will and hold in clear perspective things which are not necessarily directly ahead but which may be important above or below in the next flying second.

A friend of mine once saw a newly-released gibbon hurl itself at a glass window through which it obviously expected to pass. In the very instant of contact with the glass, against which an ordinary animal traveling at such speed would have shattered itself, the gibbon, sensing its error, recovered. With the merest featherdown touch of feet and hands, it caromed its flying body off the glass in a new direction and escaped disaster. The episode was a beautiful example of bodily coordination, but, in addition, it spoke volumes on the nature of the primate brain and eye. The vision was not all for what lay ahead. In the instant of unexpected contact with a solid, the brain, carrying some side image, knew where to divert the generated energy that was hurling it to destruction.

These acts have in them some of the insight, the flexibility of attention, the almost instantaneous internal reconstruction of external conditions which is involved in the manipulation of symbolic thought, that is, language in the other space world of time. We do not mean to imply incipient speech in the existing primates. We do, however, make bold to suggest that the arboreal environment and its demands may well have played a part in the creation of that ideational insight which is known to exist in our living relatives and which may lie close to the root of language as one of the preadaptations of our fathers of the forest world.* There is, at any rate, a remarkable analogy between the anthropoid comprehension of that world and what Chauncey Wright wrote long ago of language which "essentially consists in the power of turning back the attention from a suggested fact or idea to the suggesting ones . . . in place of the naturally passive following subserviency of the mind to the orders of first impressions or associations" (Wright, 1870, p 296). In other words, the time tracts which, in the speechless anthropoid, can be but dimly peopled with visual memories grow rich under the flow of symbolic thought. The time world comes into its own and assumes the importance and reality of the world of space.

But of that momentous crossing from the trees to the ground which is often assumed to be, as well, the passage into the world of symbolic thought and speech, we know, as yet, nothing at all. We are unsure as to what induced it, whether climatic circumstance, or the expansive powers of life itself as represented in the restless experimental habits of the primate brain. Professor Etkin is forced to take the "hunter" anthropoid for granted; and his system begins at this point. But *was* man a hunter, in any elaborate sense, when he descended upon the grass? It seems unlikely, and this may affect to some degree the validity of Etkin's comparison of the male ancestor's behavior to that of such a carnivore as the male wolf in the role of food provider. It is conceivable, since man is really an abnormal carnivore, that his first ventures upon the grass were descents into open parkland in search of seeds, grasshoppers, posibly even wild sorghums, and other items of this sort which could be harvested upon the ground. As yet, we do not have clear proof that even the Australopithecines were big game hunters, because the bones found in the sites from which their remains have been recovered may have been dragged in by hyenas. Our theories are to this extent assumptions which may or may not be true. In any case, the South African man-apes cannot be equated with the first primates who left the trees somewhere within Tertiary time. All of the existing great apes are essentially vegetarians, and indeed the arboreal brachiators have no other consistent source of food. Even the enormously powerful gorilla who has descended to the ground is a vegetarian forager and not a carnivore. It is at least worth some consideration that man is not likely to have been a meat-eater when he first came down from the trees but rather a somewhat omnivorous creature who only

---

* Sillman (1953, p. 150) says something of great pertinence in this connection:
". . . The establishment of language is essentially the transference of image evaluation of all modes of experience into the auditory vocal sphere. An anatomical basis for the domination by the auditory sphere is suggested by Meyer's loop of the visual radiation to the temporal lobe.
"A further pre-human step in the direction of language has been revealed by the experiments of Cluver and Bucy. They found that monkeys whose temporal lobes were removed lost their sense of visual discrimination so that they did not know how to respond to previously familiar objects and would mouth them as infants do. In other words, even in lower primates, temporal lobe auditory reactions acquire dominance or act as an interpretive screen between consciousness and the various forms of sense perception."

by degrees, as his numbers grew and his wit increased, turned to meat-eating in any extensive sense. Man's stomach is not that of a true meat eater. He does not possess the powerful digestive acids of the genuine carnivore, and this is why it was only with the discovery of fire that he can be said to have successfully unlocked the protein-rich food source represented by the swarming herds of the grasslands.

Man's interest in marrow and his known penchant for soft parts such as brains suggest that though he undoubtedly made some use of raw flesh in his bipedal adventure on the ground, he badly needed something that would serve as a substitute for the sort of stomach which was not his evolutionary birthright. Eventually he found it in fire. Man is thus to be seen once more as a strange anomaly among beasts, for he has been able to enhance his numbers and promote his rapid spread by literally stealing and transforming the energy of the grassland herds through the medium of fire. It is still of the utmost importance to know at what point this instrument came into man's hands, for it has undoubtedly done much to transform his habits and increase the rapidity of his diffusion (Eiseley, 1954). Although not in the beginning a true carnivore, his lack of purely instinctive controls and tremendous adaptability have enabled him to effect a transition in food habits which is unique on the planet.

The psychiatrist, Leonard Sillman (1953, p. 146), pointed out not long ago that "no other species [than man] comes into the world with so few fixed reactions for survival, knows less inherently how to maintain itself." It is for this reason that I remarked earlier in this paper that those who would disregard the higher mental characters of man, as side products of some kind of competitive struggle involving tools, have missed the real nature of the human transformation. It is this "new" brain, denuded of precise instinctive responses, growing in a curious mighty spurt during the first few months after birth that has created man and set him off from his nearest relatives. Evolution by infinitesimal competitive degrees which brings everyone out on the same potential intellectual level cannot be attributed to mechanical tool-using competition. Instead, it implies: (1) Either a true orthogenetic trend in all men, or (2) some aspect of the environment which is selective and yet common to all men everywhere.

This latter factor, if it is indeed the true explanation of the genetic mental equality of people all over the world, can only rest in the nature of man himself. In other words, the factor missed by Darwin and Wallace both, is the societal nature of human beings. The nineteenth-century biologists were confused by man because they were so taken up with the struggle for existence in the animal world that they rarely glimpsed the fact that in the case of man there was a second invisible environmental world in which he existed and which replaced for him his lost instinctive adjustments. For the first time a creature had appeared in nature who created his own world in his head, but by communication and mutual similarity of mind made of many heads a little universe in which man existed apart from exterior nature. It was this societal universe, with its institutions supplanting his lost instincts, which directed his activities. Invisible universe of dreams, it was this environment for which he was being selected in each society since the first glimmerings of that enormous change began. The naked, frail, denuded creature of which Sillman speaks could not have survived alone. In all those first societies of the years of transitional passage from the ape to the human world, the protective buffering of society for that frightened dawning consciousness must have been tremendously important. Moreover, those intellectually most able to adjust to, as well as to create, this secret universe in the mind of man, would have had the greatest opportunities for survival. Thus, the elaboration of the primary tool of *all* societies—language—went forward unceasingly. Whatever powers controlled the process, whatever institutions might arise in a given group, in the end there was only one society—the human creation in which man moved and had his being and which nurtured, in no matter what diverse ways, the essential nature of the societal creature. As Dobzhansky and Montagu (1947, p. 587) have very ably remarked:

An animal becomes adapted to its environment by evolving certain genetically determined physical and behavioral traits; the adaptation of man consists chiefly in developing his inventiveness, a quality to which his physical heredity predisposes him and which his social heredity provides him with all the means of realizing.

Rather than seeing a succession of societies graded in a series of stages leading up to Western civilization with its elaborate technology (based even among ourselves largely on the invention and use of the scientific method within the last three centuries), rather than judging the capabilities of different races on this basis, it should now be plain that the great basic innovation among all varieties of mankind was the production of the socio-cultural world itself. For this, man everywhere, whether in the far Arctic or the jungles of the Amazon, has been adapted unceasingly. It is the cultural beliefs and excrescences which vary, flux, and flow unceasingly, without, so far as we can judge, affecting man's native ability to learn the use of any tool from the hydrogen bomb to the spear thrower. The close equality of intellect seems to center around the ability of all men to use the one great socializing instrument; namely, language. Perhaps it is not surprising that Wright's remark of 1870 (pp. 295-296) that

a psychological analysis of the faculty of language shows that even the smallest proficiency in it might require more brain power than the greatest proficiency in any other direction, . . .

received so little attention, even though it was once referred to by Darwin.

It would thus appear, even though we are far from understanding the details, that the omnipresent selective force overlooked by Wallace, and which led him aside upon a somewhat mystical path, was the unseen environmental pressure implicit in the nature of society itself, rather than its individual cultural manifestations. All surviving races of mankind have, therefore, apparently been subjected to this selection to an approximately equal degree.

In answering Wallace's objection to what he regarded as a fatal defect in Darwin's treatment of man, it must be recognized that there are several aspects of man's mental life which both Etkin and Eiseley regard as somewhat mysterious but which there is not space to discuss here. Since, however, they are rather equally distributed (allowing for cultural differences) among all peoples, they do not affect the general conclusions expressed. We must, however, take note that the precise length of time involved in the production of the living species of man is still somewhat problematical. There has been a recent assumption that he is surprisingly young—a supposition that gained strength after the elimination of the Piltdown skull. There still remain, however, the faceless skulls from Swanscombe and Fontéchevade which hint strongly of *sapiens* affinities and whose datings have so far withstood all challenge. If Swanscombe, of second interglacial age, should prove to be an ancestral *Homo sapiens,* we must repeat that it will be impossible to regard the Pleistocene Australopithecines as any more than a side branch, and perhaps not even of assured human status, in spite of some human anatomical traits. In that case, we shall expect eventually to turn up creatures of possibly clear human affinities in the Pliocene. The scales at the moment are trembling but have not dipped conclusively toward either point of view. Discoveries either technical, in terms of refined measurements of time, or in the shape of new fossils should clarify this situation before long. In either case, it would appear that the evolution of the human brain has taken a shorter length of time than Wallace supposed in the older evolutionary terms of 1864. Much, in terms of time, depends upon the way in which the modern form of man was drawn out of the elder stock. Man's curious larval nakedness and extended infantile helplessness hint at pedomorphic changes whose mechanisms are ill-understood.

In the introduction to this paper, we spoke of the necessity of an assessment of our position. Perhaps it lies partly in the firm recognition of the depths of our ignorance. Even now we know practically nothing of the early dietary of the grassland primates—on what, for example, *Paranthropus crassidens* may have been chewing with those enormous molars, and with temporal muscles so massive that they demanded a sagittal crest. It is just possible that these characters are not an adjustment to flesh eating at all.

Certainly the subject is open to analysis. We should know a great many things about East African savanna that we do not know—possible foods; how much fire may have altered vegetation in post-glacial times—all these things are imperfectly understood. Finally, what must have been the frightening withdrawal of instinct in man and its replacement by the culture-building brain is a passage that the Darwinian world failed to grasp or appreciate clearly. Yet Sillman was right when he called it one of the cruelest and withal most generous endowments ever visited upon a living creature by a mysterious providence. It has surrounded him with an invisible sustaining world of pity and dignity and peace which, however much man may still struggle in the toils of his animal nature, was never built by the grossly personal selection of the stone ax and the spear. In that judgment, Wallace was correct; the world of man is a flowing world of dreams and symbols which he created long ago and which will last as long as man is man. In no other world can he now live. But the key to the secret doorway by which he came into this world is still unknown. The fortunate thing in terms of modern anthropology is that we know the disparity between man and ape is great, not small. And in that disparity of mind is locked a mystery which will not be yielded up except by serious and profound analysis. Of this also the modern anthropologist is increasingly aware.

REFERENCES

BARTHOLOMEW, GEORGE A., JR., and JOSEPH B. BIRDSELL 1953 Ecology and the protohominids. American Anthropologist, Vol. 55, No. 4, pp. 481–498.

BLAKE, C. CARTER 1864 On the alleged peculiar characters and assumed antiquity of the human cranium from Neanderthal. Anthropological Review, Vol. 2, pp. cxxxix–clvii.

BROOM, R. 1950 The genera and species of the South African fossil ape-man. American Journal of Physical Anthropology, Vol. 8, n.s., No. 1, pp. 1–14.

BROOM, R., and J. T. ROBINSON 1950 Note on the skull of the Swartkrans ape-man Paranthropus crassidens. American Journal of Physical Anthropology, Vol. 8, n.s., No. 3, pp. 295–304.

CHANCE, M. R. A., and A. P. MEAD 1953 Social behaviour and primate evolution, pp. 395–439. In Symposia of the Society for Experimental Biology, No. VII, Evolution. New York, Academic Press, 448 pp.

CLARK, W. E. LE GROS 1950 New palaeontological evidence bearing on the evolution of the Hominoidea. Quarterly Journal of the Geological Society of London, Vol. VC, pp. 225–264.

COLE, SONIA 1954 The prehistory of East Africa. American Anthropologist, Vol. 56, No. 6, pp. 1026–1050.

DART, RAYMOND A. 1954a The adult female lower jaw from Makapansgat. American Anthropologist, Vol. 56, No. 5, Part 1, pp. 884–888.

——— 1954b The second, or adult, female mandible of Australopithecus prometheus. American Journal of Physical Anthropology, Vol. 12, No. 3, pp. 313–343.

DARWIN, CHARLES n.d. The Origin of Species and the Descent of Man. New York, Modern Library Edition, 924 pp.

DARWIN, FRANCIS 1888 The Life and Letters of Charles Darwin. London, John Murray, 3 vols.

DOBZHANSKY, THEODOSIUS, and M. F. ASHLEY MONTAGU 1947 Natural selection and the mental capacities of mankind. Science, Vol. 105, pp. 587–590.

DRENNAN, M. R. 1954 Saldanha man and his associations. American Anthropologist, Vol. 56, No. 5, Part 1, pp. 879–884.

EHRICH, ROBERT W., and GERALD M. HENDERSON 1954 Concerning the

Piltdown hoax and the rise of a new dogmatism. American Anthropologist, Vol. 56, No. 3, pp. 433-435.

Eiseley, Loren C. 1953 Fossil man. Scientific American, Vol. 189, No. 6, pp. 65-72.

―― 1954a Man the fire-maker. Scientific American, Vol. 191, No. 3, pp. 52-57.

―― 1954b The reception of the first missing links. Proceedings of the American Philosophical Society, Vol. 98, No. 6, pp. 453-465.

Etkin, William 1954 Social behavior and the evolution of man's mental faculties. The American Naturalist, Vol. LXXXVIII, pp. 129-142.

Hill, W. C. Osman 1954 Man's Ancestry. London, William Heineman, 172 pp.

Hillaby, John D. 1954 Bone may be clue to ancient puzzle. New York Times, Nov. 28.

Hooijer, Dirk Albert 1951 The geological age of Pithecanthropus, Meganthropus and Gigantopithecus. American Journal of Physical Anthropology, Vol. 9, n.s., No. 3, pp. 265-282.

Howell, F. Clark 1951 The place of Neanderthal man in human evolution. American Journal of Physical Anthropology, Vol. 9, n.s., pp. 379-416.

―― 1952 Pleistocene glacial ecology and the evolution of "Classic Neanderthal" man. Southwestern Journal of Anthropology, Vol. 8, No. 4, pp. 377-410.

―― 1954 Hominids, pebble tools and the African Villafranchian. American Anthropologist, Vol. 56, No. 3, pp. 378-386.

Huxley, Thomas H. 1871 Mr. Darwin's critics. The Contemporary Review, Vol. 18, pp. 443-476.

Kingsley, Charles n.d. The Water Babies. New York, Grosset and Dunlap, 244 pp.

Marchant, James 1916, Alfred Russel Wallace: Letters and Reminiscences. New York, Harpers, 475 pp.

Miller, Gerrit S. 1928 The controversy over human "missing links." Proceedings of the United States National Museum (for 1928), pp. 413-465.

Montagu, M. F. Ashley 1952 Neanderthal and the modern type of man. American Journal of Physical Anthropology, Vol. 10, n.s., No. 3, pp. 368-370.

―― 1955 Time, morphology, and neoteny in the evolution of man. American Anthropologist, Vol. 57, No. 1, pp. 13-27.

Munro, Robert 1893 Anthropology (Opening address before the Anthropology Section of the British Asociation for the Advancement of Science, 1893). Nature, Vol. 48, pp. 503-508.

Murray, Raymond W. 1954 The place of the "Australopithecinae" among human fossils. Proceedings of the Indiana Academy of Science for 1953, Vol. 63, pp. 47-53.

Oakley, Kenneth P. 1954 Dating of the Australopithecinae of Africa. American Journal of Physical Anthropology, Vol. 12, n.s., No. 1, pp. 9-28.

Peabody, Frank E. 1954 Travertines and cave deposits of the Kaap escarpment of South Africa, and the type locality of "Australopithecus Africanus" dart. Bulletin of the Geological Society of America, Vol. 65, pp. 671-706.

Pycraft, W. P. 1917 The jaw of Piltdown man. Science Progress, Vol. 11, pp. 389-409.

Robinson, J. T. 1952a The australopithecine-bearing deposits of the Sterkfontein area. Annals of the Transvaal Museum, Vol. XXII, Part I, pp. 1-19.

―― 1952b Some hominid features of the ape-man dentition. Official Journal of the Dental Association of South Africa, March 15, pp. 1-12.

———— 1953a Meganthropus, australopithecines and hominids. American Journal of Physical Anthropology, Vol. 11, n.s., No. 1, pp. 1–38.

———— 1953b Telanthropus and its phylogenetic significance. American Journal of Physical Anthropology, Vol. 11, n.s., No. 4, pp. 445–501.

———— 1954a The genera and species of the Australopithecinae. American Journal of Physical Anthropology, Vol. 12, n.s., No. 2, pp. 181–200.

———— 1954b The australopithecine occiput. Nature, Vol. 174, p. 262.

———— 1954c Phyletic lines in the prehominids. Zeitschrift für Morphologie und Anthropologie, Vol. 46, No. 2, pp. 269–273.

SILLMAN, LEONARD 1953 The genesis of man. International Journal of Psychoanalysis, Vol. 34, pp. 146–152.

SINGER, RONALD 1954 The Saldanha skull from Hopefield, South Africa. American Journal of Physical Anthropology, Vol. 12, No. 3, pp. 345–362.

STRAUS, WILLIAM L., JR. 1949 The riddle of man's ancestry. The Quarterly Review of Biology, Vol. 24, No. 3, pp. 200–223.

———— 1950 On the zoological status of Telanthropus capensis. American Journal of Physical Anthropology, Vol. 8, n.s., No. 4, pp. 495–498.

———— 1954a The great Piltdown hoax. Science, Vol. 119, No. 3087, pp. 265–269.

———— 1954b Closing remarks. Human Biology, Vol. 26, No. 3, pp. 304–312.

TAPPEN, NEIL C. 1953 A mechanistic theory of human evolution. American Anthropologist, Vol. 55, pp. 605–607.

TEILHARD DE CHARDIN, PIERRE 1952 On the zoological position and the evolutionary significance of the Australopithecines. Transactions of The New York Academy of Sciences, Ser. II, Vol. 14, pp. 208–210.

VALLOIS, HENRI V. 1949 The Fontechevade fossil men. American Journal of Physical Anthropology, Vol. 7, n.s., No. 3, pp. 339–362.

———— 1952 L'Homme de Fontéchevade et les Praesapiens. Acts of the Fourth International Congress of Anthropological and Ethnological Sciences, Vienna 1952, Tome 1, pp. 103–104.

———— 1954 Neandertals and Praesapiens. Journal of the Royal Anthropological Institute of Great Britain and Ireland, Vol. 84, Part II, pp. 1–20.

WALLACE, A. R. 1864 The origin of human races and the antiquity of man deduced from the theory of "natural selection." Anthropological Review, Vol. 2, pp. clviii–clxxxvii.

———— 1869 Geological climates and the origin of species. The Quarterly Review, Vol. 126, pp. 359–394.

———— 1876 Difficulties of development as applied to man. Popular Science Monthly, Vol. 10, pp. 60–72.

———— 1895 Natural Selection and Tropical Nature. London, Macmillan and Company, 492 pp.

WASHBURN, S. L. 1950 The analysis of primate evolution with particular reference to the origin of man, pp. 67–78. In Symposia On Quantitative Biology, Vol. XV, Cold Spring Harbor, Long Island, New York, 415 pp.

———— 1953 The Piltdown hoax. American Anthropologist, Vol. 55, No. 5, Part 1, pp. 759–762.

WATSON, D. M. S. 1953 Africa and the origin of man. American Scientist, Vol. 41, No. 3, pp. 427–438.

WECKLER, J. E. 1954 The relationships between Neanderthal man and Homo sapiens. American Anthropologist, Vol. 56, No. 6, pp. 1003–1025.

WEINER, J. S. 1955 The Piltdown Forgery. Oxford, Oxford University Press.

WEINER, J. S., and K. P. OAKLEY 1954 The Piltdown fraud: available evidence reviewed. American Journal of Physical Anthropology, Vol. 12, n.s., No. 1, pp. 1–8.

WEINER, J. S., K. P. OAKLEY, and W. E. LE GROS CLARK 1953 The solution of the Piltdown problem. Bulletin of the British Museum (Natural History); Geology, Vol. 2, No. 3, pp. 141–146.

WRIGHT, CHAUNCEY 1870 The limits of natural selection. The North American Review, Vol. 111, pp. 282–311.

ZUCKERMAN, S. 1950 Taxonomy and human evolution. Biological Reviews, Vol. 25, pp. 435–485.

—— 1954 Correlation of change in the evolution of the higher primates, pp. 300–352. In Evolution as a Process, edited by Huxley, Julian, et al. London, George Allen and Unwin, 367 pp.

TIME, MORPHOLOGY,

AND NEOTENY

IN THE EVOLUTION OF MAN

M. F. ASHLEY MONTAGU

Discussions of the evolution of man in terms of morphology while conveying some notion of the physical changes that have progressively led to the differentiation of the varieties of man fail, however, to tell us what some of the *developmental* mechanisms responsible for those changes may have been.

There is considerable evidence that such sapiens-like forms as Swanscombe and Fontéchevade antedate in time of appearance morphologically more primitive forms such as Neanderthal man. How can this be? If it is true that evolution progresses from the simple to the more complex or more evolved forms, how can a more evolved form in any species appear earlier than a less evolved one?

The terms "simple," "more complex," and "more evolved" beg some rather fundamental questions. The truth is that evolution does not always proceed from the more simple to the more complex. *Sacculina,* which is an active crustacean in the earlier stages of its existence, swimming about by means of well-developed appendages, degenerates into a parasitic bag in its later existence which remains attached to the abdomen of a crab.

Is sapiens type of man in fact "more complex," "more evolved" than presapiens man? Are thinner skull bones and absence of supraorbital tori, for example, evidences of greater complexity or advancement? For the idea of progressive advancement is implied in these terms. We think not. Evolutionary change has occurred, but with respect to the traits mentioned it would rather seem that it has progressed from the complex to the simpler. These questions are raised here for the reader to consider, but in this essay we are concerned with a somewhat different question. It is: By what means did man come into being. What was the process or mechanism by which an apelike creature developed or evolved into a man?

We are aware that genetically the evolution of man was brought about by the accumulation of adaptively favorable mutations acted upon by natural and social selection. But what kind of mutations? Adaptively favorable to what?

Commencing with a consideration of the precursors of man we pass backward in time to the Pliocene, a geological epoch that extended over some

Reprinted by permission from *An Introduction to Physical Anthropology,* 3rd ed., by M. F. Ashley Montagu, Springfield, Illinois, C.C. Thomas, 1960, pp. 295–316.

12 million years. Man is essentially a Pleistocene form, so that many of the really important changes leading to the advent of man must have occurred mainly within the Pliocene. All the indications are that Africa is the backdrop against which these evolutionary events were enacted. There is some evidence that in Africa during the Pliocene a number of significant climatic changes occurred principally related to rainfall. The withdrawal of the rainfall further and further northward had the effect of converting vast areas of forested land into open savanna, that is, sparsely treed plains covered with low vegetation. Such environmental changes shifted the zone of adaptation from a life in the forest to one on the open savanna. Forest dwelling animals if they are to survive on the savanna must become adapted to the demands of an environment altogether different from that afforded by the forest. There are many ways in which different mammalian groups have achieved such adaptations, and even different primate groups, such as the bush babies, some lemurs, and baboons, who exhibit quite a variety of adaptations to life on the savanna or on rocky terrain.

In the case of those apelike forms which comprised the "line" that eventually led to man, their meeting of the challenges of the savanna environment, extending over a period of some millions of years, assumed the form—quite fortuitously—of the development of adaptations enabling the individual to compete increasingly more successfully in the struggle for existence. Since the yield of plant foods on the savanna, as compared with the abundant yield of the forest, is small and varies catastrophically with the seasons, it is an advantage to be able to enlarge one's dietary to include animals. Unlike plants which are stationary and have their roots in the earth, animals are mobile and have their roots in their stomachs. Animals require catching. They have to be chased. Only small game would be attempted at first, and thence one could go on to larger enterprises. But whether large or small those individuals who possessed traits that enabled them to gather an adequate number of animals would be more likely to survive and bequeath their traits to a larger and more successful progeny, than would those not possessing such traits.

The quest for subsistence would undoubtedly have placed a high premium upon the ability to cooperate, not alone in the hunt, but also in the sharing of food, the care of the young, and the care of the old. All these are highly cooperative activities, and those individuals exhibiting such cooperative traits would be more likely to leave progeny than those who did not.

To judge from the australopithecine remains it would appear that the erect posture was one of the first manlike adaptations achieved by man's early ancestors, probably in the Upper Pliocene. The erect posture frees the hands for manipulatory activities which, accompanied by increasing intelligence, enables one to command the environment more effectively. Intelligence, the ability to scan, forecast, solve problems, and make rapid adjustments to rapidly changing conditions, is at a premium. An animal narrowly confined within the walls of its instinctual equipment will not do as well under such challenging conditions as one that is free to use its intelligence unrestricted by preconditioned determinants of behavior or limited to a narrow range of responses. In short, the animal that becomes increasingly freed from its instinctual drives in arriving at decisions, becomes the driver instead of the driven, and under the unrestricted operation of natural selection would tend to be favored for survival as compared with those that tended to live by their instincts.

By means of such a selective process the immediate forerunners of man would have been increasingly freed from the limiting effects of their instinctual drives, so that by the time hominid status would have been attained virtually the last vestiges of that instinctive system of drives would have disappeared. If instinct is lapsed intelligence enabling the animal automatically to make appropriate responses to a limited range of stimuli, man's freedom for such instinctive mechanisms makes him the one creature whose responses to the environment are potentially unlimited. Man is equipped with potentialities for learning whatever he requires to know in order to grow and develop as a fully adjusted human being. In this respect, also his potentialities are unique, with the maximum capacity for phenotypic adjustment. That is to say, man possesses a genetic endowment which makes it possible for him to adapt himself to every possible environment. Man's phenotypic plasticity is the result of a long history of evolutionary adaptation which has culminated in the most plastically adaptable, the most extraordinarily educable of all living creatures.

To be educable means to be dependent. If, then, one has to *learn* to be a functioning intelligent being, with learned behavior substituted for instinctually predetermined behavior, an appreciable period of time must be available during which the trained skills of intelligent behavior may be acquired. The developmental mechanism by which this availability of time for learning was ensured appears to have been achieved by means of a process which caused a retention or persistence of the fetal or juvenile plasticity of ancestral forms in the later postnatal developmental stages of the individual. This process by which the young (fetal or juvenile) features of the ancestor are retained in the mature stages of postnatal development is known as *neoteny* —the developmental retention of fetal or juvenile characters in the adult. The suggestion is that many of the changes which led to the appearance of distinctively hominid traits were brought about by neoteny, that man, as the Dutch anthropologist Bolk pointed out, is a fetalized form. Man exhibits the retention of many characters that resemble those of fetal apes, some of which are listed below.

Neotenous Characters in Man

Retention of cranial flexure	Absence of brow ridges
Long neck	Absence of cranial crests
Forward position of foramen magnum	Thinness of skull bones

Orbits under cranial cavity	Globular form of skull
Flatness of face (orthognathy)	Hairlessness of body
Retarded closure of cranial sutures	Lack of pigment in some groups
Large volume of brain	Thin nails
Small face and large braincase	Non-rotation of big toe
Roundheadedness (brachycephaly)	Low birth weight
Small teeth	Prolonged dependency period
Late eruption of teeth	Prolonged growth period

In the fetus of all mammals and most vertebrates the axis of the head forms a right angle with that of the trunk, the cranial flexure. In all mammals, with the exception of man, a rotation of the head occurs during the later stages of development so that the head assumes an orientation that is continuous with the direction of the backbone, as, for example in the adult dog (Figure 1). Man, on the other hand, retains the cranial flexure, his face pointing in a direction at right angles to the axis of his body. The visual axis, the line of sight, of both dog and man are horizontal, the dog's body is also horizontal while that of man is vertical. In the adult great apes the position of the body is in between, being oblique, and the axis of the head is also intermediate, the foramen magnum being situated more

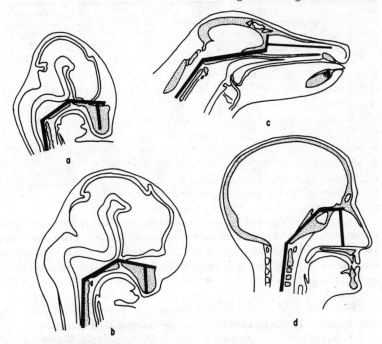

Fig. 1 Sagittal sections through the head showing the angle which the head makes with the trunk in a: embryo dog. b: embryo man. c: adult dog. d: adult man. (From Bolk.)

posteriorly than it is in either the fetal ape or in man. It thus transpires that man's erect posture is probably due to the retention in postnatal development of a fetal condition which in other mammals is limited only to their intra-uterine state of development. Man's flat-facedness is also a fetal character, and it is an interesting speculation that since orthognathy is limited to the early fetal stages of development in apes that the fetal developmental stage at which the neotenous mutations occurred in man's ancestors that led to orthognathy in man must have occurred fairly early—a point to which we shall return.

The sutures of the braincase remain open in man until all growth has been completed, and long after the brain has achieved its maximum growth. While in the apes the sutures begin to close within the first few years of life, in man they do not generally commence to close before the end of the 27th year. It is of considerable interest to note that there is a close correlation between the duration of the early learning period of man and the growth of the brain.

TABLE I

GROWTH IN BRAIN AND CRANIAL CAPACITY, BOTH SEXES

Age	Weight gm.	Volume cc.	Cranial Capacity cc.
Birth	350	330	350
3 months	526	500	600
6 months	654	600	775
9 months	750	675	925
1 year	825	750	1,000
2 years	1,010	900	1,100
3 years	1,115	960	1,225
4 years	1,180	1,000	1,300
6 years	1,250	1,060	1,350
9 years	1,307	1,100	1,400
12 years	1,338	1,150	1,450
15 years	1,358	1,150	1,450
18 years	1,371	1,175	1,475
20 years	1,378	1,200	1,500

Source: Growth and Development of the Child, Part II, 1933, p. 110.

Since the brain's growth in volume is completed by the twentieth year, the cranial sutures must remain open at least until this period of growth has been completed. Occasionally, due to some pathologic cause, the sutures unite in early childhood and prevent the brain from growing, with the result that such children remain mentally retarded all their lives. The major and fundamental part of human learning takes place during the first five years of life, and, as will be seen from Table 1, it is during this period that the greater part of brain growth is accomplished.

A point of great significance is that the human brain begins its real growth and development at birth, and continues to grow and develop in the functions of a human being, throughout the first two decades of life. The brain of a 3 year old child is almost of the size and weight of that of an adult. By the age of 6 years the brain has generally virtually achieved full adult size. In man the active growth of the brain far exceeds that of any other primate. At birth the mean weight of the brain in caucasoids is approximately 350 gm or approximately 3.9 times less than its adult weight. The growth of the brain is very different from that of the rest of the body, being quite explosive during the first year when it more than doubles to a weight of 825 gm—a gain of 475 gm. In the second year the gain is almost 275 gm, in the third year about 175 gm, and at the rate of about 70 gm up to the end of the fifth year when the brain weight reaches 1230 gm. From the sixth to the tenth year the increment varies as follows: 19 gm between 5 and 6 years, 8 gm between 6 and 7 years, 46 gm between 7 and 8 years, and 10 gm between 9 and 10 years. After the first decade and to the end of the second decade the increment is less than 3 gm a year—to a total of 1378 gm.

At birth the human brain is only 23 per cent of its adult size, and by the end of the first year the human infant has achieved 60 per cent of its total brain growth; by the end of the third year some 81 per cent. In the great apes the major part of the growth is achieved within the first year. In the rhesus monkey and in the gibbon 70 per cent of the brain growth has been achieved by birth, and the remainder is completed within the first six months. In the great apes the active period of brain growth occurs during the first eleven months, and in man during the first thirty-six months. Complete growth of the brain in man is not achieved until the end of the second decade of life. As Keith has pointed out, in this prolongation of cerebral growth and development we see an important, "if not the most important, feature of human evolution—namely, the time taken to assemble and to organize the myriads of nerve cells and of nerve tracts which enter into the structure of man's brain." This process, as Keith adds, exemplifies the "law" of fetalization or neoteny, and it is this process which is capable of explaining the evolution of that most unique of all traits, the human mind.

It seems reasonably clear that the growth (increase in size) and development (increase in complexity) of the human brain is a neotenous phenomenon. In other words, man preserves something akin to the rate of growth and development characteristic of the fetal brain or preserves and improves upon the rate of growth and development of the infant ape-brain long after the latter has ceased to grow.

The deciduous dentition of the great apes more closely resembles that of adult man than it does that of the adult apes, so that it is not surprising to find, for example, that the deciduous teeth of the australopithecines resemble more closely the permanent teeth of man than they do those of adult australopithecines.

In the long delayed eruption of both the deciduous and permanent teeth in man we again observe a neotenous trait, the prolongation of the edentulous state of the fetus.

In all the other physical traits listed man more closely resembles the fetal ape than he does the adult. The prolonged dependency and growth periods are simply prolongations of the fetal dependency and growth periods.

One of the consequences of the prolonged dependency period of man is that it involves a rather long nursing period, and it is presumed that the unique everted mucous membranous lips of man have evolved as an adaptation to the prolonged suckling period of the human infant. Just as the cheeks of the human baby with their suctorial pads of fat are very different from what they are in the later child or adult, so does the character of the lips differ in the baby from what they will later be in the child or adult. The newborn baby's lips are characterized by a median papilla (which is sometimes mistaken for an abnormal condition). This papilla, on each lip, enables the baby to secure a better hold upon the breast.

It is reasonably clear that what is inherited by the organism has in part been acquired as a consequence of interaction of genotype with environment during development. It is during the process of individual development that mutations acquire phenotypic expression. Any mutation which serves to produce a relative retardation of somatic development so that the descendant fails to pass through several of the developmental stages of the ancestor, will result in the descendant exhibiting a pattern of growth which in the adult stage represents a retention of the ancestral fetal or youthful pattern. Many such cases are known to zoologists and geneticists, in which rates of development, the retention of an embryonic or youthful character and its extension in the adult, duration of developmental periods, and termination of development are affected by mutations which may have distinct and marked effects upon adult form. Such neotenous mutations may spread rapidly in a small population, and it is suggested that under such conditions the fetal or juvenile developmental stage of a pithecanthropine or similar type could have become very quickly consolidated in the descendant group. A fetalized pithecanthropine, to judge from the juvenile Modjokerto skull, or a fetalized australopithecine, to judge from the juvenile *Australopithecus africanus,* would more closely resemble modern man than these fossil juvenile forms would the adult members of their own type. Spuhler (1954) has shown that the deciduous teeth of the australopithecines are more like the deciduous teeth of modern man, but the permanent teeth are more like those of apes. In almost all the traits in which the juvenile members of these fossil forms differ from the living apes and their own adult forms they most closely resemble modern man, for example, in the comparatively globular form of the skull, the thinness of the skull bones, the absence of brow bridges, the absence of crests, the form of the teeth, and the relative size and form of the brain. We can have little doubt as to the form and characters of the fetal forms of the australopithecine and pithecanthropine types—these would almost certainly more closely resemble the human than the anthropoid. It is by the retention of such fetal and juvenile characters in the adult, particularly in the head region, by neoteny, that a neanthropic type of man could have evolved quite early in the history of the human species. M. R. Drennan and L. H. D. Buxton and de Beer independently suggested that modern man may not be unrelated to a neanderthaloid type if he can be regarded as descended by neoteny from a juvenile form of the latter. But more recently de Beer has stated, "It is now realized that the ancestor of modern man could not have been Neanderthal man because he appeared later in time than the earliest types of modern man. But if the human ancestor was similar to *Pithecanthropus,* or *Australopithecus,* modern man would have descended from them by retention of features in the juvenile forms of their skulls, which is what is meant by neoteny."

Neotenous mutations appear to have expressed themselves somewhat differently in the different major groups. Mongoloids, for example, are rather more fetalized in their adult characters than are Caucasoids. Negroids exhibit some fetal traits that Caucasoids do not. Below are listed some of the neotenous characters in which Mongoloids and Negroids differ from Caucasoids.

Neotenous Characters
in Which Mongoloids and Negroids Differ from Caucasoids

Mongoloids	Negroids	Bushman-Hottentot
Less hairy	Less hairy	Less hairy
Larger braincase	Flat root of nose	Light skin pigment
Larger brain	Flattish nose	Short stature
More frequently	Small ears	Roundheaded
brachycephalic	Frontal bosses	(Mesocephalic)
Broader face		Small mastoid
Flat root of nose		processes
Epicanthic fold		Small cranial
More protuberant eye		sinuses
Lack of brow ridges		Wide separation of
Greater gracility		eyes
of bones		Bulging forehead
Shallow mandibular		Epicanthic fold
fossa		Relatively large brain
Small mastoid processes		Flat root of nose
Stocky build		Small face
		Horizontal penis

The varieties of mankind that fall into those broad classificatory categories we today call "major groups" were at one time very small populations, and it is evident that in these populations neotenous mutations occurred somewhat differently in each one. Similar differences in mutation could have occurred among the Pleistocene populations of man. In this manner one could readily explain the appearance of such neanthropic-like types as Swanscombe and Fontéchevade before the advent of such an apparently morphologically more primitive type like Neanderthal man. The fact that Neanderthal man got to look more "primitive" than he appeared to be in his earlier phases of evolution, suggests that our conceptions as to what is "primitive" and what "advanced" in human morphology are in need of careful study. In the Neanderthal group we see that an apparently less primitive-looking morphological type actually preceded a seemingly more primitive-looking type. If this sort of thing could happen in one variety of man it could certainly happen as between different varieties, as we have in fact seen that it happened among the living major groups.

As long ago as 1923 Keith, in commenting on the ideas of Bolk, remarked that "Man's outstanding structural peculiarities have been produced during the embryonic and foetal stages of his developmental history." In 1925 he wrote, "This intrauterine period is one which gives every opportunity for the working out of new inventions." And, again, in 1947, "It is during the intrauterine phase that nearly all revolutionary changes in structure have been introduced."

Drennan, and more recently Abbie, have argued that anthropologists have paid insufficient attention to the developing uterine organism, that is, the embryo and fetus, and too much attention to the adult form in the study of man's physical evolution. This has, in large part been unavoidable, since most of the fossil remains recovered have been those of adults. Abbie has pointed out that it is really not a sound procedure to attempt to trace human evolution by the comparison of adult forms, and suggests that the only common stem that can be found for the primates lies in an early embryonic series. Practically any of the primates in such an embryonic series could produce a sufficiently generalized precursor of man. Consequently, it would not be necessary to go very far back into primate history to find the ancestral form. And, as Abbie states, "If a common generalized foetal form could be discovered the problem of man's ancestry would be much closer to solution than it is now." As a working hypothesis he visualizes such a form as resembling a human embryo of about 7 weeks' gestation, as shown in Figure 3. Development, at that stage, is that of a generalized primate, with the digits of the hand differentiated but not those of the feet, so that there is not yet any indication whether the great toe will become lined up with the other toes as in man or will become opposable as in the apes. All that is required at this stage is a very small change in order to shift this structure either in the one or the other direction.

In Figure 3 Abbie has provided a simple scheme to illustrate the manner in which distinctive forms of the various primates may have been derived from a common primate fetal ancestor by a combination of the processes of

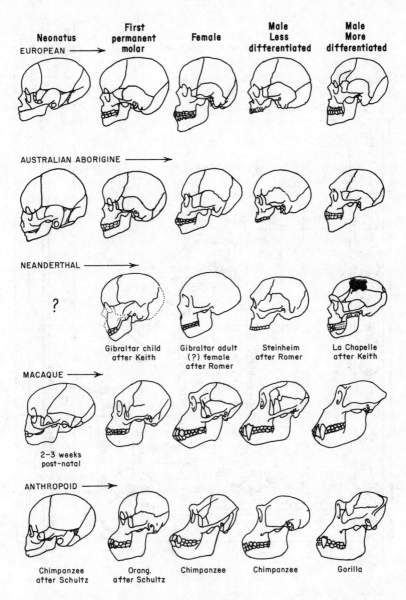

Fig. 2 From left to right, showing how the neonatal skull of various primates differentiates to varying degrees of gerontomorphism from a relatively common neonatal form. The skulls are all drawn to approximately the same size. (From Abbie. Courtesy, *Trans. R. S. S. Austral.*)

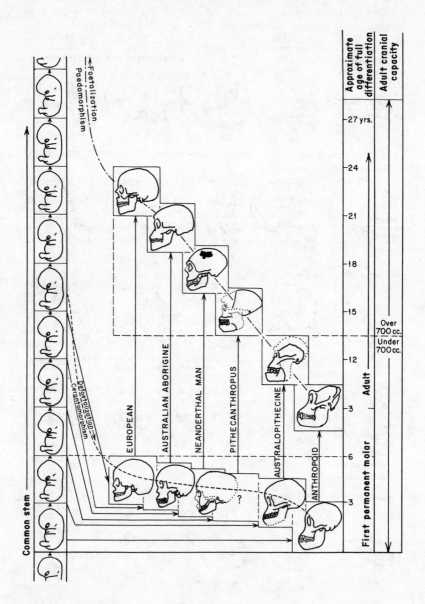

Fig. 3 A scheme to illustrate the suggested common primate stem, and the manner in which distinctive forms of various primates have been derived from it by a combination of the processes of gerontomorphism and pedomorphism.

334

fetalization and gerontomorphism.* Development from the common stem by defetalization or gerontomorphism of varying degrees leads through such juvenile forms as those shown in the lower row, which in turn lead to the gerontomorphic forms shown above, but which progressively exhibit, above the 700 cc. cranial capacity in the adult, a tendency toward the preservation of fetal traits in the adult.

THE CONTEMPORANEITY OF MORPHOLOGICALLY DIVERSE FORMS OF MAN

How can we account for the presence of probable neanthropic types like Kanjera man, Swanscombe, and Fontéchevade preceding such apparently, more primitive types as the Neanderthaloids? Let us consider some of the facts.

The hominid form most resembling the australopithecines is *Pithecanthropus robustus* from the Lower Pleistocene of Java. Middle Pleistocene *Pithecanthropus erectus* of Java, and *Sinanthropus pekinensis* of the same age from China, follow next in morphological significance—which is not necessarily morphological or temporal order. Next follows the Upper Pleistocene Java Solo man. Solo man belongs either to the end of the Third Interglacial or the beginning of the Fourth Glacial. This pithecanthropoid type is undoubtedly a descendant of the older pithecanthropines, and the persistence of Solo man possibly into the Fourth Glacial affords us an opportunity to study the evolution of a hominid group in what seems to have been a thorough geographic isolation from other hominid groups. We may thus observe the trend of evolution from *Pithecanthropus robustus* through *Pithecanthropus erectus* to Solo man. The changes over this great period of time, which we may conservatively put at 500,000 years, are both absolutely and relatively minor—but changes there have been. These changes we know to have affected the brain, in the filling out of the antero-inferior parietotemporal region, while in the skull the structure of the foramen magnum is unique in that its anterior half faces more or less downwards whereas the posterior half faces backwards. There are other interesting but minor changes. The important fact is that in Solo man we have an insular terminal hominid type which is morphologically clearly descended and but little altered from

---

* *Gerontomorphism*, the process of phylogenetic change as the result of the modification of adult traits, by means of adult variation, whereby adult ancestral traits become the traits of youthful descendants.

Defetalization, the process whereby development occurs by the loss of fetal traits by their postnatal progression toward more complex adult forms.

Fetalization, the process whereby ancestral or the organism's own fetal traits are retained in the development of the adults of a descendant group.

Pedomorphosis, the process whereby ancestral or the organism's own juvenile traits are retained in the development of the adult descendants of a group. Incorrectly used as a synonym for fetalization.

Neoteny, the process whereby the organism's own ancestral fetal and/or juvenile traits are retained in the development of the adult descendants of a group. Embraces both fetalization and pedomorphosis.

Pithecanthropus robustus. In other words, the rate of evolutionary change in the geographically isolated group of Javanese pithecanthropines was comparatively slow compared with that which appears to have been occurring in other hominid groups elsewhere. It is possible that in Solo man we have an example, in miniscule, of what Simpson has called bradytely, that is, lack of appreciable evolutionary change over a long period of time.

If, as is generally done, we assume a monophyletic origin for man in the Early Pleistocene or Late Pliocene, it should be abundantly clear that to account for such different contemporary morphological types as Solo and Fontéchevade man (each from the latter parts of the Third Interglacial) and such earlier differing contemporaneous (Middle Pleistocene) types as, on the one hand *Pithecanthropus erectus,* and Kanjera and Swanscombe man on the other, it will be necessary to consider every evolutionary process which may possibly have played a role in producing such types.

EVOLUTIONARY RATES

Starting as members of a common morphologically similar phyletic group, separated or isolated populations could, as the result of differences in rates of evolution, become significantly differentiated from one another, and this even though the trend or direction of evolution may remain the same. In this manner it would be possible to account for certain phenomena in the evolution of man which upon a naïve or orthogenetic view appear to be irreconcilable.

For our purposes an evolutionary rate may be defined as a measure of morphological change relative to a given period of elapsed time. Simpson has recently fully discussed the varieties of evolutionary rates, and for a discussion of this subject the reader may be referred to his work, *The Major Features of Evolution.* It is now fairly well understood that there has been the widest possible variation in evolutionary rates in the evolution of living forms. Simpson tells us, for example, that, "Of North American mammalian stocks introduced into South America in latest Pliocene and/or early Pleistocene, that is, perhaps from a million to 500 thousand years ago, probably all have become specifically distinct, many have become genetically distinct, but none has become so distinct as to be reasonably placed in a new subfamily or family." And Simpson adds that, as he had already noted earlier in his book of other single examples, "this represents an increased average rate of evolution accompanying occupation of new territory." The evolutionary rates of the members of the same groups which remained in North America changed in an appreciable but somewhat lesser degree.

Occupation of new territory, to judge from the wide distribution of fossil man upon the earth, and the wanderings of peoples, appears to have been a not infrequent activity of many prehistoric human populations. Such prehistoric populations seem to have been very small, so that genetic changes could have become rapidly established in them.

As Simpson has pointed out, man as a mammal must be considered to have evolved at a more than average rate, and as a mammal of quite ordinary inherent variability he owes his present great intergroup variation to the fact that he has adapted to a uniquely large number of different habitats—the habitats of man being not merely the differing physiographic environments but including also the different sociocultural environments.

PEDOMORPHOSIS, FETALIZATION, NEOTENY

Mutations have, of course, occurred—and occur—in the members of all human populations, but in accounting for evolutionary differences in man it seems unnecessary to assume substantially different mutation rates in different separated early groups of man to account for the contemporaneity of palanthropic and neanthropic types. It is here that the process of pedomorphosis may play a significant role. The original notion of paedogenesis, as he called it, was elaborated by von Baer in 1828, to describe the development of mature germ cells in a larval body. The concept of neoteny was quite clearly discussed by J. E. V. Boas in 1896 as the process by which the young features of the ancestor are retained in the adult stage of the descendant. The concepts of fetalization as proposed by L. Bolk, and neoteny by G. R. de Beer, proterogenesis by O. H. Schindewolf and bradygenesis by A. N. Ivanow, mean pretty much the same thing as paedogenesis or pedomorphosis, except that, strictly speaking, fetalization would refer specifically to fetal stages, while pedomorphosis would refer to young stages. Since the term "neoteny" embraces both these stages as well as the processes of rate implied in Schindewolf's terms, it is to be preferred as the more comprehensive term.

No one disputes neoteny as a factor of evolution in many lower animal groups. The questions for us to decide, in the light of the evidence, are whether it is at all probable that neoteny has occurred (1) as *a* factor in the evolution of man, and (2) as a factor in the early differentiation of man.

The fact that man belongs to an order of mammals in which most of its members produce a single offspring at a birth (monotocous) made possible the establishment of mutations favoring fetalization. In animals that produce several young at a birth (polytocous) competition between the intrauterine organisms for nourishment and space is considerable. Under such conditions the adaptive advantage lies with rapid development, and the emergence of fetalization becomes impossible because genes favoring a slowing down of development would be eliminated. With one offspring at a birth the case is quite different, and a slowing down of development becomes a great advantage. The longer the single offspring is preserved in the womb, the more leisurely its development can be, and the more likely it is to be preserved for the species. A fetus is, on the whole, better nourished and less exposed to danger than a newborn infant. Under the conditions of life of man's precursors and early man himself, such a prolongation of the intra-uterine period of development would have been of great advantage. Genes, therefore, favoring such a prolongation of intrauterine development by a slowing down of the rate of fetal development, would gradually have been established as part of the human genotype by natural selection.

According to the fetalization theory, then, the essential feature of human evolution has been not so much the development of new characters as the retention of embryonic, fetal, and infantile ones. It is interesting to observe that the female of the species exhibits these tendencies rather more markedly than the male.

The future of human evolution, if we are to judge by its past, will probably involve a greater prolongation of intrauterine existence as well as of child-hood and a retardation of maturity. Some of the characters now distinguish-ing adult man will be lost. As J. B. S. Haldane has pointed out, "It was not an embryologist or a palaeontologist who said, 'Except ye . . . become as little children, ye shall not enter the kingdom of heaven.'"

Respecting the evolution of such types as Kanjera, Swanscombe, Quinzano, and Fontéchevade, the suggestion is that they constitute possible examples of forms of men in which evolution by neoteny may have played an appre-ciable role. Neotenous mutations may have occurred with different, but probably insubstantial, frequencies in different early hominid populations derived from a common stock, and hence, by this means, in isolated hominid populations, very appreciable morphologic changes could have been brought about. The selective advantages of such possible neotenous changes is a subject which has received insufficient attention. What was the advantage of thick skull bones, if any, in palanthropic types? What is the advantage of thinner skull bones in neanthropic types? What were the advantages of supra-orbital tori in the pithecanthropines and neanderthaloids? What is the advantage of the absence of these tori in neanthropic types? We don't know; we don't even have good theories. We need to think more about these matters much in the manner in which C. S. Coon, S. M. Garn and J. S. Birdsell have in their book *Race*, with respect to the differences characterizing modern varieties of man. Above all, we need to investigate such matters by experimental means.

TIME AS A FACTOR IN EVOLUTION

In conclusion, a few words may be added on the dimension of secular time as a factor of evolution. Secular time is the matrix in which evolutionary change occurs. It is a universal constant, but time has no direct control upon evolutionary change. Time provides the constant against which change may be measured. Whatever it is that undergoes change is, however, develop-mentally influenced by time—change occurring as the result of the interaction of events which occur within time.

Time heals all wounds not because of its passage, but because of the occurrence of events during the passage of time which produce the healing. Were it not for those events no amount of time would be sufficient to produce the healing. Similarly, it should be clear that unless certain events occur no amount of time will serve to produce evolutionary change. However, time being the succession of instants during which events occur, time is obviously necessary for events to occur in. Time is, therefore, a factor or condition of evolution. Evolution needs time.

CONCLUSION AND SUMMARY

What we have been attempting to say thus far in this essay is that during the same length of secular time, rates of evolutionary change may vary appreciably in isolated populations of the same species. In man, with his somewhat unique breeding habits, and large differences in mobility—some early populations having been confined to a restricted habitat while others wandered over large continental areas, man having reached practically every part of the habitable globe—the possibilities of idiosyncratic variation have been greatly multiplied. Rates of evolutionary change in different early hominid groups during the same length of secular time, exhibited principally as differences in the rate of neotenous mutations—among other factors—are quite sufficient, it is suggested, to explain such apparent anachronisms as neanthropic types of man in the Middle or even Early Pleistocene and a palanthropic type of man in the Upper Pleistocene—always, providing, of course, that we are also finally able to understand the adaptive value of these neotenous changes.

The hypothesis advanced in this essay suggests that commencing with a single hominid ancestral population, which has subsequently separated into several geographically isolated populations, that in addition to such factors as mutation, natural selection, isolation, drift, and the like, neotenous mutations have played an important role in adding to the quanta of morphological difference among such populations. Neotenous mutations occurring at a more rapid rate in some early populations than in others would, at least in part, be responsible for the development of morphologically modernlike types of man at a period contemporary with the flourishing of such types as Pithecanthropus, Heidelberg, and Solo man. The hypothesis suggests that in the latter types neotenous mutations occurred comparatively infrequently.

NEOTENY AND THE EVOLUTION OF THE HUMAN MIND

A problem perennially puzzling to the student of man has been the manner in which the distinctively human brain and mind have evolved from ape-like counterparts. The mechanism of this evolution has not been understood. N. C. Tappen has pointed out that the "Ancestors of the human group must have made the shift over to symbolic communication to initiate specifically human evolution." This is reasonably certain. But what is required is some explanation of the mechanism by means of which this shift was achieved. As Tappen adds, "Once such a shift toward this new adaptive zone was initiated, a high selective advantage for individuals better adapted to learned behavior and symbolic communication must have ensued."

It is clear that the rate of structural development in man has been appreciably retarded as compared with the rate in apes. It would appear that a similar process was associated with the development of those structural elments which form the physical bases of mind. In other words, as a consequence of neotenous mutations having multiple effects both morphological characters and functional capacities may have been influenced in the hominid-human direction. ("Hominid" refers to the classificatory status of man as a morphological form; "human" refers to the psychological capacities of such a form.) On the other hand the mutations for the strictly morphological changes and those affecting the mental faculties may have occurred quite independently. One thing seems highly probable, namely, that the shift to the human mental status occurred as the result of mutations which caused the retention of the capacity for educability, so characteristic of the juvenile ape, right into the adolescent and/or adult phases of development.

The morphological chasm once separating man from his non-human animal ancestors has been steadily reduced within recent years by the discovery of such extinct forms as the australopithecines of South Africa. Morphologically the australopithecines are not altogether apes (as we have hitherto known them) nor altogether men (as we know them), but something in between —which is exactly what the forms intermediate between apes and men should be, neither altogether the one (apes) nor quite the other (men), but the advent of the past, so to speak, on its way toward the future. The australopithecines habitually stood and walked erectly as ably or nearly as ably as man. The range of brain volume exceeded that of any known ape group, the largest known ape brain being that of a gorilla with a volume of 685 cc., while the australopithecines range in brain volume from 450 to 750 cc. The highest limits of brain volume in the australopithecines may fall within the lowest limits of the range of brain volume of modern men of normal intelligence—750 cc.

The brain volume of an australopithecine such as *Telanthropus capenis*, as estimated by Robinson, namely between 850 and 950 cc. is generally agreed to be too high, but 750 cc. is not, and this is within calling distance of the lower limit of the *Pithecanthropus-Sinanthropus* group with a range of 885 to 1225 cc. Robinson believes that *Telanthropus* has virtually bridged the gap between ape and man. The gap seems, however, to be larger than Robinson suggests. Most students are of the opinion that the australopithecines do not constitute the group immediately ancestral to man, though most agree that they are closely related to the hominid ancestral group. The cerebral Rubicon which Keith placed at a mean of 750 cc. is a good distance from having been crossed by the australopithecines. "The Rubicon," writes Keith, "between apehood and manhood, so far as concerns brain volume lies somewhere between 700 cc. and 800 cc.; to be more precise, I would say that any group of the great Primates which has attained *a mean brain volume* of 750 cc. and over should no longer be regarded as anthropoid, but as human." The emphasis here is upon *a mean brain volume,* and the mean brain volume of the australopithecines is 576 cc. This is quite a long way from the mean brain volume of the pithecanthropoids of 881 cc. On the basis of brain volume the australopithecines may not have crossed the Rubicon to achieve the status of man, but on the basis of toolmaking they have.

It does not seem that many great structural changes would be necessary to produce those qualitative changes that would serve to distinguish the human from the ape mind. It would seem, on the other hand, that the principal, if not the only changes necessary would be those facilitating the ease of symbol usage. What the nature of those changes may be is at present conjectural. Increase in the number of fine connections between cerebral neurons with increased capacity for growth at axon terminals, resulting in improvement in the association, scanning, and feedback capacities of the brain, is one possibility. Thorndike has suggested that "in their deeper nature the higher forms of intellectual operation are identical with mere association or connection forming, depending upon the same sort of physiological connections but requiring many more of them." This is possibly an oversimplification. However we may describe the structural changes which have undoubtedly taken place in the human brain, they will amount to but the other aspect of what we have already stated, namely, that the difference between the human and ape brain is that the human is more educable. Indeed, educability is the species characteristic of *Homo sapiens.* The juvenile ape is more educable than the adult ape, and the suggestion here is that the preservation of the educability of the juvenile ape into the adult stage in man, by neoteny, serves to explain the evolution of a brain capable of a human mind.

The theory outlined in this section suggests that the shift from the status of ape to the status of human being was the result of neotenous mutations which produced a retention of the growth trends of the juvenile brain and its potentialities for learning into the adolescent and adult phases of development. It is clear that the nature of these potentialities for learning must also have undergone intrinsic change, for no amount of extension of the chimpanzee's capacity for learning would yield a human mind.

It is further suggested that evolution by neoteny of the mental faculties has been a gradual process from the commencement of man's origin from the apes. It is questionable whether the shift from the ape to the hominid status was saltatory either for morphological or for mental traits. It may be doubted, for example, that *Pithecanthropus robustus* was as bright as Solo man, though it is highly probable that he was brighter than any of the australopithecines. The progressive increase in the volume of the brain in the fossil

Hominidae seems to have been paralleled by a progressive increase in mental capacities. Size of brain seems to have stabilized itself in man, in fact there seems to have been a decline in gross size or dimensions of the human brain since the days of Neanderthal man. This does not, however, mean that the increase in brain mass has come to an end. Increase in mass may be achieved by deepening and multiplication of the number of cerebral convolutions, that is, by increasing the surface area of the brain without increasing its size. There is no reason to suppose that either the quality or duration of man's capacity for learning will not be subject to further evolution.

REFERENCES

ABBIE, A. A. 1952 A new approach to the problem of human evolution. Trans. Roy. Soc. S. Australia, 75:70–88.

An important study presenting the view that the morphological characters of ancient physical types, particularly Neanderthal man, lie within the range of normal variation, together with an admirable discussion of fetalization or neoteny.

——— 1958 Timing in human evolution. Proc. Linn. Soc. New S. Wales, 83:197–213.

Supplementing the foregoing discussion.

BOLK, L. 1926 Das Problem der Menschwerdung. Jena, Fischer.

——— 1929 Origin of racial characteristics in man. Am. J. Phys. Anthropol., 13:1–28.

In both these items Bolk discusses the process of fetalization as a factor in the evolution of men. In connection with man these were the earliest contributions to the subject.

DE BEER, G. 1958 Embryos and Ancestors. Oxford, The Clarendon Press, New York, Oxford University Press.

Containing an admirable discussion of neoteny in man.

KEITH, A. 1949 Foetalization as a factor in human evolution. In Keith's A New Theory of Human Evolution. London, Watts, New York, Philosophical Library, pp. 192–201.

A good discussion of fetalization in man.

CULTURAL FACTORS
IN THE EVOLUTION
OF THE HUMAN DENTITION

C. LORING BRACE

Reviewing the major anatomical developments that have taken place in the humanization of the hominid line, there are three areas in which important change has occurred: (1) postural—the assumption of the erect posture; (2) cerebral—the expansion of the brain; (3) facial—the reduction of the face and teeth.

Following the insistence of Washburn that "it is particularly the task of the anthropologist to assess the way the development of culture affected physical evolution" (Washburn 1951:69), all three of these changes can be viewed in the light of the principal adaptive mechanism employed by man in his so far successful bid for survival. This mechanism, of course, is culture, and it seems reasonable to assume a positive connection between cultural development and physical evolution.

Considering the first of the three crucial areas mentioned above, early students of human paleontology expected the immediate precursors of recognizable modern man to exhibit something less than erect posture. In this they were influenced by the fact that man's closest living non-hominid relatives, the anthropoid apes, present a semi-erect appearance even when in a quadrupedal stance. The discovery and description of the gorilla coinciding very closely with the first recognition of fossil man in the nineteenth century (McGregor 1929:531) certainly helped to influence the reconstruction of the posture of premodern forms of man.

The adaptive significance of erect posture, however, was partially overlooked in these early interpretations. Washburn has pointed out that men without culture would be "ecologically unimportant bipeds" (Washburn 1951:69). Oakley goes further and notes that bipedalism without compensating cultural factors is biologically disadvantageous (Oakley 1959:443), Hewes to the contrary notwithstanding (Hewes 1961:693; Brace 1961). When one examines the hominid fossil record, the earliest recognizable bipeds are the australopithecines (Le Gros Clark 1955:25–26) living in an area of open "grassland alternating with Savannah woodland" (Clark 1959: 68). They could neither escape predators by speed afoot nor could they protect themselves by highly specialized canines as do present-day, openground primates (Washburn 1960:69; Tappen 1960).

Anatomical equipment as poorly adapted to survival as this surely must have been supplemented by the use of tools (Bartholomew and Birdsell 1953; Montagu 1961). Although Oakley stresses the probability that the earliest hominids "must have begun as occasional tool users" (Oakley 1959:443), the occurrence of Oldowan-type tools at Sterkfontein and the association of the so-called Zinjanthropus skull with an Oldowan working floor would demonstrate that they were not only tool users but also tool makers (Oakley 1959:443; Leakey 1960:79). In view of the demonstrated continuity of the Oldowan tradition (Cole 1954:132–4; Clark 1959:113–114), one cannot deny the makers the possession of culture in Leslie White's sense (White 1949:48), and one would be forced to call them men by Oakley's definition.

It may be, then, that the development of culture and erect posture were necessarily related occurrences, and that the earliest recognizable hominids are therefore the earliest possible men.

If these considerations of the human status of the australopithecines, based as they are on the culture-posture interdependance, render the previous assertions of the characteristic stance of the "Neanderthals" somewhat suspect, a re-examination of the actual skeletal materials has shown them to be positively untenable (Morton 1926; Straus and Cave 1957).

Although the bipedal mode of progression apparently had not been completely perfected at the stage of development represented by the known australopithecines (Le Gros Clark 1955:26–7), there was only a slight amount of development remaining before the modern condition was achieved. Attainment of a bipedal mode of locomotion was evidently accomplished at the beginning of human development. Structural adaptation was soon stabilized and has not changed in any major way since that time. This means that any extensive discussion of the posture of fossil man, where the human status is undoubted, is unnecessary.

In a consideration of the second of the major changes mentioned at the outset of this paper, the selective advantage possessed by large-brained variants in a population depending upon its developing culture for survival is so obvious that it need not be stressed. It is no surprise, then, that an increase in brain size is the next gross anatomical change visible in the development of the hominids (Tappen 1953:606), and that one finds a simultaneous improvement and refinement of the tangible evidence for culture. Again, they are obviously related.

By the time the Sinanthropus level is reached, gross brain size overlaps the normal range of modern man, and by the Neanderthal level it is completely included within the normal modern range (Weidenreich 1943:113, 1946; Skerlj 1960:96). In spite of the frequently repeated claims that the gross proportions and fissure patterns of the Neanderthal brain indicate qualitative inferiority to the brain of modern man (Boule 1913; Boule and Vallois 1957:230), it appears that such confident assertions cannot be maintained (Count 1947; Spuhler 1959:9; and Comas 1961:308).

While the history of the changes in the pelvic and cranial regions is not difficult to appreciate when considered in the perspective of the selective advantage possessed by hominids with developing cultural capabilities, there are changes in the dentition on the other hand which are not quite so easy to explain. The nature of the changes themselves is somewhat difficult to specify at the earlier levels. The functional reasons for the difference between the dentitions of the groups Robinson distinguishes as Australopithecus and Paranthropus are not immediately apparent (Robinson 1956: 11,170). Australopithecus had smaller molars than Paranthropus but, then, Australopithecus was a much smaller animal. In proportion to body size, the molars may have been relatively as large as those of Paranthropus, and consequently it may not be justifiable to explain the absolutely larger Paranthropus molars as indicative of a uniquely vegetarian diet.

It has been noted that the number of different primate species simultaneously inhabiting a savannah environment is very much smaller than that inhabiting a forest area of similar size (Tappen 1960:110). Since it would follow that a diversity of contemporaneous savannah primates using culture as their primary means of adaptation is exceedingly unlikely, it behooves us to discover a logical process whereby Australopithecus, the geologically earlier form, can be transformed into Paranthropus. The fact that Australopithecus was presumably significantly nearer to the time when survival was not aided by means of systematic tool manufacturing may explain why the incisors and canines are absolutely larger, and relatively much larger, than in Paranthropus.

Certainly large canines are not a necessary sign of a carnivorous diet, witness the gorillas and baboons of today. They definitely are an important means of defense for ground-living primates, and the absence of projecting canines in the ground-living australopithecines strongly suggests that tools were being used for purposes of protection. Yet the large size of the anterior teeth of the earlier australopithecines may mean a heritage from a period in the past when they were necessary for survival.

The striking dental difference between the australopithecine and the pithecanthropine stages of hominid development is primarily the reduction of the size of the molar crowns, especially molar two, and more especially molar three. (See Figure 1.)

It is barely possible that the change may be due to a drastic modification in food preference, although this was doubted by Weidenreich (1937:161), but it is at least as likely that a change in food preparation may be the cause. Undeniable evidence for the use of fire occurs at Choukoutien, while there is as yet no evidence for it in a late Villafranchian context (Clark 1959:63, 104; Washburn 1960:69).

The inclusion of cookery in the developing cultural repertoire may well have rendered superfluous the previously necessary amount of mastication and allowed a reduction in the number of square millimeters of grinding surface.

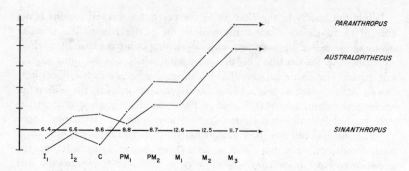

Fig. I Mandibular mesial-distal tooth dimensions. The reference line is the mean for Sinanthropus tooth measurements as given by Weidenreich. Vertical scale is marked in millimeter intervals. (Adapted from Weidenreich 1937; and Robinson 1956.)

Certainly the dimensions of the molar teeth of the Sinanthropus-Pithecanthropus stage are well within the limits of the range exhibited by recent forms of man (see Figure 2), and the selective forces operating cannot have been very different from those influencing molar size in recent hunting and gathering peoples.

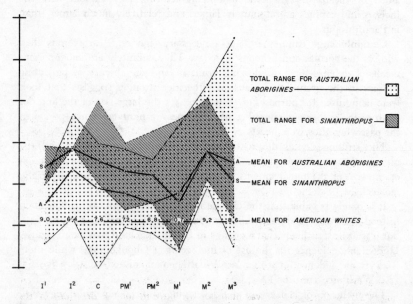

Fig. 2 Maxillary mesial-distal measurement ranges. The reference line is the mean measurements for American Whites as given by Black. Vertical scale is marked in millimeter intervals. (Adapted from Weidenreich 1937; Campbell 1925; and Black 1902.)

Still to be considered are the various changes that have occurred in the incisor region. Because of the frequently heavy wear seen in the incisors, and the consequently small number of fossil incisors available for study, many authorities have tended to dismiss the importance of the anterior teeth for odontological studies (Boule 1911–13; Hrdlička 1930; Robinson 1956). On the other hand, the frequent incidence of extreme wear is in itself an indication of the amount of use to which these teeth were subjected, and therefore of their importance.

In the Middle Pleistocene from the time of Sinanthropus to the beginning of the Upper Paleolithic, hominid incisors reach a maximum in gross dimensions and pattern complexity. (See Figure 3.)

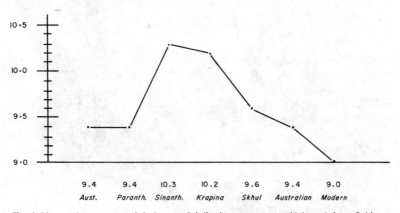

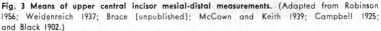

Fig. 3 Means of upper central incisor mesial-distal measurements. (Adapted from Robinson 1956; Weidenreich 1937; Brace [unpublished]; McCown and Keith 1939; Campbell 1925; and Black 1902.)

It can be seen that the morphological features which reach their greatest development during this period contribute to the total volume of the front teeth without appreciably adding to the space taken up in the jaws. The lingual tubercle provides added resistance after wear has abraded the blade. The raised margins of the lingual fossa, determining a shovel-shaped tooth, add to the volume of enamel and dentine that has to be abraded all the way down the crown. Finally, it may be suspected that the crown-height of unworn Middle Pleistocene incisors is disproportionately greater than comparable older or more recent teeth, but so few unworn teeth are available that nothing positive can be stated.

The explanation for the importance of the front teeth during this period can again be sought in cultural factors. As attempts to modify the environment increased, great use was made of the built-in tool at the front of the face. Stewart has noted that Shanidar I had used his front teeth for more than ordinary mastication, although he attributes this to the absence of a right hand (Stewart 1959:479). This same sort of wear can be seen to a marked degree in the teeth of La Ferrassie I (Boule and Vallois 1957:207, 229–30), in Ternifine (Howell 1960:214), in Krapina Mandible J (see Figure 4), in Ochos (Vlček 1958: plate xxxvi) and in other specimens. It seems likely that some sort of regular use of the mouth as a tool may account for at least part of the extreme wear so frequently seen in the incisors of Middle Pleistocene hominids.

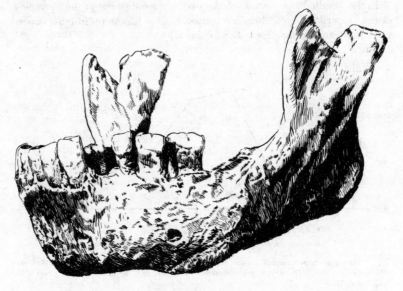

Fig. 4 Ink drawing of an original photograph of Krapina Mandible J.

An additional explanation can be offered in the characteristic mode of meat eating of hunting and gathering peoples. Excellent contemporary films show both Kalahari Bushmen and Eskimos stuffing meat into their mouths and then cutting it off at the lips with a knife. One can imagine the situation of the Paleolithic hunter before the development of an efficient cutting tool when the only means of separating the meat within the mouth from that which would not fit was by worrying and tearing with the incisors. The powerful edge-to-edge occlusion and the relatively large size of the anterior teeth of hominids from the time of Sinanthropus through the time of the Neanderthals may be a reflection of such an anatomical adaptation as well as being the result of the increasing importance of the manipulation of the environment in the bid for survival.

While the incisors of the Neanderthals are about the largest seen in the course of human evolution (Brace unpublished material), efficient cutting tools were actually being manufactured (Bordes 1961: personal communication). Still more efficient blade-type tools began to occur with increasing frequency in late Mousterian layers at sites such as La Ferrassie, Le Moustier, Fontenioux, Combe Capelle, Grotte du Renne, and Goderville (de Sonneville-Bordes 1958:432–4); to say nothing of similar occurrences in the Middle East (Garrod and Bate 1937). The form and size of the late Neanderthal incisors then may be a relict from the preceding stages in cultural development when they had important functional significance.

This delay of an anatomical response to a change in selective factors caused by cultural developments is similar to the explanation offered for the differences of relative anterior tooth size between Australopithecus and Paranthropus. In a gross sense, however, the wide variety of tool types appearing as the Mousterian-type cultural traditions are transformed into Upper Paleolithic cultures (Bordes 1958:180) indicates that tools made for special purposes became more efficient than the old built-in tool. The variability of facial morphology which follows is a sign that the particular selective forces formerly at work have been superseded. It is no surprise then that the Neanderthal face disappears with the development of the Upper Paleolithic.

If the major evident change from the Mousterian to the Upper Paleolithic peoples involved the teeth and tooth-bearing parts of the face and has a functional explanation, it would be expected that subsequent changes of a similar magnitude should also be similarly accounted for. With culture as man's primary means of adapting to the world, one should naturally look to the cultural evidence for some indications of a change in a way of life of comparable importance to the acquisition of tools for defense, of fire, and of effective cutting tools.

The final major change in human dentition has been the development of the overbite (Coon 1939:29). This change follows a change in human subsistence techniques at least as dramatic as the beginnings of culture. The food-producing revolution effected a change in diet which in the long run could not fail to affect the teeth. The delay in the development of the overbite is similar to the delay in dental change following the above-mentioned cultural developments, and illustrates the fact that genetically controlled variants must arise in their slow way by mutation and recombination in order that selective forces can operate.

While the significance of the overbite is not immediately obvious, a look at tooth-wear patterns in peoples whose subsistence depends upon cultivated plants shows that it is the molar teeth which are being most heavily worn (cf. Nelson 1938). This is in marked contrast to the Neanderthals or to contemporary hunters and gatherers where the incisors show far more wear than the more distal teeth (cf. Figure 4, also Campbell 1925; Vlček 1958; plate xxxvi; and Ritchie 1923:59).

The origin of grain cultivation is accompanied by the increasing importance of grinding tools indicating the need for fine milling of the foodstuffs before they can be eaten. Incidentally, habitual use of grinding in food preparation may be a cultural pre-adaptation to the appearance of the ground-stone tools which once were considered to be the hallmark of the Neolithic.

With the importance of food grinding indicated by the presence of milling tools and extreme molar wear, the mechanism whereby such wear is produced needs examining. It must be mentioned here that the mechanism proposed to explain the significance of the observed features is hypothetical. A series of experiments is being designed to test the hypotheses presented. It often used to be said that, because of their great interlocking canines, the great apes could not utilize the rotary sort of grinding motion found in *Homo sapiens* (Hooton 1946:174). Paradoxically, when anthropoid dentitions are examined (Schuman and Brace 1954), the pattern of molar wear resembles that of modern man far more than it does that of man during the Paleolithic or even of modern men who preserve an edge-to-edge bite. In fact those modern populations which exhibit the results of a rotary sort of grinding in the molar region have just as much restriction to free lateral movement at the front of the mouth as do the anthropoid apes. The over-bite is just as limiting as are interlocking canines.

The suspicion is raised then that the kind of molar wear seen in such situations may be partially the result of the limitation of motion at the forward end of the dental arch. As long ago as 1921 (Ritchie 1923:64), it was noted that the movements of the mandible during mastication were controlled by the relationships of the canine teeth and the cusps of the pre-molars and molars, although this does not explain how this kind of occlusion and wear is maintained after the cusps have been worn down. It has likewise been noted that the pre-articular eminence serves to translate vertical pull by temporal and masseter muscles into a mesial-distal grinding motion as the condyle slips backward into the glenoid fossa. Since the pre-articular eminence is low in anthropoid apes, this cannot be an absolutely vital part of the grinding mechanism.

Figure 5 shows how an overbite acts as a guide forcing the whole mandible to slide for a millimeter or two distally as it is being closed. The buccal surface of the lower incisors engages the lingual surface of the upper incisors and the result is a fine but powerful distal wedging of the mandible activated primarily by the vertical pull of the two strongest muscles attached to the jaw, the masseter and the temporalis. It seems likely that the interlocking canines of the anthropoid apes, coupled with their rough vegetable diet, acts in much the same way as the overbite and ground grain-powdered grinding-stone diet of Neolithic peoples.

Although these ideas must be regarded as unproven hypotheses, certainly the overbite is a significant anatomical change which separates food-producing from hunting and gathering peoples, and some sort of functional explanation for this difference is long overdue.

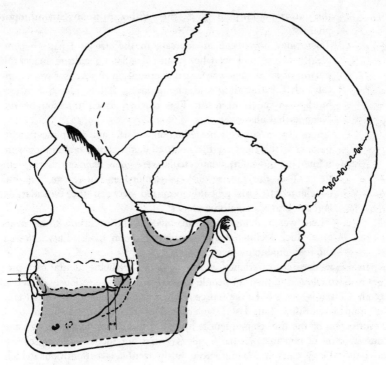

In summary there are three major anatomical developments that have left their mark on the human stock.

1. The first was the assumption of erect posture which could only have taken place with the rise of culture as an adaptive mechanism. This development has changed little since the beginning of human history. Perhaps the increase in body size deserves the status of a major development, although it does not involve a major change in form.

2. The enlargement of the brain correlated with the increase in technological development is the second obvious major change.

3. Changes in the dentition also apparently correlate with changes in ecology, although this is slightly more complex and less obvious than the first two major changes.

   a. There was an initial reduction in the incisor-canine area related to the increasing reliance upon manufactured tools and weapons. This probably occurred early in the australopithecine phase.

   b. There was a reduction in molar surface area following the acquisition of fire for cooking purposes. This probably occurred between the australiopithecine and the Pithecanthropus-Sinanthropus phases.

c. There may have been an increase in the size and pattern complexity of the incisors when man's developing culture made the pursuit of large game successful. Certainly heavy incisor wear indicates that both eating and manipulating habits placed a heavy burden on the front teeth. This reached its culmination by the Neanderthal phase.

d. There was a subsequent reduction of size and simplification of pattern of the front teeth when tool-manufacture techniques were refined to the point where tools were more efficient than teeth to perform the diverse tasks demanded by increasing cultural development. This probably occurred between the Neanderthal and the Upper Paleolithic phases.

e. There was a change from an edge-to-edge occlusion to an overbite which facilitated fine grinding of grain foods. This followed the food-producing revolution.

In this modern age of science, technology, and medicine, dental care programs have allowed millions of people to survive who have seriously defective teeth. Certainly this will be the source of another major change in the history of human dentition, but, lest I be accused of Hootonian pessimism or a resurrection of the dire consequences hinted at by former advocates of some narrow form of eugenics, let me finally say that our modern age of science and technology can also manufacture fairly trouble-free dentitions which can be tailored at will to fulfill whatever of the above-mentioned functions is deemed most desirable.

REFERENCES

BARTHOLOMEW, G. A., and J. B. BIRDSELL 1953 Ecology and the proto-hominids. American Anthropologist 55:481–98.

BLACK, G.V. 1902 Descriptive Anatomy of Human Teeth, 4th edition. Philadelphia, S. S. White Co.

BORDES, F. 1958 Le passage du Paléolithique moyen au Paléolithique supérieur. In Hundert Jahre Neanderthaler, G. H. R. von Koenigswald, ed. Utrecht, Netherlands, Kemink en Zoon (pp. 175–81).

——— 1961 Personal communication (June 9).

BOULE, M. 1911–1913 L'homme fossile de La Chapelle-aux-Saints. Annales de Paléontologie VI (1911):109–172; VII (1912):21–57, 85–192; VIII (1913): 1–70.

BOULE, M., and H. V. VALLOIS 1957 Fossil Men, Michael Bullock, trans. New York, The Dryden Press.

BRACE, C. L. 1961 Unpublished letter.

CAMPBELL, T. D. 1925 Dentition and Palate of the Australian Aboriginal. Adelaide, The Hassell Press.

CLARK, J. DESMOND 1959 The Prehistory of Southern Africa. Harmondsworth, England, Penguin Books.

CLARK, W. E. LE GROS 1955 The Os Innominatum of the recent Ponginae with special reference to that of the Australopithecinae. American Journal of Physical Anthropology n.s. 13:19–27.

COLE, SONIA 1954 The Prehistory of East Africa. Hardmondsworth, England, Penguin Books.

COMAS, JUAN 1961 Scientific racism again? Current Anthropology 2:303–40.

COON, C. S. 1939 The Races of Europe. New York, The Macmillan Co.

COUNT, E. W. 1957 Brain and body weight in man. Ann. N. Y. Acad. of Sci. 46:993–1122.

DE SONNEVILLE-BORDES, D. 1958 Problèmes généraux du Paléolithique supérieur dans le sud-ouest de la France. L'Anthropologie 62:413–51.

GARROD, D. A. E., and D. M. A. BATES 1937 The Stone Age of Mount Carmel, Vol. I: Excavations at the Wady El-Mughara. Oxford, The Clarendon Press.

HEWES, GORDON W. 1961 Food transport and the origin of hominid bipedalism. American Anthrolopogist 63:687–710.

HOOTON, E. A. 1946 Up from the Ape. Rev. ed. New York, The Macmillan Co.

HOWELL, F. CLARK 1960 European and Northwest African Middle Pleistocene Hominids. Current Anthropology 1:195–232.

HRDLIČKA, ALES 1930 The skeletal remains of early man. Smithsonian Miscellaneous Collections 83:1–379.

LEAKEY, L. S. B. 1960 The discovery by L. S. B. Leakey of *Zinjanthropus boisei*. Current Anthropology 1:79.

McCOWN, T. D., and A. KEITH 1939 The Stone Age of Mount Carmel, Vol. II: The Fossil Human Remains from the Levalloiso-Mousterian. Oxford, The Clarendon Press.

McGREGOR, J. H. 1929 Gorilla. *In* Encyclopaedia Britannica, 14th ed. p. 531.

MONTAGU, M. F. A. 1961 The "cerebral rubicon": brain size and the achievement of hominid status. American Anthropologist 63:377–78.

MORTON, D. J. 1926 Significant characteristics of the Neanderthal foot. Natural History 26:310–14.

NELSON, C. T. 1938 The teeth of the Indians of the Pecos Pueblo. American Journal of Physical Anthropology 23:261–93.

OAKLEY, K. P. 1959 Tools makyth man. *In* The Smithsonian Report for 1958, pp. 431–45. (Reprinted by permission from Antiquity, Vol. 31, 1957). Washington, Smithsonian Institution.

RITCHIE, STEPHEN G. 1923 The dentition of the Western and Central Eskimo. *In* Report of the Canadian Arctic Expedition 1913–18, Vol. XII. Ottawa, F. A. Acland.

ROBINSON, J. T. 1956 The dentition of the Australopithecinae. Transvaal Museum Memoir No. 9. Pretoria.

SCHUMAN, E. L., and C. L. BRACE 1954 Metric and morphologic variations in the dentition of the Liberian chimpanzee; comparisons with Anthropoid and human dentitions. Human Biology 26:239–68.

ŠKERLJ, B. 1960 Human evolution and Neanderthal man. Antiquity XXXIV.

SPUHLER, J. N. 1959 Somatic paths to culture. Human Biology 31:1–13.

STEWART, T. D. 1959 The restored Shanidar I skull. *In* The Smithsonian Report for 1958:473–80. Washington, Smithsonian Institution.

STRAUS, WILLIAM L., JR., and A. J. E. CAVE 1957 III Pathology and the posture of Neanderthal man. The Quarterly Review of Biology 32:348–63.

TAPPEN, N. C. 1953 A mechanistic theory of human evolution. American Anthropologist 55:605–7.

———— 1960 Problems of distribution and adaptation of the African monkeys. Current Anthropology 1:91–120.

VLČEK, E.   1958   Die Reste des Neanderthalmenschen aus dem Gebiete der Tschechoslovakei. *In* Hundert Jahre Neanderthaler, G. H. R. von Koenigswald, ed. Utrecht, Netherlands, Kemink en Zoon.

WASHBURN, S. L.   1951   The analysis of primate evolution with particular reference to the origin of man. Cold Spring Harbor Symposia on Quantitative Biology, Vol. XV:67–78.

——   1960   Tools and human evolution. Scientific American 203:63–75.

WEIDENREICH, F.   1937   The dentition of Sinanthropus Pekinensis. Palaeontologica Sinica, Whole Series No. 101. Peiping.

——   1943   The skull of "Sinanthropus Pekinensis": a comparative study on primitive hominid skull. Palaeontologica Sinica, No. 127. Lancaster.

——   1946   Generic, specific, and subspecific characters in human evolution. American Journal of Physical Anthropology n.s. 4: (No. 4).

WHITE, LESLIE A.   1949   The Science of Culture. New York, Grove Press.

CULTURAL AND NATURAL CHECKS

ON POPULATION-GROWTH

D. H. STOTT

The study of the ways in which animal populations limit themselves to their means of subsistence has yielded many surprises, and explained many hitherto anomalous features of physical growth and behaviour. The theme of the present contribution is to examine some of this work, and to ask whether certain unexplained, or poorly explained, features of human development and behaviour may be similarly understood. The writer has in mind in particular the regular appearance of reproductive casualties—infertility, still-birth, infant death, malformation, mental deficiency, constitutional ill-health —which are commonly regarded as biological accidents or genetical vestiges of no value to the species. To these must be added the behavioural maladjust-ments which, as the term implies, are viewed as failures to adapt to not very uncommon situations. Behavioural breakdown would have been many times more disastrous under primitive conditions; the capacity for maladjustment cannot thus be regarded even as a genetic survival. We must ask why, with the minutely fine instinctual equipment which regulates animal behaviour, human beings never evolved breakdown-immune patterns of conduct. The application of the criterion of survival-value to these human phenomena consequently leaves many facts unexplained.

For the individual, perinatal death, infertility, malformation, behaviour-disturbance, could obviously have no survival-value. But, as Simpson [1] points out, "selection favours successful reproduction of the population and not necessarily of any or of all particular individuals within it." It may seem implausible to suggest that the appearance of lethal disabilities could have survival-value even for the population as a whole, but if the limitation of fertility can be of advantage this might be the case. Similarly an increase in efficiency by natural selection may endanger the whole population if it reaches the point where the source of food is wiped out. A curb upon the presumed evolutionary trend towards greater hunting skill would therefore be of advantage. For human beings we thus reach the paradoxical conclusion that in times of the pressure of population on food resources any process which tended to *lower* the mental capacity, physical dexterity or perceptual acuity of a certain number of individuals might mean the saving of the race.

That the amount of food available sets the ultimate limit to the growth of all animal and human populations cannot be disputed. But this apparently self-evident proposition only holds good in a very rough way over a long period. The popular Malthusian notion that the number surviving from year to year is determined by the current supply of food, with the excess dying from starvation, is no longer supported by any student of natural populations. Even David Lack,[2] who among the authorities in this field lays the greatest emphasis upon food supply as the limiting factor, recognizes that the relationship is a complicated one. Food shortage severe enough to impair functional efficiency is critical, not because more members of the species may die than need do in order to restore the ecological balance—a state of affairs that can and often is quickly made good by the excess reproductive capacity possessed by all species—but a general weakening threatens total annihilation from predators. Thus Chitty,[3] one of the best known students of animal populations, argued that "a species which frequently exhausted its food supply might be supplanted by one whose population densities were controlled at a safer level." This caused him to look for the alternatives to starvation as the regulating factors.

All the animal populations which have been the subject of observation have been found to suffer periodic declines in numbers which are not generally the result of starvation. These declines often continue in successive generations under conditions in which there could be no question of a shortage of food, and yet may result in the near-annihilation of a local population. The possibility that they may be due to epidemic diseases has been closely examined, but no greater incidence of such has been found in "dying" populations; and the pattern of the decline and recovery does not correspond to the progress and recession of an epidemic.

Lack [4] suggests that the fluctuations may reflect predator-prey cycles: overpopulation of the "consumers" reduces their food supply, whether it be animal or vegetable, to the point where recovery is slow. Consequently there is widespread starvation among them, until their numbers are so small that their source of food can recover. As will be noted in the discussion of the field-studies, this explanation does not fit the facts, since the "crashes" often occur when food is abundant, and the mass emigrations which sometimes mark their beginning almost invariably take place in the late summer and autumn, when food is plentiful, rather than in winter. There is in addition a theoretical reason why predator-prey cycles could not be the rule. Any major advantage gained by the "consumer" species over its prey implies that it has been able to make significant inroads into the numbers of healthy adults. If though only a more efficient minority of the predator-species are able to do this, their increased hunting capacity would spread by natural selection, and still further inroads, without limit, would be made into the numbers of the prey, until they, and the predators themselves, were exterminated. It seems that predators only take a marginal toll in the form of the weakly and young animals (and the latter are naturally only at risk for a critical few weeks of their life). In his comprehensive collation of the evidence on predation Errington [5] quotes authorities on many wild animals to the effect that, on the whole, healthy adult populations suffer little from predators. In their home ranges at normal densities he observed that adult muskrats lived in noticeable security. The larger ungulates "suffer from sub-human predation chiefly when immature, aged, crippled, starved, sick, or isolated from their fellows." He advanced the theory of the *intercompensation* of factors limiting population: if predators and disease took little toll, self-limiting mechanisms came into operation to check the growth of numbers; if losses were great from external causes these mechanisms did not come into play. He concluded that "regardless of the countless individuals or the large percentages of populations who may annually be killed by predators, predation looks ineffective as a limiting factor to the extent that intraspecific self-limiting mechanisms basically determine the population-levels maintained by the prey." One might add that if predators only succeed in catching the vulnerable minority the balance would be smoothly maintained rather than cyclic, for a fairly constant proportion of the prey, other things being equal, would be eaten each year. (This argument does not hold in the case of a newly introduced predator, since time would be needed for a balance to occur by natural selection. There is also some anecdotal evidence that some ungulates, who rely for protection upon herding and flight, have at times been known in the absence of predators to eat up herbage to the point of starvation. In their case predators may be able to catch healthy adults, but since only one in a herd can be taken at a time, and the predators would be thinly spaced by territory, the toll might never exceed the replacement rate under normal conditions of abundance, and yet suffice to render other means of limiting numbers unnecessary.)

A record of typical population-cycle, that of the snowshoe hare, made by Green and Evans [6] is given in Table 1. It is seen that the decline extended over five years, and then in 1938, when extinction seemed near, the trend was reversed. In their review of possible causes the authors of this, as of similar studies, discount the likelihood of an epidemic because the mortality did not abate after a first rapid spread. Nor could the losses have been due

TABLE 1

Early spring population		Young born during summer	Per cent of yearlings surviving
1932		600	
1933	478 (peak)	1049	23
1934	374	818	29
1935	356	779	18
1936	246	541	12
1937	151	330	8
1938	32	66	91
1939	73	158	

to emigration or an encroachment into adjoining regions: the snowshoe hares were seldom found more than one-eighth of a mile from the point where they were first trapped, even after a year or more.

The decline was chiefly a matter of the poor survival of the immature hares, as shown strikingly in the last column of the table.

It is indeed remarkable that the mortality among the yearlings should be so catastrophic in 1937, four years after the presumed overpopulation, and that this should occur during the summer months, whereas the greatest mortality of adult hares was, as would be expected, during the winter. Food shortage would thus seem to be ruled out as the immediate cause of this youthful mortality. That the young born during the summer of 1937 were still severely affected despite the fact that the parental population was little over half the peak density suggests that the noxious factors persisted through four generations.

. During the peak, before the decline became general, occasional hares were found dead in the traps, the cause of which Green and Larson [7] diagnosed as "shock disease." As the decline became widespread during 1935 and 1936 this condition was observed over the entire area. The wider significance of this finding will be discussed later, but it may be noted at this stage that the parent-hares were found to be in a poor condition during the breeding season in which the generation of poor viability were produced.

In his study of a population cycle of ruffed grouse in Ontario, Clarke [8] was similarly struck by the poor viability of the young, and by the fact that "even though the first year of dying off in an area has reduced numbers to a point where the birds may be regarded as scarce, the succeeding year may show a similar reduction of summer flocks."

From the study of a number of widely dissimilar species of animal one conclusion emerges with tolerable certainty: when population density reaches a certain point, even without actual shortage of food, changes take place which have the effect of reducing the population. These changes may even be in bodily form. Wilson [9] observed that when aphides become crowded on a plant the next generation grow wings to allow emigration. Uvarov [10] reported analogous physical changes in the locust. Preparatory to swarming and emigration locusts "moult" and change their exteriors from predominantly green to a brownish colour, the two forms being originally thought to be different species. When studied in the laboratory this change was found to depend only on the density of population in a cage, and was notably independent of temperature, light or other obvious factors. The swarming is in no sense a migration, since it occurs irregularly in cycles of years. Nor, Uvarov points out, can they be driven by hunger, since they leave rich vegetation to enter the desert.

Among mammals the well known "suicidal" mass wanderings of the lemming offer a close parallel. Once again, as Elton [11] and others have shown, they occur in three to four year cycles, in periods of apparent high population in the home locality. Their emigration might be described as a behavioural aberration taking the form of always wandering downhill, which brings them to the sea, into which they then plunge, so that they are mostly drowned. The result is a periodic drastic thinning of the resident population, since none of the emigrants find their way back.

Lack draws attention to the genetic problem which these "suicidal" emigrations raise: if those who respond to this urge are eliminated while those in whom it is absent survive, why is it not rapidly eliminated by natural selection? If, however, the sacrificed individuals are the yearlings, their parents, who would as a whole be of the same genetic constitution, would have a certain advantage over other parent animals whose young caused dangerous overcrowding. In this way an inherited tendency to self-elimination, confined to the young, would be perpetuated by natural selection.

The reproductive behaviour of several species of birds shows puzzling features which can only be convincingly explained as population regulatory mechanisms. Lack draws attention to the fact that among many species of birds—the hawks, owls, storks, crows, etc.—incubating starts as soon as the first egg is laid. Consequently the earlier hatched nestling will always be stronger than the later hatched, with the result that each younger one can only get fed when its elder sibling has had so much that it is replete and inactive. The whole brood survive only when food is very abundant. Lack [4] argues that "if all the chicks had hatched on the same day and been of the same size, the food might have been divided equally between them, and all might have died." Since the passerine birds do in fact defer incubation until the clutch is complete and so produce a brood who share the available food more or less equally, this reason for a different child-rearing practice among the larger predators seems unconvincing. It would surely have been more economical for them to have evolved a slower growth rate and smaller daily food intake so that the whole brood could survive. This indeed happens among those passerines who nest in holes or roofed nests, where the young are safe from predators and there is no need for the nestling stage to be got through as quickly as possible. The ultimate value of the successive hatching would thus seem to ensure not that such of the particular brood survive as their immediate food-supply permits, but that the number of young raised should not produce a general overpopulation in the region.

Brown's study [12] of various species of eagles within a district in Kenya has brought to light yet another regulatory mechanism (that of successive hatching not being applicable because the species in question only incubate one egg). He found that in some years certain pairs failed to breed, although they were in secure possession of territories in which they had bred in previous years. This could not be related to variations in the weather, changes of mate, exigencies of nest-building or to shortage of food; but the off-years tended to follow one or two productive years. Thus the periodic infertility can best be explained, not as an adaptation to contemporary food-supply, but as a means of checking population numbers before the danger-point is reached.

Errington's study [13] of cyclic fluctuations in muskrat populations enables us to see, for this mammal at least, something of the detail of the interaction between crowding and the regulatory mechanisms. It would appear that at a certain degree of density the muskrats become intolerant of each other, as shown in greater dispersal, savage fighting among adults and attacks upon helpless young. It was significant that the friction was not a simple reaction to a threshold density-level, but seemed rather to be a "state of nerves" persisting during the phase of population decline. During the cyclic upgrade, the muskrat population congregated within the choicer feeding grounds, at a density of about ten breeding pairs per acre, while leaving the unattractive areas uninhabited. But during the peak and decline the strife was so great that they distributed themselves at densities of about one pair per acre through good and bad habitat alike.

The last of the field-studies to be considered, that of Chitty [14] in respect of voles upon a plantation in Montgomeryshire, contains an important suggestion as to the nature of the regulatory mechanism involved. He found that the offspring of the peak-generation either died prematurely or were infertile, as also was the case during the cyclic decline of the snowshoe hare. He concluded that, "in order to account for this decrease in viability and reproductive performance it is necessary to postulate a delayed effect of some previous condition . . . We cannot at present be more precise about this supposed condition than to imagine some disturbance of the hormonal balance of the mother which in some way affected the foetus." He drew attention to the strife among the adults during the early part of the season in which the affected generation were born. That this caused congenital damage may be considered a bold hypothesis, but evidence is quoted below that the harassment and strife attendant upon overcrowding may produce psychosomatic illness in animals. Chitty arrived at his theory of prenatal damage only after reviewing and dismissing all other feasible causes, such as disease, food shortage, predation and migration.

In an experiment with wild rats Calhoun [15] showed that the regulatory mechanism consisted mainly of changes in social behaviour. He bred a colony from a few individuals in a pen of 10,000 square feet, allowing them an abundance of food at all times. If over the 28 months of the experiment they had realized their breeding potential they would have numbered 50,000. If they had been content with the two square feet per rat allowed for caged rats in laboratories there could have been 5,000. In fact the population stabilized itself at less than 200. The social behaviour of the colony limited population growth in three ways. First, the rats split themselves up into local sub-colonies, between which were maintained buffer zones without burrows. Second, with crowding the normal dominance hierarchy broke down, leading to unstable groups. The effect of this was reduced frequency of conception and poor viability of the suckling young. Of the few which survived beyond weaning very few in turn had progeny of their own. Third, crowding caused increased attack upon the young, and those who received severe punishment were likely to succumb.

The behavioural breakdown of the rats living under conditions of social stress seems to have been manysided. Those which had suffered excessive punishment no longer made favourable use of their environment, that is, became "maladjusted," notably by losing their food-storage habits. The collapse of the social pattern also had a detrimental effect on fertility. Under conditions of crowding the dominant rats could no longer guard their own females from intruding males, for the latter pursued them and copulated frequently. Why the outcome was infertility may be gathered from the analogy of Bruce's [16,17] experiments with mice. From a chance observation that pregnancy sometimes unaccountably failed in the laboratory she was able to establish the cause as contact with a strange male. After mating with their familiar sire the females suffered a "blocking" of the pregnancy even if they only detected the odour of the intruder on nesting material. After some five days they came on heat again and could conceive, but a breakdown of social dominance and exposure to a succession of strange males would presumably inhibit pregnancy indefinitely.

A further effect of crowding in Calhoun's experimental colony was that "more and more individuals were stunted despite having plenty of food available. Such stunted rats seemed healthy . . . they simply failed to grow very large and attained their mature weight very slowly." These stunted rats were also characterised by behaviour-disturbances. Again one might infer prenatal damage, with a hint of the pregnancy/multiple-impairment syndrome hypothesized by the present writer in respect of human beings.[18]

The regulatory mechanisms which Calhoun observed in rats, and Bruce's "pregnancy-block" in mice, originated in the animals' becoming aware that something was "wrong" in their environment. No doubt to avoid the controversial term "psychological," Bruce described this type of influence as exteroceptive. Leaving terms aside, it can be said that a situation of a certain type, namely a relationship with other animals of their own species, was appraised as unfavourable, and that this act of appraisal initiated physiological processes which culminated in infertility. Barnett [19,20] has carried out experiments which showed that male rats in the unfavourable situation of being bullied become subject to adrenal cortical depletion, which may be followed by death, even though they suffer no actual wounding. It would appear that he induced in these bullied rats the condition of "shock-disease" which Green and Evans described in the snowshoe hare during the phase of population decline. With Larson, Green made a physiological study of a number of afflicted animals, and Christian [21] recognized their description of the disease as similar to Selye's stress adaptation syndrome: the animals had died of adreno-pituitary exhaustion.

Such a psychosomatic reaction to a situation appraised as unfavourable or disastrous does not, in itself, account for the continuance of the shock-state in subsequent generations, which did not experience the overcrowding. This could, however, result if the state of shock interferes with the reproductive processes, causing the next generation to suffer damage at the foetal stage. Two critical experiments demonstrate that the offspring can suffer prenatal damage as a result of the mother-animals' being subjected to exteroceptive or "psychological" shock. Thompson and Sontag [22] subjected pregnant rats to the constant ringing of an electric bell, to the extent that they broke down in convulsions. To eliminate the possibility that the after-effects upon the mothers retarded their young postnatally, the latter were changed around with the young of a control-group of unshocked rats. The offspring of the rats shocked in pregnancy were found to be significantly slower at maze-learning. Thompson [23] carried out a further experiment to test the effects of anxiety pure and simple during pregnancy upon the offspring. Female rats were trained to expect an electric shock on hearing the sound of a buzzer, and to escape by opening a door. After being mated they were placed each day in the same compartment, without the electric shock being applied. But the escape-door was locked, so that they were reduced to a state of fear. Once again their offspring were randomly switched with those of control-rats. The young born to the rats which had been subjected to anxiety were much more sluggish, took twice as long to reach food when hungry, and nearly three times as long before they would venture forth from an open cage. In human terms we would say that they were suffering from a congenital impairment of motivation. Their timidity and "unforthcomingness" resembled a type of personality-defect which the present writer found to be associated with pregnancy-stress in the human mother. It is reasonable to suppose that such "substandard," unassertive young would be the bullied animals, which would succumb to attacks during the strife generated in phases of overcrowding. If so, the congenital damage they suffered might rank as a mechanism for the limiting of population.

The defence of territory is found in some form among almost all animals, and must therefore have been a powerful factor in survival. Howard [24] put forward the most apparent reason why this should be so, that by defending a territory a nesting pair guarantees its family larder. Lack disputes this view, pointing out that the "territories" of some of the gregarious birds, such as the guillemot and heron, consist of a few feet or yards around their nests, which could not possibly serve as a source of food. He also draws attention to many anomalies: encroachment for feeding takes place regularly; during hard weather territoriality is suspended and birds congregate around any provision of food; and finally territories vary greatly in size for the same species (the largest held by the robins he studied being five times greater than the smallest). [25] These anomalies can better be explained if territorialism is seen as primarily a mechanism for the regulation of population-numbers.

Just as it was previously suggested that successive hatching in the larger predators serves to limit the population in general to the resources of the region rather than adjust the number of mouths in a particular brood to the resources of the moment, so the defending of territory may limit the population-density over the region as a whole from generation to generation. This is effected by preventing more than a certain number of birds from breeding. That some fail to do so is shown by the rapidity with which a new mate is forthcoming when the former one dies. Lack has himself shown that in a covered aviary, where there was insufficient space for two territories, the non-dominant pair of robins failed to breed. The territories in miniature maintained by sociably breeding birds around their nests, and the destruction by rooks of "unpermitted" additions to their rookery, would have the analogous effect of limiting the number of birds who could forage over a day's flight or over the available fishing ground. The balance of evidence thus seems to favour the view of Huxley [26] that territorialism is "one of the more important of the factors determining the population of breeding pairs in a given area"; and of Carpenter [27] that it is "an important condition for optimal population density."

It has been seen that the postulated mechanisms for the limitation of population tend to centre around reproduction and the viability of the young, these being the stages at which they could operate most economically. This consideration brings us to another sphere of biology which is fraught with unsolved problems: the study and experimental production of congenital malformations. Traditionally these have been regarded as genetic in origin, but the most persistent attempts to fit their appearance into any of the known Mendelian patterns of inheritance have met with little success. Examples of standard types of malformation crop up in a strain of animal or human being without antecedents, and even where a certain familial tendency is observed the malformation, with a few exceptions, does not occur with the regularity that would be expected if it were entirely genetically-determined. The labelling of the isolated malformation as a "phenocopy" of the true genetic prototype, or the explanation of the sporadicity in terms of the varying "penetrance" of a gene, has brought little additional understanding of the causes of malformation. In the early years of the present century Stockard [28] observed that malformations could be produced in fishes by treating their eggs with a weak solution of alcohol and other noxious substances. It was not until 1935 that an analogous discovery was made in a mammal: Hale [29] demonstrated that pregnant sows deprived of vitamin A produced piglets with a tendency to severe malformation of or total lack of eyes, together with other malformations. These findings have been abundantly confirmed in respect of a number of species of animals. The degree of deprivation proved important. Summarizing his extensive work in this field Warkany [30] reported that, "a borderline deficiency is required to induce malformations; a slight improvement of the dietary situation may result in normal offspring, while a further deterioration may lead to embryonic death." Similarly Sobin [31] found that congenital heart disease could be induced in the offspring by revolving the pregnant rat 200 times in a drum; but if it was subjected to 800 revolutions no live offspring at all were produced. The effect of these phenomena under natural conditions would be to limit population-growth in times of shortage, and the greater the shortage the more severe would be the block to fertility. It is also significant that besides vitamin deprivation the administration of hormones such as cortisone and thyroxine tends to produce malformation. With the known effects of rage and fear on the endocrine system, strife and harassment resulting from shortage and overcrowding might thus be expected to reduce fertility.

A big advance in the study of malformation was made when it was realized that they were the result, not of either genetic or environmental influences as the case may be, but of an interaction of both. This was first hinted at by Malpas [32] in 1937: "The role of an unfavourable maternal environment is to facilitate the emergence of certain lethal genetic factors." Since then this concept of the *facilitation* of a genetic propensity to malformation has been experimentally confirmed by Landauer [33] and by Clarke Fraser and his co-workers: [34] the appearance of malformation under conditions of stress was found to depend on the genetic constitution of both mother and foetus. It would thus appear that there is *regular genetic provision* for the production of malformation, or poor viability, in the offspring in times of stress. This is consistent with the view that malformation must be accounted one of the mechanisms for adapting population-numbers to the resources of the environment, and as such to have survival value.

The existence of mechanisms for limiting population in man cannot be assumed because they are found in animals. On the other hand the fact that changes in viability and in fertility as well as aberrations of behaviour leading to reduction in numbers are widespread among animals indicates a strong probability that such will be found among the human species. Moreover these mechanisms were found in their most intricate level of development —in variations of instinctive behaviour—among the large predator birds; and primitive man was the super-predator, who must have been reasonably safe against other predators in many regions of the earth.

The most evident devices for limiting human population are cultural in character. In the case of infanticide it is a self-conscious one. Among the Polynesians for example not only was any weakly or malformed child disposed of as a matter of course, but it was by no means taken for granted that even a healthy child would be allowed to live; it was left for the father to decide as a matter of policy.[35] In many cultures the taboo upon sexual intercourse during lactation, and the long nursing period, would have the effect of spacing out births. The institution of marriage, and the customs and sexual morality that go with it, must have the effect of limiting the number of children. If a bride has to be bought, or only a suitor of substantial means is acceptable, young wives would tend to get paired with old men. In peasant communities marriage had to be postponed until the suitor got possession of a holding, and by the custom of gavelkind (gable-child) the youngest son was expected to remain unmarried to work his parents' holding until eventually, at a mature age, he inherited it himself.[36] In former times in England marriage was not socially sanctioned until the couple were able to get their own cottage, which usually meant waiting many years. Just what social institutions in each civilization have militated against population-increase would be a fruitful subject of study. Under the feudal system there was a residue of landless and homeless serfs or semi-slaves, inferior in status to the peasant, who slept around the log fire of the manorial hall, and who thus had no family life. In the ancient world the institution of slavery would similarly have made marriage and reproduction out of the question for a large section of the population, not to mention the effects of physical hardship and ill-treatment. In his historical novel, *Salammbô*, Gustav Flaubert [37] makes Hamilcar, prince of Carthage, express surprise at the small number of children among his slaves. He commanded that their quarters should be left open at night so that the sexes might mix freely. Since Flaubert was noted for the thoroughness and accuracy of his historical research, it is unlikely that he invented this episode.

The aborigines of Australia are of unique scientific interest from the point of view of the limitation of numbers, since they were at the time of their discovery by Europeans the only extant example of a human population at the food-gathering stage covering a complete land mass, without anywhere to emigrate. Being subject to no predatory wild animals, they presented the exact human counterpart of the large birds of prey. If, therefore, mechanisms for the limitation of human populations exist they should be found among them. That the density of the aboriginal population was closely related to the available food was cleverly demonstrated by Birdsell.[38] He found that the lower the rainfall, and hence the poorer the vegetation and the fewer the animals able to live on it, the larger was the area occupied by each tribe. This was all the more striking among tribes without any water or shore from which to get food.

Birdsell found a remarkable correspondence between rainfall and the practices of circumcision and subincision. These were the rule in the driest central areas. The eastern boundary of the region throughout which sub-incision was practised followed the eastern 8- and 10-inch rainfall line with a closeness which made a chance relationship out of the question. That for the practice of both circumcision and subincision ran further west, along the 5-inch rainfall line. Since these rites do not impair the fertility of the affected males, it must be asked what connection they can have with austere living conditions. The explanation which will be proffered involves reference to findings which will be described more fully below. These are that the commonest form of impairment of a disturbed pregnancy is to render the infant weakly and more liable to common infections. Under unhygienic conditions the chances of survival of such weakly children would be poor. Even in 20th century Britain, the writer observed that among mentally sub-normal children—who are very liable to infection in infancy—those coming from the lowest-standard of home had the best health-records, for the reason that the poorly children in such homes would have died in infancy. Similarly it is reasonable to suppose that under primitive conditions the infliction of wounding by the above rites, and similar operations upon the girls, would eliminate those of delicate health. In times of food shortage, with the consequent harassment, fatigue and anxiety, many more delicate children would be born, so that the numbers of the rising generation would be significantly reduced. Birdsell in fact found that along the boundary marking the edge of the diffusion of these rites the tribes practising them were less numerous than those not doing so. Yet paradoxically the area in which the rites were practised had become progressively extended, which suggests that the numerically smaller tribes had gained an advantage in times of scarcity by avoiding starvation. Circumcision, subincision, and indeed the widely prevalent superficial mutilation inflicted during initiation ceremonies, may therefore be culturally effective means of adapting the size of primitive human populations to their food resources.

In the light of the work on animal populations, it would be surprising if there were no regulatory mechanisms in human beings operating at the physiological level. An observation by Smith [39] on the Ao Naga tribe of Assam may have wide implications. "The number of childless marriages is usually large, and very few women have large families. The Nagas take a pride in the strength and endurance of their women, saying they are inferior to the men by a narrow margin only. These qualities have no doubt been developed by the life of toil to which they have been accustomed from their earliest youth, but they have paid the price in a weakening of the reproductive power." Of all the hill tribes he writes, "The young women are generally stocky and plump; but this does not last long, because the hard life of carrying wood from the jungle, doing cultivation work, raising children and performing other hard tasks soon make old hags of them." Such a picture, with the women doing the hard work and the carrying, while the menfolk sit around and talk except for seasonable bursts of activity, is typical of primitive and many peasant agricultural communities. It may be that this unequal division of labour to the disadvantage of women is a cultural provision which has had survival-value by the limitation of fertility. In a study of pregnancy-factors among over 3000 women at the Watford Maternity Hospital near London, McDonald [40] found that "a statistically significant excess of mothers of children with major defects had been engaged in work they described as heavy—particularly laundry work"; work involving heavy pulling or lifting was reported in 20 per cent of the cases where the children were malformed, but in only 8 per cent where the children were normal.

If physiological mechanisms for limiting numbers in man exist, one would expect the reproductive rate to be sensitive to the quality of nutrition during pregnancy. Even in a middle-class population in Boston, women who had poor feeding habits during pregnancy were found much more likely to give birth to stillborn, malformed or otherwise defective children compared with mothers whose diet was good.[41] In Aberdeen, women belonging to the poorer sections of the community had twice as many premature babies, three times as many stillbirths and lost their infants in the first month four times as frequently, when compared with well-to-do women in a nursing home.[42] In Toronto it was found by a carefully controlled experiment that miscarriage, prematurity and stillbirth among ill-nourished women could be reduced to a small fraction of what it would otherwise have been by giving them a supplementary diet during pregnancy.[43,44]

As early as 1812 a doctor, Jacob Clesius, remarked that malformations were more frequent in times of war. Of the Thirty Years' War in Germany, Gustav Freytag wrote: "The effects which such a life, full of uncertainty and terror, exercised upon the minds of country people were very dire . . . one observed the signs of terrible misery in numerous malformations." After the siege of Paris in 1870–71 the French doctor de Saulle reported a crop of malformations.[45] Systematic evidence of this phenomenon comes from studies in several centres in Germany of the incidence of malformation during the war and in particular during the post-war phase of acute hardship, housing shortage and despondency. The malformation rate in 55 German hospitals [46] showed a startling rise after the war—the average for 1946–50 being 6.5 per cent, but there was a smaller rise for the war years themselves (2.58 per cent compared with 1.43 per cent during the pre-war and pre-Hitler Weimar period). This began from the start of the war, when there was no question of food shortage. There would however have been many reasons for anxiety and fear among the civilian population; besides the bombing, husbands and sons would have been called up, reported killed, wounded or missing and so on. From the point of view of the role of anxiety in inducing malformations, it is also noteworthy that the rate reached a minor peak during 1933, in the January of which year Hitler seized power and loosed his Storm Troopers upon the Jews and the politically opposed sections of the population; during the whole period of the Hitler terror up to the outbreak of the war (1933–39) the average rate was nearly double that obtaining during the last seven years of the democratic Weimar period. For Britain no general figures of incidence of malformation are published, but an indirect indication of the trend can be had from the death rate from malformation in the first month of life.[47] For both male and female infants it was fairly stable for the years 1932–39, but moved to a peak-level during 1940–43, the years of the heavy bombing and severest fighting, with the resulting news of casualties. Owing to full employment and the equalising effect of an efficient rationing system, the general standard of nutrition, especially of pregnant and nursing mothers, was above the level of the pre-war years.[48] One can only conclude that the increase in malformations was due to the prevalence of fear and anxiety. A study by MacMahon, Record and McKeown in Birmingham [49] confirmed the existence of a distinct peak during the years 1940–43 for anencephaly and spina bifida, the malformations which seem to act as barometers of social stress. In Scotland, where there was very little bombing, there was no significant wartime peak but only the post-war downward trend presumably reflecting the general improvement in the standard of living and social security throughout Britain as a whole.

A remarkable inverse correlation has in fact been found between social amenities and the incidence of anencephaly.[50] It is highest in Glasgow (3.1 per 1000) where overcrowding is worst, and lower in regular succession in the other three chief cities of Scotland placed in order of amenities. In the widely spaced communities of the Highlands the rate was found to be only 1.29 per 1000. Edwards, also in Scotland,[51] showed that the anencephaly rate was about four times as high among unskilled town labourers as in the highest social class. Both in the United States [52] and in Britain [53] prematurity is significantly more frequent in the lower social classes, and Stewart has shown that the same also applies to death of the infant in the first month.[54]

There are, some telltale findings concerning the greater risks attached to extramarital conception (illegitimacy and premarital conception). Stewart found prematurity to be over twice and death of the infant in the first month nearly three times as frequent among such children compared with those conceived after marriage. These findings may link up with some suggestive and unexplained features of the anencephaly studies referred to above. McKeown and Record report a consistently greater risk of this malformation in *first-born* children conceived during the summer months.[55] This could not have been due to a greater physiological risk in first-birth, otherwise the tendency would have been equally apparent in winter-conceived first-borns; nor could it have been due to seasonal infections, for second-born children conceived in the summer were not affected. But extramarital conception, owing to the greater opportunities for outdoor lovemaking, is probably more frequent during the summer months, and the resulting children would mostly be first-borns. It might be that the mental stress consequent upon becoming pregnant in the unmarried state can be one of the causes of this malformation.

This suggestion received confirmation in the above-mentioned study of anencephaly in Scotland by Edwards. Despite the general improvement in social conditions there was virtually no change in the rate between 1939 and 1956. But this global incidence disguised two opposing trends which cancelled each other out. During the peak period of the war, 1939–43, the figure for later births was consistently high, and indeed higher than for first-births. This would reflect wartime stresses. But that for first-births became markedly greater in 1944 and 1945, and except for two years when the rates were about equal, remained greater thereafter. This may well be the result of an increase in extramarital conception due to a measure of breakdown in traditional sexual morality. It is perhaps relevant that the Chief Medical Officer for England and Wales, in his Report for 1959,[56] infers an increased tendency to sexual promiscuity, especially among young people, from the steady rise in the number of new cases of gonorrhea in recent years.

It is, in short, apparent that sections of a population subjected to adverse social conditions tend to suffer more reproductive casualty. And there seems some evidence that, as in the case of some animal populations, the physiological process responsible is triggered off by exteroceptive stimuli which arouse anxiety or other emotion calculated to lead to adreno-pituitary exhaustion. That absolute infertility can be brought about by severe emotional stress was conclusively demonstrated by the well-known German anatomist, Stieve.[57,58] In the bodies of women who had been imprisoned during the Nazi terror and subsequently executed he found unmistakeable signs of degeneration in their reproductive organs which, he pointed out, must have been due exclusively to nervous shock, as they were in a well-nourished condition at the time of their death.

In his pioneer work on the effects upon the foetus of emotional disturbance in the mother Sontag observed that the children tended to suffer from gastrointestinal illnesses.[59,60] He suggested that these were in many instances of autonomic origin. In other words, the children may have already been born in the state of shock-disease found by Green and Larson in snowshoe hares during the phase of population decline. Striking also is the parallelism with Chitty's conclusion, that the poor viability in young voles during the population decline could best be accounted for by foetal damage.

The present writer made a study of 102 mentally subnormal children by case-study methods in order to make comprehensive soundings of causative factors.[18] The pregnancy was disturbed by either illness or emotional upsets in 66 per cent of the cases, compared with only 30 per cent among the mentally normal controls. Where there had been pregnancy-stress 76 per cent of the mentally retarded children were weakly and ailing or had serious illnesses other than epidemics during their first three years, as against only 29 per cent of those retarded children of whom no pregnancy-stress was reported. Among the 450 controls of normal mental ability a similarly close relationship between disturbed pregnancy and early illness was observed. Malformations in both groups followed the same pattern.

Of the pregnancy-stresses emotional upsets were more than twice as frequent as illnesses, and these showed a curious parallelism with the conditions attendant upon overcrowding in animal communities, namely strife, harassment and personal difficulties over having to share housing accommodation, shocks and anxiety-states. It is also significant that of the 24 maternal illnesses in pregnancy, 20 of which resulted in unhealthy children, all but three were stress-diseases, notably gastric ulcer, chronic heart disease, severe sickness and vomiting, and toxaemia.

It has been commonly observed that mentally retarded children tend to suffer from a multiplicity of handicaps; this was not only confirmed in the above study, but each handicap was related so closely to pregnancy-stress that the latter could be reckoned to be the common causative factor. This syndrome of pregnancy/multiple impairment, thus named, included impairment of temperament. Of this the most prevalent type was "unforthcomingness," seen in extreme unassertiveness, timidity and general lack of motivation.[61] It resembled the behaviour of the offspring of the rats which Thompson subjected to anxiety during pregnancy. There can be little doubt, also, that the other main type of impairment of temperament found in backward children, which one might term disorganized motivation (abnormal restlessness and inability to concentrate, and excitability), can also be congenital. In the important series of Baltimore studies conducted by Pasamanick, Lillienfeld and their co-workers behaviour-disturbance in the children, especially of the hyperactive, disorganized type, was found to be significantly related to certain stress-conditions of pregnancy (toxaemia and bleeding).[62] It goes without saying that these unforthcoming or disorganized children would have a very poor chance of survival under primitive conditions, and would be bullied and rejected in times of stress.

Even closer parallels can be seen between the behaviour-deterioration of animals during population-declines and that of human beings under stress. Before he was interested in the mechanics of the former, the writer, in his studies of the types of family-situation leading to maladjustment and delinquency, described the "irritable-depressive non-tolerance . . . in a severely overburdened or nervously exhausted mother (which) can assume the form temporarily of a heartless rejection of her child." During the phases of irritable-depressive character-change "the mother may express the greatest dislike of the child, or even commit some hostile act against it which earns her a prison sentence." [63] Such a reaction may be cognate with the attacks of the adult muskrats upon the young during the strife-phase of the population-cycle observed by Errington.

In the child who is the victim of parental rejection can be observed a typical and apparently instinctive behavioural-change, described as "an attitude of active hostility (which) it is hard to explain otherwise than as calculated to make its position in the family impossible." This was designated "a self-banishing reaction." Considering that at the food-gathering stage each family would need many square miles of territory per head, and that shortage and overpopulation would be likely to be general in a whole region, the chances of a rejected child being able to reattach itself to another family would be small indeed. The break-away from its own group would therefore be virtually suicidal in the same way as is that of the lemming. It is noteworthy that along with or alternative to this hostility-reaction the writer

observed a "removal impulse," which had surprisingly recurrent features:
a dislike of the home-locality, wanting to go to sea, join the army, or to get
work on a farm or with a travelling fair, besides actually running away from
home or committing such flagrant offences as will secure removal from home.
In a study of approved-school boys the writer found that this unconscious
urge for removal was the commonest motive underlying their delinquency.[64]

The most drastic way in which the reproductive capacity of a population
can be reduced, short of sterility, is to limit the number of females born.
In fact the incidence of anencephaly, which is a lethal malformation and
the commonest of those which are sensitive to social environment, is three
times as high among females. The slight preponderance of males born probably reflects the tendency for female embryos to be more subject to lethal
anomalies; hence no doubt also the slight rise in the male-female sex-ratio
during the war years, which has been explained by the myth that Providence
supplies more males to replace those killed. The wartime rise in deaths of
infants of under four weeks from malformation was more marked for female
infants: the increase in the rate during the stress-years of 1940–42 compared
with the eight pre-war years was 7.5 per cent for boys and 14.3 per cent
for girls.

On other hand, non-lethal malformations and liability to disease in childhood are more common among boys. Among the 450 normal children studied
by the writer, infantile ill-health was over twice as common among the boys,
and it appeared that a greater degree of pregnancy-stress is needed to produce
an unhealthy girl than an unhealthy boy. Boys are also more frequently
mentally subnomal, and if their ten times greater proneness to delinquency
is taken as an index thereof, they are much more liable to behaviour-disturbance. (Contrary to popular impression and certain sociological theories, the
great majority of delinquents are emotionally disturbed.) [65]

In seeking an explanation of why males thus seem constitutionally to be
the more vulnerable sex, it must be borne in mind that under primitive conditions the male was the chief predator. If a predatory species becomes too
efficient it eats up its food resources and so exterminates itself. Consequently
it would be of advantage to the species in times of too great numbers, when
the prey would be over-hunted, for the predators to become less competent.
The effects of pregnancy-stress on the male offspring is to make him more
stupid, physically less robust, temperamentally less aggressive, and possibly
more myopic and more gawky. There is indeed some evidence that deficiencies of diet in a poor community depress the level of intelligence. Harrell
and Woodyard supplemented the diet of a group of pregnant and lactating
women in Virginia (predominantly Negro); at the ages of 3 and 4 years their
children had an average I.Q. five points higher than those whose mothers
had only received dummy diet supplements.[66] Among a similar group of
White women in Kentucky, the average I.Q. of whose children was 107.6,
the vitamin supplement made no significant difference, presumably because

the untreated diet was above the level which under primitive conditions would have indicated food-shortage. Evidence that eclampsia and pre-eclampsia, which are stress-conditions of pregnancy, may result in a certain impairment of intelligence in the children has been provided by Margaret Battle in her study of school children in Rocky Mountain City.[67] It may seem paradoxical that a lowering of intelligence in the next generation should be the biological response to stress, but this is consistent with the need to maintain ecological balance.

In yet another respect the handicaps following stress during pregnancy suggest a regulatory mechanism. Those children who suffer from early chronic ailments seem to grow out of them—hence no doubt the folklore that a child's health will change for the better at 7 or 14 years. The writer has also observed that pathological unforthcomingness is often replaced at puberty in boys by normal assertiveness and confidence. Of these children who have overcome their initial handicaps one might say that under natural conditions their poor viability would have been only a provisional "death sentence": if the hardships which caused the impairment were replaced by communal well-being, so that a larger population could be tolerated, these children would be reprieved. The writer also found evidence that boys were more likely than girls to outgrow handicaps of intelligence.[68]

The tendency, to which Tanner has drawn attention,[69] for puberty to begin progressively earlier in recent generations would also seem to reflect a mechanism for the adaptation of numbers to food resources. Hammond, the leading British authority on farm animals, points out that high-plane nutrition brings earlier sexual maturity in poultry and cattle: "With seasonal breeding species like sheep, lambs reared on low-plane nutrition may completely miss the first breeding season and not come on heat for the first time until a year later." [70]

Once one gets the bit of a theory between the teeth there is no limit to the intriguing speculation in which one may indulge. The test is whether, having caused new questions to be asked, the theory can predict the answers to them better than other theories, and whether it can link into a meaningful whole what was previously thought of as separate, accounted for in a number of different ways, or just taken for granted. The case for the theory can be briefly summed up. Animal-populations would seem to be adapted to their food resources by a variety of built-in physiological and instinctive mechanisms rather than by starvation, and these come into play in response to signals of incipient overcrowding in advance of serious shortage of food. Among these signals are certain exteroceptive or "psychological" stimuli; that is to say, the perception by the animal of some factor in its environment —presumably unfavourable in the biological sense—triggers off a physiological or instinctive mechanism which has the effect of reducing fertility or the survival-rate of the young.

There was also some evidence that the same sorts of population-limiting mechanisms are found in animals and in man. In both, the severity of reproductive casualty is geared to the degree of stress upon the mother during and possibly prior to pregnancy. The most unfavourable conditions induce sterility or stillbirth; the somewhat less harsh result in a multiplicity of impairment in the young which reduces the chances of survival; more moderate hardships —sub-optimal diets, insufficient living space, strife and harassment—bring a reduction in competence, vigour or strength of motivation in the young. Perhaps the most striking and unexpected parallel is in the appearance of behavioural aberration, or perhaps more accurately, the substitution of the normal behaviour-pattern by a special pattern of stress-behaviour. In the adults this takes the form of increased irritability and intolerance of congeners, in particular of the young, who may—whether animal or human—be viciously attacked. In the young themselves the behavioural aberration is seen on the one hand in "unforthcomingness" and on the other in disorganized hyperactivity and an emigratory or "removal" urge.

The chief implication of the theory is that the predicted catastrophe of a world population increasing by geometrical progression to the point of starvation is unlikely to occur. It will be forestalled, if not by conscious human design, by the physiological mechanisms which have been evolved to obviate just such a calamity. Indeed we see that these mechanisms are already insidiously at work, and as in one region or another overpopulation and crowding cause increased hardship, so we may expect to find them more in evidence. Even among sections of the White populations of Britain and America reproductive efficiency is significantly reduced by sub-optimal living conditions.

This is not to minimize the fact that these mechanisms are themselves highly unpleasant. Nature prescribes happiness only when it has survival-value. If the survival of our species demands a certain amount of sterility, deaths of babies, unhealthy children, malformed and mentally deficient people, criminals and perverts, our feelings about these drastic measures are irrelevant. To man nevertheless is given an answer. We need not wait for the physiological killers and maimers to come upon us. Primitive man was able to evolve cultural means, even though harsh, for limiting populations. Apart from dropping the more barbarous, little real advance has been made on them by modern Western civilization. During the 18th and early 19th centuries in Britain the execution of child-delinquents, their transportation, or their being sent to sea with the poor viability which that entailed, must have been nearly as effective a means of elimination as the emigration of yearling animals. It should not, however, be beyond the capacity of man to develop cultural methods of regulating population-numbers which do not involve distress and unhappiness. The consideration of such is beyond the scope of this essay. All that can be said is that man has the choice of consciously maintaining population at a level, for each stage of economic development, at which welfare, health and ability will be at a maximum, or of allowing Nature to make the adjustment by genetic provisions which have been valuable in man's evolution but which are insensitive and amoral.

REFERENCES

1. SIMPSON, G. G. 1958 The study of evolution: methods and present status of the theory. Behavior and Evolution, ed. Simpson, G. G., and A. Roe, pp. 7–26. New Haven, Yale University Press.
2. LACK, D. 1955 The mortality factors affecting adult members. The Numbers of Man and Animals, ed. Craig, J. B., and N. W. Pirie, pp. 47–55. Edinburgh, Oliver and Boyd.
3. CHITTY, D. H. 1952 Population dynamics in animals. J. Anim. Ecol., 21:340–41.
4. LACK, D. 1954 The natural regulation of animal numbers. Oxford, Clarenden Press.
5. ERRINGTON, P. L. 1946 Predation and vertebrate populations. Quart. Rev. Biol. 21:144–77, 221–45.
6. GREEN, R. G., and C. A. EVANS 1940 Studies on a population cycle of snowshoe hares on Lake Alexander area. I, II, III. J. Wildlife Manag., 4:220–38, 267–78, 347–58.
7. GREEN, R. G., and C. L. LARSON 1938 A description of shock disease in the snowshoe hare. Amer. J. Hyg. 28:190–212.
8. CLARKE, C. H. D. 1936 Fluctuations in numbers of ruffed grouse. Univ. Toronto Studies. Biol. series No. 41. 1–118.
9. WILSON, F. 1938 Some experiments on the influence of environment upon the forms of aphis chloris Koch. Trans. Roy. Ent. Soc. Lond. 87: 165–80.
10. UVAROV, B. P. 1928 Locusts and grasshoppers. London. Imperial Bur. Entomology.
11. ELTON, C. 1942 Voles, mice and lemmings: problems in population dynamics. Oxford.
12. BROWN, L. H. 1955 Supplementary notes on the biology of the large birds of prey of Embu district, Kenya Colony. Ibis 97:183–221.
13. ERRINGTON, P. L. 1954 On the hazards of over-emphasizing numerical fluctuations in studies of "cyclic" phenomena in muskrat populations. J. Wildlife Manag. 18:66–90.
14. CHITTY, D. 1952 Mortality among voles (microtus agrestis) at Lake Vyrwy, Montgomeryshire, in 1936–39. Phil. Trans. Roy. Soc. London, B. 236:505–52.
15. CALHOUN, J. B. 1952 The social aspects of population dynamics. J. Mammal. 33:139–59.
16. BRUCE, H. M. 1960 A block to pregnancy in the mouse caused by proximity to strange males. J. Reprod. Fertil. 1:96–103.
17. ——— 1960 Further observations on pregnancy block in mice caused by the proximity of strange males. J. Reprod. Fertil. 1:310–11.
18. STOTT, D. H. 1957 Physical and mental handicaps following a disturbed pregnancy. Lancet, i, 1006–12.
19. BARNETT, S. A. 1958 Physiological effects of "social stress" in wild rats. The adrenal cortex. J. Psychosom. Res. 3:1–11.
20. BARNETT, S. A., J. C. EATON, and H. M. McCALLUM 1960 Physiological effects of "social stress" in wild rats. 2. Liver glycogen and blood glucose. J. Psychosom. Res. 4:251–60.
21. CHRISTIAN, J. J. 1950 The adreno-pituitary system and population cycles in mammals. J. Mammal. 31:247–59.

22. THOMPSON, W. R. JNR., and L. W. SONTAG 1956 Behavioral effects in the offspring of rats subjected to audiogenic seizure during the gestational period. J. Comp. Physiol. Psychol. 49:454-6.

23. THOMPSON, W. R. 1957 Influence of prenatal maternal anxiety on emotionality in young rats. Science 125:698-9.

24. HOWARD, H. E. 1920 Territory in bird life. London, John Murray.

25. LACK, D. 1953 The life of the robin. Pelican books.

26. HUXLEY, J. S. 1933 A natural experiment on the territorial instinct. British Birds, 27:270-77.

27. CARPENTER, C. R. 1958 Territoriality: a review of concepts and problems. Behaviour and Evolution, ed. Simpson, G. G., and A. Roe, pp. 224-50. New Haven, Yale University Press.

28. STOCKARD, C. R. 1910 The influence of alcohol and other anaesthetics on embryonic development. Amer. J. Anat. 10:369-92.

29. HALE, F. 1935 Relation of vitamin A to anophthalmos in pigs. Amer. J. Ophthal. 18:1087-93.

30. WARKANY, J. 1947 Etiology of congenital malformations. Advanc. Pediat. 2:1-63.

31. SOBIN, S. 1954 Experimental creation of cardiac defects. Congenital Heart Disease. 14th M and R report of the Pediatric Research Conference, Ohio.

32. MALPAS, P. 1937 The incidence of human malformations and the significance of changes in the maternal environment in their causation. J. Obstet. Gynaec. Brit. Emp. 44:434-54.

33. LANDAUER, W., and C. I. BLISS 1946 Insulin-induced rumplessness of chickens. J. Exp. Zool. 102:1-22.

34. FRASER, F. C., H. KALTER, B. E. WALKER, and T. D. FAINSTAT 1954 Experimental production of cleft palate with cortisone, and other hormones. J. cell. comp. Physiol. 43 suppl.: 237-59.

35. DANIELSSON, B. 1956 Love in the south seas. London, Allen & Unwin.

36. REES, A. D. 1950 Life in a Welsh countryside. Cardiff, Univ. Wales Press.

37. FLAUBERT, G. 1874 Salammbô. Paris, éd. définitive.

38. BIRDSELL, J. B. 1953 Some environmental and cultural factors influencing the structuring of Australian aboriginal populations. Amer. Naturalist, 87:169-207.

39. SMITH, W. C. 1925 The Ao Naga Tribe of Assam. London, Macmillan.

40. McDONALD, A. D. 1958 Maternal health and congenital defect. New Engl. J. Med. 258:767-73.

41. BURKE, B. S., V. A. BEAL, S. B. KIRKWOOD, and H. C. STUART 1943 Nutrition studies during pregnancy. Amer. J. Obstet. Gynec., 46:38-52.

42. BAIRD, D. 1945 The influence of social and economic factors on stillbirths and neonatal deaths. J. Obstet. Gynec. Brit. Emp. 52:217-34, 339-66.

43. EBBS, J. H., and W. J. MOYLE 1942 The importance of nutrition in the prenatal clinic. J. Amer. Dietetic Assoc. 18:12-15.

44. EBBS, J. H., W. A. SCOTT, F. F. TISDALL, W. J. MOYLE, and M. BELL 1942 Nutrition in pregnancy. Canad. Med. Assoc. J. 46:1-6.

45. GESENIUS, H. 1951 Missgeburten im Wechsel der Jahrhunderte. Berliner Med. Zeitschrift 2:359-62.

46. EICHMANN, E., GESENIUS, H. 1952 Die Missgeburtenzunahme in Berlin und Umgebung in den Nachkriegsjahren. Arch. Gynäk., 181:168-84.

47. Registrar-General's reports for England and Wales (1932-57).

48. GARRY, R. C., and H. O. WOOD 1946 Dietary requirements in human

pregnancy and lactation. A review of recent work. Nutr. Abstr. Revs. 15:591–621.

49. MacMahon, B., R. G. Record, and T. McKeown 1951 Secular changes in the incidence of malformations of the central nervous system. Brit. J. Soc. Med. 5:254.

50. Anderson, W. J. R., D. Baird, and A. M. Thompson 1958 Epidemiology of stillbirths and infant deaths due to congenital malformation. Lancet i, 1304–6.

51. Edwards, J. H. 1958 Congenital malformations of the central nervous system in Scotland. Brit. J. Prev. Soc. Med. 12:115–30.

52. Pasamanick, B., and H. Knobloch 1957 Some early precursors of racial behavioural differences. J. Nat. Med. Assoc. 49:372.

53. Drillien, C. M., and F. Richmond 1956 Prematurity in Edinburgh Arch. Dis. Child. 31:390.

54. Stewart, A. M. 1955 A note on the obstetric effects of work during pregnancy. Brit. J. Prev. Soc. Med. 9:159–61.

55. McKeown, T., and R. G. Record 1951 Seasonal incidence of congenital malformation of the central nervous system. Lancet, i, 192–96.

56. Chief Medical Officer for England and Wales, report 1959. London, H. M. Stationary Office.

57. Stieve, H. 1942 Der Einfluss von Angst und psychischer Erregung auf Bau und Funktion der weiblichen Geschlechtsorgane. Zbl. f. Gynäk. 66:1698–1708.

58. ——— 1943 Schreckblutungen aus der Gebärmutterschleimhaut. Zbl. f. Gynäk. 67:866–77.

59. Sontag, L. W. 1941 Significance of fetal environmental differences. Amer. J. Obstet. Gynec. 42:996–1003.

60. ——— 1944 Differences in modifiability of fetal behavior and physiology. Psychosomat. Med. 6:151–54.

61. Stott, D. H. 1959 Evidence for pre-natal impairment of temperament in mentally retarded children. Vita Humana, 2:125–48.

62. Pasamanick, B., M. E. Rogers, and A. M. Lillienfeld 1956 Pregnancy experience and the development of behavior disorder in children. Amer. J. Psychiat., 112:613.

63. Stott, D. H. 1956 Unsettled children and their families. London, Univ. London Press; New York, Philosoph. Lib.

64. ——— 1950 Delinquency and human nature. Dunfermline, Carnegie U.K. Trust.

65. ——— 1960 Delinquency, maladjustment and unfavourable ecology. Brit. J. Psychol., 51:157–70.

66. Harrell, R. F., E. Woodyard, and A. I. Gates 1955 The effect of mothers' diets on the intelligence of offspring. New York Bureau of Publ., Teachers' Coll. Columbia Univ.

67. Battle, M. 1949 Effect of birth on mentality. Amer. J. Obstet. Gynec. 58:110–16.

68. Stott, D. H. 1960 Observations on retest discrepancy in mentally subnormal children. Brit. J. Educ. Psychol. 30:211–19.

69. Tanner, J. M. 1955 Growth at adolescence. Oxford, Blackwell.

70. Hammond, J. 1955 The effects of nutrition on fertility in animal and human populations. The Numbers of Man and Animals, ed. Cragg, J. B., and N. W. Pirie, Edinburgh, Oliver and Boyd, pp. 113–20.